LAW AND GOVERNMENT
UNDER THE TUDORS

SIR GEOFFREY ELTON

LAW AND GOVERNMENT
UNDER THE TUDORS

ESSAYS PRESENTED TO SIR GEOFFREY ELTON
REGIUS PROFESSOR OF MODERN HISTORY IN
THE UNIVERSITY OF CAMBRIDGE
ON THE OCCASION OF HIS RETIREMENT

EDITED BY

CLAIRE CROSS
DAVID LOADES
AND
J. J. SCARISBRICK

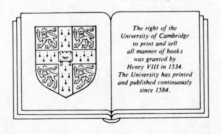

The right of the
University of Cambridge
to print and sell
all manner of books
was granted by
Henry VIII in 1534.
The University has printed
and published continuously
since 1584.

CAMBRIDGE UNIVERSITY PRESS

CAMBRIDGE
NEW YORK   NEW ROCHELLE
MELBOURNE   SYDNEY

Published by the Press Syndicate of the University of Cambridge
The Pitt Building, Trumpington Street, Cambridge CB2 1RP
32 East 57th Street, New York, NY 10022, USA
10 Stamford Road, Oakleigh, Melbourne 3166, Australia

© Cambridge University Press 1988

First published 1988

Printed in Great Britain at
the University Press, Cambridge

British Library cataloguing in publication data
Law and government under the Tudors : essays
presented to Sir Geoffrey Elton on the
occasion of his retirement.
1. Great Britain – History – Tudors,
1485-1603
I. Elton, G. R.   II. Cross, M.C.
III. Loades, D. M.   IV. Scarisbrick, J.J.
942.05   DA315

Library of Congress cataloguing in publication data
Law and government under the Tudors : essays presented to Sir Geoffrey
Elton, Regius Professor of Modern History in the University of
Cambridge, on the occasion of his retirement / edited by M.C. Cross.
D.M. Loades, J.J. Scarisbrick.
p. cm.
Bibliography: p.
ISBN 0—521—33510—8
1. Law–Great Britain–History and criticism.   2. Great Britain –
Politics and government – 1485–1603.   3. Elton, G. R. (Geoffrey
Rudolph)   I. Elton, G. R. (Geoffrey Rudolph)   II. Cross, M. C.
(M. Claire)   III. Loades, D. M.   IV. Scarisbrick, J. J.
KD606.L38   1988
349.42'09—dc19
[344.2009]   87–27215 CIP

ISBN 0 521 33510 8

WV

Contents

Contributors

BRENDAN BRADSHAW
Fellow and Director of Studies in History at Queens' College, Cambridge, and University Lecturer in History

SUSAN BRIGDEN
Fellow and Tutor in History at Lincoln College, Oxford, and University Lecturer in Modern History

CLAIRE CROSS
Professor of History, University of York

JOHN GUY
Reader in British History, University of Bristol

FELICITY HEAL
Fellow and Tutor in History at Jesus College, Oxford, and University Lecturer in Modern History

C. S. KNIGHTON
is editing the Calendar of State Papers, Domestic Series (1547–1580) for the Public Record Office

DAVID LOADES
Professor of History and Head of the Department of History at the University College of North Wales, Bangor

DIARMAID MACCULLOCH
Lecturer in Church History at the Wesley College, Bristol

GRAHAM NICHOLSON
Head of Cultural Services for Stockport Metropolitan Borough

REX POGSON
Headmaster of Lawrence Sheriff School, Rugby

PETER ROBERTS
Lecturer in History at the University of Kent, Canterbury

J. J. SCARISBRICK
Professor of History at the University of Warwick

ROGER SCHOFIELD
Fellow of Clare College, Cambridge, and Director of the ESRC Cambridge Group for the History of Population and Social Structure

Preface

And gladly wolde he lerne, and gladly teache

The six hundred years separating Chaucer's model Oxford clerk from the scholar celebrated in this volume emphasises a constant in university life, the importance of teaching, and particularly teaching by example.

In *The Practice of History*, Geoffrey Elton wrote

I put a lot of weight on teaching, . . . in my view the supervisor of research students should work very hard . . .

The collection of essays which follows is, above all else, a tribute to Geoffrey Elton's supreme skill and success as a supervisor of research, and a measure of the extent to which he has consistently followed his own precept. All the thirteen contributors studied for, and obtained, the degree of Ph.D under his guidance between 1956 and 1978. They do not constitute a majority of such successful students, and certainly not a complete list of those who have subsequently pursued academic careers. These essays are rather the work of a coherent group of scholars, linked together not only by a common supervisor, but also by a common interest in the politics and administration of Tudor England. They are also linked together by nationality. This is a British tribute. Geoffrey's American friends and pupils presented him with *Tudor Rule and Revolution* in 1983, and a similar offering with a European orientation is in hand.* So the editors of this volume make no apology for having confined their scope to scholars living and working in Britain, a country which Geoffrey Elton has made peculiarly his own since adopting it from his native Germany in 1935.

There seem to have been a number of reasons for his remarkable success as a supervisor. One of these has been a warmth and consistency of friendship, which has extended to many of us over the years, and has brought the pupils of pupils to the second and third generation up the stairs to the familiar rooms in Clare College – and more recently to the less familiar eyrie in West Road. Another has been the very high degree of professionalism which he has brought to an aspect of academic life which was traditionally undervalued in

---

* Published since this Preface was written as *Politics and Society in Reformation Europe*, ed. E. Koori and T. Scott, (London, 1987).

ix

the Cambridge to which he came in 1949. Research students in the humanities were still comparatively rare at that time, and often left very much to their own devices. But even in the days before the formation of his graduate seminar, Geoffrey Elton's guidance was precise and sensitive, consistently finding the right balance between his own knowledge and his students' ambitions. This is still a rare skill among senior academics, in spite of the great proliferation of higher degree candidates which has taken place over the last thirty years, and if more had been prompted to follow his example we might have heard fewer complaints about the lamentable completion-rate of theses in the humanities. A third reason has been the fact that he has always taken research itself very seriously, and has always been an archive rather than a library man. His students have been encouraged, or rather required, to embrace his own extremely rigorous methods of search and analysis, and to apply those techniques in ways appropriate to their own investigations.

Research, however, is not an end in itself, or an excuse for building up a school of disciples. The object of research is to uncover the evidence of the past, and nobody has been more explicit than Geoffrey Elton in discussing the nature of that evidence, or its role in the creation of interpretative history.

The historian must not go against the first condition of his calling; his knowledge of the past is governed by the evidence of that past, and that evidence must be criticised and interpreted by the canons of historical scholarship.[1]

First and foremost among those canons must be a true understanding of the purposes for which the evidence studied was originally created. Writs, proclamations and statutes, for example, although equally expressions of public authority varied considerably in their methods of application and cannot be used indiscriminately to answer the same questions. The first task of the historian, therefore, is to approach his evidence with an open mind, and then to follow where it leads. In his first inaugural lecture, delivered in Cambridge in 1968, Geoffrey Elton pursued a sustained attack on R. H. Tawney, whom he accused of '. . . the fatal propensity to fit a selection from a great mass of material into a predetermined framework . . . confirming present-based prejudices and attitudes from an investigation of the past . . .'[2] – in other words, of misusing evidence to create myth rather than history. Throughout his career, Geoffrey Elton has pursued his vision of historical truth and objectivity with consistency and passion. The whole justification for the historian's craft, and his value to an open society is embraced in that vision. The primary purpose of the historian is not to purvey information but to educate the critical faculties:

. . . to discover the truth as best he can, to convey that truth as honestly as he can, in order both to make the truth known, and to enable man, by learning and knowing the truth, to distinguish the right from the wrong reason . . .[3]

[1] *The Practice of History* (Glasgow, 1969), pp. 34–5.
[2] *The Future of the Past* (Cambridge, 1968), p. 15.   [3] Ibid, p. 22.

Consequently arguments over the 'relevance' of this or that period to the contemporary situation are totally beside the point. All historical writing is relevant if it teaches those who read it to detect false logic, bogus analogies and unsubstantiated conclusions. To this educational function meticulous research and the highest standards of professional integrity are essential. To that end generations of research students have sweated over sixteenth-century palaeography, and struggled to master the technical details of Tudor legislation and administration.

When the University of Cambridge advanced him to a personal chair in 1968, Geoffrey Elton chose the title 'English Constitutional History', and defended that unfashionable designation in characteristic style. The logic of his choice, however, was unavoidable, and required no justification. For reasons which are still debated fiercely, the machinery of the English state developed earlier and more fully than that of any other European kingdom, and by the sixteenth century its processes were mature, well-documented, and relatively efficient. To a young historian particularly concerned to apply his own tests of archival research the public administration of sixteenth-century England had proved irresistible. The plentiful material had never been systematically worked on, and generations of scholars had written the political history of the period almost without reference to this luxuriant growth beneath their feet. It was also a period subject to broad generalisations about 'the new monarchy' and 'Tudor despotism', which invited the attentions of the diligent revisionist. In 1946 Geoffrey Elton had begun to work on Thomas Cromwell, a man whose dramatic career, dubious reputation, and voluminous documentation combined to make an obvious target. In 1948 he had submitted his thesis, and in 1953 published *The Tudor Revolution in Government*. By 1968, fifteen years, and a great deal of work later, that monumental book had become the foundation of a scholarly edifice of interpretation, and a landmark to subsequent generations. It was the inevitable trademark of the newly fledged professor.

It had also, of course, been vigorously attacked and defended. The attacks came mostly from Oxford: from Gerald Harriss, Penry Williams and J. P. Cooper. Apart from semantic doubts about the use of the word 'revolution', they followed two main lines. One was to deny that anything new had happened in English public administration during the 1530s – quoting medieval precedents for all Cromwell's alleged reforms. The other was to claim that even if new things had been done in central administration, they had been much less important than was claimed, because real power still rested in the hands of the nobility and the apparent strength of the crown was largely illusory.[4] Given the commitment to accuracy which underlay the main thesis

---

[4] G. L. Harriss and Penry Williams, 'A Revolution in Tudor history?', *Past and Present*, 25 (1963), 3–58. Williams's position was eventually worked out much more fully in *The Tudor Regime* (Oxford, 1979). Similar criticisms have been voiced more recently by a younger group of

of *The Tudor Revolution*, it is not surprising that these challenges were quickly taken up, and controversial war was waged through the pages of learned journals and the lecture rooms of Oxford and Cambridge. History was the gainer by this process, because it soon became apparent that, although there were specific issues about the interpretation of particular documents, the real dispute was about priorities in historical understanding. In a cogent defence of his general position, published in 1970, Geoffrey Elton wrote 'Insofar as men are social, they *are*; as political beings, they *do* . . .'.[5] He was less interested in power structures, such as kinship groups and affinities, than in the springs of political action. Such systems might shape and condition the outcome of political initiatives, but the true focus of historical study should be upon the initiatives themselves. 'The political historian is profoundly concerned to know what happened – exactly what happened . . .' because it is in the movement of events, not in the context through which they move that the real essence of history lies.[6] So, somewhat paradoxically, a scholar who had made his reputation through an exhaustive analysis of the institutions of government, also emerged as a strong exponent of narrative history. Whatever its demerits, narrative emphasised the constant flow of events, as against the static profile of the *Annales* school, then reaching the peak of its influence in the English-speaking world. It may be easier to analyse something which can be deemed to stand still, just as it is easier for the artist to portray his subject at rest, but 'The whole difficulty of historical reconstruction and writing lies in this fundamental truth about history: it contains a multiple situation forever on the move . . .'.[7] Since water never passes twice under the same bridge, it does not greatly matter that the legal and constitutional machinery of England had behaved in some earlier periods much as it did in the 1530s. The political will was different, and consequently both the progress of events and the eventual outcome were new and unprecedented.

In a series of books and articles between the early 1950s and the late 1960s Geoffrey Elton described, demonstrated and justified his intellectual and moral stance as an historian. During those years he dominated the secular history of Tudor England, and through his two popular text books, *England under the Tudors* (1955) and *The Tudor Constitution* (1960) established a firm grip upon sixth-form and undergraduate studies, well beyond the confines of Cambridge. Always a prodigious and single-minded worker, by 1970 he had built up a formidable *corpus* of new material, both upon the crisis of the 1530s and upon the political philosophy of Thomas Cromwell himself. Some parts of this material had been revealed in a continuous succession of learned papers and reviews, but the time had come for fresh major publications. Invitations to deliver the Ford lectures in Oxford in 1971, and the Wiles

'revisionists' led by David Starkey and Christopher Coleman, some of whose researches have broken new ground in this well trodden field. *Revolution Reassessed* (London, 1986).

[5] *Political History* (London, 1970), p. 3.   [6] Ibid, p. 5.   [7] Ibid, p. 160.

lectures in Belfast in 1972 provided appropriate occasions. *Policy and Police* was partly written before the Ford lectures were delivered, and appeared with unprecedented speed in the following year. Whereas *The Tudor Revolution* had been a study of legislation and policy-making, *Policy and Police* examined the other end of the process – the impact of legislation upon the community. It was a study of enforcement, and as such revealed a grasp of popular attitudes, culture and social structures which not only added a new dimension to the study of the period, but also a new dimension to the author's reputation as an historian. This process was extended further in 1973 by the appearance of the Wiles lectures as *Reform and Renewal*. Here the focus shifted, from Thomas Cromwell the legislator, political manager and policeman, to Thomas Cromwell the social reformer, intellectual and idealist. To some it was a startling thought that Cromwell should be presented as a man of conscience and vision, but it was entirely consistent with Geoffrey Elton's own need to 'make a conscience' of what he did. It also, inevitably, pitchforked him into the debate over the development of the English reformation which, as a committed secularist both in his personal and professional life, he had hitherto largely avoided.

Religious faith, and aspirations towards a Christian commonwealth, are more elusive, and less amenable to precise archival research than the making or enforcing of specific laws. Consequently the debate provoked by *Reform and Renewal* was, and has remained, different in texture from that which followed *The Tudor Revolution*. It also led to renewed thought about such important and problematic events as the Pilgrimage of Grace, and the exact manner in which Henry VIII's mind had been poisoned against Cromwell in the spring of 1540. At a more mundane level it also set Geoffrey Elton on that somewhat improbable path which was to lead ten years later to the presidency of the Ecclesiastical History Society. Roman Catholic historians had never seen much difficulty in blaming Cromwell for the English reformation, but their tendency had been *ipso facto* to deny him any genuine religious motivation. Protestant historians, in trying to distance the Anglican church from 'Tudor despotism', had come to much the same conclusions, so *Reform and Renewal* reopened an old debate in a new way. No serious historian of the sixteenth century, however agnostic his own position, can fail to appreciate the powerful and often primitive influence of religious convictions upon the vast majority of his subjects. At the same time, one of the most important points to emerge from this debate was that strength of convictions did not necessarily mean a clear cut allegiance to the theological parties which only emerged at a later date, and the implications of that insight are still being unravelled slowly by a host of scholars.

From 1971 to 1973 Geoffrey Elton was also President of the Royal Historical Society, and from that position launched two initiatives of enduring importance for all fields of historical study in Britain. One was the monograph series *Studies in History*, which began to appear in 1977 and now runs to over forty volumes. The object of this series was primarily (but not exclusively) to assist young scholars of exceptional promise to publish works of specialist scholarship which might be difficult to place with more commercial presses. The second initiative was the annual bibliography of British history, which has appeared regularly since 1975. The comprehensiveness of this bibliography has made it invaluable, and it has largely superseded other enterprises of a similar nature. Meanwhile, not content with a second and updated version of the ever-popular *England under the Tudors* (1974), Geoffrey Elton contributed an early volume to the *New History of England* published by Edward Arnold. Entitled – in what was coming to be recognised as the 'Eltonian' idiom – *Reform and Reformation*, this book embraced twenty-five years of research, reflection and debate by the author himself, and reflected the influence of many other scholars, a number of them his own pupils. It was, as was fairly pointed out by reviewers at the time, not a history of England from 1509 to 1558 but a new and comprehensive history of the politics of the reign of Henry VIII concentrating, like the earlier studies, on the 1530s.[8] It was also, in a sense, the end of an era. Without abandoning either Thomas Cromwell or the 1530s entirely, Geoffrey Elton began to follow other leads, which led past the middle of the century into the fruitful and (from his point of view) largely unexplored reign of Elizabeth. The trail he was following was logical enough: legislation and the legislative functions of parliament. In one sense William Cecil took up this instrument where Thomas Cromwell had laid it down but there was also another, and more important, consideration. In accordance with his own first principle of research, that the historian must be able to understand exactly what his subjects were doing when they produced the evidence which he studies, Geoffrey Elton had long entertained serious doubts about the magisterial works of Sir John Neale on the parliaments of Elizabeth.

Doctoral students working under his supervision, such as Norman L. Jones, were discovering evidence and suggesting conclusions which indicated that a fresh and hard look at the work of those parliaments was called for.[9] The work of his wife, Sheila Lambert – a distinguished historian in her own right – on the procedures of the early seventeenth century, pointed firmly in the same direction.[10] Conrad Russell, Kevin Sharpe and others had already demonstrated that many accepted views about the parliaments of James I would not stand up to thorough investigation, and it was inevitable that Neale's long-standing orthodoxy should be challenged. Controversy in this case had

---

[8] E.g. Jennifer Loach in *The Times Higher Education Supplement*.
[9] Subsequently published as *Faith by Statute* (Royal Historical Society, 1982).
[10] S. Lambert, 'Procedure in the House of Commons in the early Stuart period', *English Historical Review*, 95 (1980), 753–81.

actually preceded revisionism. Geoffrey Elton's main scholarly work on the parliaments of Elizabeth, *The Parliament of England, 1559–1581*, has just appeared as these words are being written.[11] It will have been reviewed long before they are read, but in a sense the battle lines are already drawn, both on the issues of substance and upon the contingent issue of Neale's scholarly reputation. The initial salvos have been fired, and smoke is already clouding the spectators' vision, but no doubt when the heat of battle has subsided a new pattern of historical interpretation will have emerged, to be challenged in its turn in due course. Geoffrey Elton has lost none of his crusading zeal when it comes to historical accuracy, and his insistence that the business of parliament was to produce legislation, and not to fight the political battles more appropriate to the council and the court, is fundamentally and appropriately similar to his insight into the reformation parliament over thirty years ago. Ironically enough, however, his position has also been challenged in recent years by those whose perception of accuracy is even more rigorous than his own. The cliometricians led by William Fogel, the author of *Time on the Cross*,[12] have resurrected the concept of scientific history in a guise appropriate to the computer age. Basically, Fogel has argued that statistical data can and should be used to produce interpretative models of the kind used by social scientists, and that these models are valid for purposes of historical understanding. In a courteous skirmish with Fogel entitled *Which Road to the Past?*, published in 1983, Geoffrey Elton admitted the validity of statistical methods for certain purposes, but denied the priority which the cliometricians accorded them. Not only were such methods applicable only to the very recent past, he argued, but they led to an understandable over-emphasis upon the measurable (such as demography and wealth) at the expense of the unmeasurable (such as ideas and personalities). A good traditional historian should not despise either collectivities or statistics (or computers, for that matter), but must always remember that the evidence he uses was very seldom produced with such a purpose in mind. In 1983, no less than in 1953, Geoffrey Elton's prescription for the true historian was to confront his evidence upon its own terms

. . . dedicated to the unbiased study of the past, conscious of the unending variety of that past, and the great variety of techniques which help that study . . .[13]

As one of his own sources might have said, 'all is fish that cometh to the net'.

Geoffrey Elton is the elder son of the late Professor Victor Ehrenberg, at one time Professor of Classics at King's College, London. He came to England with his family to escape the Nazis, and received his English education at

---

[11] CUP, November 1986.   [12] Boston, 1974.
[13] *Which Road to the Past?* (Yale UP, 1983), p. 121.

Rydal School in North Wales, where memories of those days are still keenly recalled. From 1940 to 1943 he acted as an assistant master at the school, also studying for an external B.A. of the University of London, through University College, at that time evacuated to Bangor. After a brief period of public service, from 1946 to 1948 he was Derby Research Student at UCL, and having obtained his Ph.D was appointed to an assistantship at Glasgow University, where he remained one year. In 1949 he arrived in Cambridge as an assistant lecturer, and settled down to that remarkable and distinguished scholarly and teaching career which this collection of essays is designed to celebrate. He was elected to a Fellowship at Clare College soon after his arrival, and became a Lecturer in 1953. Owing to the traditional academic snobbery of an ancient university, he remained officially 'Mr Elton' until receiving the degree of Litt.D in 1960 – a typically Eltonian method of dealing with a minor irritation! In 1963 he became a Reader of the University, and was promoted to a personal chair, as already noticed, in 1967. The latter year also saw his election to a Fellowship of the British Academy, a body to whose affairs he has subsequently devoted a great deal of time and effort. The summit of his academic career came in 1983 when he succeeded Owen Chadwick in the Regius Chair of Modern History, an event which he celebrated with a typically outspoken inaugural lecture. It was a declaration of faith in his discipline, and in the historical importance of his adopted country, which should stand as an encouragement and as a guide to his beleaguered colleagues in these difficult times.[14] In 1986 he received the honour of knighthood in the New Year List and all his friends were delighted, not only by the recognition itself, but also by the pleasure which it clearly gave him. Although he is now retiring from his chair, it is impossible to imagine Geoffrey Elton retiring from historical scholarship, and quite certain that history will continue to need him for many years to come.

In 1952 he married fellow-historian, Sheila Lambert, and it would be unworthy to end any tribute of friendship without also recognising both her sterling professional qualities and the immensely important role which she has played in turning students, research students, visiting scholars and colleagues into personal friends. Friends moreover who continue to return to Cambridge from far away to share a meal and the inevitable glass of Glenfiddich or Jack Daniels. For many of us Geoffrey and Sheila Elton are a fixed point in a changing world, and a man who has never lacked relish for controversy has also remained a constant source of professional encouragement and intellectual stimulus.

[14] *The History of England* (Cambridge, 1984).

The three editors are Geoffrey's earliest doctoral students. In token of our gratitude, and on behalf of our fellow contributors, we offer these essays as a tribute to our mentor.

MCC
University of York

DML
University College of North Wales, Bangor

JJS
University of Warwick

1986

Abbreviations

BL	British Library
Cal. Sp.	*Calendar of State Papers, Spanish*, ed. Begenroth *et al.* (London, 1862–1954)
EETS	Early English Text Society
EHR	*English Historical Review*
HHL	Henry Huntingdon Library
HMC	Historical Manuscripts Commission
JEH	*Journal of Ecclesiastical History*
LP	*Letters and Papers, Foreign and Domestic, of the Reign of Henry VIII*, ed. J. S. Brewer *et al.*, 21 vols., and *Addenda* (London, 1862–1932)
PCC	Prerogative Court of Canterbury
PRO	Public Record Office
RO	Record Office
STC^2	*A Short-title Catalogue of Books Printed in England, Scotland, & Ireland and of English Books Printed Abroad, 1475–1640*, 2nd edn., ed. W. A. Jackson, F. S. Ferguson, and Katharine F. Pantzer. Bibliographical Society (London, 1976–)
St. Pap.	*State Papers During the Reign of Henry VIII*. Record Commission (London, 1830–52)
ULC	Cambridge University Library
VCH	*Victoria County History*
C 65	Chancery, Parliament Rolls
C 193	Chancery, Crown Office, Precedent Books
E 101	Exchequer, K.R., Accounts Various
E 159	Exchequer, K.R., Memoranda Rolls
OBS	Public Record Office, Obsolete Lists and Indexes
REQ 3	Court of Requests, Miscellanea
SP 1	State Papers, Henry VIII, General Series
SP 6	State Papers, Henry VIII, Theological Tracts
STAC 2	Star Chamber Proceedings, Henry VIII

Figures after references to *LP* are to numbers of documents; in all other cases they are to pages.

Wolsey and the Parliament of 1523

JOHN GUY

'NEWES', wrote Thomas Cromwell to John Creke on 17 August 1523, 'refresshith the spy[rit] of lyffe'. His letter followed hard upon the dissolution four days earlier of the only parliament summoned during Wolsey's chancellorship.

> Wherfor ye shall vnderstonde that by long tyme I amongist other haue Indured a parlyament which contenwid by the space of xvij hole wekes wher we communyd of warre, pease, Stryffe, contencyon, debatte, murmure, grudge, Riches, pouerte, penurye, trowth, falshode, Justyce, equyte, discayte, opprescyon, Magnanymyte, actyuyte, force, attempraunce, Treason, murder, Felonye, consyli[ation], and also how a commune welth myght be ediffyed and a[lso] contenewid within our Realme. Howbeyt in conclusyon we haue d[one] as our predecessors haue been wont to doo that ys to say, as well as we myght and lefte wher we begann.[1]

That this parliament was acrimonious thanks to Wolsey's heavy-handedness is uncontroversial.[2] The cardinal soured the atmosphere from the start by demanding supply of £800,000 on top of the £204,424 he collected from the laity by means of 'loans' in 1522–3.[3] When the commons mustered, Wolsey

---

[1] SP 1/28, fo. 153 (*LP* iii (2) 3249); printed by R. B. Merriman, *Life and Letters of Thomas Cromwell* (2 vols., Oxford, 1902), I, pp. 313–14.

[2] Previous studies are by J. S. Roskell, *The Commons and their Speakers in English Parliaments, 1376–1523* (Manchester, 1965), pp. 324–32; R. Pauli, 'Kardinal Wolsey und das Parlament vom Jahre 1523', *Historische Zeitschrift*, 21 (1869), 28–64; G. R. Elton, *Reform and Reformation: England 1509–1558* (London, 1977), pp. 88–91; A. F. Pollard, *Wolsey* (London, 1929), pp. 132–4. The significance of Thomas More's request for freedom of speech for the commons has been treated by J. E. Neale, 'The commons' privilege of free speech in parliament', repr. by E. B. Fryde and E. Miller, eds., *Historical Studies of the English Parliament* (2 vols., Cambridge, 1970), II, pp. 147–76. An account of this is not repeated here; see also Roskell, p. 42. The argument of R. L. Woods that Wolsey cemented his power and opened the door to commonwealth politics in 1523 is unconvincing: 'Politics and precedent: Wolsey's parliament of 1523', *Huntington Library Quarterly*, 40 (1977), 297–312; see also his 'The amicable grant: some aspects of Thomas Wolsey's rule in England, 1522–1526', unpublished U.C.L.A. Ph.D dissertation (1974), pp. 20–62.

[3] *LP* iii (2) 2483(3), p. 1050; J. J. Goring, 'The general proscription of 1522', *English Historical Review*, 86 (1971), 685–705; G. W. Bernard, *War, Taxation, and Rebellion in early Tudor England: Henry VIII, Wolsey, and the Amicable Grant of 1525* (Brighton, 1986), pp. 110–30. Clerical taxation and the convocations of Canterbury and York are outside the scope of this contribution.

I

blustered. He retorted 'that he would rather have his tongue, plucked out of his hedde with a paire of pinsons, then to move the kyng, to take any lesse some'; he tried to overawe M.P.s but met 'a marvellous obstinate silence'; he lied that the lords had offered the requisite taxation; he reneged on his promise of 1522 that the 'loans' would be repaid out of the proceeds of the next parliamentary subsidy.[4] Yet what proportion of the parliament was taken up by the subsidy negotiations? Did Wolsey have intentions besides taxation in 1523 that, in the event, he was unable to pursue? Although it cannot be proved beyond any shadow of doubt, documentary evidence exists to suggest that he launched policies on enclosures and collusive recoveries in parliament. These came to nothing; the subsidy bill was not ready even by mid-July. And the legislation that did emerge in 1523 deserves scrutiny. Of course, there is no question that reform by statute was ever part of Wolsey's scheme – that idea is too much for anyone to swallow. Wolsey was linked to proposals on enclosures and recoveries, but his failure to make progress with either confirms the incompetence with which he managed this parliament.

When parliament assembled on 15 April, the bishop of London, Cuthbert Tunstall, master of the rolls, delivered the speech from the throne.[5] Extant in a fully written out version, his address was a sermon on the text 'Justitia et judicium preparatio sedis tuae' (Ps. 89:14). It was a rambling and inchoate performance but it established 'justice' and 'commonwealth' as the slogans of 1523. The requirements of good law were that it should be 'honeste, juste, resonable, necessary, manifeste, and proffitable for the comon weale'. If the present parliament 'doo wele and substancyally order the lawes and statutes it ys not to be doubtede but al this roialme schalbe put yn gode order and this gode order wolde be soon hade yf that men whiche now be assembled entendyd no thynge but the comon weale'. But regal justice 'standyth yn juste exercise of batelles and warres ayenste al those that doythe invade or entendyth to destroye hys persone, hys roialme or hys subjectes'. This remark paved the way for Tunstall's advocacy of the king's necessity. When adversaries were not subject to his laws the king had no redress, for he lacked superiors to whom he might complain. No option thus existed but 'to expunge

For these and Wolsey's attempt to convoke a legatine synod, see M. Kelly, 'Canterbury jurisdiction and influence during the episcopate of William Warham, 1503–1532', unpublished Cambridge Ph.D. dissertation (1963), pp. 174–6, 306–10, 316–17.

[4] Edward Hall, *Henry VIII*, ed. C. Whibley (2 vols., London, 1904 [1550 edn.]), I, pp. 286–7; D. Hay, ed., *The Anglica Historia of Polydore Vergil* (Camden Society, 3rd series, 74, 1950), p. 306; R. S. Sylvester and D. P. Harding, eds., *Two Early Tudor Lives* (New Haven, 1962), p. 206; H. Ellis, ed., *Original Letters Illustrative of English History*, 1st series (3 vols., 2nd edn., London, 1825), I, p. 221 (hereafter cited as Ellis); *LP* iii(2) 2484; BL, Cotton MS Cleopatra F. 6, fos. 316–20; Goring, 'The general proscription of 1522', p. 700.

[5] SP 6/13, fos. 3–19 (*LP Add.* 378). Other versions of the speech are Hall, I, pp. 278–9; Supplement to the *Rolls of Parliament*, printed as an appendix to *Journals of the House of Lords*, I, p. lxxv (hereafter cited as *Rot. Parl.* suppl.); R. Brown, ed., *Calendar of State Papers . . . Venice*, III (London, 1869), p. 313.

and convince them by batele and stronge hande, and the hole roialme ys bownde to ayde and assiste ther kynge yn this cause'.[6] Wolsey reinforced these remarks in his main policy statement to the commons on 29 April. He declared 'how the Frenche kyng Fraunces the first ... had so often tymes broken promise with the kyng of England, and his welbeloved nephew Charles the Emperor, that the kyng of his honor, could no longer suffre'. Henry VIII 'of necessitie was driven to warre and defence, whiche in no wise could be mainteined, without great somes of money'. Wolsey demanded taxation at the rate of 4s. in the £ on goods and land, which he claimed would raise £800,000; 'for he saied that the yere folowing, the kyng and the Emperour should make suche warre in Fraunce, as hath not bene sene'.[7]

The 1523 parliament had three sessions, the first two at Blackfriars from 15 April to 21 May and from 10 June to 29 July, and the third at Westminster from 31 July to 13 August. The dates of the first two sessions followed those of Easter (5 April) and Whitsuntide (24 May); the third was really an adjournment to Westminster of the second on account of plague in London.[8] But the third session encroached further into the summer than any other meeting of parliament between 1433 and the Long Parliament: the nearest equivalent was the summer session of Charles I's first parliament, held at Oxford from 1st to 12th August 1625. And there were contemporary comments. Richard Lyster, Henry VIII's solicitor-general, informed Lord Darcy on 28 April that no bills had yet passed the lords or the commons, but a subsidy was demanded for the war with France.[9] The earl of Surrey's correspondent wrote on 14 May:

sithens the begynnyng of the Parliamente there hathe bene the grettiste and soreste hold in the lower Hous for payemente of lj^s. of the li. that ever was sene I thinke in any parliamente. This matier hathe bene debated and beatten xv. or xvj dayes to giddir: the hieste necessitie alleged on the Kings behalf to us that ever was herd of: and of the contrarie, the hieste povertie confessed, as well by knights, squiers, and gentilmen of every quarter, as by the commoners, citezeins, and burgessis. There hathe bene suche hold that the Hous was like to have bene disseevered; that is to sey the Knights being of the Kings Counsaill, the Kings servaunts, and gentilmen, of the oon partie, whiche in soo long tyme were spoken with and made to sey ye; it may fortune, contrarie to their hert, will, and conscience.[10]

So Wolsey's initial demand of taxation at the rate of 4s. in the £ was a bargaining ploy; real negotiations centred on the prospect of half that amount – that is, the basic rate used for the 'loans' of 1522-3. Indeed, this was unremarkable. In 1512 Archbishop Warham had asked parliament for £600,000 'to meynteyne the warys one yere' before settling for £126,745.[11]

---

[6] SP 6/13, fos. 14, 17-18.
[7] Hall, I, pp. 284-5. Wolsey's claim was extravagant; a tax of 4s. in the £ would have produced nearer £400,000. Cf. Bernard, *War, Taxation, and Rebellion*, p. 117.
[8] *Rot. Parl.* suppl., p. cxlviii.   [9] *LP* iii (2) 2982.
[10] Ellis, 1st series, I, pp. 220-1.   [11] Bernard, *War, Taxation, and Rebellion*, p. 121.

Next, Wolsey had expressly promised when instructing his collectors for the first 'loan' that the money was refundable from the proceeds of the next parliamentary grant, hence there was logic from the government's viewpoint in applying the rate of tax most likely to achieve this purpose.[12] But Surrey's correspondent continued: 'My lorde Cardinall hathe promysed on his feithe that the ij^s. of the li. of lone money shalbe payed with a good will and with thanke. But no daye is appoyntid thereof'.[13] And here is the nub. The 'loans' were not to be repaid promptly; the Crown's debt was eventually cancelled by an act of 1529 on the grounds that the 'loans' were used for the defence of the realm and might thus be deemed taxation. Also a cumulative burden of taxation had arisen by 1523. It is hardly surprising that the commons pleaded poverty when £288,814 had been levied in lay taxation between 1512 and 1517 and the 'loans' raised £204,424 from the laity.[14] In fact, those M.P.s who complained that the realm lacked adequate liquidity for taxation on this scale had some right on their side.[15]

Surrey's correspondent reported an offer of supply on 13 May at the basic rate of 2s. in the £ on goods and lands, adding 'this matier is soo ferre passid that the parliament woll sone bee endid'. But his conjecture was wrong, for according to the chronicler Edward Hall, Wolsey continued the haggling. Hall's vivid account lacks detailed corroboration, but it satisfactorily explains the long delay in drafting the subsidy bill. He wrote: 'This graunt was reported to the Cardinall, which therwith was sore discontent, and saied, that the lordes had graunted iiii.s. of the pound, whiche was proved untrue.'[16] And a revised offer on 21 May did not conclude the matter, since either Wolsey declined it, or M.P.s themselves had second thoughts over the Whitsun recess. In a period when counted votes were extremely rare in the house of commons, M.P.s divided on a third proposal on 27 June, when the motion was defeated: 'the question was asked . . . then was the house divided, and all the commons severed theimselfes, from the knightes of the sheres, so that one yea part remained onely the knightes of the shire, and the commons stifly affirmed that the mocioners of this demaunde, were enemies to the realme'.[17] Hall said that the speaker, Sir Thomas More, was obliged to recall M.P.s: 'and after long perswadyng, and privie laboryng of frendes' the rates of the subsidy were finalised.[18] This may have been about 6 July, since Sir John Hussey, one of the king's councillors most active in the commons, told Darcy that day: 'We be yet so busied with common causes in the Parliament, that there is no leisure to

---

[12] *LP* iii (2) 2484; BL, Cotton MS Cleopatra F 6, fos. 316–20; Goring, 'The general proscription of 1522', p. 700; R. S. Schofield, 'Parliamentary lay taxation 1485–1547', unpublished Cambridge Ph.D dissertation (1963), pp. 36, 329–30.

[13] Ellis, 1st series, I, p. 221.

[14] *LP* iii (2) 2483(3), p. 1050; Schofield, 'Parliamentary lay taxation', pp. 198–212, table 40 (facing p. 416); Bernard, *War, Taxation, and Rebellion*, pp. 119–20.

[15] Hall, I, pp. 285–6; Bernard, *War, Taxation, and Rebellion*, pp. 115–17.

[16] Ellis, 1st series, I, p. 221; Hall, I, p. 287.   [17] Hall, I, pp. 287–8.   [18] Hall, I, p. 288.

solicit our own particular matters . . . The Parliament goeth forth, and sums of money are granted.'[19]

Yet the decision upon the subsidy's rates did not conclude the business. The requisite legislation had to be drafted and enacted, a task still not completed by the middle of July. For Wolsey wrote to Henry VIII:

Over this, Sir, though it was thought by the Speker and [. . .] Common House, that their boke for the graunte nowe to be passed, shuld [have been] perfited and brought unto me as yesterday, yet neverthelas the same ca[nnot come] til tomorowe, at the hithermost. And for asmoche as after the [. . .] in to the Upper House, it wol require a good tracte [of time to] oversee and groundely digest the same to your most profite . . . it may th[erefore please] Your Grace to geve commaundement for ordering of your provisions [. . .] the certein tyme of your commyng to Bridewel, til suche seaon as [. . .] exhibicion of the said boke, and otherwise advertised [. . .] tyme when the same, and al other affaires of your Parliament, shal of likelihode be in good redynes; so that sone after the commyng of Your Highnes, every thing may take ende and be perfited accordingly.[20]

The letter established that, drafting delays apart, the subsidy bill required 'a good tracte' even after its introduction in the lords, but Wolsey expected the dissolution of parliament when this and 'other affaires' were completed.

Although Wolsey's letter is undated, it must have been written before the decision to prorogue parliament to Westminster, since the king would lodge at Bridewell only to dissolve a parliament held at Blackfriars, and Henry, in the event, did not stay at Bridewell but at Richmond.[21] Since, however, Wolsey began his letter by reporting receipt of a despatch from Richard Sampson sent from Valladolid on 3 July, he could not have addressed Henry VIII much before 14th, since the likely journey time between Valladolid and London was eleven days.[22] Yet the subsidy bill was still not ready for the lords then.

The subsidy negotiations therefore ruled this parliament until late July. Even after the rates of tax were agreed, extra time was needed to perfect the arrangements for collecting the subsidy. For Wolsey meant to improve the methods of assessing and collecting taxation begun with the subsidies of 1513–15 and the 'loans' of 1522–3. Innovations in 1523 were to transfer assessments of the peerage from the usual commissioners to the supervision of Wolsey and other senior officials; to define the law of distress in default of payment of taxes so as to allow defaulters only eight days' grace before their goods were sold; and to exonerate collectors at the exchequer from sums they were unable to collect, or levy by distress, if the defaulters had died or fled.[23]

[19] *LP* iii (2) 3164.
[20] *St. Pap.*, i, pp. 116–17. The document was damaged during the Cottonian Library fire.
[21] PRO, OBS 1419 (Henry VIII's itinerary).
[22] *LP* iii (2) 3150. The journey could take longer; *LP* iii (2) 3247, 3281 (letter sent 17 Aug. received on 30th).
[23] *Rot. Parl.* suppl., pp. lxxvi-xc; R. S. Schofield, 'Parliamentary lay taxation', pp. 213–14. See also *LP* iv (1) 1117; (2) 2972.

Stricter assessment of the peerage is enough to explain Wolsey's reference to 'a good tracte' but any major dispute cost time. The question is whether Wolsey fell over his own feet. What happened to his plans for 'justice' and 'commonwealth'? Did such plans exist?

The first sign that they did is given by the Welsh chronicler, Elis Gruffudd, who began to write in 1530.[24] Since his remarks have never been printed, lengthy quotation is justified.

At this time the common people of the realm were greatly angered especially by the cattle and sheep which caused much damage within the realm, so much so, that a number of preachers showed plainly from the pulpit the way sheep in many places within the realm grazed so low that they grazed towns and parishes and swallowed an innumerable number of men. Against this and to put an end to this destruction the king, on the cardinal's advice, called a parliament . . . In this parliament certain knights of the realm were created lords such as Sir William Sandes, Sir Maurice Berkeley, Sir Nicholas Vaux and others. And in this parliament a great furore was made over the damage which the sheep were then causing within the realm. The cardinal firmly and forcefully promised that no man in England should maintain or graze sheep on lowland to destroy ploughing and harrowing, and that no one from then on should enclose the land which was usually common land of that region's tenants . . . The wealthy farmers, having heard the way the burgesses in the lower house held out strongly against them concerning what is related before, made great labour to win the cardinal's favour who indeed allowed the matter to respite by demanding a tax for the king to augment his coffers and to replenish the money he spent in the triumph and to maintain him against the French, since negotiations between him and others involved were likely to be cut short.[25]

That Arthur Plantagenet, illegitimate son of Edward IV, was ennobled Viscount Lisle, and that Sandes, Berkeley and Vaux were created barons within a fortnight of the opening of parliament, is confirmed by the *Chronicle of Calais*.[26] And there is little doubt that the furore reported by Gruffudd took place, because the general pardon that accompanied the subsidy in 1523 included a section on enclosures. The act pardoned illegal enclosures, destruction of houses, or conversion of land from tillage to pasture done before 8 August 1523, provided the enclosures were down, buildings restored, and lands returned to tillage by 13 October 1524. Those in breach of the enclosure statutes would otherwise have to appear in chancery to explain why they did not comply, when they would be required to obey whatever order the court should make. Existing enclosure fines and proceedings were respited until 1524, but they were to be revived then if the enclosures were not

[24] T. Jones, 'A Welsh chronicler in Tudor England', *Welsh History Review*, 1 (1960), 1–17.
[25] National Library of Wales, MS 3054D, fos. 448ᵛ–9. I am grateful to Mr Glyn Parry of the Department of Manuscripts and Records for transcribing and translating this passage from the Welsh original, and to Dr G. W. Bernard for drawing Gruffudd's chronicle to my attention. See also HMC, *Report on Manuscripts in the Welsh Language*, 1 (London, 1898), pp. 214–21.
[26] J. G. Nichols, ed., *The Chronicle of Calais* (Camden Society, O.S., 35, 1846), pp. 32–3.

down, houses rebuilt, etc., or if satisfactory explanations had not been given in chancery according to the timetable laid down in the act of pardon.[27]

In fact, Gruffudd's account and the act of pardon harmonise if we assume that Wolsey bargained away his position on enclosures during the subsidy negotiations. According to Gruffudd, however, Wolsey had promised to extend the attack on enclosures to protect the rights of tenants in common lands. The chronicler did not say that Wolsey introduced a new bill for enclosures, and no evidence exists that he did, but it is probable that the matter was indeed raised in the terms reported by Gruffudd and that Wolsey was rebuffed in parliament. Acts of 1489 and 1514–15 had forbidden new enclosures and ordered demolished buildings to be reconstructed and land returned to tillage.[28] But customary tenants had no redress against landlords who enclosed commons, because it was not illegal to hedge or ditch lands not previously under the plough, and the statutes of approvement regulating intakes from wastes and commons (1235, 1285) covered only freeholders.[29] Customary tenants in these cases had to resort to chancery and the conciliar courts – this Wolsey knew from his experience as presiding judge there.[30] Did he mean to offer statutory protection against arbitrary intakes by landlords? There is no definitive answer but Gruffudd's report is entirely credible.

Yet far from extending Wolsey's campaign, even his current policy on enclosures was stymied by the act of pardon. For he had decreed in chancery on 12 July 1518 that enclosures made since 1485 be pulled down within forty days and the lands restored to tillage. Those not complying faced a fine of £100 unless they proved in chancery that their enclosures were 'more beneficial for the commonwealth of this realm than the pulling down thereof'.[31] Yet the pardon of 1523 enabled defendants to escape until October 1524! It was not until the amnesty expired that convictions could be obtained. And in 1525–6 many new prosecutions were brought. But they resulted mainly from Wolsey's enclosure inquiry of 1517–18 – the one that preceded his decree.[32] So these cases lay dormant for over a year under the act of pardon and Wolsey had lost more than he gained if he was serious about enclosures. All he achieved in 1523 was an amnesty for the enclosing landlords.

Another report of commonwealth initiative comes from Edward Hall. He thought parliament was summoned 'both for the remedy of mischiefes whiche

---

[27] *Rot. Parl.* suppl., pp. xc-xciv (14 & 15 Henry VIII, c. 17).

[28] 4 Henry VII, cc. 16, 19; 6 Henry VIII, c. 5; 7 Henry VIII, c. 1. J. J. Scarisbrick, 'Cardinal Wolsey and the common weal' in E. W. Ives, R. J. Knecht, and Scarisbrick, eds., *Wealth and Power in Tudor England* (London, 1978), pp. 45–67; R. W. Heinze, *The Proclamations of the Tudor Kings* (Cambridge, 1976), pp. 94–8.

[29] E. Kerridge, *Agrarian Problems in the Sixteenth Century and After* (London, 1969), pp. 94–5; A. W. B. Simpson, *An Introduction to the History of the Land Law* (Oxford, 1961), p. 107.

[30] For example: STAC 2/13/83–4; 13/144, 15/11–13; 17/396; 30/46; 30/138; 32/70.

[31] *LP* ii (2) App. 53; Heinze, p. 96.

[32] Scarisbrick, 'Cardinal Wolsey and the common weal', p. 62 n. 40.

be in the common law, as recoveries, forain vouchers and corrupt trials. And for makyng and orderyng of new estatutes which may be to the high avauncement of the common wealth.'[33] He makes Tunstall say so in his opening speech, which does not tally with other versions. But Hall was a common lawyer of Gray's Inn; his statement that one of the government's intentions in 1523 was to reform the law of recoveries must be taken seriously. Indeed there is corroboration. For when John Palsgrave, tutor to Princess Mary and the duke of Richmond, stigmatised Wolsey he wrote, 'We have begun to reform the abusions of the temporal law, especially concerning calumniation and recoveries.' Another version explained, 'We have begun to redress the abusions of the temporal law, especially that learned men should sign such books as they presented to the court, and that recoveries should no more be used.'[34] It became Wolsey's policy in both chancery and star chamber to urge counsel to sign the documents of litigation (bills, answers, etc. were sometimes called 'books' by pleaders).[35] And by 1523 the law of recoveries had reached a crucial stage of its development.

Recoveries were real actions designed to convey land but they were usually collusive, in which case their purpose could be disreputable. From the middle of the fifteenth century conveyancers used them to alienate entailed lands for a fee simple, to transmit the fee simple of lands held in use to the *cestui que use* who had come of age, or to buy and sell land safely. The method was not watertight until 1532, when it was perfected, but it was good enough. For the law was that if a tenant in tail left substitute lands of equal value to his heirs, they could not challenge his alienation of his own land: the heirs were barred from their family estates if a judgment had been obtained entitling them to recover lands of equal value. Exactly this judgment was obtained collusively in a recovery. It directed that the alienee, who was the demandant in the action, should recover the land from the tenant, who in his turn should recover different lands of equal value from a third party whom he had vouched to warranty. Here was the trick. The alienor conceded the demandant's case even though it was feigned, because he wished to sell him the land. But to bar the entail he pleaded that since he had originally bought the lands from X, that person was bound to warrant, or guarantee, his title – that is, the third party was legally obliged to compensate him out of his own estates. The plea was untrue, but it brought X into court. When X, who worked for money, appeared, the parties craved leave to imparl – that is, they sought an adjournment. In fact, X deliberately absconded, hence judgment was given that

---

[33] Hall, I, p. 278.

[34] *LP* iv (3) 5750 (pp. 2555, 2557, 2562).

[35] Signatures in chancery are tabulated by F. Metzger, 'Das Englische Kanzleigericht unter Kardinal Wolsey, 1515–1529', unpublished Erlangen Ph.D dissertation (1976), pp. 355–7. Examples of signatures in star chamber are STAC 2/1/130; 2/148; 3/1–2, 59, 314; 4/2, 19, 206, 214–16; 17/332; 19/90; 20/181, 196; 23/242; 27/31; 33/15, 68; 35/74. Documents were rarely, if ever, signed by counsel before Wolsey's incumbency.

the alienee should have the land and that X should provide compensation. And since compensation was awarded the alienor's heirs were protected in law. But they were defrauded in fact. For X was always a man of straw who had no assets; the role was sometimes taken by a minor official of the common pleas. The latter half of the judgment was wholly imaginary: its purpose was to extinguish any claim that the alienor's heirs might conceivably produce against the alienee, who acquired a safe fee simple.[36]

Hall referred to recoveries, foreign vouchers and corrupt trials. 'Foreign' meant only that a tenant litigating in one jurisdiction vouched to warranty someone from another county and asked that he be summoned; the phrase 'corrupt trials' in the context of recoveries implied collusive actions to fraudulent ends. And that they caused considerable anxiety is confirmed by Christopher St German, who discussed them at length in *Doctor and Student*. The question was whether they were unconscionable owing to the collusion involved.

For that that they that be named demaundauntis shuld haue ryght to the lande where in trouth they neuer had ryght therto: wherupon folowth a false supposel in the wryt: & a false supposell in the declaracyon & a voucher to warraunte by couyn of such a persone as hath no thyng to yelde in value & therupon by couyn and collucyon of the partyes foloweth the default of the vouchee: by the whiche defaulte the Iugement shall be gyuen / And so all that Iugement is deryuyed & groundyd of the vntrue supposel & couyn of the partyes / wherby the lawe of the realme that hath ordayned suche a wryt of entre to helpe them that haue ryght to landes or tenementis is defraudyd: the courte is desceyuyd the heyr is disherited.

The doctor spoke these words, but the student had no convincing answer: 'And so I am in maner perplexed and wot not what to say in this case.'[37]

Yet the most damaging fraud of all was that the estate of the leaseholder did not easily survive a recovery suffered by the lessor. A lessee could try to intervene pending the action and in a case of 1522 the recovery was stayed until the determination of the lease. But the lessee would rarely know of the recovery; even the alienee might remain in ignorance until it was too late.[38] Whether or not the lessee could 'falsify' the recovery was doubtful. Lessees with written agreements fared better at common law than those with verbal ones, but the best hope for redress was to petition the lord chancellor. Wolsey entertained over 450 leasehold cases in chancery during his incumbency and a smaller number in star chamber.[39] He had every reason to plug this loophole

---

[36] Simpson, *Land Law*, pp. 117–29; J. H. Baker, ed., *The Reports of Sir John Spelman* (2 vols., Selden Society, London, 1977–8), II, pp. *204–6*.

[37] T. F. T. Plucknett and J. L. Barton, eds., *St German's Doctor and Student* (Selden Society, London, 1975), pp. 160, 162.

[38] Baker, ed., II, pp. *182–3*.

[39] F. Metzger, 'Litigation in the equitable court of chancery, 1515–1529' (unpublished analysis of PRO, *List of Early Chancery Proceedings*, v [Lists and Indexes, XXXVIII, London, 1912]), p. 6. I am grateful to Dr Metzger for permission to cite his paper. Examples of cases in star chamber

by promoting new legislation. Indeed the matter was more urgent than the breaking of entails, which many landowners no longer regarded as sacrosanct but as a device to prevent heirs disposing of assets before they came of age. In fact, nothing reached the statute book until after Wolsey's fall. The requisite legislation was enacted in the first session of the Reformation Parliament. The act (21 Henry VIII, c. 15) described how leaseholders had been cheated and awarded them the same rights as freeholders to 'falsify' recoveries to which they were not parties. It was even retrospective in scope. The leaseholder was given full security of tenure during the term of his lease provided he continued to pay his existing rent to any new landowner. In his *Commentaries on the Laws of England* Blackstone praised the far-reaching nature of this reform, which guaranteed enjoyment of the long lease and enabled mortgages and family settlements to be built upon leases.[40]

Was the leasehold act some unfinished business of 1523? Since the original acts and Lords' Journals for 1523 and 1529 are lost, Wolsey's 'commonwealth' intentions must be conjectured. The chroniclers' statements are circumstantial but they cannot be ignored. Something lies behind them. And the obvious explanation is that Wolsey had plans in 1523 that went beyond taxation. If so, he failed: it is probable that his mishandling of the subsidy cost him the business that Gruffudd and Hall described.

And other 'commonwealth' business may have been lost in 1523. The editors of the *Calendar of Letters and Papers* listed five bills as belonging to that year.[41] One empowered owners of coal mines to drain off the water from them. The preamble argued that the commonwealth should be preferred to any private wealth, and that, among the commodities of the realm, 'ther is a certayne fuell of colles comonly called secolles wyche is gotten under the grounde and in many parties of this Realme the sayd colles liethes so depe undre ye gro[u]nd thatt they can nott be gottyn witheout grett soughes and trenches made under the erthe wherby the watter may voyd'. The document is incomplete but its intention was doubtless to allow drainage across the ground of other landowners.[42] Since Wolsey had just obtained the bishopric of Durham, the bill may be connected to his discovery that coal royalties numbered among his episcopal privileges. Mines at Whickham, for instance,

---

are STAC 2/2/108–12; 4/206; 4/214–16; 6/170–5; 20/249. A case brought to Wolsey in star chamber that was referred to the dean of the chapel is *Coffe* v. *Long* (REQ 3/5 [bundle]). It illustrates the loophole in unusual detail, every document of litigation being extant from bill of complaint to final decree. The lessee petitioned Wolsey following a recovery suffered in Hilary term 1509 by Lewis Pollard and others, feoffees to the use of Margaret Beaufort. The decree (30 April 1521) was a compromise whereby the plaintiff released his interest to the alienee in exchange for compensation.

[40] *Commentaries on the Laws of England*, ed. J. Stewart (4 vols., London, 1844), II, p. 164.

[41] SP 1/233, fos. 245–7; SP 1/234, fos. 43–8, 53–4, 60. Since the editors of *LP* kept no key, it is impossible to tell where these documents were found or upon what basis they were dated.

[42] SP 1/234, fo. 60 (*LP Add.* 419).

were worth 500 marks a year, and Wolsey was advised to rebuild Hartlepool harbour to stimulate the trade.[43]

Two bills, which are preserved with two copies of a working paper, restrained waste of timber. One restricted taking of the king's timber by forest officials and required those responsible for wood sales to fence off areas where trees had been felled in order that new growth might proceed without interference from grazing animals. Another bill ordered private landlords to protect 'the springs of the woods' for six years after felling. Cattle were to be kept away from the young trees and, if necessary, woodlands might be enclosed.[44]

The other two bills concerned glaziers and skinners. The London glaziers' company wanted foreign craftsmen dwelling in the suburbs of the city to be subject to civic ordinances and to employ English apprentices and servants.[45] The skinners sought free trade.[46] Those of Coventry and Bristol, in particular, wished to trade with the London skinners who had been forbidden by their company to buy lambskins tawed in the provinces. Bills of this type would have been drafted on private initiative: the process is documented for London. For on 12 March 1523 the court of aldermen named a committee of fourteen 'to devyse what thinges be most necessary & behovfull for the Co[mm]en weale of this Cite to be moved at this next parliament to be holden the xv day of Aprille'.[47] The committee may have sat through virtually the whole of parliament's first session, since it was not until 16 May that 'a bill of petic[i]on' was ready 'concernyng certeyn Offices withyn this Cite with a provyso concernyng thoffice of Co[mm]en Weyer'. Drafted by Richard Broke, a justice of common pleas, and William Shelley, serjeant-at-law and recorder of the city, the bill 'shall be exhibite & put up as it is'.[48] None of these bills succeeded in parliament but the glaziers' demands were subsumed within a general statute regulating handicrafts. The act (14 & 15 Henry VIII, c. 2) required aliens trading in the realm to employ only English apprentices and no more than two alien journeymen. Craftsmen dwelling in the London suburbs were to be subject to the jurisdiction of the city companies and their wares were to be marked for identification purposes – those of blacksmiths, joiners and coopers in every instance, and those of other trades at the discretion of the companies. The authorities of provincial towns were given similar powers but remedy was provided for craftsmen wrongfully vexed by the new regulations. The terms of the act were not retrospective: existing foreign workers could remain until the time of the next parliament. In fact, new

---

[43] BL, Cotton MS Titus B 1, fos. 295–7 (*LP* iii (2) 2946).

[44] SP 1/234, fos. 43–54 (*LP Add.* 415).

[45] SP 1/233, fo. 245 (*LP Add.* 384). [46] SP 1/233, fos. 246–7 (*LP Add.* 385).

[47] Corporation of London RO, Repertories of the Court of Aldermen 6, fo. 23.

[48] Ibid, fo. 38ᵛ. For the background to this episode, see STAC 2/24/50; HHL, Ellesmere MS 2655, fo. 17.

disputes arose which became the subject of star chamber action in February 1529.[49] Although no proof exists that the glaziers' bill and the handicrafts act were linked, the bill obviously predated the wider measure otherwise it would have served no purpose. It was corrected by Cromwell but his involvement, which may have been inside or outside parliament, is not easy to interpret.

Another act of 1523 had city connections. It sprang from a private petition of the society of physicians, which had achieved incorporation in 1518. In fact, the regulation of physicians had begun with acts of 1512 and 1514.[50] On 20 November 1522 Sir Thomas More brought to the court of aldermen in London a royal letter containing 'an ordre to be taken for the exercysyng of phesike within the Citie'.[51] The contents are unknown but the act of 1523 (c. 5) restricted the practice of medicine to graduates and those persons who underwent examination by the president and elects of the London society.

Yet the bulk of the legislation of 1523 has left few traces in the records. A draft of the act of authority for reversing attainders is extant, together with a proviso to that act.[52] And drafts survive that became provisos to the acts for Buckingham's attainder and for the duchess of Buckingham's jointure.[53] But these furnish no clues save that a proviso for Sir Richard Cornwall was corrected by Brian Tuke, clerk of the parliaments.[54] An extract of the subsidy act, which is included among the state papers, turns out to be a later copy.[55]

The sessional print of 1523 contained fourteen public acts.[56] Those chiefly affecting London were the handicrafts act (c. 2), an act regulating the Blackwell Hall cloth market (c. 1), an act repealing earlier trading restrictions on shoemakers (c. 9), and the act regulating physicians (c. 5). Acts directed at the provinces protected worsted weaving at Yarmouth and King's Lynn (c. 3), authorised road improvements in the Weald of Kent (c. 6), exempted Suffolk cloths from the size restrictions imposed by an act of 1515 (c. 11), and made perpetual an act of 1495 for rebuilding the port of Southampton (c. 13). More general acts required Englishmen sworn to foreign princes to pay customs at rates fixed for aliens (c. 4), exempted landowners worth £100 per annum from the ban on using or possessing crossbows and hand-guns (c. 7), prohibited

---

[49] STAC 2/2/44; 9/184; 10/230; 15/318; 31/140; 21 Henry VIII, c. 16.
[50] 3 Henry VIII, c. 11; 5 Henry VIII, c. 6.   [51] Repertory 6, fo. 6.
[52] SP 1/27, fos. 180–4 (LP iii(2) 2956(3)).   [53] SP 1/27, fos. 185–6 (LP iii(2) 2956(4–5)).
[54] SP 1/27, fo. 185.   [55] SP 1/27, fo. 178 (LP iii(2) 2956(2)).
[56] Peterborough Cathedral Library (at ULC), Pet. F 1. 19 (a bound collection containing copies of the statutes of 1, 3–4, 7, 11, and 19 Henry VII, and 1, 3, 4, 5, 6, 7, and 14 & 15 Henry VIII). The edition of 1523 acts is the sessional print (issued unbound) bearing the ownership signature of William Marshall. I am grateful to Dr Katharine F. Pantzer of Harvard University for advice in this matter. A slightly later edition of the acts of 1523 is Harvard University, Law School Library S 122a, MH-L. The Harvard edition has one fewer leaf than Peterborough and the woodcut depicting the royal badges is fresh in the Peterborough copy but worn at Harvard. The editions are typeset quite differently and Peterborough has an act out of sequence: c. 8 is followed by c. 12, then follow cc. 9, 10, 11, 13, 14. STC^2 9362.9 (Peterborough), 9362.10 (Harvard). The printing of public acts is discussed by G. R. Elton, 'The sessional printing of statutes, 1484–1547', in Ives, Knecht, and Scarisbrick, eds., Wealth and Power, pp. 68–86.

hare coursing by tracking prints in the snow (c. 10), exempted those serving in the king's wars from feudal incidents (c. 14), and attempted to provide sufficient small change by stipulating that half of all silver coins minted should be in groats, 20 per cent in half-groats, 20 per cent in pence, and 10 per cent in halfpence and farthings divided in the proportion of two to one (c. 12).[57] And an act permitted the six clerks of chancery to marry (c. 8). With four exceptions (cc. 1, 2, 3, 7) these acts appear on the *communes peticiones* section of the parliament roll where they are joined by an act too insignificant to be printed (that George Roll, keeper of the records of common pleas, should hold his office for life [c. 35]) and by the record of Edmond Shaa's discharge of the stigma of idiocy (a matter that got onto the roll by being made public in parliament).[58]

Supply acts and acts of pardon were printed separately from the sessional statute, but I can find no print of either for 1523. Eighteen private acts were enrolled but not printed, six of which concerned the crown. There was the act attainting the duke of Buckingham (c. 20), the act empowering the king to reverse attainders by letters patent (c. 21), an act re-grouping the manors that surrounded Henry VIII's new palace at New Hall, Essex (c. 18), and an act that manors previously held of Dover castle be held immediately of the king (c. 28). In the sphere of financial administration an act required payment of cash appropriations for the royal household direct to the treasurer of the chamber (c. 19). And a routine act continued the powers of the general surveyors of crown lands until the dissolution of the next parliament and made them responsible for auditing the expenditure of prests received by individuals from the king (c. 15).[59]

Of the other twelve private acts eleven concerned individuals and one the merchants of the Steelyard. Persons settling family and property affairs were Sir William Compton, Sir Henry Wyatt, Sir Richard Sacheverell, the earls of Shrewsbury and Northumberland, Sir Andrew Windsor, Lord Marney, Thomas Kitson, and Sir George Tailboys and his family. All but two of these acts arose, however, from the need to protect estates in the aftermath of Buckingham's fall. The exceptions were the act that discharged Wyatt's Kentish estates from the customs of partible inheritance (c. 32) and that which settled estates on Elizabeth Tailboys (c. 34). In addition the duchess of Buckingham secured her jointure (c. 22), and Buckingham's heir and daughter-in-law obtained enactment of the letters patent by which Henry VIII had restored various properties to them (c. 23). Lastly, the merchants of the Steelyard received exemption from any legislation of the parliament prejudicial to their privileges (c. 29); presumably they had in mind the act regulating the wholesale cloth market.

[57] C. E. Challis, *The Tudor Coinage* (Manchester, 1978), p. 202.
[58] C 65/137, mm. 13–17, 44–7. G. R. Elton, 'The rolls of parliament, 1449–1547', *Historical Journal*, 22 (1979), 14–15, 19.
[59] The body of the act and the schedule were introduced as separate bills; C 65/137, mm. 17–23.

Although superficially impressive this legislation was, in fact, minor. The bulk arose from two issues: Buckingham's conviction for treason – this had taken place in May 1521 and the various acts merely awaited the summoning of the next parliament; and the need to renew the lapsed powers of the general surveyors, which was a technical matter.[60] The most important public acts concerned the minting of small change and the Blackwell Hall trade, but little was achieved in either sphere. For the prescribed proportion of coins of the smallest denominations was so low as to be useless, while the problems of the wholesale cloth market were still engaging the council's attention in May 1527.[61]

Yet Wolsey's reputation as a parliamentary manager plummets when we realise that the rates of tax he secured in July 1523 were only marginally better than those offered on 13 May. The commons' first offer was spread over two years: a subsidy of 2s. in the £ on lands, or 2s. in the £ on goods worth over £20, whichever assessment yielded the greater revenue from individual taxpayers; 1s. 4d. in the £ on goods valued between £2 and £20; and a poll tax of 8d. on everyone else – this was to be the.total amount.[62] The final rates were 2s. in the £ on lands, or on goods over £20 as before; 1s. in the £ on goods valued between £2 and £20; and a poll tax of 8d. on wages of £1 to £2 per annum or goods worth £2 – these amounts were spread over two years. In the third year a surcharge of 1s. in the £ was to be levied on lands valued at £50 or more. And in the fourth and last year 1s. in the £ was due on goods worth £50 or more.[63] The third and fourth year surcharges brought in £5521 and £9116 respectively.[64] So the question is whether these amounts compensated for the difference between the rates of tax offered on 13 May and the standard rates of the first two years of the final subsidy. Rates in both cases included 2s. in the £ on lands or on goods over £20, and a poll tax of 8d., though the final grant exempted those with wages under £1 per annum from the poll tax. The main difference, however, was that the final grant taxed goods worth between £2 and £20 at the rate of 1s. in the £, which was 25 per cent less than 1s. 4d. as offered in May. Was this loss of taxation from the middle band compensated for by the aggregate value of the third and fourth year surcharges?

It is sometimes assumed that in July Wolsey accepted rates of tax which were in total less than those he had declined in May, but this is an exaggeration.[65] For the aggregate value of the two surcharges (£14,637) fractionally exceeds 25 per cent of the receipts of the second of Wolsey's 'loans'. This 'loan' raised £56,992 from the laity; so 25 per cent amounts to

---

[60] B. P. Wolffe, *The Crown Lands 1461–1536* (London, 1970), pp. 80–1.

[61] HHL, Ellesmere MS 2652, fo. 12; Challis, *The Tudor Coinage*, pp. 202–3.

[62] Ellis, 1st series, I, pp. 220–1.

[63] *Rot. Parl.* suppl., pp. lxxvii–lxxviii, lxxxi–lxxxii. Resident aliens paid double. The rates stated in *LP* iii(2) 2956(1) are incorrect.

[64] Schofield, 'Parliamentary lay taxation', table 40 (facing p. 416).

[65] Cf. Bernard, *War, Taxation, and Rebellion*, p. 121.

£14,248.[66] But the 'loan' assessed middle band taxpayers at higher rates of tax than either the commons' offer of 13 May or the final subsidy. The rates of the second 'loan' were 2s. in the £ on goods valued between £5 and £20, or 2s. in the £ on lands valued between £1 and £20.[67] So by negotiating surcharges upon higher-rate taxpayers, Wolsey potentially secured a better tax yield in July 1523.

Yet the margin is likely to have been slim. The 'loan' rated lands over £1 at 2s. in the £, and if we conjecture that this met the cost of exempting goods below £5 from tax, a basic tax rate of 1s. in the £ in 1523 when levied on persons worth less than £20 per annum produced £28,496 if valuations of goods and lands remained the same.[68] On this basis, Wolsey's remission of 4d. in the £ for the middle band of taxpayers in July 1523 cost £9498. His estimated net gain from negotiating the subsidy's third and fourth year surcharges therefore falls to £5139. True, this is a rough and ready calculation, but it tells us something. Whatever Wolsey's haggling achieved between May and July 1523, it was not a king's ransom.

So Wolsey wasted his own time and that of parliament after 13 May. He originally demanded £800,000, but the 1523 subsidy's total yield of tax over the four-year period was £151,215.[69] Cromwell gave vent to his frustration in his letter to Creke but did not, I think, question government policy in parliament. It is impossible to tell whether the speech among the state papers marked 'Imp[erator] et R[ex] Anglia[e]: de regno Gallia[e] recuperando' was Cromwell's or whether it was delivered.[70] Either way its contents were unremarkable if drafted before the end of June 1523, because the abandonment of the Anglo-imperial 'Great Enterprise' against France in favour of Henry VIII's conquest of Scotland, essentially the policy the speech advocated, was actively considered by the council that month.[71] About 2 June the earl of Surrey, the king's lieutenant in the north, was recalled to London for consultations. Already informed that Henry VIII planned to invade Scotland with 20,000 men, Surrey replied that he hoped to be with the king and Wolsey on the 9th.[72] And the agenda was revealed by Wolsey in a letter to Lord Dacre, warden of west march, whom Surrey had appointed his deputy. Dacre was told why the king sent for Surrey; what had passed in the council concerning

[66] *LP* iii(2) 2483(3), p. 1050.   [67] E 101/518/43.

[68] The 'anticipation' of the subsidy apart, the 1523 grant was eventually levied on the basis of new and, for taxpayers worth £40 or more, possibly lower valuations. Schofield, 'Parliamentary lay taxation', pp. 332–3; Goring, 'The general proscription of 1522', pp. 694, 701.

[69] Schofield, 'Parliamentary lay taxation', table 40 (facing p. 416).

[70] SP 1/27, fos. 189–204 (*LP* iii(2) 2958); printed by Merriman, I, pp. 30–44.

[71] Essential diplomatic background is *LP* iii(2) 2948, 2952, 2966–7, 2984, 2996, 2998, 3071–2, 3107, 3114–16, 3118, 3123, 3134, 3138, 3149, 3153–4, 3194, 3203, 3207, 3215, 3220–5, 3232–3, 3268, 3271–3, 3281, 3291, 3307; G. Mattingly, ed., *Further Supplement to Letters, Despatches and State Papers . . . Preserved in the Archives at Vienna and Elsewhere* (London, 1940), pp. 20–5, 28–9, 190–4, 202–3, 209–19, 229–36, 247, 257–62.

[72] *LP* iii(2) 3071–2.

the projected invasion; and what the current plan was.[73] The upshot was that it was 'made and spoken of, though not expressly concluded, that an inv[asion] should with convenient celerity and diligence be made into Scotla[nd, with] the number of 25,000 men'. The object was to recover the king's honour and safety, and perhaps sever France and Scotland for ever, which 'were no small act'.[74] And it was just such a policy that Cromwell's speech recommended when it glossed the old adage, 'Who that entendyth Fraunce to wyn with Skotland let hym begyn.'[75]

When Henry VIII took Dacre's opinion, however, the warden did not think the plan 'to reduce the Scots to the King's grace' militarily feasible.[76] (That he was right was proved by Protector Somerset's inability to establish permanent garrisons in Scotland.) Yet what finally killed the idea was the treason of Charles, duke of Bourbon, constable of France, against Francis I. Although Henry's and Wolsey's policy oscillated in late 1522 and early 1523 between their continued wish to attack France and their negotiations for peace or a papal truce,[77] immediately they became convinced that Bourbon was willing to rise in revolt, they altered their Scottish strategy and began shipping an army of 11,000 troops under the duke of Suffolk into France. The army was expected at Calais in late August 1523, while the policy switch was cemented by a league early in September between the Habsburgs, Henry VIII, and Bourbon.[78]

Yet Cromwell's speech (if his it was) several times cited Wolsey's main policy statement before the commons as if it were a recent event.[79] As Wolsey's statement was given on 29 April, it is indeed probable that the speech was prepared before Lord Dacre vetoed the attempted conquest of Scotland on 26 June. Nothing is certain, but if this reconstruction is correct, the 'opposition' element of the speech evaporates. On the contrary, the address becomes one that any man of business might use to test reactions to the idea of uniting the crowns of England and Scotland by conquest. Or one that a man with his ear to the ground might prepare to attract attention during a council debate on the same subject. Of course, the fact that the speech questioned Henry VIII's *supposed* policy in 1523 is irrelevant. For although Henry and Wolsey were committed to the 'Great Enterprise' by the treaties of Bruges and Windsor, they were constantly attempting to delay the project because they feared the expense, the Scots and the possibility of a separate peace between Francis I and the emperor.[80] In this respect Wolsey's policy statement was a sham.

[73] *LP* iii(2) 3114–15. [74] *LP* iii(2) 3115. [75] Merriman, I, pp. 42–3.

[76] *LP* iii(2) 3315, 3134.

[77] *LP* iii(2) 2952, 2966, 2984, 2996, 2998, 3107, 3153.

[78] *LP* iii(2) 3153–4, 3194, 3203, 3217, 3225, 3232, 3307; *St. Pap.*, VI, pp. 174–5; Mattingly, ed., pp. 247, 249, 256–7, 261–2; S. J. Gunn, 'The duke of Suffolk's march on Paris in 1523', *English Historical Review*, 101 (1986), 596–634.

[79] Merriman, I, pp. 30, 31, 35, 38, 42; Hall, I, pp. 284–5.

[80] Mattingly, ed., pp. 63, 160, 162, 164, 176, 180, 184, 207, 210, 219, 225, 236–7, 239.

To sum up. So few source materials are extant for the 1523 parliament that a balanced perspective of that event, and of Wolsey's role, will be hard to obtain. But more can be said than has hitherto been allowed. For Wolsey wasted time by browbeating the commons, who believed that they had offered the largest subsidy on record. Surrey's correspondent opined: 'I have herd no man yn my lif that can remembre that ever ther was geven to any oon of the Kings auncestours half somoche at oon graunte.'[81] And Cromwell told Creke: 'Whe haue in our parlyament grauntyd vnto the Kinges highnes a right large Subsydye, the lyke wherof was neuer grauntyd in this realme.'[82] While these opinions were arguable, they signalled the mood of contemporaries.[83] Yet the subsidy Wolsey finalised in July was only marginally greater than the offer Surrey's correspondent had reported in May with which the cardinal was 'sore discontent'. Wolsey's slogans, too, had been 'justice' and 'commonwealth'. His name is linked to policies launched in parliament on enclosures and collusive recoveries; and the reports of Gruffudd and Hall make sense because they described two obvious injustices – the grievances of customary tenants against enclosing landlords and the frauds that accompanied the rise of recoveries – that Wolsey knew required remedy from his personal experience as a judge. These injustices were best tackled by legislation as the leasehold act of 1529 illustrated. But Wolsey achieved nothing; he even lost ground on enclosures. Other 'commonwealth' business may also have been lost. For Wolsey's rapacity ruled; that he coerced M.P.s with court connections to the point of dividing the commons indicates the seriousness of his fiscalism. And he left hostages to fortune. In the wake of the 'loans' of 1522–3 the political cost was considerable. There was hypocrisy in his dissolution speech that thanked the two houses for 'long pain, travail, study, costs and charges' over both the king's subsidy and acts 'for the common weal of this his realm'.[84]

And this should serve as an historiographical corrective. After centuries of vilification Wolsey's reputation has been boosted by recent studies of his judicial work, his policy on enclosures, and his foreign policy.[85] A sense of proportion must, however, be retained. For Wolsey was both good and bad. In star chamber he was creative and, with minor blemishes, constructive but in parliament he was arrogant and insensitive. Often the consummate politician, his fiscal policy lost touch with reality. For the mood of 1523 was electric

---

[81] Ellis, 1st series, I, p. 221.   [82] Merriman, I, p. 313.

[83] Cf. Bernard, *War, Taxation, and Rebellion*, p. 122.

[84] SP 1/27, fos. 187–8 (*LP* iii(2) 2957); *Rot. Parl.* suppl., p. cxlix.

[85] J. J. Scarisbrick, *Henry VIII* (London, 1968), pp. 67–162; his 'Cardinal Wolsey and the common weal' (see above n. 28); Metzger, 'Das Englische Kanzleigericht' (see above n. 35); J. A. Guy, *The Cardinal's Court: the Impact of Thomas Wolsey in Star Chamber* (Hassocks, 1977). Scarisbrick's argument that Wolsey's was a peace policy which for fifteen years he struggled to implement, has been challenged by P. J. Gwyn, 'Wolsey's foreign policy: the conferences at Calais and Bruges reconsidered', *Historical Journal*, 23 (1980), 755–72. For a revisionist reading of Wolsey's fiscal policy see Bernard, *War, Taxation, and Rebellion, passim.*

compared to that eleven years before when Warham asked for £600,000 and settled for £126,745. In 1512 no lay taxation had been granted since 1504, while major sums had not been exacted since 1497.[86] By contrast, total lay taxation between 1512 and 1517 amounted to £288,814, while the 'loan' from the laity raised during 1522 raised £104,285, plus £43,147 from the nobility, leading knights, the city of London, and the town of Calais.[87] And in 1523 itself, the second of Wolsey's 'loans' was announced; a total of £56,992 was collected between March and the end of June, overlapping with the subsidy debate in parliament.[88] True, the 'loans' of 1522–3 were paid, but Wolsey's instructions to the collectors expressly promised that this money was refundable from the next parliamentary subsidy.[89] So when he reneged in parliament, the atmosphere was soured.

Yet perhaps the final straw was Wolsey's attempt to 'anticipate' payment of the first instalment of the 1523 subsidy on the basis of rigorous assessments. On 2 November 1523 he named commissioners to 'practise' with all persons having £40 and above in lands or goods whose names he obtained from the returns of the 1522 commissioners for musters.[90] They were to pay their first instalment of tax immediately, instead of at the date specified in the subsidy act, using the assessments of 1522 which may have over-estimated their wealth.[91] Only five per cent of this 'anticipation' was paid by the due date, though seventy-four per cent was realised within another month.[92] And although the subsidy was eventually levied on the basis of new and, possibly for richer taxpayers, lower valuations, it provoked dismay. Indeed, when the second instalment fell due in February 1525, late payments by the vast majority of all taxpayers signalled burgeoning resistance to Wolsey's fiscal ambitions, culminating in the *débâcle* of the Amicable Grant.[93]

[86] For earlier taxation, see Schofield, 'Parliamentary lay taxation', pp. 160–212.

[87] *LP* iii(2) 2483(3), p. 1050; Schofield, 'Parliamentary lay taxation', table 40 (facing p. 416); Bernard, *War, Taxation, and Rebellion*, p. 119.

[88] *LP* iii(2) 2483(3), p. 1050; *LP* iii(2) 2895; Bernard, *War, Taxation, and Rebellion*, p. 119.

[89] *LP* iii(2) 2484; BL, Cotton MS Cleopatra F 6, fos. 316–20; Goring, 'The general proscription of 1522', pp. 700–1; Bernard, *War, Taxation, and Rebellion*, p. 120.

[90] Ellesmere MS 2472; E 159/303, *communia* Mich. rot. 1; C 193/3, fos. 24–5; *LP* iii(2). 3504; Schofield, 'Parliamentary lay taxation', pp. 312–33; Goring, 'The general proscription of 1522', p. 701.

[91] Goring, 'The general proscription of 1522', pp. 694, 701; Schofield, 'Parliamentary lay taxation', pp. 331–3.

[92] Schofield, 'Parliamentary lay taxation', p. 435; Bernard, *War, Taxation, and Rebellion*, p. 132 n. 80.

[93] Schofield, 'Parliamentary lay taxation', table 41 (facing p. 432); Bernard, *War, Taxation, and Rebellion*, pp. 118, 122–3. Only if new evidence were forthcoming that Wolsey's actions in 1523 were the product of direct and specific royal instructions might his reputation as a parliamentary manager be salvaged: that Wolsey blustered because Henry had told him to secure £800,000 on top of the 'loan' money – a cool £1 million for the war chest; and that Wolsey's was a posture motivated by shrewd political calculation in the face of Henry's unrealistic demands. Such conjecture lacks substance; the evidence does not exist. Cf. Woods, 'The amicable grant', p. 61.

The Act of Appeals and the English reformation

GRAHAM NICHOLSON

AT MID-SUMMER in 1530 there were distinct signs that the English government was in a panic. The king wanted the annulment of his marriage to Catherine, but he seemed further than ever from achieving his purpose. A year earlier his attempt to have his case decided quietly, indeed stealthily, in a legatine court at Blackfriars had misfired completely; Catherine appealed to Rome for judgment and in due course Henry was cited to appear there. The case was to open at the Rota in June 1530. The government can have had little confidence that the canon law case it had assembled would carry the day, and so William Benet and Edward Carne in Rome had instructions to use whatever means were necessary to prevent the case proceeding. Meanwhile English agents were harrying canonists and divines in Italy and in the universities to speak out for the king.

These tactics of prevarication and pressure could not delay the hearing for ever nor prevent a judgment being given in Rome, in the fullness of time, and almost certainly against Henry. In the ensuing months the king's men rapidly assembled evidence for the radical propositions that the king, not the pope, was the fountain-head of all ecclesiastical jurisdiction, and that England, not Rome, was the place of final appeal for an English case. In time these propositions were translated into the Act of Appeals, and saved the day for the king. Our purpose here is to discover how, and incidentally by whom, the king's case was constructed and to suggest that there was, contrary to some suggestions, a largely consistent direction in policy from the autumn of 1530 to Archbishop Cranmer's declaration of the nullity of the king's marriage to Catherine in May 1533.

The first hint of the new direction came in the early autumn of 1530. The king's agents in Rome were told to assert Henry's immunity from papal jurisdiction by virtue of a *privilegium regni* which was 'ne Angli extra Angliam cogantur'. No doubt this was rather too cryptic an expression for so momentous a proposal – Benet and the rest seemed less than sure of its meaning – but the change of approach was to be no flash in the pan. In the weeks that followed, the papal nuncio and the emperor's ambassador in London were

19

treated to a series of lectures on the king's determination to have the divorce settled within the realm, either by the archbishop of Canterbury, or by the clergy of the realm. Soon, many of the most important ministers were expressing the new sentiments. Norfolk and Gardiner spoke to the nuncio on the matter early in September, while Wiltshire and Suffolk told him there was nothing to fear in England from pope or popes, even if they rescuscitated St Peter, because the king was emperor and pope, absolute in his own realm.[1]

The idea of a *privilegium regni* was not going down well in Rome, however. There was a shortage of detailed information. Henry's letters to his agents were suspiciously more full of assertions than proof. He asked them to sift through all the papal registers in the Vatican for evidence of his 'imperial' status, but Benet baulked at the sheer magnitude of the task, and complained of the delays they suffered at the hands of suspicious librarians.[2] Nor did Benet have good news for Henry at the end; the imperial authority of past English kings had mysteriously left no mark on the papal archives. For a time Benet hesitated to put the idea forward to the pope, because, he said, doctors to whom they had mentioned it were full of scepticism. But when Clement did eventually hear of the *privilegium regni*, he understood it as a threat that Henry might take independent action. As a serious basis for a repudiation of the pope's authority the *privilegium regni* was not credible, and Clement told Benet so. Henry's assertion rested only on national custom, while the pope claimed a God-given universal jurisdiction, which Henry had customarily accepted.

Though the energetic searches of registers and libraries in Europe had failed to produce a single shred of evidence for Henry's claim, another search was going on at home, with considerably more success. There is no evidence of it in the form of instructions from the king, and nothing to show who was engaged in it – nothing, that is, beyond what can be deduced from the collections of texts which are preserved in the Public Record Office and in the Cottonian papers at the British Library. The collections are important because they supply some of the background thinking to the government's policies and pronouncements in the reformation period and show more clearly than is otherwise possible the grounds on which Henry began to deny that he was answerable to papal jurisdiction. They can also help us to understand how, and by whom, important legislation of the period was framed.

The main collection is catalogued in the Cottonian Library as 'Collectanea satis copiosa, ex sacris scriptis et authoribus Catholicis de regia et ecclesiastica potestate'.[3] It is a substantial volume of texts, running to 120 folios, written in a number of hands and on paper from at least two sources. It is evident, in fact, that it was expanded in the course of two or three years by the addition of

---

[1] *Calendar of State Papers, Spanish*, ed. Begenroth *et al.* (London, 1862–1954), iv. 429, 433, 445.

[2] *LP* iv 6602, 6605, 6607; BL Add. MS 40884 fos. 31–31a, 366. J. J. Scarisbrick, 'Henry VIII and the Vatican Library' in *Bibliothèque d'humanisme et renaissance*, 24 (1962), 211ff.

[3] BL Cleopatra E 6, fos. 16–135.

further texts, an index and marginal comments. One section added later appears to have been the source book for the *Glasse of the Truthe*[4] a piece of government propaganda of 1532. But this collection was not simply a quarry for literary endeavours. Its very appearance makes that unlikely. In the original sections of the text especially, the references are set out with a neatness and care well above the ordinary. This was a book for circulation at court, and in particular for presentation to the king. His hand is to be found on it in forty-six places (not including sundry underlinings and scratchings which may or may not be his) recording his comments in brief marginal notes. A good number of the entries simply note the content of the head – on one page, for instance, we find only 'de carolo rege', 'de investituris' and 'sententia excommunicationis';[5] in other places there is no more than a casual 'bene nota'. Nowhere, it should be said, does Henry show that he is working out arguments for himself from the notes of others. It seems much more likely that the 'Collectanea satis copiosa' was made to enable Henry to look over his scholars' arguments at leisure, to query, to approve, and in the fullness of time to adopt as his own. This interpretation accords with such annotations as 'nota diffinitionem nicene concilii',[6] and 'ubi orta ibi terminandi'[7] – observations which he repeated publicly on a number of occasions – with the somewhat puzzled response 'nota et perquiri', against a sentence about the granting of the keys of heaven to Peter,[8] and with the more enthusiastic 'pulcherimum privilegium' that he placed opposite the head 'Rex Anglie excommunicare & interdicere prohibet'.[9] Despite the brevity of his comments, the king read the book with unwonted thoroughness, for apart from a few skipped pages here and there, the whole book bears the marks of his diligent if not particularly perceptive study.

Some of the customs of the realm which the king had thus far failed to enumerate are to be found in two smaller collections of historical texts, one endorsed 'Quaedem pertinencia ad regis officium',[10] the other 'Non est novum Regem esse vicarium dei in terris'.[11] It is reasonable to suppose that they represent an early stage in the research, for their contents were later transcribed by the same hand into the 'Collectanea'. The paper 'Quaedem pertinencia' assembles some precedents. King Edgar (according to Aelred) reproved clerical morals, asserting that judgment pertained to him. The Constitutions of Clarendon and Northampton are recalled, and the assertion is made (on no more authority than Ralph de Diceto) that because of the scandal of the rivalry of two popes, Urban and Clement, the English church had refused obedience to the pope after the death of Gregory Hildebrand.

---

[4] *A Glasse of the Truthe*, T. Berthelet, London, n.d. (1532) is in part based on Cleo. E 6, fos. 98–109b.
[5] Cleo. E. 6, fo. 32a.
[6] Ibid, fo. 38a.
[7] Ibid, fo. 97b.
[8] Ibid, fo. 41a.
[9] Ibid, fo. 69a.
[10] SP 1/236 fo. 204f; (*LP Add.* i 673).
[11] PRO SP 1/238 fo. 238f; (*LP Add.* i. 912(1)).

This is scarcely an impressive list, even when bolstered by some quotations from Augustine and Aquinas about the need for Christian princes to use their coercive powers against the enemies of the church, for the salvation of their subjects' souls. The second paper 'Non est novum' relies on the legal formulas of Bracton and Britton. The king, Bracton seems to be saying, is the 'vicarius dei' and his rule is of God. Moreover the king has no equal in his own kingdom 'quia par in parem non habet imperium'.[12] The compiler is attempting, so far with very modest success, to prove that the king has *imperium* or final authority extending equally to matters temporal and of spiritual jurisdiction.

By the time the 'Collectanea' had been assembled, many more sources had been plundered. The compiler had discovered the two kings of Israel who rapidly became familiar in Henrician propaganda – Hezekiah who destroyed the bronze serpent which Moses had set up when it became an object of idolatry, and Jehosaphat who led the people of Israel back from apostasy. The means of Jehosaphat's reforms were most important – he established judges in each city to hear spiritual causes. Moreover he appointed priests and others to decide disputed cases or appeals at Jerusalem.[13] An effective shot came, surprisingly, from English experience. The compiler found a letter of Pope Eleutherus, a fabrication of John's reign, which was supposedly the reply to a letter from the newly converted King Lucius.

Petistis a nobis leges Romanas et Caesaris vobis transmitti, quibus in regno Britanniae ut voluistis. Leges Romanas et Caesaris semper reprobare possimus, legem Dei nequaquam. Suscepistis enim nuper, miseratione summa, in regno Britanniae legem et fidem Christi. Habetis penes vos in regno utramque. Vicarius vero Dei estis in regno.[14]

Here was perhaps the most straightforward attribution of spiritual jurisdiction and supremacy that the compiler had found, and he repeats it several times in the 'Collectanea'. The idea surfaced again a couple of years later in several of the drafts of the Act of Appeals where we read that

dyeurs the kingis most roiall progenitours kingis of this said realme and Impier by the epistolis from the sea apostolik have be named called and reputed the vicars of god within the same, and in their tymes have made and devised ordinauncis rules and statutis consonant to the lawes of god . . . for the due observyng and executyng of thingis spirituall as temporall within the lymytis of the Imperiall crown of this realme.[15]

The obvious weakness in a case for the jurisdictional supremacy of the king in spiritual matters was that the church exercised authority day by day in the

---

[12] The quotations are from the 'Introductio' and first chapter 'De Personis' of Bracton. See G. E. Woodbine, ed., Bracton, *De Legibus et Consuetudinibus Angliae* (4 vols., New Haven, 1915–42), vol. II.

[13] Cleo. E 6, fo. 24a. The text is from 2 Chron. 19.

[14] The compiler of the 'Collectanea' probably derived the letter from an extracted section of the thirteenth-century *Liber Custumarum* of the city of London, now BL, Cotton MS Claudius D 2, fos. 1–135, 269–80, and in particular fos. 32a–33a. See below p. 24.

[15] Draft of the Act of Appeals (24 Henry VIII c. 12) SP 2/N fos. 78–9.

courts Christian, and when it enacted constitutions in convocation – both of which were activities recognised and accepted by the crown from time immemorial. So the compiler goes on to make the case, already implicit in the example of Jehosaphat appointing lay and clerical judges, that while the king holds God-ordained sovereignty, he may from time to time 'lend' a part of his authority, without loss of his rights, to the priesthood.[16] To prove the point, the compiler has a catalogue of authorities, from Malmesbury and Gervase of Tilsbury to Hugo of St Victor and Origen. The most appealing of the arguments is derived from a novel interpretation of the Donation of Constantine. If the Emperor Constantine gave power in the western part of the empire to Pope Sylvester, it demonstrated that the emperor was the origin of the church's wealth and of its spiritual jurisdiction. The compiler goes on to gloss the texts with the proposition that these powers may never be alienated finally from the king's divinely-granted prerogative. This interpretation implicitly recognises the Donation's historicity, and was out of line with the subsequent government-inspired publication of Valla's celebrated treatise of demolition.[17] It does, however, support the contention of several drafts of the Act of Appeals that

... the Englisshe churche ... is sufficiently endowed by the kingis most noble progenitours ... as well in honour as possessions for the due declaracion and admynystracion of the same ... (the laws of Almighty God) ... and ... their auctorites and iurisdiccionis ys deryved and dependyth from and of the same Imperiall crown of this realme.[18]

But how was the English crown of sufficient status to be called imperial? We have seen that ministers of the crown had been speaking of the king as emperor and pope in his realm as early as September 1530. In January 1531 Norfolk told Chapuys that the king had a right of empire in his kingdom and recognised no superior. He spoke in similar terms on another occasion.[19] Phrases such as these have been said to demonstrate a reliance on the definitions of Roman and French jurisprudence,[20] but one need look no further than Bracton's sentences on the 'imperium' of the king within his realm, quoted in the 'Collectanea', to find very similar words and ideas, commonplaces of legal language in England. Norfolk was also anxious to bring to Chapuys' notice the inscription on the seal of Arthur: 'Patricius Arcturus, Britanniae, Galliae, Daciae Imperator', which Chapuys took to be a boast of the extent of English dominion; he remarked disparagingly that it was a pity that Arthur was not also entitled 'Imperator Asiae', as he might have left Henry successor to that vast territory. If Chapuys had understood this second point correctly, Norfolk was making 'empire' a matter of an aggregation of

[16] Cleo. E 6, fo. 276.
[17] *A Treatise of the Donation Gyven unto Sylvester Pope of Rhome* (T. Godfrey, London, 1534?).
[18] PRO SP 2/N, fos. 78–80.
[19] *LP* v 805.
[20] R. Koebner, *Empire* (Cambridge, 1961), p. 55 n. 2.

kingdoms, rather as in the usual modern sense of the word. It would be easy to dismiss the reference as a meander of the duke's somewhat unchannelled imagination, but for some remarkable passages in the 'Collectanea' which suggest that he may have caught something important. The first is an extract from the city of London's *Liber Custumarum*, a compilation of around the end of the thirteenth century; or rather it was taken from a portion torn from the unique manuscript, presumably by an eager researcher employed by the king.[21] Here, in what purport to be the laws of Edward the Confessor (but which were a compilation of John's reign drawing its inspiration and much of its information from Geoffrey of Monmouth),[22] is an unambiguous statement of the imperial status of the English crown, a status derived from or demonstrated by, its authority over a number of realms:

De numero provinciarum et patriarum et Comitatuum et insularum quae de jure spectant et sine dubio pertinent corone et dignitati regni Britanniae scilicet quo modo vocatur Regnum Anglorum in tribus divisorum consuetudineque tres leges dicuntur scilicet Essexenelaga Mircenelage et Denelage verum de jure potius appellari potest et debet excellentia illustrissime predicte corone imperium quam regnum.[23]

The next entry in the 'Collectanea' is from an historical survey prepared for Edward I in 1301, in defence of the king's claim to overlordship of Scotland.[24] A number of monastic houses which kept historical records were requested to supply evidence for Edward's claim, and the resulting mixture of fact and fantasy showed how for centuries – indeed from the remote days of Brutus – English kings had been the lords of Scotland and had received homage from its kings. The text of this survey is included in Rishanger's chronicle, which the compiler of the 'Collectanea' certainly knew. He also quotes from the chronicle of Walter of Guisborough, recording how the king's claims to Scotland and Wales were maintained by parliament at Carlisle in 1307.[25] All this is, in effect, to argue with the celebrated opening of the Act of Appeals, that 'by dyvers sundrie olde autentike histories and cronicles it is manifestly declared and expressed that the Realme of England is an Impire, and so hath ben accepted in the worlde . . .'. The practical point of these references from the chronicles, and, we may surmise, of Norfolk's allusion to Arthur's empire, was simply that they showed the English king to be a feudal overlord, and thus without a superior. Or as a similar phrase of Bracton has it 'rex superiorem non recognoscens in regno suo est imperator'.

The act goes on, of course, to refer to the imperial crown. The crown was an

---

[21] BL, Cotton MS Claudius D 2, fos. 1–135, 269–80.

[22] See Walter Ullmann, 'On the influence of Geoffrey of Monmouth in English History' in C. Bauer, L. Boehm and M. Muller, eds., *Speculum Historiale* (Munich, 1965), pp. 257–63.

[23] BL, Cotton MS Claudius D 2, fo. 1a; cf. 'Collectanea', Cleo. E. 6, fo. 41b.

[24] 'Collectanea', Cleo. E 6, fo. 42a; ULC MS Dd 2.5 is the text from which the compiler worked.

[25] See M. Powicke, *The Thirteenth Century* (Oxford, 2nd edn., 1962), p. 705. In the 'Collectanea' the reference is given as 'ex libro gest. pont. Dunelm', but none of the historians of the church of Durham have a corresponding passage.

ambiguous word, because well before the sixteenth century it was possible to distinguish beween the person of the monarch and the effective political authority of the state. Earlier, however, the crown had been the personal insignia of the monarch, 'representing a body of special rights, "leges, jura, consuetudines, placita – omnes consuetudines quas rex habere potest".' Thus, to give an illustration, the inheritance of the 'crowns' of both England and Normandy united in one person a body of private rights which far surpassed that enjoyed by any other in those realms.[26] Now clearly the evidence for the imperial status of the English crown in the 'Collectanea' is a recital of the feudal and customary rights of the kings of England, and builds on this earlier idea of the 'crown'. Thus the crown can be said not only to be imperial but, as the laws of Edward the Confessor have it, to be an 'empire'. The argument runs from the personal status of the king to the consequent nature of his crown; in the 'Collectanea' at least, empire is no less an attribute of the king's personal authority than is his supremacy in spirituals.

Who was behind these theories of church and state? The task of gathering references from continental libraries had been undertaken chiefly by Croke and Stokesley, with Gardiner and Foxe perhaps issuing instructions from London.[27] Later in 1530, abroad, Benet and Carne had joined in the unrewarding search for the privileges of the realm. By comparison the labours of scholars at home are obscurely documented. There is only circumstantial evidence, but that points strongly to Edward Foxe, the king's almoner, as the prime-mover. Foxe's public career was from the beginning linked with the divorce. While serving as Wolsey's secretary in 1528, he went with Gardiner to Orvieto to persuade the pope to grant a commission for the hearing of Henry's divorce. When More, about the same time, argued with the king about the divorce, he was 'commaunded . . . to commune ferther with Mr Fox'.[28] A year or two later, Reginald Pole who had been given the king's leave to study in Paris, received instructions to press for opinions on the divorce in the university. Pole found the prospect distasteful and asked for the assistance of someone more learned in such questions, and Foxe was dispatched to join him. Intriguingly we know that Pole and Foxe called from Paris for luggage;[29] Foxe's items were in two black chests; of the contents we know only one item: 'ii bookis for mr. fox. librum conciliorum. Et librum mercatoris' – a reference to Merlin's recently published edition of the Pseudo-Isidorean decretals and later conciliar acts.[30] This work is a major source for the 'Collectanea', in particular for sections which are the main source-book for the *Glasse of the*

---

[26] J. E. A. Joliffe, *Angevin Kingship* (2nd edn., London, 1963), pp. 19–20.
[27] There is a large volume of correspondence calendared in *LP* iv (3), especially from Croke in the first half of 1530, and *LP* iv 6232, 6235.
[28] J. Merlinus, ed., *Conciliorum Quatuor Generalium Tomus* . . ., 2 vols. (Coloniae, 1530).
[29] E. F. Rodgers, ed., *The Correspondence of Sir Thomas More*, pp. 493–5 (*LP* vii 289).
[30] *LP* iv 6004.

Truthe. Later, when leading members of the king's council were pressed to take up their pens in defence of the royal supremacy, Foxe turned the 'Collectanea' into a treatise. The texts were shuffled, sorted and pruned, the argument filled out and turned into Foxe's elegant Latin prose. None of this can hide the angular framework beneath the surface of his *De Vera Differentia.*[31]

But to go back to 1530 and 1531: the sudden talk, first of the privileges of the realm and then of empire, from Norfolk, Wiltshire, Suffolk and the king himself was, we may reasonably conclude, a slightly less than coherent version of Foxe's carefully documented theories of church and state. There existed as early as 1530 the germ, at least, of a theory of empire, which is seen fully grown in the Act of Appeals in 1533.

If this is correct, it begs the question: why the lengthy delay in taking action upon it to give the king the divorce he required? The key may well lie in a meeting between the king and certain lawyers and divines sometime before the middle of October 1530. Henry asked whether, by virtue of the privileges of the realm, parliament could and would enact that the king's cause be heard by the archbishop of Canterbury, the pope's prohibition notwithstanding. The idea was flatly rejected, for what reasons we are not told; (Chapuys' account is the only record).[32] It had evidently not yet been established that the king's suzerain authority extended to matters within the ecclesiastical jurisdiction, nor that the church in England derived independent jurisdictional authority therefrom. This was a major setback; in a choler Henry postponed the session of parliament until January 1531 and, for the time being, the simplest and most effective solution to Henry's problem – an act of parliament – was set aside.

The next three years saw a series of government manoeuvres against the church, and in particular the Pardon of the Clergy and the enforced Submission of the Clergy. Unless this assault on the church is seen in the context of Henry's pursuit of a divorce it becomes difficult to interpret. There was little for the king to gain from it, and indeed if his policy still centred on the hope that the pope would allow the English clergy to judge the divorce,[33] it was an absurd error to demonstrate the dependence of the clergy on the will of a party to the case. It becomes 'an extraordinary manoeuvre' and 'like so much of royal policy in these years . . . full of uncertainty'.[34] On the contrary, there was a concerted effort to establish the king's position as supreme head of both temporal and spiritual jurisdictions, and to persuade or intimidate the church to accept the idea.

Within a few days of the abortive October 1530 meeting with the lawyers

[31] *Opus Eximium de Vera Differentia* . . . (T. Berthelet, London, 1534).
[32] *Cal. Sp.* IV 460.
[33] Thus J. J. Scarisbrick, 'The Pardon of the clergy', *Cambridge Historical Journal*, 12 (1956).
[34] J. J. Scarisbrick, *Henry VIII* (London 1968), pp. 274–5.

and divines, a charge of *praemunire*, laid first against fifteen clerics, was turned against the whole clerical estate.[35] The substance of the charge (eventually at least) was that the very exercise of jurisdiction by the spiritual courts constituted a *praemunire*. When convocation met in January 1531, the clergy soon found themselves bargaining with the king over the terms of a settlement. Convocation wanted three safeguards: the restoration of their old privileges, by which was meant the protection of laws and immunities which guaranteed the existence of the clergy as a community outside the king's jurisdiction; the restoration of their 'volition' – presumably their right to exercise their jurisdiction in the courts Christian; and a definition of the scope of the statutes of *praemunire*, so that the conditions under which they could use their jurisdiction in the future would be known.[36]

The king granted only the second of these demands, and this partial concession was well judged. It acknowledged the existence of ecclesiastical jurisdiction yet refused to guarantee his recognition of its legality while it rested on immunities, while it stood apart from the king's law, while it had some other head than the king. The final demands of the king presented as five articles,[37] required that he be declared protector and supreme head of the English church and clergy. The third article proposed to allow only such clerical immunities as did not detract from the power of the king or laws of his kingdom – which hardly sound like immunities at all. The others would be confirmed and defended by the king. In other words, the strength of clerical jurisdiction and other privileges was their sanction by the king.

Clerical resistance persuaded Henry to accept the important clause 'quantum per Christi legem licet' qualifying his headship. Few believed, however, that this form of words would really protect the independence of the church.[38] Chapuys was gloomy; in June he reported that Norfolk and others of the council were still trying to persuade the queen to withdraw her appeal to Rome. The king could not be dragged to judgment in Rome, she was told, for he was 'entirely sovereign chief in his kingdom, as well in regard to temporalty as the spiritualty, as had been lately recognised and approved by the Parliament and clergy of England'.[39] The king now claimed to be the highest point of both jurisdictional systems in England; no appeal could go further. The corollary – Chapuys missed it perhaps – was that the spiritual courts in England might function legitimately, and judge the king's case without reference to the pope.

The following year, Henry, by enforcing the Submission of the Clergy,

[35] R. B. Merriman, *The Life and Letters of Thomas Cromwell* (2 vols., Oxford, 1902), I, p. 334.
[36] The three demands of the clergy (Chapuys, *Cal. Sp.*, IV 635) have been expanded by reference to the 'Petitio Cleri Cantuarensis Provincie' (BL Cleo. F 6, fo. 240) which Scarisbrick, 'Pardon of the clergy', p. 32 n, has convincingly ascribed to this time.
[37] D. Wilkins, *Concilia Magnae Britanniae et Hiberniae* (4 vols., London, 1737), III, p. 725.
[38] R. Hall, *Life of Fisher* (London, 1921), p. 79.   [39] *LP* v 287.

pushed the advantage home. There was thought of securing the submission by parliamentary means. A draft bill claims that all the king's subjects, spiritual and temporal, are 'but one body polytyke' and that all laws take their vigour and effect from him, their 'allonly Supreme emperyall hede', the true minister and vicar of God.[40] The bill's notion of royal authority follows the thinking of the text-collections; the important innovation is the use of parliament to declare and give effect to legislation in spiritual matters, as, of course, it did in the following year in the Act of Appeals. But the bill was put aside. The time was not yet ripe. The reasoning of the preamble presupposed that the spiritual authority of the prince was an established fact; but this was not the belief of all or even (to hazard a guess) of the majority of the clergy. The English church had never committed itself to such a principle. The act would have been open to the objecion that it was beyond the competence of the king or parliament to legislate for the spirituality. Its passage would surely have been a grave error, likely to precipitate a confrontation between laity and clergy, and to throw doubt on the validity of the subsequent Act of Appeals.

The king pressed on instead for a submission by convocation. Someone had been doing more research. A late addition to the 'Collectanea' is a section of references culled from Merlin's *Conciliorum . . . Tomus*. In particular it draws upon decrees of the early provincial councils of the church, and on the letters of Pope Leo. The references show kings summoning and dominating synods and giving confirmation to the edicts and laws enacted. We read of the Emperor Constantine ordering councils to be held in every province of the church, and of Spanish Visigothic kings summoning the councils of Toledo in the seventh century.[41] The significance of the materials is that they furnished examples of kings who actually exercised a *potestas jurisdictionis* in the church, where hitherto the argument of the 'Collectanea' had been somewhat theoretical. When Foxe appeared in the convocation on 10 May 1532, no doubt armed with the proof-texts, he advanced very concrete demands – three articles 'quibus rex omnes subscribere voluit'; that in future clerical legislation would require the royal assent, that existing 'constitutions provincial' be examined and where found objectionable suppressed, and that all other canons which 'stand with God's law and the king's' should remain in effect, with the assent of the king.[42] A fourth was added as an aside to the first, on the morning of 15 May, to the effect that convocation could only be assembled by the king's commandment.[43] Convocation was forced to accept these articles of submission without gaining any significant concession. It accepted that the king was the fountain-head of all jurisdiction, spiritual as well as temporal.

---

[40] *LP* v 721(1).

[41] BL Cleo. E 6, fos. 18–216. This section, placed before the main body of the book, was added *after* the index had been compiled.

[42] Wilkins, *Concilia* III, p. 749.

[43] Kelly, 'The Submission of the clergy', pp. 114–15; F. Atterbury, *The Rights, Powers and Privileges of an English Convocation* (2nd edn., London, 1701), pp. 546–7.

Now it was possible to enshrine this principle in statute. Yet, as is well known, before the bill to prohibit appeals to foreign courts was introduced in the commons on 14 March 1533, it passed through a number of drafts.[44] In the earliest extant version, all jurisdiction is described as 'deryved and depended of the Imperiall crown of this realm'. The words were in and out of the bill several times – here cut out by Cromwell, there restored by the king's own hand. In the final version of the act, such phrases were suppressed wherever they had occurred, even though the opening flourishes about the realm being an empire, and the king's supremacy were retained. It has been argued that these brave words were, after all, irrelevant to the content of the act, and were employed only in propagandist fashion for their emotive force. The act's declaration of the sufficiency of the English church to fulfil all the offices of the spirituality 'without the intermeddling of any exterior person or persons', has been taken to be a claim for 'a traditional jurisdictional autonomy for the English church'.[45] But, in fact, the act did not entirely abandon the concept that spiritual jurisdiction depended from the king or from his imperial crown. It ascribed to the king God-given authority to render justice in all manner of causes arising within the realm – which would seem to include spiritual causes. Moreover, the king was no 'exterior person' to the English church – he was its supreme head. The independence of each province of the church was in no way incompatible, in Henry's book, with the spiritual supremacy of a Christian prince.

But if the king did not give up any fundamental principles as a result of the revisions, the bill appeared less contentious than the earliest draft. With Henry's over-hasty marriage to Anne Boleyn already solemnised in secret, on 25 January, the government desperately needed a swift and sure resolution of his case. It could not afford to stir up once more the volume of opposition that had met its bill to restrain annates. Cromwell's response was to shift the focus of the bill away from theological principles and from the nature of the king's supremacy, to parliament's defence of the temporal interests of the realm. Where the earliest draft discusses the failings and usurpations of Rome for about a quarter of its length, the final version of the act has almost nothing to say on the matter. There is no hint that a reformation of the church is required or implied in the statute. The explicit statements of the derivation of all jurisdiction from the king, which Cromwell cut out, would have run counter to at least two centuries of progress towards the notion of the authority of the whole realm in parliament. Instead Cromwell spelled out the 'dyvers and sondry inconveniences' – the costs and delays – which the current system of appeals engendered. The complaints of the act are strictly limited to the political interference of Rome within the realm. The act, therefore, suggests a

---

[44] The drafts have been studied by G. R. Elton, 'The evolution of a reformation statute', *EHR*, 64 (1949), pp. 174–97.

[45] G. L. Harris, 'Medieval government and statecraft', *Past and Present*, 25 (July 1963).

political solution. It implies that the new restrictions are only an extension and necessary revision of existing parliamentary law protecting the sovereignty and temporal interests of the realm – the statutes of provision and *praemunire*.

By Cromwell's skilful re-drafting, and by the deliberate association of the new measures with old, the revolutionary nature of the act is partially glossed over. But revolutionary it nonetheless was. The anti-papal legislation referred to in the preamble amounted to no more than an attack on certain specified activities of the papacy in England, especially its exercise of patronage. It established that where spiritual jurisdiction touched on the temporal rights of the crown or of lay subjects, statute might modify canon law, and even afford protection against spiritual censures. It did not touch on the wider proposal, now on hand, to ban all appeals to Rome. And while the 1393 statute claimed that causes of ecclesiastical patronage belonged to the king's temporal courts, divorce was indisputably a spiritual cause. Of necessity, therefore, the Act of Appeals retains and builds on the royal supremacy; it places the king at the head of the spiritual jurisdiction. All use of papal jurisdiction becomes a usurpation, not merely its use to frustrate the temporal affairs of the realm. Moreover, the act hedges the king's authority about with the imperial status of the realm, so that there can be no recourse to any exterior jurisdiction. This solution is as much a part of the earliest draft as of the final version of the act. It is no more, in principle, than the king's ministers were threatening to achieve as early as September 1530.

Thomas Cromwell and the 'brethren'

SUSAN BRIGDEN

DURING the 'progress time' of the reformation, as he furthered the 'cause of Christ', Thomas Cromwell ventured into unknown political territory.[1] The reformers hailed him as God's special 'instrument', and promised him that if, 'for the zeale ye beare unto the trouth' he ensured that 'the pure worde of god may ones go forth', then 'the whole realme . . . shall haue . . . you after in more hye remembrance than the name of Austen that men saye brought the faith fyrst into englonde'. They prayed God 'to preserve him long to such good purposes, that the living God may be duly known in his spirit and verity', and besought 'in our lorde Jesus, you maie liue Nestor in yeres'. Who would not, asked Richard Taverner, extol Cromwell's 'most circumspect godliness and most godly circumspection in the cause and matter of our Christian religion?'[2] But most could not believe Cromwell to be circumspect at all, such were the risks he took. He himself knew well enough the mutability of political fortune, especially at the court of a king as restless and insecure as Henry VIII. Like Wolsey, and like his old friend Ralph Sadler, he understood that 'the fair hests and promises of court are hely water', sprinkled randomly.[3] Cromwell had faced the wilderness in 1529, when his master Wolsey fell, and in the 1530s the stakes would be higher still.

Cromwell received daily reminders of the dangers of serving such a master as Henry VIII, and he always knew that his time was short. Was not 'my lord Cardynall a gret man and ruled all the reallme as he wold?', asked Cromwell's enemies; 'what be cam of hym, ys he not gone? Allso Sir Thomas More, highe

---

[1] *LP* x 644 (Luther to Cromwell, 9 April 1536). For Cromwell's part in the making of the English reformation and his religious beliefs, see (apart from the works of G. R. Elton) A. G. Dickens, *Thomas Cromwell and the English Reformation* (London, 1959); B. W. Beckingsale, *Thomas Cromwell: Tudor Minister* (London, 1978) and S. E. Lehmberg, 'The religious beliefs of Thomas Cromwell' in R. L. de Molen, ed., *Leaders of the Reformation* (London, 1984), pp. 134–51.

[2] *Sermons and Remains of Hugh Latimer*, ed. G. E. Corrie (Parker Society, Cambridge, 1845), p. 411; PRO SP 1/96, fo. 36 (*LP* ix. 226); Latimer, *Remains*, pp. 395, 386–7; SP 1/141, fo. 127ᵛ (*LP* xiii(2). 1223); Richard Taverner, *The Confession of the Faith of the Germans* (*STC* 909, [1536]), prefatory letter; cited in G. R. Elton, *Policy and Police*, p. 424.

[3] *The Lisle Letters*, ed. M. St Clare Byrne (6 vols., Chicago, 1981), V, 1244; cf. also *St. Pap.* 1 (i), clcix.

Chauncellor . . . and nowe my lord prevy seale in like maner rewleth all, and we shall se onse the day that he shall haue as gret a ffawle as eny of them'.[4] 'Who hastis to clyme sekes to reuerte.'[5] In April 1536 Cromwell told the imperial ambassador that 'it was only now that he had known the frailty of human affairs, especially those of the court . . . and if fate fell upon him as upon his predecessors he would arm himself with patience, and leave the rest to God'. Yet, all the while he struggled to conceal a smile. Even as he spoke, far from submitting to providence, he was plotting to strike before he was himself struck down, for Queen Anne, so he told Chapuys, 'would like to see his head cut off'.[6] Through speed and guile Cromwell might survive the attacks of his rivals, but he could not last long if ever he angered the king. Yet Cromwell insistently led the king towards reform in religion more radical than the king could countenance, aware that he might revert, and that when he did his minister was likely to be sacrificed. *Ira principis mors est.*

So it was. By 1540 Henry had been persuaded that Cromwell held the darkest heresy, against the sacrament of the altar, and charged with this belief Cromwell went to the block on 28 July 1540.[7] The act of attainder against Cromwell claimed that he was 'a detestable heretic', who would stop at nothing to spread 'his damnable Errors and Heresies'. So committed was he to the cause of reform, so his accusers alleged, and to the heretics he gathered about him, that he 'did arrogantly say in defence of their preaching':

That if the King did turn from it [the Gospel], yet I would not turn; and if the King did turn, and all his people, I would fight in the field in my own person, with my sword in my hand against him and all other.

This vow was made, so it was said, in St Peter le Poor on 31 March 1539.[8] Most would have found nothing fantastic in these charges against him. For Cardinal Pole, Cromwell was no less than the 'messenger of Satan', endowed with all 'the arts of the old Serpent': God 'in his anger at the King' had spared Cromwell's life in 1529 to give it to the Devil to use 'as an instrument' to afflict Henry's soul.[9] From around the country reports came of people saying that Cromwell was 'a starke hereticke and . . . all his withholders', who would hang in Hell one day.[10] A servant was abused as if 'he had been an heathen and not your mastership's servant'.[11] In 1536 the prior of St Alban's said that the

[4] SP 1/128, fo. 110 (*LP* xiii(1) 95); see also SP 1/114, fo. 6 (*LP* xii(1) 193(2)).
[5] *Collected Poems of Sir Thomas Wyatt*, ed. K. Muir and P. Thomson (Liverpool, 1969), CLXXVI.
[6] *LP* x. 601.
[7] G. R. Elton, 'Thomas Cromwell's decline and fall', in *Studies in Tudor and Stuart Politics and Government*, I, pp. 189–230; J. J. Scarisbrick, *Henry VIII* (London 1968), pp. 375–81.
[8] *LP* xv 498(60); *The Acts and Monuments of John Foxe*, ed. G. Townsend and S. R. Cattley (8 vols., 1837–41), v, p. 399.
[9] *LP* xvi 404; xiv(1), 200, p. 82.
[10] See, for example, SP 1/116, fo. 187 (*LP* xii(1) 567); SP 1/114, fo. 227; SP 1/115, fos. 6, 122, 166 (*LP* xii(1) 163, 193, 275, 308); Elton, *Policy and Police*, pp. 6–9.
[11] *LP* ix 1169.

reformation statutes were made 'by a sort of lyght brayned merchauntes and also heretyckes, Cromwell being one of the chief of them'.[12] How was it that Thomas Cromwell, so brilliant a pragmatist and so astute, had come to espouse ideas so dangerous, and to be confederate with reckless evangelicals who might make him a martyr as well as themselves? Among Cromwell's old associates were men whom it was folly for him even to know.

The 'euangellycall bretherne' vowed to spread the Gospel in England. These were men determined that the word, hidden from the faithful for a thousand years, must go forth by whatever means and whatever the risk. An underworld of the 'brethren' sheltered and sustained each other under persecution; converts bound together lastingly in common cause. The networks of those 'godly lerned men which labour in the vyneyarde of the Lorde to bryng the people of this realme to the knowledge of Christes gospell' were shadowy, but in the early days the 'brethren' were to be found in the universities, in the inns of court, in the merchant community of the capital and among English merchants abroad. Cromwell was part of all these worlds, and had known some of the 'brethren' of old. That he was acquainted with some of them is no proof of his sympathy with their convictions, for no man is his friend's keeper, but his protection of them might be. Cromwell was renowned for his loyalty to his friends. John Foxe, who had spoken to some of them, headed one chapter of his life of Cromwell: 'The Lord Cromwell: Not Forgetting his Old Friend and Benefactors'. 'My lord yor joy and comforth maye be greate that you almost alone of all men that euer were in your place haue neuer forgotten your old [friends]', wrote Morison in 1538.[13]

I

On 19 November 1530 four men rode from the Tower through the City to the Cheapside cross. Facing their horses' tails, wearing papers on their head proclaiming *Pecasse contra mandata Regis*, their clothes festooned with copies of William Tyndale's forbidden works, they were penitents, to be publicly shamed. Yet one of them rode upon a 'lofty gelding and fierce', which would have no basins rung by it, and having always 'loved to go handsomely' in his apparel, he sported his books as a ruff. Into a great fire in Cheapside they cast the 'infected books', and then were set in the pillory as a dread warning to others. These four men – John Purser, John Tyndale, Thomas Somer, and an unnamed apprentice from London Bridge – were leading lights among the 'brethren'. Their penance brought knowledge of William Tyndale's works to the citizenry, now curious but hitherto oblivious of them, more effectively than

---

[12] PRO E 36/120, fo. 78 (*LP* xi. 354).

[13] PRO, Prerogative Court of Canterbury, Prob. 11/31, fo. 158 (Henry Brinklow's will, 1545); Foxe, v, p. 391; see also R. B. Merriman, *Life and Letters of Thomas Cromwell* (2 vols., Oxford, 1902), I, pp. 19–23; SP 1/133, fo. 254 (*LP* xiii(1) 1297).

ever their clandestine book-running could have done.[14] These men had scattered through London three thousand copies of *The Practice of Prelates*, Tyndale's attack upon the king's divorce and his cardinal. They had been sent before the lord chancellor, and thence before the council in star chamber, 'for having books against the King's proclamation'.[15] All had hopes of Cromwell's intervention, for they had known him in the City, and since early in 1530 Cromwell had been high in the counsels of the king.[16]

Cromwell was acquainted with these men before his rise to political eminence. An anonymous suitor from the Middle Temple, seeking service with Cromwell later, excused his audacity by reminding the minister of his old friendship with Thomas Somer.

I reducing into my memorye of olde youer manifolde gentill kyendnesse at such tyme (in especiall) as my late ffrende Thomas Somer, whiche in his lifetime was youer owen assured bothe harte and bodie (to whose solle godde gyue reste) he and I then at diuerse tymes untoo youer mastershippe resorting, your inhabitacion that tyme beyng agayn the gate of the ffryars Augustynes.[17]

It may have been this Mr Somer's advice which Margaret Vernon took about finding a suitable tutor for her young charge, Gregory Cromwell, and his opinion which she relayed to his father.[18] Thomas Somer was a citizen and stockfishmonger of London, 'a very honest merchant and wealthy', yet by 1524 grown unlucky in his business ventures. In that year Somer, with his partner Henry Barnes, sustained heavy losses when the ship carrying their cargo of wine from Italy was detained at Cadiz; and when spermaceti which he was bound to buy was seized by the crown, according to ancient right, he lost a further £20. It was Thomas Cromwell who drafted petitions for Somer to Wolsey (and to Tunstall?) seeking aid in settlement of his disputes. He also lent Somer £60: a loan which proved hard to recover.[19] On behalf of 'my frende Mr Somer', Cromwell would try to sell a horse to raise some money.[20] John Copland, a London merchant taylor, called at Cromwell's house in 1527 to intercede for Somer, who 'hathe ben wt me dessireng me ffor to speke wt you in his be halffe & ryght glad he wold be at a poynt wt you'. Cromwell was

---

[14] *Calendar of State Papers, Venetian*, III, p. 642; *Cal. Sp.* IV(1), pp. 820–1, 847–8; *Two London Chronicles, from the Collections of John Stow*, ed. C. L. Kingsford, Camden Miscellany, XII (Camden Society, 3rd series, XVIII, 1910), p. 5; Foxe, V, pp. 452–3.

[15] HHL, Ellesmere MS 2652, fo. 15; J. Guy, *The Public Career of Sir Thomas More* (Brighton, 1980), p. 173; R. W. Heinze, *The Proclamations of the Tudor Kings* (Cambridge, 1976), p. 280 n. 90.

[16] Elton, *The Tudor Revolution in Government* (Cambridge, 1953), p. 83; Guy, *The Public Career of Sir Thomas More*, p. 130.

[17] SP 1/88, fo. 50 (*LP* vii 1618). Cromwell lived at the Austin Friars from 1527 until he moved to Stepney in 1533.   [18] SP 1/65, fo. 40 (*LP* v 17).

[19] Foxe, V, p. 453; SP 1/234, fos. 113–17 (*LP Add.* i 429); Bracton, *De Legibus et Consuetudines Angliae*, Tractatus secundus, de corona; SP 1/47, fo. 149 (*LP* iv(2) 4107; *LP* iv(3) 5330(2).

[20] SP 1/59, fo. 39 (*LP* iv(3) 6800). The editor of *Letters and Papers* dates this letter to December 1530, but it is likely to have been written earlier.

out, so Copland invited him, as a friend might, 'to send ffor me to my garthen when that ye might be at leysser or ellis and yef ye be dysspossyt ffor to seke the aire of the ffeldes ye shalbe sure ffor to ffynd me at my garthen'. Copland lent Somer the 'lofty gelding' for his penitential ride through London, for he too was of the 'brethren'.[21] Somer returned from his penance to the Tower, never to leave it, despite his supplication to Cromwell. He died there by the summer of 1532, 'for the testimony of his faith', his will witnessed by two priests of the Tower.[22]

John Purser and Thomas Cromwell were joint signatories to an award early in 1524. Later, Purser became one of the 'vowbrekynge brethern' whom Sir Thomas More denounced. With others, Purser had bound himself for the appearance of John Byrt, a bookbinder troubled for religion, but, far from delivering Byrt, they 'force not to forfayt theyr bonde for bretherhed, but let hym slyppe asyde', hiding him until he could make his escape to the 'brethren' in the Low Countries.[23] In Purser's house, a 'comon taverne', the brethren met. One of them, George Gower, implored Cromwell from prison in July 1532, 'Refuse not the sighes of an opprest herte'. In trouble, Purser looked to Cromwell for help. Scribbled on the back of a letter to Cromwell in 1529 was this message: 'here hathe be Pursar ij tymes to speke wt yow desyryng yow that in any wayse he may speke wt yow thys nyght'. By Christmas 1533 Purser lay dying, and at his deathbed were Thomas Parnell, Robert Barnes's 'scholar' and George Tadlowe, both won to reform.[24] Purser left a son, Dick, whom he had 'nowseled up' in heresy. Sir Thomas More took this child into his own household, hoping to wean him away from the pernicious influences found in his father's house. But it was too late, for George Joye had already taught the boy 'vngracyouse heresye agaynst the blessed sacrament of the aulter'. This Joye denied: 'I had ben an vndiscreit Maister so sodenly in so lytell space to haue taken forthe the chylde owte of his Pater Noster vnto the Sacrament of the Auter.'[25] When Dick began to impart his heresy to another child in More's household, More had the boy whipped and cast him out. What would become of Dick? He was taken into Thomas Cromwell's household by 1537, and there given charge of his new master's leopard.[26]

[21] SP 1/45, fo. 313 (*LP* iv(2) 3720); Foxe, v, p. 453. When Copland made his will in July 1533 he had with him William Carkeke, the reformist scrivener whose servant was already in trouble for importing Tyndale's works; PCC, Prob. 11/25, fo. 89; Foxe, v, p. 39; *LP Add.*, i 420.

[22] *LP* vii 923(26); PCC, Prob. 11/24, fo. 113^v. Somer's executors also sent a supplication to Cromwell; *LP* vi 299(3).

[23] *LP* iv(1) 87; More, *The Apology*, ed. J. B. Trapp, in *The Complete Works of St Thomas More*, vol. IX (New Haven, 1979), pp. 29, 90.

[24] SP 1/70, fo. 184; SP 1/55, fo. 19^v (*LP* v 1176; iv(3). 5809). PCC, Prob. 11/25, fo. 49.

[25] *The Apologye of Syr Thomas More, Knyght*, ed. A. Taft (Early English Text Society, original series, 180, 1930), p. 301; More, *The Apology, CW*, IX, p. 117; George Joye, *The Subuersion of Moris false foundacion* (1534; *STC* 1489), sigs. 1$_2$–1$_3$; cited in *The Apologye*, ed. Taft, p. 314.

[26] More, *The Apology, CW*, IX, p. 118. Joye said that More had the boy whipped naked 'tayed vnto the tree of his trowthe'; *LP* xii(2) 300; xiv(2). 782.

In January 1532 a young man wrote to Cromwell from Rouen, beseeching him 'for the passion of crist', as the only one who could help him. No merchant in London dare employ Richard Hilles 'ffor ffear of the byshopes'. Hilles had written a treatise expounding 'how I dyd understand that part off Sancte James pystell that sayd how Abraham was iustiffyed by workes', and now he sent it to Cromwell ('howbeyt no man lyvynge do know that I do wryte to youre mastershyppe'). His master Nicholas Cosyn, merchant taylor at the sign of the anchor on London Bridge, pleaded with him, weeping, 'to reuoke rather than to dye'. Hilles explained how, when challenged with 'worldly reasons', he 'shewyd . . . how S. Paull sayth that the naturall man can nott perceave spirituall thinges . . . as your mastership maye conjecture'. From London Bridge, his distraught mother implored Cromwell, 'ffor cristes sake to remember my pore sonne Rychard Hylles'. It was surely Hilles who was the penitent apprentice of London Bridge in November 1530; who, with John Tyndale and Thomas Patmore, confessed himself guilty of 'receauing of Tindalls testaments & dyuers other bokes and deliuering and skatteryng the same abrode in dyuers places of the Citie of London'. Now in 1532 he looked confidently to Cromwell, as to one who would know why he could never 'returne ageyn from crist', and who would come to his aid.[27]

Latimer wrote to the king on 1 December 1530, protesting the innocence of the penitent merchants – 'there is no man, I hear say, that can lay any word or deed against them that should sound to the breaking of any of your grace's laws' – but maybe he was wrong about John Tyndale. In February 1528 John Tyndale, a London merchant dwelling by the Austin Friars, declared to a Colchester clothworker that he could see no remedy for the desperate slump in the cloth trade, 'excepte we coode cause the comons to arise and complayne to the kynges grace And schewe hym how the peple be not halff set awourke'.[28] This John Tyndale was among the 'brethren' from the earliest days. In his house at St Martin by the Well with Two Buckets Rowland Phillips had married in 1525 'non in facie ecclesie'. Later, in Mary's reign, Phillips went to the stake, and one of the witnesses to his marriage, Thomas Benet, died for the faith much sooner. By May 1529 John Tyndale was excommunicate.[29] Foxe wrote that John Tyndale abjured in 1530 'for sending five marks to his brother William Tyndale beyond the sea, and for receiving and keeping with him certain letters from his brother', yet whether this John Tyndale was more than an evangelical brother to William remains doubtful.[30]

[27] SP 1/74 fos. 107ᵛ–108, 109 (*LP* vi 99); BL, Harl. MS 425, fo. 15; Foxe, v, p. 804.
[28] Latimer, *Remains*, p. 306; SP 1/47, fos. 176–7 (*LP* iv(2) 4145(1, 2)); J. F. Mozley, *William Tyndale* (London, 1937), pp. 121–2.
[29] W. H. Frere, *The Marian Reaction and its Relation to the English Clergy* (1896), p. 67; Foxe, v, pp. 15–26; SP 1/236, fo. 224 (*LP Add.* i 683); H. C. Porter, *Reformation and Reaction in Tudor Cambridge* (Cambridge, 1958), p. 41; PRO, C 85/188/28.
[30] Foxe, v, p. 29; G. R. Elton, *Reform and Renewal: Thomas Cromwell and the Common Weal* (Cambridge, 1973), p. 18, n. 30.

Martin Tyndale, fellow of King's College, Cambridge, sent his translation of Erasmus' life of Colet to Cromwell, in hope of patronage ('the Lord aboue . . . registers the benefites done to his litell ones in the courte Roules of his remembraunce'), and in thank offering, because Cromwell had 'so louingly helpide my brother one John Tyndall . . . in his troubles'.[31] Martin wrote of his brother 'now departide' (and he should have known) but in 1539 a John Tyndale, now a servant to Latimer, was involved in a sinister conspiracy with John Sheriff, a founder member of the Christian Brethren, to frighten Thomas Pylson into resigning his fellowship at King's College. Subsequently John Tyndale witnessed the will of John Gough, an evangelical even more reckless and determined than he; perhaps even an anabaptist.[32] The only communication from Cromwell to John Tyndale hardly suggests his sympathy or support; it would be surprising if it had. Thomas Jermyn informed Cromwell, 'I have sent to Master Tyndall thys monday . . . my servant in his house delyvered the kynges letter to hym selff so that he can nott deny the receyte thereoff.'[33] Yet why then should Martyn Tindale have thanked Cromwell for helping John 'in his troubles'?

A letter of early 1530 was copied in the early seventeenth century from a manuscript which was subsequently lost, perhaps in the great fire in the Cottonian library. It shows that the 'brethren' were wrong to presume too far on their old acquaintance:

Cromwell to the Card. That he hath disovered lately some who favour Luther's sect, and read his books, and Tyndale's. The books he hath taken are *The Revelacion of Antichrist* and *Supplication of the Beggers*, pestiferous books, and also if they be scatired among the comon people so destroy the whole obedience and policy of this realm. He exhorts the Cardinal to stop this doctrine.[34]

The seventeenth-century scholar who transcribed this letter was puzzled by Cromwell's religious stance. In the margin of a letter from Stephen Vaughan he noted, 'it may be judged that Cromwell was no Lutheran', yet by the side of a letter written by Shaxton at the fall of Anne Boleyn, pleading 'in visceribus

---

[31] SP 1/77, fo. 148 (*LP* vi. 751).

[32] Tyndale had persuaded Pylson to go to Sheriff, a barber surgeon in Colman Street, to be cured of the 'vulnus meretricis' he had contracted in the Stews: E 101/348/38; SP 1/162, fos. 1–31 (*LP* xiv(2) 255; xv 936); Guildhall Library, MS 9171/11, fos. 132ᵛ–3.

[33] SP 1/66, fo. 60 (*LP* v 304). The editor of *Letters and Papers* places this letter in June 1531, and suggests that it refers to William Tyndale. J. F. Mozley plausibly proposes that it refers to John, not William, and was written on 19 December 1530; *William Tyndale*, p. 172. Yet his surmise that the letter was a royal demand that John divulge where William was is less probable, for Cromwell knew Tyndale's whereabouts through Vaughan. Monday fell on the 19th in September as well as December in 1530.

[34] Bodleian Library, Jesus College MS 74, fo. 192. I am grateful to Dr Steven Gunn for this reference. The books to which Cromwell referred are: Richard Brightwell (alias John Frith), *The Revelation of Antichrist* (*STC* 11394, 12 July 1529); Simon Fish, *A Supplicacyon for the Beggers* (*STC* 10883, printed early 1529); A. Hume, 'English Protestant books printed abroad, 1525–1535; an annotated bibliography' in *The Confutation of Tyndale's Answer*, ed. L. A. Schuster *et al.*, *CW*, VIII(ii), Appendix B, pp. 1071–3.

Jesu Christi that you will now be no less diligent to set forth the honor of God and his Holy Word', he wrote, 'Is this Cromwell?' (it was); 'if it were it seems he favoured the Protestants'.[35] The perplexity about Cromwell's faith remains, and perhaps not only because it was private, nor because it was politic to keep it secret.

II

If there was speculation about Cromwell's belief while he lived, and misunderstanding about it when he died, still harder is it to discover it now, but there are signs. On All Hallows Day 1529, when Cardinal Wolsey was fallen, and his servants seemed likely to follow him, George Cavendish came upon a disconsolate Cromwell in the great hall at Esher. He was 'leanyng in the greate wyndowe wt a prymer in his hand sayeng of our lady mattens'. But this, wrote Cavendish, 'had byn synce a very straynge syght'. 'He prayed not more earnestly than the teares distilled frome his eyes'.[36] Cromwell was still, to all outward appearance, of conventional piety. In July 1529 he had made his will, commending his soul, as a good catholic would

to the grete god of heuen my maker Creatour and Redemer besechyng the most gloryous virgyn our blessed ladie Saynct Mary the vyrgyn and Mother with all the holie companye of heuen to be Medyatours and Intercessours for me to the holie trynytee So that I may be able when it shall please Almightie god to call me out of this miserable worlde and transitorie lif to inherite the kingdome of heuen.

He willed that a priest 'of contynent and good lyuyng' should sing for his soul in purgatory for seven years.[37] In May 1530 Cromwell, now his master's 'only comfort' and 'moste assuryd refugye in this my cala[mity]', wrote to tell Wolsey what Wolsey would have liked to hear: 'The fame is that Luther is departed this Life. I would he had never bin borne.'[38] There is no reason to doubt his sincerity. Yet for all the signs that Cromwell was conventionally pious, there were already others that he was not.

On Passion Eve 1528 Stephen Vaughan wrote to Cromwell, his old friend and former master, of his search through London to recover a debt from the evasive Mr Mundy. At last Vaughan had found him, as befitted the day, at evensong at St Faith's, but Mundy was 'otherwise disposed to serue God', and declined to discuss money. Vaughan was 'bolde to answer him' that 'sythe it

---

[35] Bodleian, Jesus College MS 74, fos. 156, 248^v. The original letter is to be found in the Cottonian manuscripts: BL, Cotton MS Otho C. 10, fo. 260^v (LP x 942). Where the original and the seventeenth-century copy are compared, and found to be identical, as here, the transcription of the lost letters may be given more credence; see above n. 34; and below n. 85.

[36] The Life and Death of Cardinal Wolsey by George Cavendish, ed. R. S. Sylvester (EETS, original series, 243, 1959), p. 104.

[37] The will is printed in Merriman, Life and Letters, I, pp. 56–63.

[38] St. Pap. I(i), pp. 349ff; Bodleian, Jesus College MS 74, fos. 192–3, 194; Merriman, Life and Letters, I, p. 327.

was hys mynde in suche place to serue god that better he coulde not serue hym then with restoryng the ryght unto his brother whom he had wrongfully defrawded'. Mundy's discomfiture and hypocrisy might amuse Cromwell, Vaughan knew, yet beyond the joke lay their shared belief – rational, practical, sceptical – that true piety lay not in ritual observance and conventional obsequies. This was the message of Erasmus and his followers, and in Vaughan's letter also comes perhaps a hint of who might have influenced them. Describing an ambassador newly arrived in London, Vaughan explained that he was 'a good deal like Dr Colet, late dean of Powlys, both in person and gesture', as if they had both known him.[39] When Martin Tyndale offered his translation of Erasmus' lives of Colet and Vitruvius to Cromwell, his desire was that they

but speciali Collet, may walke a brode in his owne contre, where he may visite his kinffolke, his frends, his familieres, and his scoleres, or rather godsones (for full many he did regender and get to god) for all be not yet dede . . .[40]

Among Colet's 'godsons' may have been Cromwell, Vaughan and their friends.

In Cromwell's house at the Austin Friars were pictures of the Virgin and saints, and to his new house at St Peter the Poor in 1534 came an image of the child Jesus, pictures of our Lady of Pity and the Passion of Our Lord.[41] (Did these belong to Cromwell or to his mother-in-law who lived with him?). Still in 1533 the bishop of Ely sent Cromwell a 'poor token' of St Audrey, 'whereof ye shall be sure for your life',[42] yet soon, and probably already, Cromwell was known to oppose vehemently trusting in images. His would be the campaign against abused images – idols which duped the faithful into believing that the pictures and shrines had power in themselves – and his the concern, following Colet and Latimer, to relieve rather the 'poor image of Christ', the starving poor.

In the cardinal's household, and elsewhere, those 'gnatomical elbow hangers', clerics, enjoyed privileges and found a way to wealth denied to laymen. The lesson went deep with Cromwell. When Wolsey lamented that he could not reward his loyal lay retainers at his fall, Cromwell stormed against his master's pampered chaplains; let them pay, for they had 'had all the profettes and avuntages at your handes And thes yor seruauntes non at all And yet hathe yor por seruantes taken myche more payn for you in oon day than all your Idel chapleyns hathe don in a yere'.[43] Among Cromwell's papers in the early 1530s was a copy of the 'Jestes' of Skelton, and a treatise about the most

[39] SP 1/47, fo. 149 (*LP* iv(2) 4107).
[40] BL, Harl. MS 6989, fo. 45 (*LP* vi 752), cited in J. K. McConica, *English Humanism and Reformation Politics* (Oxford, 1965), pp. 119–20.
[41] *LP* iv(2). 3197; xv 1029(6).   [42] Ibid, vi 218; see also ibid, vii 763.
[43] 'A Supplication of the Poore Commons', ed. J. M. Cowper (EETS, extra series, 13, 1871), p. 77; *The Life and Death of Cardinal Wolsey*, p. 106.

anti-clerical of states: 'A book of the Venetians' life, and of their prelates and curates'.[44] Cromwell's friends and servants wrote to him with tales of discomfited prelates. 'I wold to God . . . that ye had ben there to here hym', wrote Richard Cromwell in 1537, describing the bishop of Ely in a rage; swearing by 'Goddis bodye', 'his cullor and countenaunce chaunged so often that I was affayred that he had ben helf lunatique; . . . I have not seen a man of his ordre so ientle to entertayne his sewtors; suerlye suche jentle hartis be worthie of good promocions'. The most savage jest of all was the burning of Friar Forest.[45] Nothing amused Cromwell better than teasing sanctimonious clerics. He told Chapuys in 1535 that he would have given £1,000 for the emperor to have heard Bishop Stokesley preaching – all against his will – upon the invalidity of the king's first marriage and the usurpation of the pope. Hearing Stokesley parade his 'old rusty sophistry and unwritten verities' early in 1537, Cromwell and Cranmer 'smiled a little one upon another'. Cromwell's particular animus against Stokesley had much to do with the bishop's traduction of Wolsey, and something to do with Stokesley's refusal to translate the Acts of the Apostles into English, 'whiche were symple poore felowes; and therfore my lord of London disdayned to have to do with any of thair actes'.[46]

Cromwell had been among the very first to study Erasmus' Latin translation of the New Testament. To obtain a copy in 1517, as Cromwell did, was in itself a mark of considerable intellectual and theological curiosity. On his journey to Rome in 1517–18 to acquire papal pardons for the gild of Our Lady at Boston – still 'good religion' then, before Luther's protest – he took the New Testament with him. 'By learning without book the text . . . in his going and coming from Rome . . . he began to be touched, and called to a better understanding.'[47] Perhaps he soon came to know men of like mind. In 1537 a Cambridge reformer 'strengthened by the Holy Ghost so to set forth and bring to light the verity of the Gospel', would claim that 'I more than xv yeres agoye dyd then perceyue yor mere and naturall goodnes'.[48] In 1527 Miles Coverdale besought Cromwell, 'for the tender love of god & and for the fervent zeall that you have to vertue and godly study', for a 'diversyte of bookys' that he might advance his studies. Reminding Cromwell of a conversation they had had at 'master moorys' house on Easter eve, Coverdale, now with Robert Barnes at the Cambridge Austin Friars, avowed that 'now I begyne to taste of holy schryptres, now (honor be to God) I am sett to the most swete smell of holly lettres'. A year later Coverdale had gone over the wall, and his mentor, Friar Barnes, was 'free prisoner' at the London Austin Friars, reading

[44] *LP* vii 923 (7); vi 299 (11); Elton, *Reform and Renewal*, pp. 12–13.
[45] SP 1/122, fo. 225 (*LP* xii(2) 241); Latimer, *Remains*, 391.
[46] *LP* viii 1105; Foxe, v, p. 383; William Roper, *The Lyfe of Sir Thomas More, Knighte*, (EETS, original series, 197) pp. 38–9; *Narratives of the Reformation*, ed. J. G. Nichols (Camden Society, o. s., 77, 1859), pp. 277–8.
[47] Foxe, v. 363–5; G. R. Elton, 'Thomas Cromwell *Redivivus*' in *Studies*, III, pp. 375, 378.
[48] SP 1/118, fos. 90–1 (*LP* xii(1) 876–7); Elton, *Policy and Police*, pp. 38–9.

Tyndale's New Testament to eager City 'brethren'.[49] In Cromwell's own house at the Austin Friars the table talk was by 1531 or 1532 of the interpretation of scripture, of evangelical theology. John Oliver wrote with gratitude for 'divers dinners' at Cromwell's house, 'where in verie dede I did here such communicacion which were the verie cause of the begynnynge of my conuersion'. And he 'fownd allwaies the conclusions you mayntenyd at yor borde to be consonent with the hollie worde of god'. From Cromwell's house he would go home to compare the Latin translation of Erasmus 'with the vulgare which they call Saint Jeromes translacion', and then, because 'I wolde not haue this gere after a vulgare sort', he studied the New Testament in Greek.[50] For all those who did want the Gospel in their own tongue Tyndale had made an English translation, but how was it to go forth?

'Thys is the newys in ynglond now, Rychard Harman', wrote John Sadler to one of Tyndale's agents in Antwerp in September 1526, 'non other but that the new testament in ynglyshe schuld be put down & bornt, whyche god fforffend'. Only the most determined evangelicals read Tyndale's New Testament, especially once More and Stokesley began their fierce campaign to repress it. The brothers John and Ralph Sadler were early won to reform; Ralph was, from his youth, Cromwell's servant.[51] Among the leading 'euangelycall bretherne' were some of Cromwell's associates. John Sadler may have been despondent, but others were convinced that the Word must soon go forth. 'Beholde the signes of the worlde whiche be wondrous',[52] wrote Stephen Vaughan to Cromwell in 1531, as if to one who shared his hopes.

III

In the autumn of 1531 Sir Thomas More challenged George Constantine:

There is beyond the sea, Tyndale, Ioye, and a great many mo of you. I know thei cannot liue without helpe, some sendeth theim money and succoureth theim . . . I pray thee who be thei that thus helpe them?[53]

Cromwell sent Vaughan warning that Constantine, under interrogation, would name him 'not only a fautour and adherent to the Lutheran secte', but also a book agent. 'Withe [many] frendly, louyng, ernest and discrete exhortacions' throughout that autumn, so Vaughan admitted, Cromwell had urged him 'to be circumspect, clerely . . . alyenatyng myself from suche sectes and erronious opinions only to applye . . . myself truly [and] unfaynedly to

[49] SP 1/65, fo. 254 (*LP* v 221); Foxe, v, 415–17; Dickens, *Thomas Cromwell and the English Reformation*, pp. 109–10.

[50] SP 1/141, fos. 126–7 (*LP* xiii(2) 1223); Elton, *Reform and Renewal*, pp. 26–8.

[51] SP 1/50, fo. 75 (*LP* iv(2) 4693); A. Slavin, *Politics and Profit: A Study of Sir Ralph Sadler, 1507–1547* (Cambridge, 1966), pp. 15, 166.   [52] SP 1/68, fo. 57 (*LP* v 533).

[53] Edward Hall, *The Union of Two Noble and Illustre Families of Lancaster and York*, ed. H. Ellis (London, 1809), p. 763.

serve the king'.[54] If Vaughan was suspect, and rightly, then Cromwell was suspect also. The story of how Vaughan had left England for Antwerp in December 1530, set on a rash venture to bring Tyndale back to England, is well known.[55] Robert Barnes was at court in December; Simon Fish was in the City; both promised a safe conduct,[56] and there were hopes that Tyndale might return, reconciled, to serve the king. This scheme, ever ill-conceived, foundered when Henry read Tyndale's *Answer* to More, 'fyllyd with Scedycyous Slanderous lyes and Fantastycall opynyon[s]'.[57] Cromwell's own anxiety and turmoil, fearing that his own position at court would become yet more precarious, is evident in every line of the letter, crossed through and through, that he wrote at the king's command to his indiscreet friend in May 1531. He pleaded with Vaughan 'vtterlie to forsake ... Tyndale and all his secte', for the king suspected

that *ye should* {ye} in such wise {by yo*ur* lett*er*es} *lene vnto and favo*ur *the evill doctryne of so peruerse and malycyous a person and so moche prayse him* {prayse Setforth and avaunse hym} {*bothe to lake lernyng*} {to be envyous and to lake lernyng gra|ce|} {*vertue and all good discrecyon*} *who nothing* {*whiche nothing elles*} {pretendyth} *goeth about or pretendeth* but *onelie to Seduce deceyue and disquiet the people and comenwelth of this realme Whose* {*Repayre thether ys to be estuyd*} *cummyng into Englonde the kinges highnes can right well forbere and* {sowe sedycyon among the peopull of this realm.[58]

With heresy would come subversion: so Cromwell had warned Wolsey in 1530. Yet the postscript, a personal message, expressed the opinion that 'if it were possible, by good and wholesome exhortations to reconcile and convert the said Tyndale ... I doubt not but the King's highness would be much joyous of his conversion'.[59] Perhaps Cromwell still shared Vaughan's hopes. Yet when in November 1531 Vaughan, with supreme indiscretion, sent him a book so clearly reformed that even Vaughan thought that its author 'shall seale it with his blood' – Robert Barnes's *Supplication* to Henry VIII – Cromwell at last made politic moves to distance himself. Vaughan, bound to his patron 'nolens volens', protested his innocence. 'Whatsoeuer the worlde bable of me ... I am neyther Lutheran ne yet Tyndalyn', he vowed, and for good scriptural

---

[54] BL, Cotton MS Galba B, 10, fos. 21–3ᵛ (*LP* v 574).
[55] Vaughan was first accused of heresy in Antwerp in 1528; *LP* iv(3) 5823. For Vaughan's mission, see R. Demaus, *William Tindale: A Biography* (1886), ch. X; Mozley, *William Tyndale*, ch. IX; Elton, *Reform and Renewal*, pp. 38–46; W. C. Richardson, *Stephen Vaughan: Financial Agent of Henry VIII* (Baton Rouge, 1953), ch. III.
[56] *Cal. Sp.* IV(i), no. 549, p. 848 (21 December, 1530), Foxe, IV, p. 657.
[57] Merriman, *Life and Letters*, I, p. 336. The book was *An Answere made vnto Sir Thomas Mores dialoge made by Vvillyam Tindale* (STC 24437; 1531).
[58] Words enclosed thus {...} are inserted above the line in the original. Words printed in italics are crossed out. Merriman, *Life and Letters*, I, pp. 335–9. A similar agitation is betrayed in another letter of Cromwell's, perhaps written for the same sort of reason: SP 1/81, fo. 80 (*LP* vi 1625). [59] Demaus, *William Tindale*, p. 355.

reasons would not 'esteme them . . . for my goddes'; 'maledictus qui confidit in homine. Cristes churche hathe admitted me a lernyng sufficient and infallible and by crist taught whiche is tholy scripture'.[60] Vaughan did not heed Cromwell's warning; neither did Cromwell follow his own advice. He continued to use as his agents and messengers in the Low Countries fervent evangelicals, with a mission to bring the Gospel into England.

'I [have] made an end of my book', so Vaughan informed Cromwell in January 1532, 'and do la[ck only a] trusty bearer, which I find not'. At last Vaughan was circumspect: in this book, now unknown, 'I have declared things . . . which I should not wish to be known to come from me, and have used so strange a manner that few men will think it mine', and now again he insisted, 'I am no heretic, nor will be made one'. Though the book, it seems, concerned the cloth trade, not evangelical theology, the bearer he found was 'my frende', Richard Downes, dwelling in Cornhill.[61] Downes was, and would remain, a leading light within the underworld of City 'brethren'. In 1540, when a new reaction began, one of the 'good willers' wrote to Downes for 'godly news', for he was

nat only associat & in compeny dayly wt suche maner of men as be favourable to the worde of god But also wt suche as can partely delate whether that it be of any licliod (likelihood) that godes worde shall have free passage or no.[62]

When in December 1531 Vaughan recommended Agrippa's *De Vanitate Scientiarum* to Cromwell 'for your pastime', he suggested that his 'brother' William Johnson could procure a copy. 'Help my brother William Johanson to live', asked Vaughan in August 1533, and by December Cromwell had done so, for he thanked Lord Lisle 'for your great cheer made to my servant [Will]yam Johnson'. This was probably the William Johnson who, in a London garden in 1527, had avowed that 'the works of Martin Luther were good and laudable, and that were it within his power they should be published throughout the realm of England'.[63] John Coke, secretary to the merchant adventurers at Antwerp, was another adherent of Tyndale's and another servant of Cromwell's, and in October 1531 he was sent to the Fleet for possessing Tyndale's New Testament.[64] Yet still in 1533 Coke was in touch with 'Brother William' (Tyndale), taking his part against Joye in their controversy about the sleep of the soul.[65] In February 1532 Coke had thanked

[60] SP 1/68, fos. 56–7 (*LP* v 533); Elton, *Reform and Renewal*, pp. 41–2; *A supplicatyon made by Robert Barnes* (*STC* 1470; 1531). BL, Cotton MS Galba B 10, fos. 21–3ᵛ (*LP* v 574).
[61] *LP* v 739; SP 1/69, fo. 82 (*LP* v 753).
[62] PRO, STAC 2/34/2811; Elton, *Policy and Police*, p. 36. Downes's will, made in December 1542, reveals his ardent evangelical views and his links with the 'brethren'; PCC, Prob. 11/29, fo. 113ᵛ.   [63] *LP* v 585; VI 934, 1413; Greater London RO, DL/C/330, fo. 138ᵛ.
[64] HHL, Ellesmere MS 2652, fo. 15; M. L. Robertson, 'Thomas Cromwell's Servants: The Ministerial Household in Early Tudor Government and Society' (Ph.D thesis, University of California at Los Angeles, 1975), p. 468; Guy, *The Public Career of Sir Thomas More*, p. 174.
[65] SP 1/75, fo. 210 (*LP* vi 402(2)); Mozley, *William Tyndale*, pp. 271–2.

Cromwell for declaring his favour towards him to Mr Locke, another who imported evangelical books.[66] All this while, the chancellor and Stokesley hunted 'the brethren', knowing well that such men had powerful protectors. They waited their chance to strike them down.

John Petyt, burgess for the City, was 'one of the fyrste that wyth mr. Fryth, Bylney, and Tyndall cowght a swheetnes in Godes worde'. He, too, knew Cromwell. In 1529 when a committee of men learned in the law was appointed to draw up statutes for the reformation of the clergy it is almost certain that Cromwell was on it, and likely that Petyt was with him.[67] While Robert Barnes lay imprisoned in 1526, Petyt went to Tunstall to plead for him: 'Thys is a yong man, and hathe good frendes, which wolde be ryghte lothe to haue hym cast away'.[68] Perhaps it was Petyt, as warden of the grocers' company, who brought Dr Forman to All Hallows Honey Lane to master-mind a heretical book trade;[69] certainly More and the bishops suspected him to be 'a fawtore of the religione that they called newe, and also a bearer with them in pryntyng of their books'. Thomas Somer at Somer's Key and Petyt at Lyon Key were neighbours at Billingsgate: soon they were neighbours in the Tower also, after the chancellor called at Petyt's house in search of forbidden books. In the Tower Petyt, like Somer, 'caght hys dethe', and upon his grave the priests poured soap ashes, 'affyrmyng that God would not suffer grasse to growe upon suche an heretyckes grave, and many of the Balaamytes came to see'.[70] Soon after the widow of this pariah married another of the 'brethren', John Parnell, who had gone with Petyt to plead for Barnes. Thomas Parnell (perhaps John's son) was Barnes's 'scholar', and his apprentice too was won to reform, for in November 1531 he bore a faggot at St Paul's for his heresy. Parnell was the chancellor's enemy, as Petyt had been, though not for reasons of faith alone. Cromwell did not forget this when the time came to find jurors to try the chancellor in 1535, for Parnell was among them.[71] Cromwell petitioned the

[66] LP vi 118. For William Locke, see BL, Add. MS 43827, fos. 2–3ᵛ; printed in M. Dowling and J. Shakespeare, 'Religion and Politics as seen through the eyes of an English Protestant woman: the recollections of Rose Hickman', Bulletin of the Institute of Historical Research, 55 (1982), 94–102.

[67] Narratives of the Reformation, p. 25. S. E. Lehmberg, The Reformation Parliament, 1529–1536 (Cambridge, 1970), p. 83. For Petyt's career, see The House of Commons, 1509–1558, ed. S. T. Bindoff (3 vols., London, 1982).

[68] Barnes, Supplicacion to Henry VIII (1534), sigs. I_2ᵛ–I_3.

[69] The grocers' company had the advowson of All Hallows Honey Lane; Novum Repertorium Ecclesiasticum Parochiale Londinense, ed. G. Hennessy (London, 1898), p. 76.

[70] Narratives of the Reformation, pp. 26–8. The A to Z of Elizabethan London, compiled by A. Prockter and R. Taylor (Lympne Castle, Kent, 1979), 7s; John Stow, Survey of London, ed. C. L. Kingsford (2 vols., Oxford, 1908), I, p. 206.

[71] Barnes, Supplicacion to Henry VIII (1534), sig. I_2ᵛ; Foxe, V, pp. 416–17; Original Letters Relative to the English Reformation, 1531–1558 (2 vols., Parker Society, Cambridge, 1846–7), II, p. 617; Two London Chronicles, ed. Kingsford, p. 5; Roper, The Lyfe of Sir Thomas Moore, pp. 61–3; Nicholas Harpsfield, The Life and Death of Sir Thomas Moore, Knight ed. E. V. Hitchcock (EETS, original series, 186, 1932), pp. 343–4, 349–50; Guy, The Public Career of Sir Thomas More, pp. 75–7.

court of aldermen on Lucy Parnell's behalf, reminding them that the late John Petyt had been 'a true and loving citizen, and from time to time exceeding painful in the procurement of your common affairs'.[72] This was in October 1532, after More had withdrawn from politics ostensibly to contemplate 'last things', and with Cromwell now high in the royal favour, yet the 'brethren' remained always at risk.

In the 'progress time' of the 1530s Cromwell moved again and again to protect the reckless evangelicals who looked for him for aid: John Bale, Richard Hilles, Stephen Caston, John Goodale, Robert Watson, Robert Barnes, William Hewytt, Robert Wisdom, Matthew Parker, George Browne, Robert Ward, John Erley, Hugh Rawlyngs.[73] Yet he could not save all of them, and would not save himself. In November 1536, as the Pilgrimage of Grace threatened all the advances which had been made for the Gospel, Robert Packington was murdered in Cheapside on his way to mass.[74] Packington was another City burgess who 'used to bring in English bibles from beyond the sea', and another of Vaughan's messengers sent from Flanders to Cromwell. 'Cherysshe hym and geve hym thankes, ye shall fynd he deserveth them', promised Vaughan. After Packington's murder William Locke's daughter no longer dared to read evangelical books to her children, 'for fear of trouble', but the preachers were less circumspect.[75] Barnes preached an impassioned sermon at Packington's funeral, and in the days which followed Barnes, Goodale, Field, Marshall and 'another of that sort of learning' (John Bale?) were imprisoned by their patron, who was more prudent than they, lest they stir a further conservative backlash, and to save them from themselves.[76] Cromwell's protection of 'the newe secte' was ultimately to destroy him.

IV

'Ayde me for Chrystys sake that I may preche chryst', wrote Thomas Willey in 1537, 'fatherlesse and forsaken'. He sought to win Cromwell's favour by dedicating to him 'a reverent receyvying of the Sacrament as a Lenton matter, declaryd by vj chyldern representyng Chryst, the worde of god, Paul, Austyn, a chylde, a Nonne caulyd Ignoransy'.[77] The theme of this interlude proved its

[72] Corporation of London RO, Repertory 8, fo. 242.
[73] Elton, *Policy and Police*, pp. 35–43, 101–6, 122, 138–41.
[74] Hall, p. 824; C. Wriothesly, *A Chronicle of England during the Reigns of the Tudors*, ed. W. D. Hamilton (2 vols., Camden society, new series, XI and XX), I, p. 59; Stow, *Survey*, I, p. 261; for Packington's career, see *The House of Commons, 1509–1558*, ed. Bindoff.
[75] BL, Add. MS 43827, fo. 4; SP 1/90, fo. 212 (*LP* ix 346); *LP* viii 303.
[76] SP 3/4, fo. 4; SP 1/111, fo. 187; SP 1/114, fo. 54 (*LP* xi 1097, 1111; xii(1) 40); *LP* xi 1164. For Field's earlier troubles, see Elton, 'Sir Thomas More and the opposition to Henry VIII', in *Studies*, I, pp. 159–60. Goodale had sought Cromwell's protection earlier, and was given his protection later: SP 1/81, fo. 112 (*LP* vi 1650); Elton, *Policy and Police*, pp. 101–6. For Marshall, see Elton, *Reform and Renewal*, pp. 26, 62, 76.
[77] SP 1/116, fo. 158 (*LP* xii(1). 529).

author a gospeller, but no sacramentary. This distinction was critical. By 1538 the 'error of the sacrament of the altar was . . . greatly spread abroad . . . and daily increasing more and more', and the leaders of reform – Cromwell, Cranmer and Barnes – feared that the passage of the Word would be threatened 'if such sacramentaries should be suffered'.[78] In August 1539 George Constantine, long one of the 'brethren', wrote to Cromwell, appalled that he should be 'sklandered . . . for a Sacramentary, which ys, yf any thinge can be worse, more heynous then treason', and 'greved' because Cromwell had believed these charges against him.[79] Certainly, since the immutable penalty for those guilty of this heresy was now death, Constantine's denial was politic, but it was probably also sincere. Even Richard Downes, the 'good willer', in 1542 bequeathed a candle to burn before the blessed sacrament.[80] But if ever Cromwell's adherents moved to more radical heresy they would threaten their patron and his cause.

In September 1538 Cromwell's dream of making the 'very lively word of God' freely available to the people was realised when the order came for an English bible to be placed in every parish church. Yet within months this greatest advance for the Gospel was compromised. On 16 November John Lambert, denounced by Barnes for his denial of the real presence, was tried before the king himself: 'I will not be a patron unto heretics'. It was Cromwell who read the sentence of condemnation, and soon he wrote to Sir Thomas Wyatt, telling him how Henry, 'the mirror and light of all other kings and princes in Christendom', had triumphed in disputation over a 'miserable heretic sacramentary', who had just gone to the flames.[81] Yet Foxe tells the tale, pitiful and heroic, of Lambert stopping at Cromwell's house on his way to Smithfield, 'and so carried into his inward chamber, where as it is reported of many, that Cromwell desired him of forgiveness'.[82] Cromwell's own letter to his friend and fellow reformer should be given more credence but, knowingly or unknowingly, he had himself been sheltering sacramentaries.

Calais had become an enclave for reformers in the 1530s, and there sacramentarian heresy was preached along with scripture. Letter after letter came to Cromwell from Lord Lisle in 1538, warning him that the darkest heresies were spreading, and urging action.[83] Cromwell ignored his pleas, and to Calais still sent his own men, of reforming views.[84] All through 1538 Cromwell kept his knowledge of the heresy in Calais secret. Some of the

---

[78] SP 1/133, fo. 174 (*LP* xiii(1) 1237); Foxe, v, p. 228; *LP* vi 402.
[79] 'Memorial from George Constantyne to Thomas Lord Cromwell', *Archaeologia*, 23 (1831), p. 77.
[80] PCC, Prob. 11/29, fo. 113ᵛ.
[81] Foxe, v, 229–234; *The Works of Henry Howard, Earl of Surrey, and of Sir Thomas Wyatt the Elder*, ed. G. F. Nott (2 vols, 1815–16), II, pp. 326–7; see also p. 343.
[82] Foxe, v. 236.
[83] *Lisle Letters*, v, 1160, 1166, 1178, 1189, 1190, 1498, 1498A. Three letters written by Lisle around Easter 1538 are missing.
[84] See, for example, *Lisle Letters*, v, pp. 391, 489–91, 675.

correspondence between Cromwell and the terrified Lisle is lost, but the seventeenth-century historian discovered in the Cotton library

A sharpe letter of Crumwell to Lord Lisle, taxing him for persecuting those who favor and set forth God's word and for favouring those who impugn it. Allso for suffring bruites to be scatired that the Bp of London is Vicar generall of England and all English books shall be called in &c.[85]

In February 1539 Clement Philpot, Cromwell's body servant, sent word to the gospellers in Calais: 'my lord doth know them all in Calais . . . that doth favour the word of God, and them that do not favour it'.[86] But that same month Hertford was sent 'to view the strength of Calais', and then Cromwell's secret would out.[87] Soon Henry knew the truth; how far heresy had spread through his garrison town, even among 'the saddest sort'. The discovery appalled him. Cromwell wrote to Lisle on 6 May, feigning astonishment: 'I cannot a little marvel' that Lisle, knowing Cromwell's desire to repress error and establish 'one perfect unity in religion', should never have vouchsafed the news that Calais 'should be in some misorder by certain Sacramentaries alleged to be in the same'. The beliefs of sacramentaries were 'very pestilent'; 'most detestable and cankered heresy'.[88] Yet now Cromwell's enemies could the more easily traduce him to the king as a favourer of sacramentaries, even a sacramentary himself, and the king would believe them, for a time.

From the Tower in June 1540 Cromwell, 'most hevye and most myserable prysoner & poore slave', wrote beseeching Henry's pardon: 'I Crye mercye, mercye, mercye.' 'Falslye accusyd' like Susan, he tried to exonerate himself, though 'I haue medelyd in So many matyers vnder yor Highnes that I am not able to answer them all'. One admission he made might perhaps be seen as an acknowledgement that he had been less than diligent in seeking out the 'brethren': 'Yf I haue herde of Any conbynacyons Conventycles or suche as wer offenders of your lawse I haue, though not as I sholde haue done, for the most parte reuealyd them'.[89] The talk at court was that Cromwell was 'imprisoned because he should say that He wolde stande againste the King and agt the Emperor . . . in these maters of the Bp of Rome, and cast his Gantlet agt them all': treason.[90] For treason and the sacramentarian heresy he was 'convyctyd & Attayntyd'. To the king he protested his horror and his innocence of the one charge and the other: it

[m]oche grevyd me that I sholde be notyd [a traitor when always] I hadde your lawse in my brest and [that I should be a sacra]mentarye god he knowythe the [truth and that I am of t]he ton and the other gyltles. I a[m a faith]full Crysten man and so will I [die].[91]

[85] Bodleian, Jesus College MS 74, fo. 198ᵛ.   [86] *Lisle Letters*, V, pp. 391–2.
[87] Ibid, V, 1362; Bodleian, Jesus College MS 74, fo. 275ᵛ.   [88] *Lisle Letters*, V, 1403, 1443.
[89] BL, Cotton MS Titus BI, fo. 273; Merriman, *Life and Letters*, II, pp. 348–9.
[90] Bodleian, Jesus College MS 74, fo. 300.
[91] BL, Cotton MS Otho C 10, fo. 247; Merriman, *Life and Letters*, II, pp. 350. I have followed Professor Scarisbrick's reconstruction of this damaged letter: *Henry VIII*, pp. 379–80, n. 4.

Henry was unmoved by all Cromwell's denials and entreaties, and on the very day of Cromwell's execution he celebrated his fifth marriage.[92] At the scaffold on Tower Hill Cromwell made a last speech to the crowd:

I am come hither this day to dye, & I have offendyd God, & that from my yought, & in especyall from my yeares of discretion, I have hitherto offendyd God. Secondarily it is sayd & thought of dyvers sundry persons that I would excuse or pourge my selfe on this day, which I intend no suche thinge . . . Masters all, I desire you to marke well that I shall say, I have travayled the world when I was younge, & came of a lowe stock, & synce I have bin in the Kinges service, the King of his goodnesse hath set me in dignity, which his grace hath not taken from me, but I have bin the causer of my fall, for I have first offendyd God, & also I have offendyd my King.

To confess guilt at the last, to acknowledge the justice of the penalty, and to ask forgiveness was conventional; this was to die well. Yet in protesting his innocence of heresy, his belief in the sacrament of the altar, and his loyalty to God, Cromwell never wavered.

My lords & masters all, I desire you to pray for mee, & if there be any man or woman here present, or in any other parte in Londone which I have offendyd in word or Deed I pray you in Godes behalfe to forgive mee, And of charity I forgive all the world. And last of all I intend this day to dye Godes servant, and beleive in the holy Catholique fayth. I beleive in the lawes ordeined by the catholique church, & in the holy sacrament without any grudge. & I pray you all to pray for mee that the spirit which is in this body, that it may depart from this mortall body unto the father of heuen, liftinge up his eyes to heaven. And sayd, O father forgive mee, O X forgive mee, O holy ghoost forgive mee, O 3 & one forgive mee.[93]

Cromwell's death left his evangelical friends bereft, leaderless; they feared for themselves and for the Gospel:

> The pillar pearisht is whearto I Lent
> The strongest staye of myne vnquyet mynde;

so Wyatt lamented. William Gray, who had written *The Fantasie of Idolatrie* for Cromwell, wrote in defence of his fallen master in the autumn of 1540; though Cromwell had died justly, a traitor, yet

> The sacrament of the aulter, that is most hyest
> Crumwell belieued it to be the very body of Chriest.[94]

Returning to court in September 1540, John Lascells asked, 'what news there were pertaining to God's holy word, seeing we have lost so noble a man that did love and favour it'.[95] Lascells was one of those servants of Cromwell's who

---

[92] Ibid, pp. 429–30.
[93] Bodleian, Fo. Δ 624, facing pp. 462 and 463. Gary Hill gave me this reference and sent me his transcription, for which I am extremely grateful.
[94] *Collected Poems of Sir Thomas Wyatt*, ed. Muir and Thomson, CCXXXVI; E. W. Dormer, *Gray of Reading* (Reading, 1923), p. 80.
[95] *LP* xvi 101.

joined the royal household at their master's fall; one of those also who moved to the sacramentarian heresy for which Cromwell had died. Around the king in his last years, in daily attendance, were men whose religious sympathies were much closer to his fallen minister's than to his own.[96] Some were zealous protestants, even sacramentaries. Lascells would die at the stake, and others were lucky to escape the same fate. Whether Cromwell knew how far his friends and clients held such extreme convictions, whether he might have moved to them himself, can never be known. For himself, he admitted in 1538 to some Lutheran envoys that he believed much as they did, but would 'as the world stood, believe even as his master the King believed'.[97]

[96] See the biographies of Nicholas Arnold, Maurice Berkeley, George Ferrers, Philip Hoby, William Morice, Richard Morison, Ralph Hopton, Thomas Sternhold, Ralph Sadler, Thomas Cawarden in *The House of Commons, 1509–1558*. Dr Robertson found that of 56 of Cromwell's servants for whom it is possible to make a surmise about their faith 'at least 26, and possibly 46, were protestant in the Continental sense, or at least reformers'; 'Thomas Cromwell's Servants', p. 373.

[97] Merriman, *Life and Letters*, I, p. 279: Elton, 'Thomas Cromwell *Redivivus*', *Studies*, III, p. 377.

Henry VIII and the dissolution of the secular colleges

J. J. SCARISBRICK

I

THE SURRENDER of England's last monastery, Waltham Abbey, on 23 March 1540 marked the end of medieval English monasticism but not of the crown's attack on the possessions of the English church. On the contrary: it marked the end of only the first phase thereof.

From 1540 to 1553 the campaign developed in five new directions. First, bishops found themselves often entering into unfavourable 'exchanges' with the crown which resulted, in particular, in parting with London houses and choice rural manors.[1] Next, there was intermittent pruning of the resources of cathedrals, i.e. their deans and chapters, by similar methods. The cathedrals concerned were those which, like Exeter, Lincoln and London, had always had secular chapters, as well as those which had previously been served by monastic communities, an arrangement almost unique to England. Of these, the two that had been 'twinned' with secular cathedrals (Bath with Wells, Coventry with Lichfield) had already been suppressed and their churches seized. But there were eight others (Canterbury, Durham, Ely and Worcester among them) that were formerly staffed by monks and were re-founded in 1540/1 as secular cathedrals – though with considerably less landed endowment than their Benedictine or Augustinian forebears had enjoyed.[2] These, too, were thereafter liable to further depletion of income at royal hands. So were the six quite new bishoprics of Bristol, Chester, Gloucester, Oxford, Peterborough and Westminster which, between 1541 and 1543, had been granted ex-Benedictine abbey churches to serve as cathedrals of the new sees carved out of existing dioceses, notably Lincoln.

---

[1] F. Heal, *Of Prelates and Princes. A Study in the Economic and Social Position of the Tudor Episcopate* (Cambridge, 1980), pp. 117–25. Cf. Gina Alexander, 'Victim or spendthrift? The Bishop of London and his income in the sixteenth century', in E. W. Ives, R. J. Knecht and J. J. Scarisbrick, eds., *Wealth and Power in Tudor England. Essays Presented to S. T. Bindoff* (London, 1978), pp. 128–36.
[2] M. D. Knowles, *The Religious Orders in England*, III. *The Tudor Age* (Cambridge, 1959), pp. 389–92.

Though meanly 're-modelled' in the first place, they were subsequently as vulnerable to royal pilfering as any cathedral of the Old Foundation. And all cathedrals, old or new, had meanwhile lost their shrines.

Thirdly, from the early 1540s there was a trickle of suppressions of chantries, decayed hospitals, religious guilds and the like. This was accelerated by the so-called Chantries Act of 1545 and turned into a deluge by the act of 1547. Five years later, with the final establishment of protestantism, the crown could begin to harvest the wealth of parish churches: their plate, bells, vestments and other furnishings of catholic worship.

Finally, there were the secular colleges. Some of these were plump fruit indeed. Most were brought down between 1547 and 1549; but during the last years of his reign and with the help of some subjects, Henry VIII had been able to shake off nearly a quarter of the crop.

II

The word 'college' has today such strongly educational significance that we can forget that its basic meaning – still reflected in, say, 'electoral college', 'College of Cardinals' or 'College of Arms' – is simply a community of people carrying out a particular function. In the middle ages the word was used primarily to describe communities of secular priests who lived together and staffed 'collegiate' churches or chapels. Some – like Chester's two colleges, Crediton's Holy Cross, Derby's All Saints', St Mary's in Stafford or St Stephen's, Westminster – were royal free chapels of pre-Conquest foundation. Beverley, Ripon, Southwell and Wimborne, no less ancient and yet more splendid, carried the title of 'minster'. All could be described as communities of canons, vicars choral, lay clerks, choristers, etc., belonging to a pre-monastic or non-monastic tradition who had either not succumbed to the magnetic pull of monasticism or had failed to grow into cathedral chapters, as had the college of York, for instance. Thus, though leading communal lives similar to that of monks, they were in fact autonomous communities of secular priests.[3]

Several colleges developed alongside royal castles: in Bridgnorth, for instance, Hastings and Windsor. Many more were founded in the twelfth and thirteenth centuries: in Howden (Yorks.), Lanchester (Co. Durham), Penrhyn and Warwick, to name but a few. College-founding had a special heyday, however, in the next two centuries, when dozens were added to the list. But these were rather different in character from their precursors in that

[3] G. H. Cook, *English Collegiate Churches of the Middle Ages* (London, 1959) is a good introduction. Much light was thrown on secular colleges by A. H. Thompson (see note 5). A useful list of all known colleges, plus notes thereon, is given in M. D. Knowles and R. N. Hadcock, *Medieval Religious Houses in England and Wales* (revised edn., 1971), pp. 412–46.

they were essentially large-scale chantries, that is, communities of secular priests whose first duty was to offer mass for the souls of the founders and their ancestors. Some of these 'chantry colleges' also ran almshouses; many had a greater interest in education than previous colleges had shown, so much so that for Winchester College or All Souls', Oxford, for example, this was to become the dominant purpose and do much to give the word 'college' its primarily academic connotation.

As in earlier centuries, prelates were conspicuous founders. In 1395 William Courtenay, for instance, grafted a college of a master and 24 chaplains onto a hospital for ten poor people in Maidstone and made its parish church collegiate. Another Kentish college was founded by Archbishop Kemp of York in his birthplace, Wye. Archbishop Chichele's large establishment at Higham Ferrers included a school and beadhouse. In 1483 Archbishop Rotherham founded Jesus College in his namesake–birthplace and provided for three schools for its choristers and local boys, as well as for a butler, cook and barber. Had Wolsey's immense plans for a boys' school in Ipswich, run by a large college of priests and feeding a massive college in Oxford (he envisaged a hundred canons alone) been achieved, the story of pre-reformation archiepiscopal foundations would have been magnificently concluded.[4]

However, ecclesiastics were outdone by laymen. In 1433 Lord Cromwell began to build alongside his castle at Tattershall a college and hospital which was simply a more ambitious version of a foundation which fellow-noblemen, gentlemen and wealthier burgesses were now increasingly likely to undertake. The grand establishment at Fotheringhay, built by a son and grandson of Edward III and completed in 1411, still had in 1545 a master and precentor, eleven other fellows, nine lay clerks (including one in charge of the clock), thirteen choristers, an organist and thirty servants – among these a cook, under-brewer and seventeen farmhands. There were ninety-three books in the chained library and a rich collection of vestments and plate. Staindrop College (Co. Durham) was founded a few years previously by the earl of Westmorland to provide for prayers for him and his family, and to run a poor house for his aged retainers. In 1548 it still boasted a master, four priests, two choristers, two lay clerks and eleven elderly poor, of whom six in 1546 were noted as gentlemen who had been in the service of the then earl. Manchester's large college, suppressed early in Edward VI's reign but resuscitated by Mary, had been founded in 1421 by Thomas de la Warre. Newark College of the Annunciation in Leicester had begun as a hospital in 1330 and been transformed in 1353 by John of Gaunt into a college staffed by twenty-six clergy and four lay assistants, its hospital being enlarged to cater for a hundred

---

[4] Cook, *English Collegiate Churches*, and Knowles and Hadcock, pp. 412–46.

poor under the supervision of ten female attendants. A dean and thirty clergy acknowledged the royal supremacy in 1534.[5] The college in Tong (Salop) was set up as a large chantry by Lady Isabel Pembridge in 1410. Moated Battlefield nearby was founded to supply prayers for those who fell in the battle of Shrewsbury in 1403. Whittington College, completed in 1424, needs no comment on its wealthy founder. Herringby College (Norfolk) was established in 1447 and run by ten lay feoffees. It received a large new endowment in 1518 and looked after eight almsmen. Lord Dacre founded a college in the early 1520s in Kirk Oswald (Cumbria).[6] The list could continue for pages.

The essential feature of a college was the presence of a community of secular clergy who, like monks and whether or not they also functioned as chantry priests, were responsible for maintaining the daily round of divine office in their churches and such other services as the founder laid down. They lived and sometimes ate together. They were often required to wear uniform clothing. Their lives were governed by statutes usually drawn up by the founder.

Some boasted the full panoply of dean and canons (prebendaries), vicars choral and a large lay staff of clerks, choristers and servants which rivalled the complements of many cathedrals. Smaller ones – including a large proportion of those founded in the later middle ages – often consisted of only a master, provost or warden and a handful of chaplains or fellows. The scale of building varied accordingly. Some, as Windsor or the remains at, say, Maidstone or Manchester still show, were on a grand scale, with fine houses for canons and vicars, cloisters and chapterhouses, and perhaps dormitories and refectories, libraries, gatehouses, gardens, etc., not to mention the adjacent almshouses and schoolhouses.

Older colleges had simply grown up with the churches or chapels in which their members officiated. But when a new college was founded in later times the local parish church was commonly appropriated to it, an event which in turn often occasioned or coincided with a major rebuild. Archbishop Sudbury completely rebuilt the parish church in his home town to accommodate his new college there, founded in 1375. The promotion of the church of North Cadbury (Somerset) to collegiate status some fifty years later coincided with a complete rebuilding; and when Maidstone acquired its college Kent gained its grandest perpendicular church. Nearby, Ashford's parish church was largely reconstructed by the founder of its college, Sir John Fogge, between 1475 and 1483, and there was much rebuilding not far away at Wingham when its

---

[5] *VCH, Lincs*, II, p. 237; *VCH, Northants*, II, pp. 170–6; *VCH, Durham*, II, p. 129; *VCH, Lancs*, II, p. 167; A. Hamilton Thompson, *History of the Hospital of the Annunciation of St Mary in the Newarke* (Leicester, 1937) and his *English Colleges of Chantry Priests*, Ecclesiastical Society Transactions, n.s. 1, pt. 2 (1945).

[6] *VCH, Salop*, II, p. 131; *VCH, London*, I, p. 578; J. C. Cox, *Churches of Norfolk* (1911), I, p. 95, and *LP* xx(i) p. 102; *VCH, Cumbs*, II, p. 208.

college was set up. When Sir Thomas Astley founded a college at Astley (Warwickshire) beside his castle, he embarked on massive church-building for it. That Darlington has one of the finest churches in County Durham is largely due to the coming there of St Cuthbert's College. Elsewhere it might be necessary only to enlarge a chancel or equip it with stalls. Thus Sir Reginald Cobham rebuilt the east end of Lingfield parish church when he founded his ambitious college in 1431. Stratford-on-Avon's chancel was transformed into soaring perpendicular fifty years or so later and given handsome stalls and misericords about 1500 – the college having originally had its chapel in the south aisle. In Lanchester a chapel for the college was added to the north side of the chancel. The college in Mangton (Rutland) seems to have used the Lady chapel for its liturgy.[7]

Where parish churches were appropriated to colleges, the normal parish duties would be looked after by the college clergy, who might also have served nearby chapels of ease as well. The chancel was usually taken over by the college and the parochial high altar placed in the nave, to the west of the rood screen, as was often the arrangement in monastic churches. Archbishop Rotherham's statutes for his Jesus College explicitly required that the provost should preach widely in the locality.[8] More difficult to define exactly is the relationship between collegiate clergy and local chantry priests. As has been said, some colleges were, from the start, simply communities of chantry priests. Others began as small chantries but were enlarged and given collegiate status later. Two Nottinghamshire colleges, in Clifton and Sibthorpe, are good examples of this evolution. Occasionally what were intended to be colleges never developed beyond the simple chantry stage – or by the 1540s had degenerated into mere chantries. Thomas Rotherham wanted his college, among other things, to tackle what could be a serious problem of indiscipline among the throngs of chantry, guild and stipendiary priests to be found in and around many larger parish churches, by bringing Rotherham's into a collegiate structure. Other colleges reflect the same concern to place unattached clergy under the wing of a college and away from the taverns and dubious company. In 1455, for instance, Henry VI licensed the then archbishop of York to gather no less than twenty-three chantry priests in his cathedral into a college, St William's, which had acquired four more chantries by the time it was suppressed in 1548.[9] In London, St Paul's army of cantarists already lived together in the 'Priesteshouses'. A vicar of Northampton's main church himself formed into a college the numerous guild and chantry priests who celebrated in his church, and gave them a common lodging.[10] Thoresby

[7] *VCH, Suffolk*, II, pp. 150–1; *VCH, Somerset*, II, p. 171; *VCH, Warks*, II, p. 117; *VCH, Rutland*, II, p. 163. Architectural detail from N. Pevsner, ed., *The Buildings of England* (Harmondsworth, 1951–74).   [8] *VCH, York*, III, p. 372.

[9] *CPR, Henry VI*, VI, p. 218. Allegedly the chantry priests had previously been living in lay households.

[10] *VCH, London*, I, pp. 426–7; *VCH, Northants*, II, pp. 180–1.

College in King's Lynn, founded by the mayor in 1502, had a similar purpose and so did the colleges in Newark and Garlickhithe in London. St Chad's in Shrewsbury had absorbed the cantarists by making them vicars choral, a not uncommon practice. Elsewhere some chantries were staffed by non-prebendal canons. In Southwell the chantry and guild priests formed a separate community, whereas sometimes the clergy serving chantries added after the college was begun might be 'conducts', that is, members of the community but not of the foundation. There were many different arrangements.

There was and is inevitable difficulty in exact definition. The line between a guild and a college is not always easy to draw, for instance, especially when the large contingent of clergy serving, say, Coventry's Holy Trinity guild, were formed into a 'college'. Contemporaries were uncertain whether Holy Trinity in Pontefract was a hospital or a college, a not uncommon hesitation; and Edward VI's commissioners wondered whether what they viewed in Halstead (Essex) was 'a chauntrie or collegge', another familiar uncertainty.[11] Such blurring of edges should surprise no one. Nor need it frighten us away from attempting a grand total. Excluding academic colleges like Winchester's or those in the universities, and also excluding colleges of various kinds to be found in cathedrals (of deans and prebendaries, vicars choral, minor or 'petty' canons, etc.) but not colleges of chantry priests officiating therein, and finally excluding the most dubious of the doubtfuls (i.e. those institutions which never had been or were no longer colleges in even a dilute sense), we can say that there were some 140 colleges in England and Wales when the reformation came upon them.[12]

They were a significant feature on the late-medieval ecclesiastical landscape. Their demise is an important (and neglected) episode in the story of the English reformation. They were a European phenomenon; that is, colleges were to be found in much of late-medieval western Europe. They hark back to an early-medieval, pre-monastic tradition and have strong echoes of eigenkirchentum, the proprietary church. That princes, prelates and the richest of the laity of much of Latin Christendom should have poured wealth and energy into what were often ambitious foundations should also affect our judgment on pre-reformation Christianity. These 'super-chantries' spring from, and are inexplicable without, the doctrine of Purgatory, belief in the propitiatory character of the mass and the efficacy of other prayer for the living and the dead, and in the veneration of saints. Thus they proclaimed on a grand scale both material wealth and commitment to the dominant features of traditional, late-medieval piety. They warn us again not to suppose that a decline in endowment of, say, monks and nuns indicates a lay disenchantment

---

[11] VCH, Essex, II, p. 193.
[12] My total is based on the checklist in Knowles and Hadcock, Medieval Religious Houses, pp. 413–19, corrected as seemed necessary.

with an allegedly clericalised, inflexible and often unworthy church. The truth is that many lay people were bestowing their favour on other religious institutions – the wealthiest on colleges and chantries, others on guilds and obits, and their parish churches. The flowering of collegiate foundations is yet another (and perhaps the most impressive) indication of how much initiative and control the laity enjoyed in the late-medieval church. For a layman to found a college with a community of priests wholly subject to him, living under statutes written by him and charged with the duty of incessant prayer for the repose of his and his family's souls as well as the education of young dependants and their care in declining years, was to make more comprehensive provision for both this world and the next than any monastic founder had ever essayed. This was some compensation for the loss of influence brought about by Gregorian clericalism and the development of religious orders jealous of their autonomy. True, except for those that were royal and 'free', colleges were normally subject to episcopal visitation. Nonetheless, had clerics ever been more completely and clearly subject to layman?

<h2 style="text-align:center">III</h2>

It is difficult to assess the spiritual condition of English colleges on the eve of their dissolution. Their besetting disease was absenteeism: deans and prebendaries were often non-resident and even expected to be so. Colleges in general, and royal colleges in particular, were happy hunting-grounds for careerists, especially those king's clerks whose pluralism the crown openly encouraged. Bishops' visitations reveal the familiar and predictable catalogue of human failure: absence from choir and presence in taverns, suspicious female company, financial mismanagement, squabbles within the community and without, and the like. The testimony of others is often equally difficult to interpret. For instance, in 1545 Edward Seymour denounced Beverley Minster, saying its provost and some of the prebendaries were 'but children'; on the other hand, no less a person than Matthew Parker, then dean of Stoke by Clare in Suffolk, in 1546 eulogised his large college, saying that it distributed alms and hospitality daily, instructed in the word of God and taught children grammar, singing and playing.[13] But since Seymour was trying to acquire Beverley and Parker to ward off suppression, both statements should be taken with a pinch of salt.

Maybe we can settle for the following generalisations. First, though a few were undoubtedly badly run down and some (perhaps also a few) in good condition, the majority were probably betwixt and between. Over the centuries colleges had come and gone, and the survivors had had their ups and downs. But the same could be said of all religious institutions – monasteries,

---

[13] PRO, State Papers, Henry VIII (SP 1), 204, fo. 55 (*LP* xx(1) 1031); *LP* xxi(1) 968.

friaries, guilds, hospitals, etc. There is no reason to suppose that colleges were in noticeably worse condition before the reformation than they had been fifty, a hundred or two hundred years previously. Indeed, some Tudor bishops (like Archbishop Warham) seem to have kept a close and fairly effective eye on them. Finally, when the end came, there was no official attempt to justify their suppression on the ground that they were scandalous or unwanted.

Out of the total of c. 140, some 34 colleges had been dissolved by 1547 (almost a quarter). The first handful of suppressions, in 1540/1, must be treated separately, however. In January 1541 the bishop of St David's, who presumably had taken the initiative in the matter, was licensed to suppress a small college in Carmarthen to help endow a new school in Brecon.[14] Kingston College in Surrey dropped into the crown's hands by accident ten months earlier.[15] The disappearance of Attleborough College (Norfolk), whose church still possesses fine stalls and roodscreen, is a mystery. Two colleges, Thompson in Norfolk and Cobham in Kent, were also suppressed privately, the crown licensing Sir Edmund Knevet to acquire the first and the Cobham family the second.[16] Then there is the strange story of Southwell. This famous college surrendered to the crown in November 1540. The reason must have been that Southwell was a candidate for promotion to cathedral status, in which case its surrender was no more than a formality to make way for that conversion. In the event, this did not take place; and three years later Southwell was fully restored to its previous existence by act of parliament.[17] There may have been little interruption of its daily life while it remained in that legal limbo – but one may still wonder whether what happened had been entirely innocent.

Southwell was reprieved – only to fall again finally in 1548. But those other five early suppressions were apparently not the result of any calculated royal policy. They were either accidental or procured by private initiative which the crown merely licensed.

The remaining twenty-nine suppressions of Henry's reign, however, were of a different character. Though often owing a good deal to the promptings of the king's subjects, as we shall see, they were direct and (until the act of late 1545) 'voluntary' surrenders to the crown, which was then free to do what it liked with the properties which had come into its hands.

The royal suppressions proper began in late 1541 with the surrender of Rushford College (Norfolk), a small institution founded in 1342 by the same man who endowed Gonville Hall in Cambridge. It had a master and five chaplains in 1534, fed and clothed seven boys and contributed £1 a year to a

---

[14] *LP* xvi 503(30). [15] *VCH, Surrey*, II, p. 126.

[16] *LP* xv 611(2); xvi 779(13); xviii 66. *LP* xvi 88(60) shows that Cobham College was dissolved before early 1541. Knowles and Hadcock (*Medieval Religious Houses*, p. 414) say it fell in 1539, but this seems too early.

[17] House of Lords RO, Original Acts, 35 Henry VIII, no. 42.

priest who instructed them. Five colleges went down in 1542, including Chichele's Higham Ferrers, rich St Martin's le Grand in London and Vaux College in Salisbury, an unusual foundation that supported both a college of priests in Salisbury and some poor scholars in Oxford, which it was still doing at its demise. There was a lull in 1543. In the following year, however, six more colleges fell, including those in Arundel, Lingfield, Warwick and Westbury-on-Trym. In 1545 there were thirteen victims. Some, like St Mary's in the Field in Norwich and South Malling (Kent) were small enough; but there were also three major establishments: Crediton's Holy Cross, Tattershall's celebrated college, and Ottery St Mary's, which had a staff of thirty-eight, including eight prebendaries and eight choristers.

These and later suppressions involved seizure of the college's landed possessions, residential buildings and other properties, and the subsequent sale of most, if not all, by the court of augmentations. Plate, precious stones, vestments and other valuables went to the king's jewel house. The inmates were mostly pensioned off; twelve in the case of St Martin's le Grand, for instance, eight at Wingfield, which was suppressed in 1548.[18] Ottery St Mary's pension bill was no less than £210 per annum.[19] Thus in many respects the dissolution of secular colleges followed the same course as had the dissolution of monasteries. But there were differences between the two events. First, only rarely did collegiate churches themselves suffer. True, only the huge chancel at Astley (Warwickshire), suppressed in 1545, survives; and when Dudley acquired Fotheringhay in 1548 he immediately pulled down the choir, as well as stripping the lead off the rest of the college buildings. But most collegiate churches were unharmed when their colleges were dissolved. Secondly, quite often the spiritual needs of the local parishioners would thereafter be met by a vicar, perhaps plus a curate of two, who were former members of the dissolved college, sometimes even the ex-dean or master; and sometimes they retained for their use one or two houses or other buildings formerly belonging to the college. So something survived, therefore – as did the title 'collegiate', albeit the churches had once more become ordinary parish churches, served by ordinary secular clergy. Though redundant stalls and misericords survive in chancels – along with perhaps an incongruous chapterhouse or a tell-tale blocked-up door that once gave access to nearby college buildings, and odd ruins around the churchyard outside – most of today's 'collegiate' churches are but shadows of their former selves.

Care was taken to see that collegiate schools and hospitals were protected. The man who acquired Higham Ferrers, for instance, took over responsibility for maintaining the school and paying £24 a year to support thirteen poor men in the hospital, a sum which would provide 7d. a week for every inmate and pay

---

[18] *LP* xvii 74 (cf. *LP* xviii(1) 436, at fo. 32); xviii(1) p. 548.
[19] So Edward Seymour reckoned when he was bidding for the college's former possessions. PRO, SP 1/204, fo. 144 (*LP* xx(1) 1284).

for eight cartloads of wood, a barber and a lamp in the dormitory. He was also to find £18 a year for two clerics, named by the crown, who would staff the church.[20] When Holy Cross College, Crediton, was dissolved in 1545 the countess of Bath and her son, Sir Thomas Darcy, were granted the bulk of its former possessions. But responsibility for looking after the church and its now much-reduced clergy, and for the 'kynges newe gramar scole', successor to a previous small school for the choristers, was vested in a corporation of twelve 'governors of church goods'. The inhabitants of Crediton paid £200 for this deal.[21] A similar arrangement was made for Ottery St Mary: four local men were named as governors of the hereditaments and goods of the church, with responsibility for maintaining the fabric, paying the vicar, two chaplains and a schoolmaster, and giving them accommodation. They were granted tithes and properties of the former college worth £45 a year for this purpose.[22] When St Mary's in Warwick fell, the townsfolk rallied and secured a charter of incorporation which bestowed the church on the new borough and gave it responsibility for the new boys' school.[23] The demise of a college, therefore, could occasion an important forward step in a town's constitutional development.

All of these colleges were suppressed before the first Chantries Act of December 1545. Before that act, one must presume, the crown's title to the colleges and other institutions it was acquiring was as dubious as had been its title, before the act of 1539, to the larger monasteries which had already come into its hand by surrender. And perhaps Henry had again proceeded piecemeal on purpose. After December 1545, however, the royal title was secure and further suppressions would be lawful. In the event, only five more colleges had fallen before the king and the act of 1545 expired in January 1547. These included the college in Tong, another in Salisbury, namely, St Edmund's, and Holy Trinity in Pleshey (Essex), a moderate-sized establishment with a staff of six priests, two clerks and two choristers.

It was rumoured earlier in 1546 that Fotheringhay was 'lyke to goe downe' and Matthew Parker reported that he was being pressed and bribed (by unnamed persons) to surrender his college of Stoke by Clare.[24] The bishop of Chester, about the same time, was making bids to the crown for Manchester College.[25] But though Henry had destroyed some large colleges, he had not brought down any of the giants. Indeed, when Edward Seymour cast his eyes on a prize like Beverley and then Newark College in Leicester, he was roundly told that the king would not 'deface any of his great colleages, though percase uppon some respectes his grace might determyn to alter their foundacions hereafter as the case shall requyre', i.e. he might slim them down.[26] He had certainly done this to Fotheringhay and to St George's, Windsor, by the time

20 LP xviii (1) 474(27).
21 LP xx(2) 496(38); CPR, Edward VI, I, pp. 43–4.
22 LP xx(2) 1068(45).
23 LP xx(1) 846(41).
24 LP xxi(1) 528 and 968.
25 LP xxi (1) 967.
26 PRO, SP 1/204, fos. 55, 144 (LP xx (1) 1222, 1284).

he died.[27] When Henry's son came to the throne that same Seymour would have few qualms about pulling down anything. In his first year as protector over forty colleges were felled. Almost as many came down in 1548, leaving a mere handful intact. Of these, ten had gone by 1553. Some half dozen survived, most (it seems) by accident.[28]

Henry's caution had probably owed less to religious scruple or sentiment than to political instinct. It is possibly significant that not a single college in the north was touched and only Tattershall (Lincs) in any of the counties affected by the risings of 1536. As has been said, things would be different when the deluge came in the next reign. For the moment, the crown was in no great hurry, partly perhaps because the sales of ex-monastic property was by then in full flow. Thus, when Stephen Vaughan wrote eagerly to ask that, 'If any colleges be putt down I wold I had a good pece of some thing for my money', he was unlucky.[29] An offer of 1000 marks from Lord Lisle for any well-endowed college, plus the added bait that he would found a school in Henry's name and pay the pensions of the ex-collegiate clergy, earned only the gruff reply from the king that that sounded like a bad bargain for Lisle.[30]

The crown seems to have responded better to precise proposals than to such general bids. Thus two colleges, Sibthorpe (Nottinghamshire) and St Mary in the Field in Norwich's splendid church of St Peter Mancroft, were acquired by the very masters who surrendered them – Thomas Magnus and Miles Spencer. Both were voracious pluralists and had probably paid little attention to their colleges. Magnus was granted his for life; Spencer, who has been accused of duping his colleagues into surrender, had £805 ready for the purchase of much of his former establishment.[31] It is difficult to suppose that these two men had not taken the first steps towards suppression. Other colleges were so often snapped up by 'founders', royal servants and courtiers that the latter probably took the initiative in procuring their downfall, in which case the crown would simply have acted as broker between its subjects and the objects of their desire. The king's secretary, Thomas Wriothesley, had acquired Wolvesey College – dedicated to St Elizabeth of Hungary and standing in St Stephen's meadow at the gate of the bishop of Winchester's castle outside that city – within twelve days of its surrender in March 1544. He paid £500 for it.[32] Since he was a local man and already active in the market for ex-monastic property, it is likely that he precipitated the fall of the college. The earl of Arundel paid a thousand marks for his college in Arundel, the

[27] *LP* xxi(2) 581, 738.

[28] St George's, Windsor, was exempted by statute (as were Eton, Winchester and the Oxford and Cambridge colleges – which have been excluded from consideration in this essay because they were primarily educational institutions). Colleges in Axminster, Burford and St Endellion (Cornwall) escaped inexplicably. Jesus Commons in London lasted until c. 1568; a college in Middleham (Yorks.) until the nineteenth century.

[29] PRO, SP 1/200, fo. 231 (*LP* xx(1) 700).

[30] *LP* xx (2) 412.   [31] *LP* xx(1) 846(71) and 1335(46).   [32] *LP* xix (1) 278(74).

grant also being dated a mere twelve days after the surrender in December 1544; another royal secretary, Ralph Sadler (and his wife Ellen), acquired Westbury-on-Trym's college for the same sum.[33] An exchequer official paid £437 for part of the possessions of Vaux College in Salisbury, which in total yielded well over twice that amount.[34] Sudbury College went for £1280 to Sir Thomas Paston, a local man (of course) but also a gentleman of the privy chamber, just three weeks after its surrender. Another gentleman of the privy chamber secured Pleshey College almost as quickly.[35] Likewise Charles Brandon acquired Tattershall's massive possessions (for 4000 marks) soon after they came into the crown's hands.[36] In many of these cases, the eventual grantees may well have been the first movers of the surrenders. But there were also cases which involved casual purchases and hence remind one of the sales of most ex-monastic property. Thus the considerable residue of possessions of St Mary's in Warwick – manors, messuages, water and fulling mills, fisheries, woods and advowsons, etc. – were sold over several months to a variety of local people and speculators, and must have yielded many hundreds of pounds. And, as with the monasteries, buildings and lands were not the only prizes: there were the jewels, church plate and often sumptuous vestments with which some colleges had been endowed over the decades, as well as lead and bells. St Martin's le Grand, for example, possessed 520 oz of plate and no less than 46 copes.[37] St Mary's Warwick was famous for its vestments, its collection of relics and its library.

The total wealth of the colleges may have been but a fraction of that of the religious houses. But they were more than trifles: and they mattered enough to the king for him sometimes to receive the cash for them in person. Sir Thomas Palmer, chief baron of the exchequer, allegedly paid 1000 marks 'to the king's own hands' for the possessions of South Malling's college;[38] and we are told that Edward Seymour paid 1000 marks to the king in person when he acquired the college of Ottery St Mary in May 1546.[39] A few months before that, William Paget was granted all the possessions of Burton College, with licence to fortify the buildings and impark 500 acres, together with some lands recently shed by the bishops of Coventry and Lichfield and Chester after he had been able 'to practice with the said bishops'. In return, he parted with a

---

[33] *LP* xix (1) 278(68); ii 800(35).

[34] *LP* xvii (1) 981(5).

[35] *LP* xx (1) 125(2); xxi(2) 648(61).

[36] *LP* xx (1) 465(38). The surrender was made on 4 February; the grant to Brandon on 13 March.

[37] PRO, Augmentations Accounts (E 323), B, pt. 1, fo. 114$^{\rm v}$.

[38] *LP* xx (1) 1335(35).

[39] *LP* xx (1) 970(41): 2000 marks were due to the court of augmentations in two equal instalments. J. Youings, ed., *Devon Monastic Lands: Calendar of Particulars for Grants 1536–1558*, Devon and Cornwall Record Society, n.s. 1 (1955), p. 82 suggests 'there is no record that he ever paid any of the purchase money'. But the grant says that 'one thowsande merkes sterlynge are delyvered into his majesties owne handes'. Seymour may not have paid the remaining two-thirds of the purchase price, but he seems to have delivered a substantial sum to the king.

hospital in Durham which he had acquired and some other lands, plus over £5000, of which £2708 was apparently paid directly to the king himself.[40]

There was a final virtue in these sales from the crown's point of view: the grantees seem usually to have taken over responsibility for paying pensions to former college staff, as well as the stipends for the parish clergy and schoolmasters who took over their work. No wonder that Seymour blanched when he found that he would have to pick up the bill for Ottery St Mary's large community! 'Yt wolbe no present relief unto me', he exclaimed.[41] But further reflection persuaded him that the investment was sound, and he accepted the king's terms.

IV

Burton College, bought by Paget in January 1546, had been founded by the crown as recently as August 1541. Six months later, a second new college was established at Thornton (Lincolnshire). Both were reconstituted monasteries, that is, were communities of ex-monks living in some of the buildings of former monastic houses and endowed by the crown with some of the landed possessions of their medieval forebears. Their story is an interesting one.

By late 1538 it was widely understood that the king planned to turn many of the surviving larger monasteries into secular colleges. Lord Audley proposed that two major abbeys of Essex – Colchester and St Osyth's – be so used. Hugh Latimer suggested Malvern's grand Benedictine house. Evesham Abbey took the initiative and offered itself for the metamorphosis, as did a house near Pontefract. From Coventry came the suggestion that the cathedral priory could go the same way and, as well as supplying local preachers, could provide accommodation for former abbots of suppressed houses in the area, who could live there on their pensions and not 'lie lurking in corners'. So the belief was that the king intended, in Evesham's words, 'to alter and change' – not to suppress, nor to allow greater houses to be emptied, pulled down or pass into lay hands for private, secular use.[42]

The government was also considering long-overdue plans (which Wolsey had come near to implementing) to establish some new dioceses, again using some of the largest religious houses. Their endowments would support the bishops and chapters, and their churches become cathedrals. Three distinct plans survive.[43] One would have created thirteen new sees, all coterminous with counties or pairs of counties (e.g. Cornwall, Essex, Berkshire, Oxfordshire, and Staffordshire with Shropshire) and employing apparently the whole

[40] *LP* xxi(1) 149(39); ii 199(137) and 332(76).
[41] PRO, SP 1/202, fo. 182 (*LP* xx (1) 1031).
[42] See my *The Reformation and the English People* (Oxford, 1984), pp. 71, 77–9.
[43] BL, Cotton MS Cleo. E 4, fos. 362ᵛ–3, 365; PRO, E 315/24, fos. 1–80 (printed in H. Cole, *King Henry the Eighth's Scheme of Bishopricks* (London, 1838); SP 1/154, fos. 86–93.

wealth of twenty large abbeys for the purpose – singly, in pairs or, in two cases (including Cornwall's), three at a time. A second scheme would have set up two new colleges (Burton and Thornton) and twelve new dioceses, employing thirteen abbeys and Southwell College for these. The third envisaged ten new bishoprics, founded on fifteen former abbeys and two former colleges (Beverley and Leicester), and three new colleges in Burton, Thornton and Thetford.

The second Act of Dissolution of 1539, which swept away all the surviving monasteries, was accompanied by another measure empowering the king to establish new 'bishoprics, collegiate and cathedral churches'. Its preamble is unique, as far as one knows: it was written by Henry himself.[44] It promised that all manner of good things (almshouses, highways, teaching of Greek and Latin, etc.) and not just new dioceses, would result from the suppression of those dens of idleness, the rich abbeys, and the dispersal of their inmates. There was no obvious need for this statute. Henry could have founded all the new sees and colleges he wanted by letters patent and as supreme head of the church. The need was political. That second act, rushed through parliament, and perhaps even an afterthought, was calculated to facilitate the passage of the first. Thanks to it, and especially its preamble, what parliament would have thought it was voting for when it ratified the crown's title to the larger abbeys (many of them already in royal hands) was the large-scale conversion of monastic wealth to religious, as well as social and educational, purposes. Since the abbeys being considered for use as cathedrals or colleges included the richest houses in England, such adaptation would have saved for religion a significant proportion of the total wealth of medieval English monasticism.

In the event, only six new sees and two new colleges were founded; and these cost the crown less than might have been expected because their endowments (like the re-endowments of the ex-monastic medieval cathedrals, often compiled from former possessions of several religious houses) were only a portion of the wealth of the former monasteries from which they took their names. All this is not proof that previous plans for many more bishoprics, etc. had been completely insincere; but one may suppose that the government would always have wanted to keep its outlay to a minimum. However, there had been so much talk of new colleges and numerous bishoprics that sooner or later the promises would have to be honoured. Presumably the six new sees and two colleges were the most that the king judged that he needed to concede.[45]

---

[44] BL, Cotton MS Cleo. E 4, fo. 366.

[45] Perhaps the re-founding of Burton and Thornton as colleges was also meant to allay fears that the crown had designs on colleges in general. In 1537, amidst the first stages of the dissolution of monasteries, Henry had founded two religious houses (Bisham – Chertsey Abbey reconstituted – and Stixwould). A third followed in 1538. Presumably there were intended to persuade his subjects that whole suppression was not envisaged. Were the two new colleges of 1541/2 likewise decoys?

It is only fair to add that 'royal' grammar schools were set up with the new cathedrals and that the latter's statutes required them to distribute some £500 a year in alms to the poor and over £300 on repairing roads. Some were also responsible for maintaining students and readers in divinity at the universities. We can hear strong echoes here of the preamble to that act of 1539. The king's promises were being honoured, though on nothing like the scale that could have been expected. Moreover, by the time he died, several of these new foundations had been squeezed and two had been suppressed.

Like their elder brethren, some of the new sees were soon shedding possessions as a result of 'exchanges'. Westminster, for instance, was particularly badly hit.[46] Thornton College, which had been granted only a part of the former abbey's lands and buildings, surrendered considerable possessions just before Henry died in exchange for rectories and advowsons.[47] Several cathedrals lost lands after being exempted from maintaining students at the universities[48] and in July 1546 a royal commission was appointed to enquire into how deans of the new cathedrals and colleges were discharging their liabilities for almsgiving and highway repair. Though it was allegedly the king's intention to have 'better success' therein, there was ominous talk about the money perhaps being 'better bestowed otherwise to God's pleasure and the king's honour'.[49] Then came actual suppression. It having been perceived that St Frideswide's church in Wolsey's college in Oxford, by then known as King Henry VIII's College, was grand enough to be a cathedral, it was decided to abandon the cathedral which had been given to the new see of Oxford in 1542, namely, the former church of nearby Osney Abbey, and to transfer its chapter, stalls, bells and episcopal *cathedra* to St Frideswide's. A complicated series of events ensued. In May 1545 both the new see and its cathedral church of Christ and St Mary were formally surrendered to the crown, and so was King Henry's College. By December 1546 the latter had been reconstituted as a cathedral and college, Christ Church, and re-endowed with lands and a vast collection of vicarages and rectories worth £2200 a year.[50] Thus two became one. Osney Abbey's large church, now an ex-cathedral, was abandoned – like Coventry's and Bath's (except that Bath Abbey was eventually saved and survives). There may have been some good reasons for the merger, but in the course of it the crown was able to claw back a mass of

---

[46] See *LP* xx (1) 465(94 and 100), 620(3) (11 and 53), etc. Chester and Gloucester also suffered noticeably. Canterbury and Rochester were among the worst affected ex-monastic medieval cathedrals. Exeter and York were probably the chapters of the old foundation which suffered most. Nor did Eton and Winchester escape completely.

[47] *LP* xxi (i) 760, 963(36); *CPR, Edward VI*, I, p. 147. Ibid, p. 153 shows that the crown had not handed over major buildings formerly belonging to the monastery when the college was founded in January 1542. Its landed endowment, too, had been but a fraction of the abbey's.

[48] See *LP* xx (1) 400 and 777 (Durham and Ely), for examples.

[49] *LP* xx 1335(52).

[50] *LP* xx (i) 775–6; xxi (2) 648(25) and p. 443 (pensions for the displaced dean and canons of St Frideswide's).

properties which it had only recently bestowed on the new diocese of Oxford, as well as to bite into Wolsey's foundation for his college.[51] While all this was happening, Burton College, too, was dissolved and in January 1546 sold to secretary Paget. Henry's other recent collegiate foundation, Thornton College, was suppressed in 1549. In 1550 the new see of Westminster was discontinued and its cathedral reduced to a college. By then, of course, the chantries, guilds, obits, 'lights' and all the rest were falling thick and fast, along with the remaining colleges. But Burton and Thornton, as well as the new bishoprics, had long since served their political purpose.

[51] As the subsequent sales by the crown show. See, e.g. *LP* xx (2) 496 (22, 29 and 36), 910(3), 1068(46 and 50).

God's law and man's: Stephen Gardiner and the problem of loyalty

REX POGSON

I

'We have had here disputacion for wordes, and that is a gret parte of that the wourlde is nowe troubled with' (Gardiner to Paget, 21 December 1545)[1]

A CENTRAL PROBLEM of the reformation was the need to express new, or newly recognised, doctrinal and political realities in the inherited language of the canon law, while adjusting or denying its implications. Revolutionary ideas are of necessity couched largely in familiar words and concepts, whatever the startling underlying assumptions, and this was certainly true of the sixteenth century when newfangledness was taken for falsehood. But sharing the problem with other revolutionary eras did not make it easier for leaders and clerics to distinguish between divine and human, eternal and temporal, with intellectual tools and ancient examples which could be taken to justify any stance. As Melanchthon said, either in humour or resignation, if the early Fathers had only known what trouble future generations would take in their interpretation, they would surely have made their meaning more clear.[2]

This was far from a simply academic problem. As consensus broke down, the tendency was, as Cranmer observed, to call 'divine institution' anything that people think well done;[3] yet it was precisely at such moments of fragmentation that winning the intellectual argument seemed so critical. The story of the schismatic and doctrinal conflict in mid-Tudor England can be written round the theme of legal and scriptural authority. In the 1520s Henry VIII's desire for Anne Boleyn and a male heir was expressed in (rival) glosses of Leviticus and Deuteronomy, however irrelevant Charles V's control of Rome makes such antics seem in retrospect. In the subsequent confrontation with the papacy no medieval or dimly pre-historical exemplum was neglected.

---

[1] PRO, SP 1/212, fo. 84.
[2] H. Latimer, *Sermons and Remains* (Parker Society, 1848), II, p. 268.
[3] T. Cranmer, *Miscellaneous Writings* (Parker Society, 1846), p. 76.

And when the unprecedented breach was justified by ancient precedent, words looked the same but changed their meaning – for some. Chapuys, Charles V's ambassador, contrasted divinely-ordained jurisdiction with the transitory nature of national decrees, and saw that the Henrician councillors knew not what to say.[4] He thought he had confounded them with truth, but it is more realistic to suppose they were experiencing that frustrating lack of communication which comes from sharing a vocabulary without admitting any mutual understanding. For those councillors the lines between levels of spiritual jurisdiction had been shifted and the medieval debate re-written by stature.[5]

Loyalty to erastian statute was likely to be least complicated for the papacy's doctrinal enemies. The schism gave heresy its great chance, and Tudor governments acknowledged it with a mixture of negative complaisance, positive support and incompetent persecution over the next twenty-five years. The argument over God's will and man's interpretation was thus extended from jurisdiction to the means of salvation and the nature of the church itself. Protestantism had a double revolutionary potential, in the unwitting encouragement to secularism of surrendering visible ecclesiastical control to the prince, and in challenging the fabric of law and government by accepting only the authority of scripture. That these stark prospects were blurred and softened in most individual reformers, and that for much of the time the language of secular relativism advanced unperceived at the expense of traditional concepts, only served to increase the dilemma of those who had to decide when to obey, when to compromise, when to resist.

II

Stephen Gardiner is the cleric whose view of God's law and man's is taken to illustrate the dilemma of loyalties. As Henry VIII's most gifted canon lawyer in the 1520s, trained as an administrator under Wolsey, he was marked possibly for the highest offices of all when he rose to the secretaryship in 1529 and to Winchester in 1531. His orthodox medieval clerical career was disrupted by the annulment, for Thomas Cromwell had solutions more radical than Gardiner was qualified or trusted to provide. Gardiner faced royal displeasure for defending clerical independence prior to his decision to write *De Vera Obedientia*, the most scholarly defence of erastianism. Although he showed no further qualms about Henry's royal supremacy, Gardiner was involved in constant in-fighting against Cromwell and Cranmer, and showed increasing

---

[4] *LP* VI, 1501; Chapuys to Charles V, 6 December 1533.
[5] S. Gardiner, *Obedience in Church and State* (ed. P. Janelle, Cambridge, 1930, hereafter cited as Janelle, *DVO*), pp. 103–5, 117; Gardiner on new words for ancient rights. But cf. W. Ullmann, 'This realm of England is an Empire' (*JEH* 30(2), 1979), 179–80, 203, for old words acquiring new meanings.

anxiety over the spread of heresy. The six articles of 1539 and the king's book four years later reassured him, but in 1547 he was excluded from Edward VI's regency council and then endured the rapid advance of protestantism under Seymour and Dudley. He underwent extensive interrogation following a test sermon, and spells in the Fleet and Tower, whence he emerged to be Lord Chancellor under Mary, to face the problem of reconciling his past with the return to Rome.

This formidable career, marked by Gardiner's unattractively combative style, contains the confrontation of orthodox values with jurisdictional and doctrinal upheaval which so strained concepts and loyalties alike. But when with hindsight we see a career which weathered two decades of such an upheaval, we tend to play down the pressures on the survivor, and assume self-interest as an explanation for administrative flexibility and the absence of martyrdom. In Gardiner's case, this view has a long pedigree: Foxe dismissed him as 'a good lawyer, but yet a naughty divine and a worse bishop' and as 'neither firm in his error nor steadfast in the truth';[6] Pole, from the other side of the ideological divide, commented repeatedly on Gardiner's schismatic record with a contemptuous superiority which seems easy enough for a cleric who viewed Henry's and Edward's changes from the comparative security of a distinguished exile.[7] They have thus left us a number of important assumptions: that political expertise is not conducive to spiritual commitment; that failure to identify with one extreme or the other makes a bad churchman; and that changes of mind over twenty years of revolution prove insincerity. These propositions may appeal to us – perhaps we hanker for an age when moral issues were allegedly clearer-cut than in our own, or perhaps we like our historical trends tidy – and may indeed be fruitful; but it is important not to take them as precepts, for they remain propositions to be weighed.

In his standard biography, Muller tried to resist these received assumptions and to emphasise Gardiner's positive principles, but his summary of Gardiner's character loses credibility because it makes too little mention of self-interest and – a more subtle but perhaps more significant criticism – because it makes Gardiner's support for the supremacy a straightforward tactic in pursuit of a conservative church: this loses the crucial sense of tension between conflicting, entangled and deeply-entrenched loyalties.[8] Most comment, in any case, takes a very different line from Muller's, and echoes Foxe's and Pole's assumptions. Thus Janelle's editorial introduction to some of Gardiner's most important works, while finding some underlying continuity in his thought, takes his political motivation and periodic insincerity for granted;[9] L. B. Smith contrasts Gardiner's wiliness and chicanery with the

---

[6] J. Foxe, *Acts and Monuments* (ed. S. R. Cattley, London, 1837–41, hereafter 'Foxe'), VI, pp. 266, 258.
[7] BL, Add. MS 41577, fos. 57–61: three letters of 1553 illustrating Pole's view.
[8] J. A. Muller, *Stephen Gardiner and the Tudor Reaction* (1926), pp. 295–302.
[9] Janelle, *DVO*, p. lxviii, 'underlying continuity'; pp. xiv–xv, lii–liii, lxv.

reformers' otherworldliness, assumes that Henrician conservatives were not of a deeply pious nature, and only just draws back from the notion that with deeper thought Gardiner might have finished up a protestant.[10] More subtle appreciations of the conservatives' dilemma, Baumer's and McConica's, for instance, sometimes drop similar hints: Gardiner chooses his principles as he finds them 'convenient'; and his changed view of the supremacy in Edward's reign shows that his loyalty to 'the Henrician ideal' had been reluctant, and was now revealed as error.[11] It is legitimate to ask: if circumstances were changing rapidly, why can there not be a logical and spiritual basis for both positions and for the shift between them? And this is a relevant question to ask of very recent comments: Guy, summarising Gardiner's character, chooses Cranmer's hardly unprejudiced remarks as a vehicle, dismisses Gardiner's manoeuvring in the early 1530s as 'plainly . . . to further his advancement', and tries to suggest 'prudence' as Gardiner's motive even when he did risk his neck;[12] and even Skinner's sensitive work on the development of early modern thought offers the opinion, apropos of Gardiner, that consistency over time is a gauge of sincerity.[13] It is worth noting that most of these works have placed Gardiner in passing in the context of a much wider subject – the theory of kingship, or English humanism or the notion of the state, and so on. Valuable though it is to unravel major strands of thought or historical development, there is a danger in belittling legitimate discrepancies in an individual's response to revolutionary pressures; the discrepancies, of course, affect the picture of the development.[14] It is indeed in his study of the individual dilemmas of Latimer, Ridley and Cranmer that Loades gives a coherent and more sympathetic analysis of Gardiner's consistency as part of the backdrop to his story.[15]

This paper picks out this theme of the individual's distinctive response to change by looking afresh at aspects of Gardiner's view of law, authority and obligation. It is not intended to challenge the main thrust, conclusions or values of the works mentioned: but to ponder this general and often implicit idea that it is disreputable to contrive to balance loyalties for any length of time; and to appreciate the peculiar pressures on a conservative in this time of rapid change. We shall, of course, find self-interest and political manoeuvring; but we shall not assume that therefore we shall find little else. And there are broader benefits: any standpoint overlooking the familiar but vast area of the reformation is likely to offer angles which help the total view.

[10] L. M. Smith, *Tudor Prelates and Politics, 1536–58* (Princeton Studies in History, VIII, Princeton, 1953), pp. 96–100, 123–4, 139, 230, 280.

[11] F. L. V. Baumer, *The Early Tudor Theory of Kingship* (New Haven, 1940), pp. 125, 188; J. K. McConica, *English Humanists and Reformation Politics under Henry VIII, and Edward VI* (Oxford 1965), p. 236.

[12] J. Guy, *The Public Career of Thomas More* (Brighton, 1980), pp. 145, 146, 194–5.

[13] Q. Skinner, *The Foundations of Modern Political Thought* (Cambridge, 1978), II, p. 98.

[14] Cf. M. Oakeshott, review of Skinner's book (note 13) in *Hist. Journal*, 23(2), 1980, 445–53.

[15] D. M. Loades, *The Oxford Martyrs* (London, 1970), pp. 50–8.

III

One false step which can lead us to expect life-long coherence of belief is to attribute fore-knowledge, not of events but of their implications. There was no reason for Gardiner to suppose that the king's great matter would broaden beyond the question of marriage. In 1529, English diplomats (to Chapuys' amazement) actually expected something from Campeggio's mission to England; Gardiner was talking confidently of a middle way in 1532; Cranmer was envisaging reconciliation with Rome in 1534.[16] What with hindsight was a revolution had impermanence in contemporary eyes.

Moreover, Gardiner took a pragmatic professional view of the matter. Truth, he once said, had a habit of emerging over a long time; he was too busy trying to swing votes at Cambridge or bargain with the Curia to ponder philosophical implications.[17] Besides, he had observed Clement VII at close hand, had diagnosed him as beyond reason through malice or fear, and was quite sure that it would be absurd to put such a pope's view of God's law above that of the Henrician church.[18] The prospect of an open breach did not bear consideration.[19] It was better to play it down as a jurisdictional squabble on a human scale, where the dilemma of conflicting loyalties and instructions could be expressed not in More's terms of God and man, but in earthly terms in English and Italian interests.[20] Rome, said Gardiner, was like a contentious lawyer, obscuring truth and inventing new arguments.[21] We may wonder if he saw the self-portrait in that.

But one of Henry VIII's weapons in the struggle was the status of the clergy in England, and Gardiner was a committed clericalist. It was because of this loyalty, and not because of any demonstration of regard for the pope, that Chapuys was able to describe Gardiner as a consistent champion of apostolic power.[22] Clement could be despised, but Gardiner outspokenly defended the English clergy's right to keep their own house in order, and said that oaths to Rome were not derogatory to the king's power – if they were legal.[23]

Quite so. The quandary which was avoided by Gardiner in the papal argument appeared over clerical privilege. The phrase 'so far as the law of

[16] *LP* iv 5572: Campeggio to Salviati, 20 May 1529; BL, Add. MS 28584, fo. 174; BL, Cotton MS Cleo. E 6, fo. 234.

[17] BL, Cotton MS Tit. B 1, fo. 379: Gardiner to Cromwell, 30 June 1532; BL, Cotton MS Vit. B 13, fo. 51, for Gardiner in Cambridge on the annulment.

[18] J. A. Muller, ed, *Letters of Stephen Gardiner* (Cambridge, 1933), p. 13: to Henry VIII, 21 April 1929.

[19] The prospect of the fall or non-recovery of the English church: PRO, SP 1/53, fo. 276.

[20] PRO, SP 1/76 fos. 40–1: Bedyll to Cromwell, 12 May 1533 – Gardiner's useful legalistic approach: cf. Gardiner's own arguments in Janelle, *DVO*, pp. 89–91.

[21] Janelle, *DVO*, p. 43.

[22] *LP* ix 965; Chapuys to Granvelle, 13 December 1535.

[23] Ibid, v 1058: Chapuys to Charles V, 31 May 1532; Muller, *Letters*, p. 49, for Gardiner's argument with Henry over the Supplication; cf. Gardiner's boldness on the divine prescription of episcopal powers, Guy, *Public Career of More*, pp. 194–5.

Christ allows', used to extricate king and convocation from a predicament in 1531, was deliberately vague, but the vagueness itself clarifies the dilemma. If God's authority had been handed down to clerics, said Gardiner, they ought not to give it away.[24] Easily seen as equivocation because of that use of the conditional, this was a brave stand to take with Henry in that mood, and Gardiner must have known precisely the risk he was running.[25] The conditional was an honest indication of indecision: for while it is commonplace to sneer at the disloyalty shown to the pope by these conservatives, it is not always made so plain that the alternative, disloyalty to Henry's dearest wish, was genuinely shocking to them. Much use had been made in Henrician propaganda of the notion that the canon law was no more universal than local custom, but merely represented sectional Italian interests, so that the Carthusians, for instance, died not for eternal truth but for a transitory tradition falling rapidly into decay.[26] This line in historical relativism finds a consistent echo in Gardiner's regard for statute and was as strongly part of him as his clericalism. So when he argued for ecclesiastical privilege against the common law, and yet soothed his conscience over appeals by referring to his obligation to obey statute, the discrepancy is more likely to be a symptom of unprecedented choices than time-serving.[27]

For he allowed his mixture of reactions (he was 'jumbled' in his mind before writing the De Vera) to give him a reputation for 'coloured doubleness' which he never shook off.[28] Very inefficient time-serving. Hardly surprising that in 1534 and 1535 Gardiner faced the choice of oblivion or rehabilitation, or that he chose to write the book and survive. He has been severely castigated for this piece of writing. He loses all ways: it was shameful to bow to pressure and write the book; having done so, it was shameful to employ the biblical arguments we associate with protestants; but, if he had to use them, it was insincere not to mean them when he did so.[29]

It would be absurd to deny that the De Vera was written to save his skin; but absurd too to suggest that precludes any additional motive, and absurd to assume that the only acceptable way out of his complex dilemma was to die in

[24] Muller, Letters, p. 49: a letter to Henry VIII showing Gardiner's courage; cf. Muller, Gardiner and Tudor Reaction, p. 300.

[25] Cf. Guy, Public Career of More, p. 146; M. Bowker, The Henrician Reformation: the Diocese of Lincoln under John Longland, 1521–1547 (Cambridge, 1981), pp. 68–9; J. Scarisbrick, 'The Conservative Episcopate in England' (unpublished Ph.D dissertation, Cambridge, 1955), pp. 237–45.

[26] W. Zeeveld, Foundations of Tudor Policy (London, 1948), p. 124. Cf. the intense national and historical relativism in the 'Collectanea Satis Copiosa' (J. Guy, 'Henry VIII and the praemunire manoeuvres of 1530–1' (EHR, July 1982), 481.

[27] Baumer, Early Tudor Kingship, pp. 172–3, 189; Muller, Letters, p. 392, for the Audley discussion; BL, Cotton MS Vesp. F. 13, fo. 71; Foxe, VI, p. 46; cf. Muller, Letters, p. 269 – 'I have gret feare of the comen lawe in a doubte'.

[28] Janelle, DVO, p. 69; Skinner, Modern Thought, II, p. 94.

[29] Janelle, DVO, pp. liv, lv, for a version of this argument.

it. Pole said the book was inspired by hope and fear: we do not need to agree that all the hopes were selfish ones.[30] Just as More saw the chancellorship in 1530 as a weapon for orthodoxy, in spite of the annulment, so Gardiner could develop his existing contempt for the pope and retain a position to defend essentials of clerical and doctrinal orthodoxy. The primacy could be jettisoned: the *De Vera* continued Gardiner's earlier arguments – Henry's accuracy on Leviticus, scripture as the 'plummet' of God's will, the arrogance of the bishop of Rome. The spirit and authority of the church would have to be preserved without the pope: Gardiner stressed the king's obligation to rule rightly, the divine law of the subjects' obedience to the prince, and the position of the crown in the mainstream of imperial and ecclesiastical tradition.[31] Pole called the book a cowardly betrayal, and Cromwell viewed it as a useful piece of apostasy; Baumer concludes that Gardiner had 'turned King's evidence'.[32] But all these implications of betrayal need examination. From Gardiner's point of view, there can have been nothing to die for in 1535: More did not stop any juggernauts by dying. The clerical rearguard had been fought to its standstill, and the mood of the reformation parliament was such that the king's conservatism offered the only clear hope. There seemed no reason why Henry VIII should not have his heir, the English church its traditions, and Gardiner his high office. It is one-sided to concentrate only on the last: all these things mattered to Gardiner. It is one-sided to suggest that his use of scriptural quotations makes him a hypocrite: he could stress fashionable scriptural quotations rather than papal decrees because Henry's record did not suggest the king's interpretation would be different from his own.[33] It is one-sided to assume that he placed schismatic England in the continuing tradition of the universal church just to impress foreign observers and give Henry room for diplomatic manoeuvre: his view was a logical extension of his conclusions about Clement.[34] Where was the alternative, anyway? It is understandable that a conservative cleric who had been through the supplication and submission would finally settle for Henry VIII rather than nothing. And – here's the nub – if we were viewing his decision from 1543 or the accession of Mary, could we not argue that he had got it right? Hindsight does not only operate from 1558.

IV

There were times in the next few years when Gardiner was far from happy that he had got it right. Between the publication of the *De Vera* in 1535 and his

---

[30] BL, Add. MS 25425, fol. 204: Pole to Gardiner, 22 March 1554.

[31] Janelle, *DVO*, pp. 69, 87, 121, 127–9, 147.

[32] *LP* x 7; Pole to Contarini, 1 January 1536; PRO, SP 1124, fos. 148–9, for Cromwell's view of *De Vera* as a useful balance to Pole's 'Pro Unitate'; Baumer, *Early Tudor Kingship*, p. 64.

[33] But cf. Janelle, *DVO*, p. liv, for the argument that the protestant quotations indicate insincerity.

[34] Cf. Baumer, *Early Tudor Kingship*, p. 532 n.

polemic against Bucer, the 'Contemptum' of 1541, and throughout the closing struggles of Henry's reign, Gardiner met the classic problem of the conservative who shares in an initial revolutionary step, only to be appalled by the prospect of accelerating innovation glimpsed, for example, in his close encounters with Barnes at the end of the 1530s.[35] In the six years after the *De Vera* he saw the dissolution, liturgical and sacramental experiments, the English bible, the negotiations with German heretics – and much of this he saw from Paris, an exile which he felt was another symptom of the reformers' victory.[36]

Not surprisingly, he became alarmed at heresy's advance, concentrating his venom in the 'Contemptum' against protestantism's extreme potential to dissolve all respect for existing law. Protestants' claims of loyalty were paradoxical, he said (not like his own?), since they professed allegiance to the crown yet taught a rejection of all authority except scripture, thus causing anarchy. Gardiner's fears were confirmed for him by the reformers' disillusionment with the results of the schism: still later even the cautious Cranmer affirmed that popery's grip on doctrine and administration had not yet been loosened.[37] Alarming sentiments, since in that sense Gardiner had supported the pope's removal partly to retain popery.

Protestant disappointment, of course, was accentuated by Gardiner's skilful use of the supremacy as a weapon of conservative propaganda, a tactic which confirms that he supported the breach with his eyes open and not merely in selfish panic. Two examples demonstrate his polemical skill: the reformers' continuing use of the language of canon law was turned against them when Gardiner accused Cranmer of praemunire because he retained papal wording in archiepiscopal visitation;[38] and he applied erastian theory to the Schmalkaldic League, castigating German protestants for disobedience to Charles V, their secular head.[39] This later argument was tendentious, for it made Gardiner appear an ardent erastian, pushed England towards an imperial rather than heretical alliance, and hinted at protestant treachery in consorting with German rebels. Gardiner was seeking to be seen as the moderate centralist; he always admired Henry's claim to be 'newter', to stand alone in diplomacy and to favour neither papist nor heretic.[40] Protestant

[35] Muller, *Gardiner and Tudor Reaction*, pp. 79–94. See also note 108, for references to G. Redworth, 'The Political and Diplomatic Career of Stephen Gardiner, 1538–51' (Unpublished Oxford D.Phil. thesis, 1985).

[36] S. Gardiner, 'Contemptum humanae legis', in *Obedience in Church and State* (see note 5) hereafter Janelle, 'Contemptum'. Examples of Gardiner's feelings of exile, *LP* xii(1). See also note 108.

[37] Muller, *Letters*, pp. 166–7, 490; T. Cranmer, *Writings and Disputations on the Lord's Supper* (Parker Society, 1844), p. 240.

[38] BL, MS Cotton MS Cleo. F 1, fos. 249–50; Cleo. F 2, fos. 123–7.

[39] Muller, *Letters*, pp. 72–5.

[40] E.g. Muller, *Letters*, pp. 97–8: Gardiner to Russell *et al.* on diplomacy, 1542; BL, Add. MS 29546, fos. 1–9: to Cranmer, on Henry's ability to 'reforme and thenne moderate religion'.

groups could be compared with friars, subversive to the supremacy: heretics were a threat to royal authority, for they would destroy the good with the bad, and pull down without building a proper replacement.[41] It is symptomatic of Gardiner's bad press that this eminently tenable moral position has been associated with his mastery of 'chicanery' and contrasted contemptuously with the reformers' idealistic search for truth.[42]

The threat to authority was the central theme of the 'Contemptum'. Bucer had asserted that a ruler's first priority is to enforce God's scriptural law, and that the breach of merely human law is of little consequence in comparison.[43] Gardiner's impatient administrative mind, conscious that law-making is an eclectic and haphazard occupation,[44] pointed to problems of absurdity and political credibility in Bucer's position. If, say, drunkenness had to be punished by human authority simply because it involved transgression of divine law, it would have to incur stiffer penalties than breaches of merely human law, because of its divinity; but it would be absurd to pitch the punishment higher than for major social upheaval. Besides, there are so many sins that minute gradations of penalty would make the system a mockery. No, said Gardiner, divine laws which are not taken up by rulers as matters for earthly concern are God's to protect. More important in Gardiner's mind is contempt for human legislation, since Bucer's distinction is invalid, and the contempt touches God through the ruler. Since he put even heresy laws into the category of human legislation, Gardiner clearly saw law-making as human even if the protection offered was to divine truth.[45] So any heretic seeking the escape route of elevating his belief above the mundane power of secular rulers would not get away with it. General agreement on doctrine was essential to princely authority, social unity and thus respect for God.[46]

Bucer's response – a reasonable one – was to point out that Gardiner rated efficient government above justice.[47] This put the finger on Gardiner's short-term emphasis on the power of statute. Gardiner's position was that, even in post-schismatic England, Roman ceremonial must be obeyed because it was required by statute law.[48] The inference that anything parliament wanted was

---

[41] Muller, *Letters*, pp. 170, 483; Foxe, VI, p. 187.

[42] E.g. Smith, *Tudor Prelates*, pp. 123–4.

[43] Janelle, 'Contemptum', pp. 189, 201, 205. Cf. P. Avis, 'Moses and the Magistrates', *JEH*, 26 (1975), 160, 163, on Bucer's doctrinaire view of applying scripture to contemporary problems, cf. Muller, *Letters*, p. 137, for Gardiner on Greek pronunciation.

[44] E.g. Muller, *Letters*, p. 484 (answer to Turner): 'no common welthe but it hath taken in sum poynte other nations' laws'.

[45] Janelle, 'Contemptum', pp. 177, 179, 193, 205.

[46] Cf. Gardiner's 'Preface to and Explicacion of the true Catholique faythe' (in Muller, *Letters*, p. 249): 'Conforme knowledge to agree with obedience where Goddes truthe repugneth not unto it'. Cf. Baumer, *Early Tudor Kingship*, p. 161.

[47] Janelle, 'Contemptum', p. 185, cf. BL, Royal App. 87, fos. 34–8, for Gardiner on accepting even faulty justice as truth.

[48] Cf. Foxe, VI, p. 91: Gardiner was still producing this argument under interrogation in Edward's reign.

an imperative is so obvious that Gardiner must have seen it: indeed, he attached a familiar disclaimer – 'in so far as a statute does not stand against God's precepts' – which showed he anticipated the possibility of legislative change and was prepared to 'stay' – as indeed he did – on forms of worship which enshrined traditional doctrine. Why then did he base his attack on heresy on such shifting human sand? When he mocked the protestants for trying to reach truth by common assent, what other basis was there for his defence of ecclesiastical tradition by existing statute?[49]

The likely answer is that he felt nothing else was immediately available to him. His continuing references over the next decade to the six articles and the king's book suggest that Henry's apparent rejection of doctrinal experiments in the early 1540s was a landmark for Gardiner.[50] He remained sure that this conservatism was the true expression of Henry's beliefs, and even though it led him into some problems of logic, he was content after an extremely confused period to stick to that conviction as the best defence of orthodoxy.[51] Since there was some talk of his rising to the vicegerency after Cromwell's execution, he had reason for optimism.[52] It may be, too, that he could not believe that any government, seeing heresy's potential for subversion, would seriously encourage it: by the end of the reign he was sure that doctrinal concessions would open the way for the collapse of all authority.[53] After all, heresy had always been an undercover protest, never an alternative orthodoxy espoused by a government. Before 1547 Gardiner may have been unable to envisage a genuine governmental programme which was not conservative. Judging from the reaction of those close to Henry in 1547, Gardiner may have shared the general feeling that the king would last for ever.

There are plausible explanations here for Gardiner's immediate thinking in the 1540s, and there is consistency too, if we mean what we should by that word, that changes in approach are consistent with the entire picture of a man's values and his circumstances at a given time. But our understanding of his position must not conceal the significance of a conservative bishop's relativism, and the emphasis on positive law. The protestant Turner said that if Gardiner argued the correctness of the royal breach with Rome, and also the royal right to punish clerical lapses, from celibacy, for instance, then the king, like the pope before him, was afforded the right to create sin, since celibacy was not scriptural law.[54] It was all very well for a secular humanist (St

---

[49] Muller, *Letters*, p. 72: to Cranmer, February 1536; cf. BL, Royal App. 87, fos. 34–8, for Gardiner's accusations that his opponents change the meanings of words; cf. Baumer, *Early Tudor Kingship*, pp. 139–40.

[50] BL, Cotton MS Cleo. E 6, fo. 129; Muller, *Letters*, p. 352, for Henrician influence on the Edwardian situation.

[51] BL, Add. MS 29546, fos. 1–9; the argument over Henry's rightness or gullibility.

[52] Muller, *Gardiner and Tudor Reaction*, p. 91.

[53] M. Bowker, 'The supremacy and the episcopate' (*Hist. Journal* 18(2), 1975), 234; BL, Add. MS 29546, fos. 1–9, on breaches in the wall of authority.

[54] Muller, *Letters*, p. 489: Gardiner, meeting Turner's point, seems to bear out his misgivings.

German) to say that statute could do what it liked, but quite another for Gardiner to get close to saying the same thing.[55] The dangers lay in directions Gardiner least wanted to travel: first, in Edward's reign he was to defy statute through conscience, having helped to sell that particular pass himself; secondly, the threat to royal authority was a fear which proved self-fulfilling, since if only royal law blocked heretical advance, the demand for change would beat upon the crown itself;[56] thirdly, and connected with the second, the identification of conservative ideas with changeable statute rather than immutable divine law advanced the case for rebellion theory, as Henry VIII's apparently definitive supremacy turned into a confrontation of alternative programmes in the next two reigns.

We have said that Gardiner should not be expected to have read the future. We know that he believed genuinely in the authority of common law. We can accept that he was more likely to win moderate support in the 1540s with this sort of legislative argument than with any re-statement of papalist claims. Nonetheless, his stance represents the conservative's dilemma, for to have a chance of winning the argument it seemed he was in danger of surrendering the core of his case. And, of course, rapid changes in policy and statute laws were likely to increase doubts about the legitimacy of the source of authority too.[57] These are the shifts in assumptions which can tempt historians to talk of changes in the spirit of an age.

V

Certainly, there was a new spirit after 1547. Gardiner was alarmed by largely unchallenged shifts in the meaning of words: history was reinterpreted so that Gardiner was now seen as a hinderer of Henry VIII; for after all his efforts to be catholic without being papist, Gardiner was now called the latter for being the former; God's word, individually declaimed, was superseding God's law as defined by the church.[58] Cranmer, said Gardiner, was ignoring history as if he had suddenly dropped out of the skies with a brand-new version of the truth: Gardiner mocked this transparency as a 'jolly easy way' in commenting on Cranmer's first Prayer Book.[59] And Cranmer was a cautious moderate:

[55] Guy, *Public Career of More*, p. 154.
[56] BL, Add. MS 29546, fos. 9–24: Gardiner to Cranmer, July 1547, on turning hatred from Rome to the crown; cf. R. Pineas, 'William Turner and Reformation Politics' (*Bibliothèque d'Humanisme et Renaissance*, 37, 1975), 196, on the fading of the myth that the crown was above the doctrinal conflict.
[57] E.g. BL, Add. MS 25114, fo. 244: Henry VIII's concern in 1537 about parliament's future attitude to the validity of succession laws.
[58] BL, Add. MS 29546, fo. 9: Gardiner to Cranmer, July 1547; cf. Muller, *Letters*, pp. 249–52: Gardiner to Paget 1546, on the challenge to long-accepted truth: PRO, SP 10/1, fo. 105: 'God's truth against that they call God's Word'.
[59] Cranmer, *On the Lord's Supper*, p. 63; Muller, *Letters*, p. 448; Foxe, VI, p. 160. See note 108; Redworth, 'Stephen Gardiner', p. 246, for an analysis of Gardiner's attitude to the Prayer Book.

how much more did Gardiner fear the protestant view that 'little by little' was failing, that radical steps had to be taken to remove what Hooper called the 'human things' of surviving traditions.[60]

These traditions were precisely the issues over which Gardiner's whole career showed he would 'stay'. While his defence of images, for instance, seems a classic statement of 'things indifferent' (images are admirable so long as they express truth), this does not detract from the intensity of doctrinal commitment behind his regard for ceremonial.[61] Although in Henry's and Mary's reigns Gardiner's letters were dominated by admininstrative concerns, that does not justify the conclusion that they were all he cared about: he was, after all, a very busy man. It is likely that, with time to reflect in isolation and later under threat in prison, he concentrated on issues which ultimately mattered to him. Cranmer certainly thought so: he said that Gardiner brought all arguments back to a defence of transubstantiation, and this is such a striking comment on an allegedly political animal that we should pause to register it. Cranmer judged transubstantiation to be the root of surviving popery, and he and Gardiner spent much time and ink in disputation of it.[62] Gardiner emphasised that scripture is not easy: although it has divine authority, it can wilfully be misinterpreted, and fallacies set up in men's minds.[63] Just as the king breathes life into the dead body of the law by interpreting it (inevitably Gardiner used examples of Henry's strict limits on religious change late in his reign) so the church has given visible shape to God's law.[64] This is why Gardiner propagated what Loades has rather dramatically called a 'total denial of intellectual curiosity';[65] Gardiner had to use the church's authority to justify as divine those things which Hooper had called merely 'human'. The official support for heresy ended any pretensions to neutrality in Gardiner's tone; he protested that he retained outward obedience, he agreed at first with Ridley that England was better without the pope, but on doctrine and clerical traditions the debate left less and less room for compromise as time passed. Whereas in the past it had been possible to hate the idea yet love the man, Gardiner found such luxuries no longer possible, and he blamed himself for his 'condescension' in involving himself in experimentation in Henry's reign. On Erasmus, too, he changed his tone, noting, as Rome did, that the Dutchman's criticism of the clergy made him a Trojan horse in the catholic camp. So much for all that shared humanist excitement in the Cambridge of thirty years before.[66]

---

[60] *Original Letters Relative to the English Reformation* (Parker Society, 1846), I, p. 100.
[61] Foxe, VI, pp. 27, 69; cf. Muller, *Letters*, p. 217.
[62] Cranmer, *On the Lord's Supper*, pp. 4, 6, 10, 240, 302.
[63] E.g. BL, Add. MS 29546, fo. 1; Gardiner to Cranmer, June 1547; 'a dangerous enterprise to dispence lyes from the trewth'.
[64] Foxe, VI, p. 51; Baumer, *Early Tudor Kingship*, p. 150.
[65] Loades, *Oxford Martyrs*, p. 82.
[66] Muller, *Letters*, p. 255: Gardiner to Ridley, 1547; PRO, SP 10/1, fos. 103–6: Gardiner to

We should expect this doctrinal emphasis to alter Gardiner's arguments on obedience, and to some extent this is so. He saw that even if, and when, the statutes preserving traditional beliefs were repealed, he would not desert the beliefs.[67] He had to use conscience, the separation of divine from human direction in worldly affairs which he so mistrusted in Bucer. When interrogated in Edward's reign, he emphasised that this was consistent, that unlike his questioners he had always been of the true catholic faith, that there was no scriptural justification for the doctrine of faith alone, that no king should use a servant's obligation to obey as a means to make him do wrong.[68] He even indulged in the sort of cheek which so infuriated him when used by protestants: when the council forbade him to preach controversially, he expounded the eucharist on the grounds that the doctrine of the altar was clearly established by scripture and therefore not controversial![69]

And yet: the short-term constitutional arguments for orthodoxy which we noted in the early 1540s still survived under these less promising circumstances.[70] Gardiner fought a holding action against the council, literally hour by hour: 'this is the law of the realm this day', he stated, hanging on to the non-repeal of the six articles, as if the passage of time could somehow be suspended.[71] Although he was saying repeatedly that he would stand by God's laws even if protestants repealed godly legislation it was still a comfort to reflect that what Cranmer imagined was truth was not yet even man's laws.[72] He bombarded the council with technicalities which he claimed would invalidate any repeal of Henrician legislation: Henry had produced reform through common assent, whereas the Edwardian council was a mere clique, manipulating a monarch into contentious legislation which lacked support. The case could be strengthened by dwelling on Edward's youth: the supremacy could not be employed by a minor to upset his father's blend of reform and essentials, for the six articles and king's book were based on God's law – 'or so the realm hath agreed'.[73] This mixture of scriptural certainty with positivist afterthought raises rather than dispels doubts. Gardiner seems to be using God's name to halt positive law at a point which suits him. The Edwardian council felt that Gardiner's constitutional arguments came into the

Somerset, 1547, with episcopacy under siege; Muller, *Letters*, pp. 372, 398, 418: Gardiner to Somerset on Erasmus, and the dangers of the 'lower sort'; Muller, *Gardiner and Tudor Reaction*, p. 18; Foxe, VI, p. 190; Muller, *Letters*, p. 207, on toughness; Baumer, *Early Tudor Kingship*, p. 61; McConica, *English Humanists*, pp. 236–7. See note 108; G. Redworth, 'Stephen Gardiner', pp. 200–41, has uncovered the tensions between conciliation and disagreement in this period.

[67] Muller, *Letters*, pp. 311–12; Foxe, VI, pp. 72, 190.

[68] Foxe, VI, p. 76: Muller, *Letters*, p. 447.

[69] Foxe, VI, p. 110; Muller, *Letters*, p. 402.

[70] Loades, *Oxford Martyrs*, pp. 54–61, for good coverage of this point; cf. Muller, *Gardiner and Tudor Reaction*, p. 300.

[71] BL, Add. MS 32091, fos. 142–3; Add. 28571, fos. 6–9, to the Council 1547.

[72] Foxe, VI, p. 48.

[73] Muller, *Letters*, pp. 420–1, on Edward's youth; Foxe, VI, p. 52; PRO, SP 10/1, fos. 103–6, on the status of bishops.

same category: what made Edward's parliaments unrepresentative, apart from Gardiner's own exclusion from the Lords?[74] And what made it acceptable to prepare secular legislation in a minority, but taboo to touch anything involving the supremacy?

So there were obvious weaknesses in his constitutional arguments, and the short-term adherence to statute confused or detracted from the appeal to God's precepts and conscience. As we have seen, this mixture reflected Gardiner's training and pragmatic temperament; using the small print to defend unwritten verities of faith was second nature. But it is too easy to stop there, or to suggest that he was avoiding real issues by escaping into general theories of parliamentary sovereignty.[75] The pragmatic touches were severely and minutely tactical, as they were in the dispute with Bucer. Gardiner had seen Bucer's challenge to the authority of law as his most vulnerable point, and had attacked it: in Somerset's case, he knew the protector relied heavily on proclamation, showed impatience or fear of parliament, and lacked unanimity on the council for his Scottish policy.[76] So a conservative who stressed Henry's greatness, recalled the solidity of support for the Henrician legislation and the thrust of the proclamations act in exalting statute, pointed to the signs from Mülhberg that defiance of an erastian conservative monarch leads heretics rapidly to ruin – such a conservative could hope for nods of anxious approval on the council and considerable support in the political nation.[77] He played the card for all it was worth: the illegal persecution of a cleric today would be the laity's problem tomorrow; the repeal of Henry's statutes would imply the impermanence of Edward's.[78] Cranmer acknowledged the potency of this argument by advising against religious innovation in a troubled minority.[79] In this context, the mixture of appeals to conscience with observations (however flawed) on the supremacy shows acumen and bite rather than mere 'convenience'.[80] Scoring points off Cranmer on the details of patristic interpretation and off Somerset on the moral and political obligation to obey Henrician statute, was designed as a defence for what Gardiner saw as spiritual essentials.

This interpretation is not, naturally, the only possible one, and it can coexist with others. Gardiner's position in 1550, when he showed signs of obeying the ecclesiastical laws of 1549 after all, so long as he did not have to say his earlier objections were erroneous, looks very similar to the line he took in 1532 on clerical privilege, and in 1554 on Mary's marriage – namely, resistance, then

---

[74] Muller, *Letters*, pp. 443–4. [75] Cf. Baumer, *Early Tudor Kingship*, p. 61.

[76] M. L. Bush, *The Government Policy of the Protector Somerset* (London, 1975). Cf. Foxe, VI, p. 25, for tactlessness on Scots; Baumer, *Early Tudor Kingship*, p. 188.

[77] Foxe, VI, pp. 140–50, for the council's confidence that Gardiner must acquiesce; Muller, *Letters*, pp. 388–91, on Somerset's disregard for law; BL, Add. MS 29546, fo. 9, leading into the Mülhberg reference.

[78] BL, Add. MS 32091, fos. 142–3: Foxe, VI, p. 311.

[79] Foxe, V. p. 563. [80] Cf. Baumer, *Early Tudor Kingship*, p. 188.

attempted modification, then making the best of a bad job, a balancing of loyalty to statute with a troubled conscience. But the Edwardian council was not content with that level of conformity, heresy was in any case accelerating, and Gardiner spent the rest of the reign in prison.[81] The point is that this gives further insight into his agonised line-drawing: he wanted to conform, for legislation and legal manoeuvring provided for Gardiner the process by which truth was advanced in this world, and he wanted to be out there, scheming;[82] yet for Gardiner the truth was also manifestly receding in these laws. He drew his line rather later, and with more tactical curves in it, than historians at their comfortable desks may think respectable; but an ambitious timeserver should have opted for obedience with much less ambiguity and saved himself all that trouble.

The complexity of this picture of motivation is consolidated by a doctrinal postscript to the reign. Gardiner's ambiguity of approach is reflected in uncharacteristic touches of humility which illustrate the uncertainties of the period. He admitted he 'might percase chaung' over doctrine; he confessed he could not precisely explain how Christ was present at the eucharist.[83] And yet he 'stayed' on this very issue. Like Cranmer in his repeated Marian recantations, like so many clerics in this period with their mixture of conventional and controversial beliefs, he was acknowledging the confusion of the schism, and the pressure to conform. We are under no obligation to assume with Foxe that uncertainties prove insincerity, or to accept the notion that Gardiner's Edwardian heart-searching condemns his earlier hopes as foolish errors.[84] The stark battle-lines which we can see with hindsight in the English reformation were drawn up over time through tough individual choices.

VI

Gardiner lived just over two years after the accession of Mary, and from that period has left us two particularly interesting problems concerning consistency and loyalty: the return to Roman obedience, and the posthumously published treatise on English history written for the benefit of Philip of Spain. First, we consider his chancellorship, in which he faced obvious problems of credibility. The author of the *De Vera* was credited by protestants with the decision to return to Rome; the man who bastardised Mary, said Turner, was himself the spawn of the papacy.[85]

[81] Loades, *Oxford Martyrs*, pp. 56, 227; cf. Muller, *Letters*, pp. 440, 441, 449, for the pressures. See note 108.

[82] Cf. W. S. Holdsworth, *A History of English Law* (London, 1921–52), II, p. 129, on the significance of legislation for the moral statesman.

[83] Muller, *Letters*, p. 395; Cranmer, *On the Lord's Supper*, p. 59. See note 108.

[84] Foxe, VI, p. 259; cf. Smith, *Tudor Prelates*, p. 100, for an extraordinary contrast of Gardiner's attitude with Cranmer's alleged certainties.

[85] R. Pineas, 'William Turner and Reformation Politics' (see note 56), 196; R. Pineas, 'William Turner's Polemical Use of Ecclesiastical History' (*Renaissance Quarterly*, 33, 1980) 607.

No protestant would allow Gardiner to forget the *De Vera* or the oath to Henry. Whatever continuity we may seek in his lifelong hostility to Pole, or his abhorrence of clerical marriage, he faced the accusation of double perjury.[86] In fact, although it would not satisfy an opponent, Gardiner had been leaving himself an escape route on the papacy since his fear of heresy mounted in the 1540s: he dropped hints that popes had only 'exceded' from the truth; good remained in an idea 'whosoever hathe abused it'.[87] From such a stance Gardiner could deny the need of the pope in preserving tradition, or justify his return. But it would be a pragmatic, human view of the office. In his oath to Henry he had sworn that Roman authority was 'set up only by men'; in Edward's reign, by arguing that the whole church, or parts of it, can produce good customs, he placed papal and national decrees as parallels or alternatives; he pointed out that a bad pope can pass a good law just as Richard III put good statutes through parliament, a fascinating parallel which weighs both papal decrees and English law against something more constant; early in Mary's reign he was accused of supporting altar rather than pope, and supporting the primacy for reasons of national stability; and at the very end of his life, the Machiavellian treatise to Philip discussed below, maintains this utilitarian analysis of institutions to be neglected or preserved in the interests of peace and security.[88] It was Gardiner's advice in 1553 and 1554 to define royal power clearly and leave the pope's vague, and to respect English titles to ex-monastic land.[89] This is severely practical; it is clear that he appreciated the value of Roman reconciliation in restoring and preserving doctrine and worship, but it is too romantic to suggest with McConica that he had come to see how right More and Fisher had been.[90] Gardiner's beliefs did not reflect Fisher's or More's in the 1550s any more than in the 1530s. Many of the curiosities of interpretation of Gardiner come from regarding him as a sort of shop-soiled, malfunctioning and cowardly Fisher.

After his death came the treatise, published in 1556.[91] This is a wide-ranging historical survey of changes of dynasty and leadership, intended as advice for Philip as he sought to gain full advantage of his marriage to Mary. There has been scholarly debate on authorship, which needs no long rehearsal here.[92] There is a balance to be struck between circumstantial evidence for Gardiner's authorship, and textual errors and idiosyncrasies

[86] Muller, *Letters*, p. 180; *Cal. Sp.* XI, p. 202; Foxe, VIII, p. 73, Janelle, *DVO*, pp. 165–7, for embarrassment in Mary's reign and its causes.

[87] Muller, *Letters*, p. 482.

[88] Janelle, *DVO*, p. lix, on 'variation' and Gardiner's dislike of it; BL, Add. MS 25425, fo. 204, on the altar; Foxe, V, p. 72 on the oath; Muller, *Letters*, pp. 261, 482; P. S. Donaldson, *A Machiavellian Treatise of Stephen Gardiner* (Cambridge, 1975), p. 35.

[89] BL, Add. MS 25425, fo. 241.

[90] McConica, *English Humanists*, pp. 236–7. See note 108; G. Redworth, 'Stephen Gardiner', p. 244, for an assessment of Gardiner's motives in his view of Rome.

[91] See note 88, for reference to Donaldson's edition and close analysis in the introduction.

[92] D. Fenlon, review of Donaldson (note 88), in *Hist. Journal*, 19 (1976), 1019–23.

which cast doubt upon it. Within the limits of this paper, there is no attempt to enter the detail of that debate. Our concern is to test whether or not the postulated authorship of Gardiner would fit our pattern of his development. Donaldson, in claiming Gardiner as the author, indicates that despite the writer's debt to Machiavelli, his secular pragmatism, and his alignment with the Habsburgs, there are links with Gardiner's immediate circumstances in Mary's reign, and with his earlier outlook.[93] In these circumstances, we need to assume Gardiner's authorship in order to make our own parallels between our emerging picture, and the treatise's author as he explained himself to Philip.

Because Gardiner has been identified by Harbison and later commentators as an opponent of the Spanish marriage, this detailed advice to Philip can present further suggestion of deviousness.[94] It would be foolish, indeed, to discount self-interest in giving service to the most powerful ruler in Europe. Gardiner had seen Mary's capabilities, and as a result she hardly gets a mention in the treatise; he expected Philip's son to rule England; and – a general human characteristic – he would not have expected to die before Philip read his advice. But there is no problem in fitting the treatise into Gardiner's diplomatic record without resorting to self-interest. His enforced exile in Paris in the 1530s gave him a deep mistrust of the French; he was commissioned by Henry VIII in the 1540s to negotiate imperial marriage alliances; his reaction to Mühlberg and the protestant league show his imperial sympathies; and standard humanist belief on European peace and defence against the Turks had singled Philip out as the best hope.[95] It is in line with Gardiner the realist to doubt the wisdom of the match at first, and then settle for the necessity in the end, given the right legal limits for which Gardiner fought in parliament and which are mirrored in the treatise.[96] Support for Philip was also logical in the context of Gardiner's hatred of heresy. Once more, we must beware of expecting hindsight in Gardiner: the Spanish influence at court and the degrading loss of Calais heightened Mary's unpopularity and identified protestants with patriotism, but those developments should not prevent our appreciation of Gardiner's motives at the time. It is difficult for a politician to see that his strongest card may enable his opponents to win the game.

We also know that Gardiner, throughout his career, was a clericalist rather than papalist. So there is no difficulty in accepting as Gardiner's the comments in the treatise on the diplomatic cunning and insincerity of popes. Gardiner's memories of Clement VII would give him sympathy with Philip's problems with Paul IV. The relativism and historical perspective displayed in

---

[93] P. S. Donaldson, 'Bishop Gardiner, Machiavellian' (*Hist. Journal*, 23 (i), 1980), 1–16.
[94] E. H. Harbison, *Rival Ambassadors at the Court of Queen Mary* (Princeton, 1940).
[95] PRO, SP 1/211, fos. 130–1; Donaldson, *Treatise*, p. 13.
[96] *Cal. Sp.* XI, pp. 338, 347; XII, pp. 5, 242; cf. Donaldson, *Treatise*, pp. 27–33, 132–5.

the treatise find echoes right through Gardiner's career, from his assessment of the pope's claims in the *De Vera*, through his arguments with Cranmer in Edward's reign about judging the truth of ideas by their longevity and history, to the pragmatic line on the primacy we have already noted in Mary's reign.[97] Certainly, the treatise does not look like the book of a Roman clericalist; but it could certainly have been written by the sort of clericalist we have seen Gardiner to be.

Then there is the vexed question of morals, the picture of a Machiavellian Gardiner as advocate of underhand amorality and superficial godliness to flatter the crowd and keep the throne; the values of Machiavelli's 'Prince', extensively quoted in the treatise, seem distant from the Gardiner we noted in Edward's reign. Donaldson notes that Gardiner's justification for offering pragmatic Machiavellian advice to Philip was two-pronged: first the separation, with Machiavelli, of what is from what ought to be; then the rather strained application of Machiavellian precepts to the notion of sacred kingship, either by equating the unpredictability of God's ways and kings', or by elevating unity and obedience into a justification for any means of government.[98]

There are several observations to be made on this prospect of Gardiner's view of God's law and man's. First, Gardiner relished some aspects of his reputation for 'wiliness', and took scholarly pleasure in disputation; we should expect him to gain positive enjoyment from the exercise of applying Machiavelli to English conditions. Secondly, although the plagiarism of large sections of Machiavelli is most interesting, it may be suggested that if Machiavelli had not existed English politicians of the mid-sixteenth century would have had little difficulty in inventing him. The arguments of renaissance political thought in Italy arose from a confused and hectic confrontation of an ailing church and a large number of princes and cities, divided and febrile; for different reasons, the pressures of Edward's and Mary's reigns, light years rather than half a century from Henry VII, threw up another rich confusion of dilemmas. There is nothing remarkable about the appeal of 'what is' when there are so many dangerous and conflicting versions of 'what ought to be'. Thirdly, it is not surprising to find an able polemicist borrowing from appropriate sources at need. We saw Gardiner quoting in the *De Vera* from the scriptural sources of reformers he mistrusted, in order to make immediate ecclesiastical points against the pope; it did not mean that he was a protestant, any more than his emphasis on royal authority meant that he discounted parliament.[99] No more do the massive quotations of tactics from Machiavelli prove he shared the underlying moral assumptions of the *Prince*. Important though the *De Vera* and the treatise are, these set pieces are less likely to reveal

---

[97] Donaldson, *Treatise*, p. 149; Janelle, *DVO*, p. 151; Cranmer, *On the Lord's Supper*, p. 13; Donaldson, *Treatise*, pp. 143–4.   [98] Donaldson, *Hist. Journal* (1980), 12–13.
[99] Baumer, *Early Tudor Kingship*, pp. 61, 84, 166; Janelle, *DVO*, liv.

the inner Gardiner than his letters or his long disputations with Cranmer. We are back with Foxe's condemnation again: does Gardiner's facility with worldly argument (a good lawyer) automatically make him a 'naughty divine' and a 'worse bishop'?

For the blend of Machiavellian pragmatism with the sacred notion of kingship is reminiscent of balancing acts Gardiner was performing throughout the period.[100] We have seen him (often uncomfortably) mixing secular relativism with eternal verities. Here he distinguishes between political rules and individual morality, and then adds the conventional pieties: even though they are unnecessary to the argument, they were obviously necessary to Gardiner's peace of mind. Necessary, because this is the bishop who, five years before, was accused by Cranmer of an obsession with transubstantiation. The advice to Philip to use his English power cautiously, and his concern for his own advancement, are compatible with the Gardiner who strove for strict limits in the marriage treaty, to secure Philip as a guardian of catholic belief and internal order, to protect peace and orthodoxy without involving too many Spaniards.

VII

We are now in a position to consider a few conclusions. Not easy answers, for those are precisely what the evidence here suggests we must shun. Wolsey, Fisher and More indicated in their dying rhetoric that the distinction between serving God and obeying the king was simple and fixed. Gardiner, like them, was in fact pulled by more loyalties than two, none of them straightforward.

To begin with his loyalty to his own advancement and survival, the one which tends to dominate assessments of his work. Since legists in the church were civil servants, trained for administration and high office, Gardiner's worldly ambition was natural. He was noted for pulling rank and fretting at disagreements. He poured rancour on those who thwarted him. When he denied plotting, he was preaching subversively. The *De Vera* was a life-saver, the treatise a bid for influence. There need be no argument about that.

But it is important not to stop there. Gardiner was consciously staying in the battle and fighting for his beliefs: as he said in 1547, he had lived long enough in the crisis to judge religious issues over an extended period, and he clearly saw the longevity and acquired experience as achievements and a recommendation in themselves.[101] As we have seen, not everyone would agree: both papists and protestants resented Gardiner's line in the 1530s because it offered hope to both that he might be an ally, only to prove in the end a disappointment to both. His erastian conservatism, his administrative attempt

---

[100] Donaldson, *Hist. Journal* (1980), 9: 'one is struck by the congruence of the religious argument and the Machiavellian one'.
[101] Muller, *Gardiner and Tudor Reaction*, p. 297.

to adjust and preserve traditional beliefs and customs under unpromising conditions, could be brushed aside as time-serving. Latimer summed up the extremist viewpoint, familiar in all ages, when he said that half a papist was worse than a whole one.[102] But in Gardiner's polemics we can see his rancour often taking the form of a fierce loyalty to his training and background in royal service and the episcopate, and this combined pride, condemned as arrogance by Bucer and Cranmer, or by catholics at Louvain, had a much wider significance than self-importance. It mattered to Gardiner to ridicule the pope's claims, impugn the expertise of reforming theologians who mocked him as a mere lawyer, even win squabbles over the pronunciation of Greek at Cambridge, because one man's reputation as a controversialist could decide his influence over others in the definition of God's law and right policy: the credibility game had high stakes.[103] Paradoxically, of course, prejudice and political in-fighting accelerated the fragmentation of authority, and led to scepticism as much as to certainty, but that has never been a reason for one side to back down. Gardiner's position on the erastian compromise was similar in this respect to Hooker's on Elizabethan unity: once he had to explain in painful detail why his ecclesiastical traditions were better than his opponents', the cause was lost anyway. Acts of uniformity only multiply when uniformity is a thing of the past, and no one who drafts them wins many thanks.

Like the erosion of the authority of the Roman church, the triumph of nationalism over such ideas as the seamless garment of united Christendom is seen as another modern trend which took a giant step in the schism. Against such a summary, Gardiner's *De Vera* seems an important influence for the new, and the return to Rome and the treatise to Philip look like retrograde steps. But again it is not so simple. On the one hand, national feeling was nothing new in the sixteenth century: on the other, the scholarly and diplomatic network which criss-crossed Europe continued to influence reformers just as much as conservatives for a long time, with Cranmer blithely anticipating union with the German protestants, and Elizabethan puritans looking towards Zurich or Geneva as home. So Gardiner's intensely personal feeling for Henry VIII is not to be seen as sophisticated modern nationalism, or a mystical aura, but the direct result of two outstandingly able Tudor kings; and the vulnerability of their work can be seen in Gardiner's contrasting and less than reverent attitude to Edward in minority, to Mary's naïveté, and to Elizabeth as a nuisance in Mary's reign. He looked for conservative stability, doctrinal and political, from Henry VIII; he despaired of it under Edward; and in the context of Mary's weakness, the treatise to Philip was a shrewd appeal for the same stability to the person most likely to provide it. There is

---

[102] Latimer, *Sermons* (Parker Society, 1844), p. 266.
[103] E.g. BL, Add. MS 28571, fos. 15–16; Cranmer, *On the Lord's Supper*, p. 157; Muller, *Letters*, p. 137, on Greek; cf. Muller, *Gardiner and Tudor Reaction*, p. 297.

consistency in Gardiner's attempt thus to freeze a revolutionary situation at a stage he most desired or least feared. His choices between Henry and the pope, Mary and Elizabeth, and Philip and an English husband for Mary, were comprehensible in these terms as well as the parallel factor of personal ambition. There is nothing shocking about that; it only looks an incoherent performance against a foreshortened perspective of the inexorable march of English nationalism.

And it does bring us back to Gardiner's loyalty to God's law. We have seen him persistently juggling with short-term constitutional arguments and pragmatic tactics in support of his beliefs, but it is important to do him justice by quoting his statement of priorities to Cranmer in Edward's reign. Traditional beliefs, he said, had the support of 'the scriptures plain, the plain doctors, and plain Acts of Parliament'.[104] His regard for statute was deep and sincere but when all is said and done, statute is placed third here. That list of 'plain' supporters for his beliefs shows both the now desperate insistence that questions of doctrine were straightforward, and the same mixture of loyalties and influences which proved that they were not. Life did not get easier for these conservatives as they sought a path through the maze. Muller speculates that Gardiner would have found the eventual defiance of the Edwardian supremacy to the point of martyrdom as illogical in himself as he later found the obstinacy of the Marian protestants:[105] but this cannot be so, for the centre and exit of this maze were 'the scriptures plain', and Gardiner was slowly working towards a point where the logic of conscience overrode obedience to statute.

Nonetheless, if sincerity is to be judged over twenty years as a refusal to bend in the fierce winds of change then Gardiner fares shakily. But it is worth considering the idea that one form of consistency is shown when a politician and thinker, faced by developments he did not anticipate, reacts in a manner not previously explicit in his work but very much in line with values previously maintained. Gardiner met situations in which some of his various loyalties, none of them negligible or slight, were incompatible. The secular and transitory nature of his manoeuvres does not as a matter of course invalidate the spiritual integrity of his goal. His unpleasing personality does not as a matter of course make his motives unworthy. If we do ultimately conclude that this flexibility was blameworthy, we should make sure we have understood it first.

For he was suffering the pressures of a revolution. That word has itself been a battleground in reformation studies, and needs no re-play here. It is enough to say that just as the radical Calvinists used the traditional vocabulary of canonical debate to change the political thought of the century, so the fertility of the English schism can be seen in the erastian, theocratic, passive and

---

[104] Foxe, VI, p. 47.   [105] Muller, *Gardiner and Tudor Reaction*, p. 298.

rebellious theories which emerged from the same texts and examples.[106] We have fastened on one symptom – the penetration of relativism and secularism into the thinking of a strong conservative. Just to show that Gardiner was not alone in being battered by the changes and in absorbing them, consider Aske in the 1530s. In defending northern traditions against Cromwell's alien assaults, Aske mentioned the invalidity of many reformation statutes if Catherine of Aragon should prove after all to be truly married to Henry. What an 'if' from Aske, and what an example of accepting an opponent's scepticism while arguing against its results![107]

So at a time when canon law was proving ineffective in answering key questions, when old certainties were increasingly uncertain, when statute was moving into the area of doctrine yet was itself seen as vulnerable, Gardiner's choice of secular legalism, consciously and unconsciously, to cut at the ground round heresy is understandable. That was one way to play the game of the moment.

But playing the game that way did not prove the way to win. One of the reasons for Gardiner's bad reputation is that he lost; and however much we try to absolve Gardiner from the unreasonable demands of hindsight, we can still use our hindsight to suggest why he was wrong. There was another way for another loyal and confused cleric, also accused of wavering unworthily, to respond to the schism: Cranmer said that in so great a confusion of things so like, how shall a man know truth except by scriptures? Gardiner would have disagreed over what the scriptures meant, but would have agreed with the words themselves: but the point is that Cranmer's appeal to scripture had a credibility that Gardiner lacked. For Edwardian protestantism, having suffered from a reputation for greed and secular opportunism comparable with that which so bedevilled the English church before the schism, was released by Marian persecution to project a simplified, cleansed scriptural truth, all the more appealing because of the generation of confusion which preceded it. This did not occur overnight, but it was dramatic for all that, and Marian conservatives were caught between the conviction that the outrage of heresy must be seen to be attacked, and the growing awareness that persecution can be counter-productive. Although the Roman church in Europe found inspiration to fight fire with evangelical fire, this was a line which Gardiner was ill-qualified to pursue. He was the product of a church whose legalism and lack of evangelism had outweighed its traditions and authority and had invited the reformation; and he carried its instincts into the 1540s and 1550s, and helped to colour Mary's reign with the same shade of grey. His brand of conservatism did not take heresy lightly, kept sight of underlying spiritual values and visible traditions of worship beyond which it would 'stay', and re-thought its

[106] Cf. Skinner, *Modern Thought*, I, pp. xiv–xv.
[107] PRO, Exch. TR Misc. Books, vol. 119, fo. 105; cf. D. M. Loades, *Reign of Queen Mary* (New York, 1979), p. 49, on the contrast of conservative language and revolutionary implications.

relationships with secular authority and positive law. But his was a consistency which rather than offering a visionary escape from his predicament of conflicting loyalties, only gave him nimble, pugnacious footwork within it. And that, while assisting understanding rather than dismissive condemnation of Gardiner, helps to show why heresy was ultimately so successful.[108]

[108] This paper had almost gone to press before I had the opportunity to read Dr G. Redworth's stimulating and important DPhil. thesis: 'The Political and Diplomatic Career of Stephen Gardiner, 1538–51' (Oxford, 1985). I am deeply indebted to Dr Redworth for his kind permission to read, use and make reference to his work. In a number of my footnotes, I have added a reference to this note 108 to acknowledge the important material in many areas and indicate some issues of interpretation. These particular acknowledgements deal with Gardiner's role in ecclesiastical policy-making in Henry VIII's las years (my notes 35, 36; thesis, early chapters); with Gardiner's attempts to find a modus vivendi with Edward VI's Council (my notes 66, 81; thesis, pp. 200–41); and with Gardiner's reasons for changing wording and attitude on doctrine and the papacy in Edward's reign (my notes 59, 83, 90; thesis, pp. 223–4, 244, 246). In general, the discussion in Chapter 8 (pp. 200–41) of Gardiner's relations with the Edwardian Council is most enlightening on his attempts to conform, and on the confusion, negotiation and hope involved in the process. There is also a picture of a misunderstood Gardiner, genuinely striving to be conciliatory on doctrine, not grasping why he should be considered such a threat: this is a different image from the tactical Gardiner, winning time, hoping for re-gained influence, delaying ominous change, which has emerged in this paper. I look forward eagerly to the prospect of seeing Dr Redworth's present and subsequent research in this area in print, and only regret that the timing of publication has placed this limit on my response to his work.

Bondmen under the Tudors*

DIARMAID MacCULLOCH

IMITATION being the sincerest form of flattery, this paper borrows its title directly from a study published eight decades ago by Alexander Savine, one of the great pioneers in the generation of F. W. Maitland who sought to use legal history to illuminate the social and economic history of England. Its purpose is to provide an interim report on our present knowledge of serfdom in the Tudor age. Savine made it clear that serfdom remained a reality into the sixteenth century; what can be done now is to paint this picture in even brighter colours. For serfdom was an institution surprisingly tenacious and widespread through the early Tudor age, and its eventual disappearance was the subject of legal and financial campaigns of thoroughness and ingenuity.[1]

The survival of personal unfreedom has been largely concealed from us because after its practical demise at the end of Elizabeth's reign, it was in no one's interest to remember it outside antiquarian circles. Indeed, there were some surprisingly influential people who had a vested interest in forgetting the whole institution. The case of the mayor of Bristol who was harassed by Lord Stafford during 1586–7 about his supposed villein status is well known; the mayor was probably safe as citizen of a great city with a custom of conferring legal freedom on serfs after a year and a day's residence.[2] However, there were

---

* I am most grateful to the following who have helped in the preparation of this paper: Simon Adams, John Baker, Christine Cook, Nesta Evans, Steve Gunn, Christopher Haigh, Felicity Heal, Phyllis Hembry, Roy Hunnisett, Eric Kerridge, Christopher Kitching, Peter Northeast, Dorothy Owen, Conrad Russell, Sir Robert Somerville, Ann Warden, Katherine Wyndham, Joyce Youings, Michael Zell. The greatest (though indirect) debt is to Geoffrey Elton, who many years ago warned me that if I had to work in Common Pleas, 'Heaven help you'.

All county locations mentioned have been standardised to the 1900 county boundaries.

[1] A. Savine, 'Bondmen under the Tudors', *Trans. Roy. Hist. Soc.*, 2nd series, 17 (1903), pp. 235–89 (hereafter Savine). The best recent discussions of serfdom, both with valuable references, are E. Kerridge, *Agrarian Problems in the Sixteenth Century and After* (London, 1969), pp. 90–3, and J. H. Baker, ed., *The Reports of Sir John Spelman*, Selden Society, XCIII–XCIV (1976–7), II, pp. 187–90 (hereafter Baker, *Spelman*).

[2] *Acts of the Privy Council*, XIV, pp. 48, 100, 153, 190; XV, pp. 69, 303–4. On Bristol and freedom cf. e.g. PRO, C 1/739/22.

some serfs in prominent places during Elizabeth's reign whose status cannot be in doubt; among the bondmen of the crown were a fellow of All Souls, Oxford, and a fellow of Peterhouse, Cambridge. Dr Daniel Dunn built on his All Souls fellowship to become a master of requests and dean of arches; several times an M.P., he would gain a knighthood and employment on foreign embassies from James I. The inquisition into bondmen of the Suffolk honour of Eye in 1576 tactfully glossed over both his name and that of his brother William (fellow of Exeter College, Oxford), but the patent rolls were necessarily more pitiless in recording the Dunns' manumissions later that year. Nevertheless, Sir Daniel would posthumously fool the *History of Parliament* into thinking that he was of Welsh rather than of servile East Anglian descent.[3] Dr John King (bondman of the duchy of Lancaster's Norfolk soke of Gimingham) went on from his Peterhouse fellowship to die in 1608 as a canon of Windsor; three clerical relatives from the King clan mentioned in his will included a fellow of Merton and a scholar of Trinity, Oxford. It is in the light of the sensibilities of such clerical escapees from the world of villeinage that one must view the assertion by King's fellow-canon of Windsor, William Harrison, that there were no 'slaves and bondmen' in England, or the dismissive remarks about the continued existence of English serfdom made by Dunn's fellow-civilian Sir Thomas Smith. The truth was uncomfortably different: secular lawyers and surveyors gave a more accurate picture, as Savine was quick to point out.[4]

Our difficulties in assessing the survival of bondage under the Tudors are compounded by the problems of the sources. There is no doubt that letters of manumission were still commonly being granted to villeins by royal and private lords throughout the sixteenth century, but their survival is rare; once safely free, few families showed the pride in their villein origins which led one fifteenth-century chief baron of the exchequer to treasure the letters of freedom granted to his father and uncle.[5] Otherwise, survival even of copies in royal and private registers is remarkably patchy: very little of crown manumissions, for instance, before the last great campaign managed by Sir Henry Lee during the 1570s, although we know that major royal commissions for raising funds through manumissions were issued for augmentations and duchy of Lancaster manors in 1544 and 1550, and also that manumissions provided a steady source of fees for the clerks of the signet and privy seal up to the 1570s.[6] Apart from this, some of the most significant sources on Tudor villeinage lie concealed in the formidably effective hiding-place provided by the plea rolls of

[3] Eye inquisition: PRO E 178/2151. Manumissions: *Calendar of Patent Rolls, Elizabeth I*, VIII, nos. 705–6. Cf. *History of Parliament 1558–1603*, II, p. 66. Knighthood would have brought Sir Daniel automatic manumission in the end: cf. Baker, *Spelman*, II, p. *189*.
[4] PRO, D.L. 41/13/20, no. 7; King's will is PCC, 114 Windebanck. Savine, pp. 238–43.
[5] R. A. Griffiths, ed., *Patronage, the Crown and the Provinces* (Gloucester, 1981), p. 173.
[6] Commissions: *LP* xix(1), nos. 278/5, 278/67, 812/77; xix (2), no. 800/8 (all 1544); *Calendar of Patent Rolls, Edward VI*, III, p. 215 (1550). Fees dispute: PRO, SP 12/151/58–63.

the court of common pleas, as will be demonstrated; turning to other sources, chasing villeinage into private archives would require a full-scale research team to face the vast but miscellaneous storehouse of sixteenth-century manorial records scattered throughout England.

The figures given in Table 1 are therefore in no sense complete, but they do give a picture of the distribution and ownership of Tudor serfs which is unlikely to be altered by further investigation. From the limited material available in his time, Savine was able to find serfs on some eighty manors in twenty-six counties (in reality twenty-four) at any time during the Tudor period:[7] I can say that on the day when King Richard III was alive and dead, there was a minimum of four hundred manors in thirty English counties and in Wales which retained serfs. In the first decade of Elizabeth's reign, there were still one hundred manors in twenty-one English counties and in Wales; the Elizabethan figure in particular is likely to be a gross underestimate, and it would probably not be wildly wrong to double both figures.

The figures in the table also help us to demolish another myth assiduously propagated by Sir Thomas Smith: that it was the clergy who were particularly slow to free their villeins, lagging well behind the laity. In fact in 1485 well over half the manors known to retain villeins were in the hands of the crown or private lay owners; in the 1560s, when the church had lost the majority of the other half, about ninety per cent of recorded villeins were in the hands of the crown or of private lay owners. Savine's scepticism about Smith's reliability as a witness is amply justified. One can indeed point to certain ecclesiastical lords who did act as the backbone of the feudal institution; Glastonbury Abbey, with its great west country estates, is an obvious and oft-quoted example.[8] Yet even Glastonbury was granting manumissions piecemeal in the decades before its dissolution: among churchmen, one could also contrast the very large-scale programme of manumission being carried out on the Ely cathedral estates between the 1470s and the 1510s, or the lesser campaign under Abbot Braunch of St Peter's Gloucester between 1505 and 1510.[9] Among secular lords, the Howard family was as tenacious of villeins on its manors as any ecclesiastic; it was indeed two former Howard manors in East Anglia which provide us with the last known case at common law concerning villeinage and the last reference to villein status so far found.[10] It is particularly noticeable

[7] Savine, pp. 246–8, 281–6. His references to serfs in Kent and Nottinghamshire are wrongly located.
[8] Glastonbury dissolution survey by Richard Pollard and Thomas Moyle, pr. T. Hearne, ed., *Peter Langtoft's Chronicle* (2 vols., Oxford, 1725), II, pp. 343–88; cf. the surveys of 1515–18, BL, Add. MS 3034, BL, Egerton MS 3134, BL, Harley MS 3961, with references to manumission at Add. 3034, fos. 108ᵛ, 134ᵛ, 141ʳ; Harl. 3961, fos. 19ᵛ, 123ʳ.
[9] ULC, EDR, G/2/3, between nos. 255 and 471; Gloucester Cathedral Library, Register C, beween nos. 88 and 175.
[10] *Pigg* v. *Caley: English Reports* LXXIV, Noy 27: PRO, CP 40/2009, m. 1966, referring to a dispute at Wroxham (Norfolk). Suffolk RO, Ipswich, HA 66/3/26, custom roll of Earl Soham manor, 1635 (pr. *East Anglian Notes and Queries* new series II, 1887–8, *passim*).

Table 1   *Distribution of manors with serfs in England 1485–1560*

County	1485					1560			
	A	B	C	D	Total	A	B	C	Total
Beds.	–	–	–	3	3	3	–	–	3
Berks.	1	2	–	3	6	1	1	–	2
Bucks.	2	4	–	1	7	2	–	–	2
Cambs.	–	2	9	–	11	–	–	3	3
Cornw.	5	–	–	–	5	5	–	–	5
Derbys.	1	4	–	–	5	–	–	–	–
Devon	1	10	4	3	18	–	2	–	2
Dorset	2	3	–	1	6	2	–	–	2
Essex	1	4	–	1	6	2	–	–	2
Gloucs.	–	7	1	15	23	–	4	–	4
Hants./IW	3	1	5	4	13	5	–	1	6
Heref.	–	–	–	1	1	1	–	–	1
Herts.	1	1	1	2	5	–	–	–	–
Hunts.	–	–	2	2	4	–	–	–	–
Leics.	–	5	–	–	5	–	–	–	–
Lincs.	3	21	1	5	30	5	1	1	7
Norf.	2	49	7	8	66	4	10	3	17
Nthts.	1	–	–	2	3	–	–	–	–
Notts.	1	2	–	–	3	1	–	–	1
Oxfs.	1	–	1	–	2	–	1	–	1
Rutl.	–	1	–	–	1	–	–	–	–
Soms.	–	21	9	36	66	4	9	1	14
Staff.	–	1	–	–	1	–	–	–	–
Suff.	–	39	6	4	49	4	13	1	18
Surr.	–	3	1	2	6	1	1	–	2
Suss.	–	17	3	2	22	1	2	–	3
Warws.	2	1	–	1	4	–	–	–	–
Wilts.	1	6	3	13	23	–	7	–	7
Worcs.	–	–	2	2	4	–	1	1	2
Yorks.	–	2	–	–	2	–	–	–	–
Totals	28	206	55	111	400	41	52	11	104

Key to symbols above
A   Crown, duchy of Lancaster and duchy of Cornwall manors
B   Manors with private lay lords
C   Manors owned by monastic and secular cathedral chapters/bishops or by secular ecclesiastical corporations
D   Manors owned by monasteries or nunneries

that Norfolk's and Suffolk's large number of small manors in lay hands were even more prominent in preserving serfdom than the great manors of ecclesiastical giants like Ely cathedral or Bury abbey.

What else can one learn from the distribution patterns of manors with serfs? The most obvious fact is that by 1485, serfdom was virtually dead north of the Trent. For instance, the 'bondagii' or 'bondagers' of the Durham cathedral estates were far from being in a state of personal unfreedom, even though (like many non-servile copyholders in the south of England) they were in theory bound to perform labour services on the demesne as part of their tenure; there had once been genuine bondmen on these estates.[11] In many areas of the north, the classical manorial system had never taken firm roots; already in the thirteenth century there was little practical difference between villein and freeman in Northumbria. The demands of defence on the border with Scotland had meant that many tenures had developed in their own way to provide military manpower: tenant right, for example, or the cornage tenure of the Lake Counties.[12]

Within the lowland zone, the survival of serfdom was markedly regionalised. It was at its strongest in the coastal counties, with the ancient exception of Kent, and at its weakest in the Midlands. Looking at the distribution patterns, it seems that most serfs had no head for heights and an affinity for water. Three patterns of survival are prominent: wetlands, river-valley systems and the heavy soils of East Anglia. Consider wetlands: in the west country, the Somerset Levels provided one of the largest concentrations of Tudor serfs in England. In eastern England, the fens from Norfolk to Northamptonshire and the Lincolnshire marshes running from the Wash right up to Grimsby formed another area of large-scale survival. Along the south coast, survival can be described almost entirely in terms of river-basins: from west to east, the Tamar, the Dart and its adjoining coast, the Exe and its tributaries, the Dorset Stour, the Hampshire and Wiltshire Avon and its tributaries, and the Sussex Ouse. The exception in the sequence to prove the rule is a curious little group of manors, divided between several secular and ecclesiastical lords, on the South Downs between Steyning and Lewes. The Severn valley, with the western fringe of the Cotswolds, was also a centre for serfs. East Anglia fits into neither of these patterns: here, distribution was fairly even within the heavier soils of the 'wood-pasture' county of east Suffolk and south and east Norfolk, spreading into north-east Norfolk but otherwise less frequent in the lighter-soil 'sheep-corn' region.

---

[11] J. T. Fowler, ed., *Extracts from the Account Rolls of the Abbey of Durham* (3 vols., Surtees Society, XCIX, C, CIII, 1898–9, 1901), pp. 196, 558, 623, 670, 674, 676, 679, 896.

[12] E. A. Kosminsky, *Studies in the Agrarian History of England in the Thirteenth Century* (Oxford, 1956), p. 135 (hereafter Kosminsky); M. E. James, *Family, Lineage and Civil Society* (Oxford, 1974), pp. 80–1, 83, 118; S. M. Harrison, *The Pilgrimage of Grace in the Lake Counties 1536–7* (Roy. Hist. Soc. Studies in History, XXVII, 1981), pp. 66–70.

Wales was as variable as England in its patterns of survival. North Wales retained substantial numbers of bondmen in its predominantly royal lordships down to the Tudor period, with some lordships providing evidence for their survival into the mid-sixteenth century, long after the royal charter of 1507 had freed them all in Anglesey, Caernarfonshire and Merioneth. In the south-west, the evidence suggests almost total disappearance of serfdom before the Tudor period, but in the south-east a pattern more akin to the neighbouring English west country counties is apparent, thanks to such conservative English lords as St Augustine's abbey, Bristol or the dukes of Buckingham. In the case of the Buckingham estates and lordships, a determined effort was made after 1500 to revive serfdom as part of the programme of estate exploitation which made the last Stafford duke so unpopular among his tenants: a comparable move to the tightening-up by the third duke of Norfolk on his lands in eastern England some decades later.[13]

How does one explain these varied patterns? Everywhere, of course, serfs tended to be retained on manors with a settled, continuous history: great ecclesiastical corporations like cathedrals or Benedictine monasteries or estates which passed as units from lay owner to lay owner. One of the most conservative manors in England in Elizabeth's reign must have been Long Bennington in Lincolnshire, where tenurial change had been exceptionally retarded by the austere unworldliness of the Carthusians of Mount Grace before the manor was absorbed into the duchy of Lancaster.[14] However, a sample from the parade of secular owners of serfs in the Tudor period hardly suggests unworldliness: inheritors of ancient noble estates like the dukes of Norfolk, Suffolk and Buckingham, the marquises of Dorset, the earls of Oxford, Northumberland, Bath, the lords De la Warr, Bergavenny, Willoughby of Eresby; or among the county elites, such long-established families as the Pomeroys of Devon, the Copuldikes and Skipwiths of Lincolnshire, the Knyvetts and Sheltons of Norfolk, the Wentworths and Wingfields of Suffolk or the Shirleys of Sussex.

Considering this, one can perhaps hazard the suggestion that continuity in estates was greatest in the rich soils of the river estuaries and valley systems, which had proved such a magnet for the landholdings of early Benedictine foundations. In the pastoral economies of the upland regions in southern

[13] S. L. Adams, 'The Composition of 1564', *Bull. of Board of Celtic Studies*, 26 (1976), pp. 484, 489–91; T. Jones Pierce, ed. J. Beverley Smith, *Mediaeval Welsh Society* (Cardiff, 1972), pp. 61–2, 315, 322 (hereafter Jones Pierce), E. A. Lewis and J. Conway Davies, *Records of the Court of Augmentations relating to Wales and Monmouthshire* (Cardiff, 1954), pp. 310–11. On Bristol Abbey, A. Sabin, ed., *Some Manorial Accounts of St. Augustine's Abbey, Bristol*, Bristol Record Society, XXII (1960), p. 25. On Buckingham, T. B. Pugh, ed., *The Marcher Lordships of South Wales 1415–1536* (Board of Celtic Studies, Univ. of Wales History and Law series, XX, Cardiff, 1963), pp. 249, 268, 273; K. B. McFarlane, *The Nobility of Later Mediaeval England* (Oxford, 1973), pp. 51, 221, 224–6.
[14] On Long Bennington, see Savine, pp. 273–6.

England, as in the north, manorial organisation may never have been as well-developed as in the lower contours. The wetland manors which retained serfs were often late developments of the high middle ages; a significant number of manors with Tudor serfs in the Somerset levels and in the Cambridgeshire fens represent places not mentioned in the Domesday survey. These probably continued to be closely regulated by manorial organisation. In the Somerset Levels in particular, the lead in retaining serfs given by the estate management of Glastonbury Abbey and the bishop of Bath and Wells was followed by lay owners: some Levels manors which had always been in secular hands were still exacting servile dues at the beginning of the seventeenth century.[15]

Geographical factors might be complemented by trends in lordship, mode of tenure and levy of labour dues during previous centuries. The relative rarity of serfdom in the Midlands (where most of the Tudor references relate to grants of freedom before 1500) contrasts with strong sixteenth-century survival in East Anglia; one might predict this, considering the thirteenth-century evidence that even then peasant conditions were much freer in the Midlands than elsewhere, at a time when labour dues were actually increasing in the south-east and were at their heaviest in East Anglia.[16] Explanations of the survival of villeinage in Wales are complicated by the distinctively Celtic patterns of tenurial custom and the different political history of much of the country; yet north Wales retained villeins when they had long disappeared from Cardiganshire, despite the common Celtic origins of their institutions.[17] The discrepancy here would bear further investigation.

Given that serfdom's survival was considerable in the Tudor period, did it have any real meaning? It is unlikely that villeinage meant much in terms of labour dues; formalised though they are, most manorial records do not suggest that such services were of great significance by this stage. However, serfdom was a real and ever-present threat to the serf's purse: traditional payments like chevage for living out of the manor were quite clearly regularly exacted and regularly inventoried. Such fossils of the feudal system were the equivalent of the burdens which wardship imposed on tenants-in-chief higher up the social scale; if the Tudor crown was able to make a reality of a feudal survival at the top of the social pyramid, there is no reason to suppose that its subjects would neglect their own opportunities. After all, a bondman's legal status (or lack of it) remained unaltered: although he was liable to all the king's taxes and exactions of military service, he was a non-person in the eyes of the king's law. In the prerogative courts at least, a bondman might get away with entering litigation, as when in 1533 the duke of Norfolk's bondman John

---

[15] Orchard Wyndham (Somerset) MSS, surveys of customs and rentals, manors of Churchill, Rolston and Edingworth, early seventeenth century. I am most grateful to Dr Katherine Wyndham for allowing me to use these documents in the custody of her family.
[16] R. H. Hilton, *The English Peasantry in the Later Middle Ages* (Oxford, 1975), pp. 64–7, 126–7, 139; Kosminsky, pp. 175, 192–3. [17] Jones Pierce, pp. 315, 322.

Grosse of Kelsale in Suffolk headed a village crusade in star chamber litigation against the abbot of Leiston; however, the correct form was observed by chancery in the same decade, when the duke of Suffolk had to be brought in to act as the ostensible plaintiff on behalf of one of his villeins of the Suffolk manor of Frostenden.[18] Villeins could not even give evidence in the king's courts: depositions in chancery could still specify that the deponent was 'free of Blode' in the opening decades of the sixteenth century, while the church courts were still using similar formulae as late as the 1580s.[19]

Above all, there is overwhelming evidence from the fourteenth century onward that people simply hated the stigma of serfdom. This is readily apparent in sixteenth-century sources. Christopher St German expressed it in his *Doctor and Student* (1523) when he made his doctor ask if claims of villeinage 'stande with conscyence . . . yt semeth he loveth not his neyghbour as hym selfe that doeth so to hym'.[20] However, righteous indignation might shade off into prejudice. Among ordinary folk, servile status could stand in the way of marriage: two breach of promise cases in the Norwich consistory court in 1509 and 1524 hinged on the fact that the bride-to-be would not marry a bondman, and in 1520 one disappointed suitor from Buckinghamshire took his case to common pleas, claiming that an accusation of villein status had robbed him of a rich bride. As late as 1559, a Dorset bondman sent in a pathetic petition to the queen in which he spoke of 'the wante of charitie amongste som froward parsons who obiecteth ageynste your maiestyes seide poore subiecte the name of bondeman in the waye of reproch whereof your Maiestyes saide poore subiect cannott matche his poore children in matrymonye'.[21]

Two of the most striking testimonies to the reality of Tudor serfdom are two related statements from the heartland of East Anglian villeinage in the 1540s. The first came from an association of bondmen themselves: twenty-six heads of families from four Suffolk manors lately owned by the Howard family. The sudden fall from power of the third duke of Norfolk in 1546 and the seizure of his estates by the crown gave them the opportunity to seek their freedom, and they lost no time in petitioning Protector Somerset for manumission by letters patent.[22] First emphasising their service as taxpayers and soldiers alongside the king's other subjects, they went on to describe in detail their experiences as bondmen to the third Howard duke:

---

[18] Grosse: PRO, STAC 2/25/4. Frostenden: PRO, C 1/934/17.

[19] Chancery: C 1/293/11 (1510). Church courts: cf. D. Cressy, *Literacy and the Social Order* (Cambridge, 1980), p. 111 and n. (although Cressy has not seen the point of the phrase), and Canterbury and York Society, XI (1913), pp. 132–3 etc.

[20] T. F. T. Plucknett and J. L. Barton, eds., *St German's 'Doctor and Student'*, Selden Society, XCI (1974), p. 213 (hereafter *St German*).

[21] E. D. Stone and B. Cozens-Hardy, eds., *Norwich Consistory Court Depositions, 1499–1530*, Norfolk Record Society, X (1937), pp. 95, 308; PRO, CP 40/1028, m. 623 (*Boeller v Serjeaunt*); PRO, DL 44/7.

[22] PRO, C 1/1187/9.

the saied late Duke and his auncestours ... through that colour and pretense of bondage have at all tymes at their pleasure as oft and whatsoever theim lusted by their servantes and officers spoiled your saied oratours of any their landes and tenementes, gooddes and catalles that them lyked and that not onely with the most cruell and uncharitable woordes of reproche that maie be imagined and with such extremitie void of any compassion pietie or reason that your said oratours have been cast in suche despair of the world that some have dyed for thought and no small nombre have forsaken this Realme and gon prively into foren countreyes to live there and many have willfully fallen in ruine and decaie because thei knewe aforehande that whatsoever thei truly gotte with the sweate of theire broughes should by plain force and violence bee taken from them in suche sorte as neyther theimselfe should peaceably enioye any parte thereof nor yet any relief or coumforte should redounde to their wives and children by their peinfull labours and travaillis. For the saied late Duke and his officers usyn [-----] tyme to tyme towardes your saied oratours and their auncestours muche more extremite then his auncestores did, would not in any wyse permitte any of your oratours to marrye acordyng to the lawes of god ne yet to sette any of their children to schoole or to any kynde of learnyng without exaccions and fines to them to bee paied suche so great and so unreasonable as should be to thextreme detrimente and hynderance of the same so that through occasion of that and other the premisses and partely by reason of such obloquie and slaundre as ther been emongest their neighbours and other the kynges subiectes concernyng the said bondage your oratours shall not onely bee in utter discomforte and despair but also bee continually spoiled and at length undoon ...

One would hardly expect an unbiased description of the third duke of Norfolk with Protector Somerset as audience; however, the serfs' words fit the unflattering picture of the duke which emerges from his own writings. This petition was presented within two years of the East Anglian explosion of 1549 generally known as Kett's rebellion, which can be seen at least in part as a celebration of the Howards' fall. The programme of the Mousehold camp in 1549 contained a more succinct statement of bondmen's grievances which echoed their earlier appeal to 'the charitee of Christe': 'We pray thatt all bonde men may be made fre for god made all fre w^t his precious blode sheddyng'. It was appropriate, and resonant of that plea, that a quarter of a century later Robert Kett's eldest son William should be a member of two Wymondham juries on an exchequer enquiry which studiously avoided naming any living person as a bondman.[23]

This groundswell of impatience, even anguish, was eventually to meet with success. The brief and puzzling career of the 1547 act of parliament which sought to introduce slavery for vagrancy is a mark of Tudor Englishmen's distaste for personal unfreedom. By the end of the century, bond status was virtually at an end as a practical vexation, and so in contrast to its gradual consolidation in central Europe during the same period, its story during the

[23] Mousehold articles: BL, Harley MS 304, fos. 75–8. Inquisition: PRO, E 178/1550. Cf. D. N. J. MacCulloch, 'Kett's Rebellion in context', in P. Slack, ed., *Rebellion, Popular Protest and the Social Order in Early Modern England* (Cambridge, 1984), pp. 58–60.

Tudor period is one of gradual wasting illness and eventual death.[24] But why was death not more sudden? The precedents for large-scale moves to dispense with bond status were there in Wales. In 1447, for instance, Richard duke of York had shown what could be done in a single lordship by manumitting all his bondmen in the Lordship of Cydewain for a lump sum payment of 1000 marks.[25] In 1507 Henry VII followed this precedent by granting a charter for the counties of Anglesey, Caernarfon and Merioneth which among other things proclaimed general manumission for 'nativi' in these counties. What was particularly remarkable about this charter was that it made clear that the king was granting manumission for serfs who were not his property, specifically mentioning 'nativi' who were bound to the bishop of Bangor or to 'any abbots whatsoever'.[26] General manumission was therefore possible. However, the sort of wide-embracing action which could be taken in the semi-colonial setting of Henry VII's Wales would not be tolerated by the political nation of England. The Lords made that quite clear in 1536 when they rejected a general bill 'concernens Manumissionem servorum vocat. Bondmen'.[27]

The Lords knew that any such sweeping step would not simply be a blow to the common law rights of every propertied Englishman; it would be a blow to many highly placed people's exploitable assets. Throughout the sixteenth century manumission was acknowledged to be a profitable business. In 1544 the crown looked to manumission as one of its many expedients in raising cash for the bottomless pit of Henry VIII's French wars. Similarly, when the young duke of Norfolk required to act as if out of wardship in order to raise the vast sums needed to complete the reconstruction of the Howard estates after their Edwardian destruction, the act of parliament authorising his actions specified four means of getting the cash: land sales, raising finds on leases, wood sales, 'and manumysyng of bond men'.[28] Later on, Sir Henry Lee would not have gone to the considerable trouble and expense involved in research and lawsuits over his campaign of manumissions on crown estates during the 1570s and later if there had not been good money in it. Savine's work made it clear that bondmen by the sixteenth century tended either to be miserably poor or substantially prosperous, in the latter case taking advantage of their enforced security of tenure.[29] This second group's keen interest in gaining relief from the humiliation and financial exactions of serfdom would coincide with their lords' search for a quick profit.

---

[24] E.g. on serfdom in Brandenburg, see W. W. Hagen, 'Peasant rents and seigneurial profits in sixteenth-century Brandenburg', *Past and Present*, 108 (August 1985), pp. 80–116.

[25] *Calendar of Patent Rolls, Henry VI*, II, pp. 523–4.

[26] Charter pr. *Archaeologia Cambrensis* (1847), pp. 215–22, and cf. the discussion of the context in S. B. Chrimes, *Henry VII* (London, 1972), pp. 245–57.

[27] Baker, *Spelman*, II, p. 192.

[28] *LP* xix (1), 278/5, 278/67, 812/77; xix (2). 800/8 (all 1544); House of Lords RO, Original Acts 2 and 3 Philip and Mary, 23. [29] Savine, pp. 276–80.

This coincidence might simply lead to an agreement on straightforward manumission, but it might also lead elsewhere. To build a foolproof road to freedom for England's serfs, the common law created the most bizarre of its collusive legal fictions: certification of bastardy. The principle of the fictitious action involved was simple: serfdom could be passed only through the male line, and therefore no bastard could be a serf, since his father was unknown. Bastardy could bar villeinage. From this maxim, fifteenth-century lawyers constructed a fiction of abstract beauty, which would serve its purpose for more than a century and then fall into near-oblivion.

The action took an incongruous origin in a private act of parliament of 1430–1 legislating for a family row among the heirs of the earl of Kent. To stop an alleged bastard of the earl getting a favourable judgment that she was legitimate from a bishop of her choice, a procedure of open proclamation in chancery was laid down in order that all interested parties should have time and warning to make their respresentations to the ordinary concerned.[30] However, the subsequent history of this certification procedure took it far down the social scale from the Holand family. We do not know which quick-witted Lancastrian lawyer spotted the potential of the act, but the first chancery writ ordering an episcopal certificate to be discovered so far, issued twenty-nine years later, already involved a claim of villeinage. After this there is a hiatus in extant writs until 1470 or 1471, but from then on there is a continuous sequence of cases traceable into the 1570s. These can be recovered partly from a fragmentary series of the writs filed in chancery, partly through cases traceable in the plea rolls of the court of common pleas, and partly through occasional references in episcopal records: the secretary of Bishop Parkhurst of Norwich, for example, kept a meticulous record in one of his letter-books of cases involving the bishop during the 1560s and 1570s.[31] Our knowledge is supplemented by various references and quoted cases in contemporary legal commentators; in all, 240 cases have so far been discovered. Making estimates about the gaps in our knowledge during this period, particularly during the fifteenth century, one can confidently say that a minimum of seventy further cases remains to be found on the plea rolls.[32] For a hundred years, therefore, there was a minimum average of three suits a year involving certification of bastardy, and at the height of the action's popularity,

[30] *Statutes of the Realm*, II, p. 269. For an earlier instance of bastardy claims in a manorial context, see J. Hatcher, 'English serfdom and villeinage', *Past and Present*, 90 (February 1981), p. 38 n.

[31] The filed writs are PRO, C 263/1/1–3; cf. Parkhurst's Letter-Book, Norfolk RO, SUN/3, contents list and fos. 101ᵛ–151ʳ.

[32] Cf. cases quoted in W. Rastell, *A Collection of Entrees*... (London, 1596, STC, no. 20732), fos. 681ᵛ–682ʳ, and collection of entries by Robert Maycote, Library of Congress MS Ac. 1093.2, fos. 116–17 (I am indebted to Dr John Baker for allowing me to use his photocopy of this document). Cf. also the discussion by other contemporary lawyers, conveniently summarised in P. Vinogradoff, *Villainage in England* (Oxford, 1892), pp. 59–60, and Richard Broke's reference to the action in a reading of 1504–9, Baker, *Spelman*, I, p. 225. A handful of cases refer not to villeinage but to Kentish gavelkind tenure: PRO, C 263/1/3, nos. 5, 6, 5 (1509, 1521).

between the late 1490s and the late 1510s, the average was about six a year.

What was the procedure in such cases? The action invariably began with the villein as plaintiff, bringing an action against his lord. Several actions would do; a writ of entry sur disseisin was a favourite, particularly in the last decades of the process, but trespass was also commonly used. From there the case could go in two ways: the lord as defendant could either claim that the plaintiff had no title to the land in question because he was a bastard, or he could make an explicit claim that the plaintiff was his villein and therefore had no right of action against his lord. In the latter case, it would be the plaintiff who in response claimed bastardy and hence the impossibility of villein status. In either case, the result was the issue of a chancery writ directing the bishop to investigate the bastardy. By the provisions of 9 Henry VI, c. 10, this could not be awarded to the bishop until three proclamations had been made in chancery in three successive months; once these were complete, the bishop would be directed to hold his inquisition. If he certified bastardy, the result of the action would follow the two lines of defence outlined above. In the first instance, the plaintiff would lose his suit, and the defendant would be dismissed *sine die*. In the second, the plaintiff would win, and a writ would be issued to the sheriff of the county named in the plaint to assess damages and costs.

Certification of bastardy seems to have been a speciality of common pleas. King's bench did employ the action, but seems to have preferred to develop actions on the case which incidentally tried a plea of villeinage; this was not as neat nor as foolproof as certification of bastardy, nor does it seem to have been used as much.[33] Certification became such a routine part of common pleas procedure that it entered the scale of fees: 'wryttes of Bastardy into the chauncery and to the busshop' carried a two shillings fee in the sixteenth-century fee list, like such writs as *supersedeas* or *certiorari*.[34] The plea roll docket rolls survive in common pleas from 1509, and in them (fortunately for the historian) the bastardy cases were already distinguished by the clerk by some variant on the phrase 'bastardia placitata': this piece of routine probably implied that there was a standard charge among attorneys for the various stages of the action besides the court's formal fees. Once the clerk, greatly daring, put down the action as 'bastardia contra villenagium'.[35]

It is clear that certification normally involved untruth. It is beyond the realms of possibility that the hundreds or even thousands of people affected by the action could all have been born out of wedlock, even considering the known reluctance of some people to be married to a villein; nor is it likely that

[33] For a king's bench action of 1470, see Selden Society, XLVII (1930), p. xxvi (PRO, KB 27/836, m. 31, *Comper* v. *Bartelot*). On case, see Baker, *Spelman*, II, pp. 190–1.

[34] M. Hastings, *The Court of Common Pleas in Fifteenth-Century England* (New York, 1947), p. 254.

[35] PRO, IND 1/7 m. 13 (*Chylde* v *Sherley*, 1538). I have examined the docket rolls from 1509 to 1567 with some of 1568–9, IND 1/1–27, and have taken samples from 1583 and 1587 (IND 1/63, 75).

bond families deliberately planned their bastardies for future use at law, rather like putting one's son down for Eton. The routinisation and the very number of instances of the action over a century suggest fiction, but that this was so in an overwhelming majority of cases is proved by an examination of the proceedings. Very quickly the pleas settled down to stereotyped descriptions of wrongs: identical descriptions of goods seized, or from the 1490s a general preference for naming entries or trespasses on a single messuage or close or on one acre of land. If damages were awarded, they tended to be nominal sums like half a mark with a mark's costs, and very often these were remitted by the successful plaintiff. Only in the earliest decades is it difficult to discount the possibility that a genuine trial of bastardy was involved: the second oldest known case, for instance, from 1470 or 1471, included the description of a thorough inquisition by the bishop, with dates and places of birth and the name of the putative father given.[36]

Perhaps the most striking indication of fiction comes from the places alleged to be the birthplaces of bastards. Villeins might well allege that they were bastards born in the manor where their bond status lay, or in some nearby place, but quite frequently they alleged that they were born in an entirely different county and diocese. Sometimes the writ ordering certificate quite patently leaves a gap for the place and diocese of the alleged bastard birth to be filled in at a later stage. Norfolk and Norwich were the most frequent county and diocese to be the subject of such allegations: Norwich was in any case the most frequent diocese to be involved in certification suits. Between 1502 and the 1540s, at least fifty plaintiffs from such widely separated counties as Berkshire, Buckinghamshire, Leicestershire, Lincolnshire, Dorset, Kent, Derbyshire and Somerset all claimed to be bastards born in Norfolk. Why? Brushing aside unworthy speculations about Norfolk Broads, we can see that the explanation is to be found in the reluctance of some diocesan administrations to become involved with the downright lie necessary to sustain a successful action. Thirty-one of the above actions would have lain within the jurisdiction of the diocese of Lincoln if the plaintiff had claimed to have been born in the vicinity of the manor where his villeinage lay. In contrast with Norwich's constant turnover of certificates, the diocesan officials of Lincoln do not seem to have dealt with any cases of certification between the 1490s and the 1550s: the period of the action's greatest popularity. Indeed, two cases alleging bastard birth in the Lincoln diocese entered by the same attorney in 1551 are instructive: the plea roll records that the bishop of Lincoln did nothing, and the case peters out.[37] Bishop Sherburne of Chichester took nearly sixteen years, doing nothing from term to term, before he finally made a grudging certificate on a revived action for the unfortunate John Borde in Hilary Term 18 Henry VIII. In fact, only one other bastardy case involving the

---

[36] Maycote, Entries fo. 117ʳ (see n. 32 above).
[37] PRO, CPO 40/1146, m. 38 (*Sune* v *Earl of Sussex* and *Dyconson* v. *Grevell*).

Chichester diocese can be found during Sherburne's time after 1515; in 1518 Sherburne, himself a former archdeacon of the Lincoln diocese, is known to have speeded up major reforms of his diocesan courts, bringing in new officials previously connected with Lincoln.[38] Chichester cases of certification began once more after the arrival of Richard Sampson as bishop in 1536.

Other dioceses which seem to have been noticeably reluctant to get involved with the bastardy procedure were Ely, with no case discovered after 1473, Exeter, with only one after 1512, Salisbury, with none between 1502 and 1550, and Winchester, with a solitary case in 1511: all dioceses where we might expect to find use of the action. None of the new dioceses founded by Henry VIII ever became involved in certification. The Norwich officials seem to have been happy to act as general broker for the process, and it is instructive to look at the limited number of places in Norfolk where the 'foreign' plaintiffs or defendants alleged bastardy: Worstead, Flitcham, Aylsham, Wymondham, Attleborough, Bishop's Lynn, Stanford and Buxton. In nearly all these cases one can demonstrate a close connection between the parson of the parish and the episcopal machine, generally because the bishop had the right to nominate the incumbent. Since it would be the incumbent who would be the obvious person to lead any parish enquiry into bastardy, it would be convenient to go to parishes with such episcopal connections. Significantly, in two Norfolk cases so far discovered, the parson of the parish where the bastardy was alleged was himself the subject of the action, and probably certified his own bastardy.[39] Can it have been coincidence that Norwich's genial if morally dubious role in this process began soon after the arrival of Richard Nix as bishop in 1501?

Clearly certification of bastardy was an involved and expensive process. To succeed, it would have to be a collusive action between lord and villein, and this would presumably involve a substantial composition to be paid by the villein. Two cases give us an indication of what this might be. The accounts of Charles, duke of Suffolk for 1523–4 reveal a receipt of 'xx^{li} of one Whele bondeman to the seid duke of Suff. for his manymyssion to be opteyned': we can identify this Whele as Thomas Whele of Norwich, bondman of the duke's Norfolk manor of Kerdeston, who gained his freedom by a bastardy action in 1523. A second case is even more striking. John Dosy of the Howards' Norfolk lordship of Forncett gained his freedom by certification of bastardy with several other Forncett villein families in 1556, and we know that he was bound immediately to pay his lord the duke of Norfolk no less than £120.[40] Perhaps

[38] CP 40/999, m. 127, 40/1053, m. 522 (*Borde* v. *Underhill*, 1511 and 1527). S. Lander, 'Church courts and the Reformation in the diocese of Chichester, 1500–58', in R. O'Day and F. Heal, eds., *Continuity and Change* (Leicester, 1976), pp. 219–21.

[39] Incumbents have been ascertained from F. Blomefield and C. Parkin, *An Essay towards a Topographical History of the County of Norfolk* (11 vols., London, 1805–10). The two cases concerned the parsons of Brancaster and Walpole (CP 40/1013, m. 346, *Abbys* v. *Smith*, 1516, and CP 40/1050, m. 326, *Wheteholme* v. *Copuldyke*, 1526).

[40] Whele: PRO, LR 12/21/636, fo. 15^v, and CP 40/1040, m. 340, *Whele* v. *Stowe*, 1523 (the case

this was a package deal which included the costs of his action in common pleas, and of fees to chancery and episcopal officials: at least the nature of his action (a plea of bastardy in defence by the duke) spared him the costs of a sheriff's inquisition to assess the plaintiff's damages. There can be no better tribute to the reality of serfdom in the reign of Philip and Mary than that a bondman was prepared to make such a major investment to gain his family's freedom.

What was the particular attraction of this complex charade? There were, after all, common law methods for proving bastardy: the Norfolk common pleas plaintiff John Bordyop, for instance, proved the bastardy of his grandfather and hence his freedom from villeinage in the manor of Saham Toney by *nisi prius* jury trial at Thetford assizes in Lent 1495.[41] The disadvantage of such a common law process was that by the public nature of the trial, an allegation of bastardy had better be true if it were to succeed; indeed, Bordyop's allegation has the ring of conviction about it. In addition, the certificate of the ordinary was legally accepted as unchallengeable even when it was likely to be wrong. St German said as much in his discussion of bastardy: 'this certifycate of the bysshop is the hyest tryall that is in the law in this behalfe', and no further writ in the question could be suffered to go forth once such a pronouncement has been made. Against certification, the only appeal for any remedy such as return of land to a third party not involved in the original case was to the conscience of the party certified bastard; in a jury trial there was a legal remedy for a party strange to the original suit.[42]

Above all, the attraction of certification of bastardy to lord and villein alike was its bar to reversionary interests of ownership. Like its greater cousins in fiction the fine and the common recovery, certification was a key to unlock perpetuities and a safeguard against the heir. It is clear that many cases were defended by manorial lords and ladies who had no more than a life interest: tenants in tail, tenants in the wife's right, or widows, for instance. Several cases specifically state this in their writ to the bishop. A tenant for life could only manumit for his own life, like any other alienation, but certification evaded this handicap. At least one aggrieved heir tried to reverse the emancipation of a Wiltshire villein resulting from a collusive action of bastardy with his grandfather, a tenant in tail: John Mompesson the younger complained to the court of requests that the action had been 'by covyn bytwene the seid John Mompesson thelder and the seid John Snelgar and Richard Snelgar to

has some slightly unusual features); cf. Blomefield and Parkin, *Norfolk*, VIII, pp. 243–4. Dosy: F. G. Davenport, 'The decay of villeinage in East Anglia', *Trans. Roy. Hist. Soc.*, n. s., XIV, p. 135; cf. the bastardy actions in CP 40/1167, mm. 623, 265. I am grateful to Dr Steve Gunn for the LR 12 reference.

[41] CP 40/930, m. 314d (*Bordyop*, v. *Coo*, 1494; I am indebted to Dr John Baker for drawing my attention to this case). For another example, see CP 40/1038, m. 528 (*Reymond* v. *Lord Fitzwalter*, 1522).

[42] *St German*, pp. 187–8, and cf. Richard Broke's comment on certification: Baker, *Spelman*, I, p. 225.

thentente to defraude and disheryte the seid John Mompesson nowe defendaunt of his seid bondemen, the seid John Mompesson theldere at that tyme beyng seased only of a state taile . . .'.[43]

From the point of view of heirs like the younger Mompesson, the grant of any sort of manumission to villeins by a precedessor was the equivalent of felling woodland or levying large entry fines on long leases at low rents: it was an unprincipled expedient to raise cash quickly which deprived them of an exploitable asset. Manumission might thus seem to be of dubious morality; more than one lord would feel that manumission represented an unwarrantable encroachment on an inheritance which was greater than their temporary occupancy – at least when such a view suited them. Thus Dr London, the warden of New College, Oxford, told Thomas Cromwell in 1538 that it was against the college statutes to alienate either lands or bondmen. Such solicitude for the rights of perpetual corporations does not seem to have concerned him further than the walls of New, as he pursued his busy activities on behalf of the crown in the dissolution of monasteries and friaries. William, earl of Arundel expressed similar feelings in the same year when trying to refuse another of Cromwell's requests to free a bondman: such an action, he said, would be to the prejudice of his inheritance for ever.[44]

Arundel's son does not seem to have shared this view, for he used the certification process at least twice.[45] Any lord so doing would be safe from claims for redress from an heir. After all, the form of the action meant that the lord had actually defended his title against the villein as complainant: an heir could do no more than fume impotently like John Mompesson the younger. It may be because certification was devised to be an effective bar to the heir in private suits that the action was confined almost exclusively to secular private lords. Only three cases have come to light where the action was used by the crown, all in the reign of Henry VII, and all among the few examples which do not seem to be connected with villeinage. Only one ecclesiastical owner of serfs is known to have availed himself of the action: the abbot of Halesowen in Worcestershire, evidently determined to bid for the affections of twentieth-century social historians alongside his predecessors of the high middle ages.[46] The crown's absence is to be expected, since a villein's lord was always cast as defendant in the suit, and the crown was not open to process except of grace, but why did the church hold back? Perhaps ecclesiastical lords shared the distaste evidently felt by several episcopal administrations for the whole sordid business.

[43] PRO REQ. 2/4/327, rejoinder of Mompesson. This case is datable to mid-Henry VIII; the earlier case, probably late fifteenth century, has not yet been found.

[44] On London, *LP* xiii(1). 324, and cf. D. Knowles, *The Religious Orders in England* (3 vols., Cambridge, 1959), III, pp. 272, 354–7, 379, 385, 411–12, 487. Arundel: *LP*, xiii(1). 1263.

[45] PRO, CP 40/1132, m. 146 (*Jenyns* v. *Earl of Arundel*); CP 40/1161, m. 120 (*Carter* v. *Earl of Arundel*).

[46] Crown cases: PRO, C 263/1/2, nos. 1, 2, 11 (1498, 1502). Halesowen: ibid, no. 46 (1506).

Although the peak year so far discovered for cases of certification is 1504 (with a total of eleven actions), the number of cases seems to have remained steady until the end of the 1530s. A lull followed in the 1540s, succeeded by a revival in the 1550s and 1560s which was spearheaded by the fourth duke of Norfolk, in a reversal of his grandfather's repressive policies. The last case of the sequence traced so far was on the Somerset estates of Lord Grey of Pirgo in 1574; the one solitary writ to certify bastardy in Merionethshire in 1592 has several distinctive features which make it unlikely to refer to a villeinage case.[47] There is more than one explanation for the disappearance of the action after the 1570s. Protestant bishops may have been less ready to co-operate with the procedure than some of their precedessors; after all, reformist-minded catholic bishops had already shown their distaste for it. One cannot imagine that John Parkhurst, back from his Marian exile in Zurich to become bishop of Norwich in 1560, can have been best pleased to find his officials playing the leading role in the bastardy charade, but in any case he was at loggerheads with most of them for a decade, terming all his first four archdeacons 'popish lawyers or unlearned papists'. Certification cannot have been far from Parkhurst's mind when he spoke bitterly of his officials' 'pettyfogging, juggling and hypocrisy'. Dominating them was Miles Spencer, archdeacon of Sudbury, and an appropriately unreformed figure to act as broker in bastardy: a comfortable pluralist, a pronounced religious conserva-tive, and a nephew of Cardinal Bainbridge. There were only two more bastardy cases in Norwich after Spencer's death in 1570.[48] The co-operation between ecclesiastical and common lawyers which the action represented may have been less easy as their relations worsened in the 1580s. Perhaps more directly, the action may have been losing its value. The universal English revulsion against serfdom may have meant that from the middle of Elizabeth's reign, all but the most thickskinned of lords were unwilling to exact the full potential of their servile assets, and so the trouble and expense of certification no longer seemed commensurate with the reward. Thereafter, serfdom is very sporadic in its appearance on private estates.

However, it was precisely in the decade when the battle against villeinage had been won among the private lords that the last drama of English serfdom would be played, on the estates of the crown. The round-up of the majority of the remaining crown bondmen was made into a grant for the private profit of Elizabeth's well-loved courtier, Sir Henry Lee: a rather similar grant to the various patents to search out concealed crown lands made to private individu-als from the 1560s onwards. The first patent of 1574 covered only shires in the

---

[47] C 263/1/3, nos. 61, 63.

[48] On the archdeacons, R. A. Houlbrooke, ed., *The Letter Book of John Parkhurst* (Norfolk Record Society, XLIII, 1974–5), p. 27, and Houlbrooke's second quotation in R. O'Day and F. Heal, eds., *Continuity and Change* (Leicester, 1976), p. 249. On Spencer, see D. N. J. MacCulloch, *Suffolk and the Tudors* (Oxford, 1986), pp. 164, 185–6.

west country; it was a commission not to Lee but to Cecil and Sir Walter Mildmay, and purported to have been on the petition of the queen's 'poore faithful and loyall subjects' who were bondmen. However, even if there had been some genuine move from west country bondmen, Cecil made it clear in a private letter that the 'benefitt' was intended for Lee; the letter asked Henry Fanshaw of the exchequer on the queen's instructions to make plans for a wider patent explicitly made out to Sir Henry.[49] Perhaps those familiar with crown lands had pointed out to Lee that most crown bondmen were to be found outside the area included in the first commission. The new patent came in January 1575, still talking of the bondmen's petitions, and it gave Lee the right to search out and manumit two hundred bondmen or bondwomen with their children, 'compoundinge with theim for such reasonable fynes or somes of money to be by theim paied'. A second patent in June added a further hundred to Sir Henry's total, and gave teeth to the earlier grant, implying that he was meeting some resistance to his schemes: if any bondmen were rash enough to look a gift horse in the mouth and refuse manumission, Lee could enter all their possessions without impeachment of waste; moreover, in terms even more reminiscent of the 'concealed lands' grants he could search out and seize bondmen's lands aliened without official permission.[50]

Sir Henry set about his task with enthusiasm and a determination to make a good profit; the surviving detailed returns from the Lincolnshire manor of Long Bennington make it clear that wealthy bondmen would not get away without paying a sum proportionate to their wealth, while refusers faced confiscation of property. It is not surprising that few persisted in defiance, although one can note juries at Spalding (Lincs.) and Wymondham (Norfolk) helping along the process of obstructing Lee by finding no definite bondmen alive.[51] Lee's work was completed between 1575 and 1580; with a few stragglers brought in on his patent from 1589 to 1599, 137 villein families and 495 named individuals can be shown to have been affected.[52] He did not make a completely clean sweep, for various manumissions and references to serfs can be traced on crown manors into the reign of James I; however, the back of a venerable social institution was finally broken.

Bastardia contra villenagium: it was better to be a bastard in Tudor England than a bondman. For the *favor libertatis*, bondmen were prepared to lose all

[49] 1574 patent: T Rymer, *Foedera* (20 vols., London, 1704–35), XV, p. 731. PRO, SP 46/30, fo. 49.

[50] *Calendar of Patent Rolls, Elizabeth I*, VI, nos. 3068, 3294. The originals of Lee's patents and related documents were sold at Sotheby's in 1973: for a description, see Sotheby's catalogue, 20 November 1973 (I am grateful to Prof. Conrad Russell for drawing my attention to this).

[51] Long Bennington: Savine, pp. 273–5, commenting on PRO, DL 41/13/19. Spalding: PRO, DL 44/258, m. 8. Wymondham: PRO, E 178/1550.

[52] These figures derive from the listing of duchy manumissions in PRO, DL 42/102 and of other crown manumissions in *Calendar of Patent Rolls, Elizabeth I*, VI, VII, VIIII. I am grateful to the Public Record Office for allowing me to use their unpublished typescript calendars of the Patent Rolls up to 1603.

rights of legal inheritance, clerics of servile descent willing to imperil their orders and preferment, bishops and lawyers to tell lies at law. With the disuse of certification, bastardy ended its brief flirtation with legal respectability; with the coming of the systematised poor law of 1601 and the various acts of settlement, bastardy would become one of the ways in which ordinary people were deprived of dignity rather than gaining it. Yet serfdom had been defeated, and England's social institutions continued to diverge from the path of many northern nations. Many unfreed serfs must walk England's streets today, for the personal status has never formally been abolished: but as Hargrave observed in the eighteenth century, it is thanks to this existence of a strictly circumscribed and hereditary state of unfreedom that a new slavery can never enter the realm.[53] This happy state of affairs was brought about by the lords and bondmen of the Tudor age.

[53] Savine, p. 252.

Wales and England after the Tudor 'union': crown, principality and parliament, 1543–1624*

PETER R. ROBERTS

THE CONSTITUTIONAL ANNEXATION of Wales to England, begun under Edward I and completed by Henry VIII, extended the respective powers of king and parliament first over parts and finally over the whole of the country. In the 'act of union' of 1536 what was proposed was a parliamentary arrangement of laws and justice, an enlargement of the Edwardian settlement designed for all Welsh lands. The historic principality – the territory ruled over by the Welsh princes of Gwynedd until the conquest of 1282 and since 1301 reserved for the eldest sons and heirs of the kings of England – appeared to have been extinguished in the Tudor 'union'. In 1543 the 'second act of union' of Henry's reign (as it is known in modern Welsh historical accounts) contained a proviso which tempered the parliamentary union of laws previously proposed by reaffirming the royal powers to legislate for Wales that Edward I had originally assumed in 1284. This proviso supplies a key to the constitutional relationship of crown and principality over the previous two and a half centuries. Neither that relationship nor the proviso itself has always been well understood, and it was an anachronistic reading of the latter that led to its repeal in 1624. The original legislative intention in 1543 was to be subjected to conflicting interpretations in James I's reign by those who sought to identify the historical nature of the principality and the crown's prerogative in Wales in order to define their present extent and future potential. The Jacobean commentators, for immediate political reasons, subjected the statute of 1543 to closer scrutiny than it has received since from historians, who have always treated the second act as a mere appendage of the first 'act of union'. For all their misconceptions and special pleading, some at least of these later legists and legislators arrived at a plausible reading of significant clauses of the original statute which illuminate rather than distort the record.

* I am grateful to Professor Robert Ashton and Professor Ralph Griffiths for reading this paper in draft and making valuable suggestions.

I

The Tudor 'union' of Wales with England was a protracted legal and administrative settlement legislated in and out of parliament in a series of measures between 1536 and 1543. The key act 27 Henry VIII, c. 26, passed in the last session of the reformation parliament, inaugurated a policy the full implications of which had not been worked out and for which little practical preparation had been made. The act's immediate effect was to unite the diverse lands of Wales, hitherto owing different kinds of allegiance to the crown, with the realm of England, and to introduce English common law without abolishing Welsh or marcher customs. Partible inheritance was to be preserved, at least pending the report of a commission set up to investigate the land laws. Another commission was to collect information on the division of the new shires into hundreds. To complement the provisions made in the contemporaneous act 27 Henry VIII, c. 5, authorising the lord chancellor to appoint J.P.s in the old shires of Wales, it was decreed that the laws to be administered in the newly created shires of the Marches were to be an amalgam of English common law and such of the native laws and customs as the king and his council would allow to continue. Henry was empowered for five years to erect courts and appoint justices to administer these laws in imitation of the existing practice in the three shires of the old principality of north Wales. Clearly the emphasis lay not on a union of laws but on uniformity in the administration of justice throughout Wales. That the policy was tentative and provisional as well as ill-prepared is shown by the clause enabling the king to suspend or revoke the act in whole or in part within the following three years. Any such decision, made in writing under the great seal and affixed to the parliament roll, was to have the authority of statute law.[1] This conditional discretion granted to the king had a recent precedent in the first act of annates and was in fact resorted to in February 1537, when a proclamation suspended until 1 November of that year all the act's provisions except those which transferred certain marcher lordships to English border shires.[2]

In this hesitant fashion began the settlement which, after a number of postponements, was to be consolidated in parliament seven years after its introduction. By September 1541 the shiring was complete and the courts of great sessions and of quarter sessions had begun their work in Wales. The great act of 1543 (34 & 35 Henry VIII, c. 26) rehearsed and elaborated regulations for the administration of justice that were most of them already in operation. Its title is revealing: 'An acte for certaine Ordinaunces in the Kinges Majesties Domynion and Principalitie of Wales.'[3] In the preamble it is

[1] *Statutes of the Realm*, III (London, 1817), pp. 385–8, 534–5, 563–9. Further acts in June 1536 (28 Henry VIII, c. 3) and in 1539 (31 Henry VIII, c. 11) renewed the three-year right for the king to allot townships in the new shires, such assignments to be made as if by authority of parliament. Ibid, pp. 653, 730.

[2] PRO, SP 30/26/116, fos. 13–15.   [3] *Statutes of the Realm*, III, (1817) pp. 926–37.

claimed that these regulations were enacted in parliament at the suit of the king's subjects of Wales. This can be taken to refer to the Welsh M.P.s recently arrived in Westminster as a result of the granting of parliamentary representation in 1536. There had been a decision to gather up orders already enforced, in fulfilment of the discretion granted to the king in the original act, and to codify them in a statute in whose making the Welsh members would have a voice. Although the document does not survive, the indications are that these 'ordinances' had been formulated in 1540–1 as a single legislative instrument and promulgated by the king in council. Between its first statement and its final enactment a number of significant changes had been considered by Henry and his councillors in the character and extent of the 'union' to be effected. At one stage a scheme was drafted to institute a new and augmented principality as a distinct province of twelve shires under the nominal rule of the young Prince Edward.[4] Under this arrangement the system of new courts would have been supervised by a Welsh court of chancery as a replacement for the council in the Marches, which had continued to function as the king's commissioners under a lord president since the recall of the Princess Mary in 1527. The shiring of the marcher lordships had therefore led to a new definition of the principality, conceived not as an apanage of estates but as a separate jurisdiction to be exercised by the prince under his father's sovereignty. The whole of Wales would have formed this province, not merely the territories formerly ruled by the prince's council in the Marches of Wales. In the event, Henry decided against the establishment of a formal principality – perhaps Edward's extreme youth did not make it a practical proposition for the near future – and the council was confirmed in existence in a clause at the beginning of the act of 1543 (section III). This decision had been taken before the revised ordinances were brought before parliament, and so it was after the rejection of an alternative dispensation that the council received its statutory recognition as a prerogative court. The apparatus of assize courts – the act's apparent innovation – was likewise confirmed in existence by parliament.[5]

The 'effectes devised for Wales' of 1540–1 would have conferred on Edward the profits and supervision of justice in the twelve shires while reserving for the king 'his Royal auctoritie to chaunge, adde and reforme' all the provisions. This amounted to a larger power than that to repeal or suspend conferred for three years in the enabling clause in the act of 1536. The enabling clause in the 'breviat' of 1540–1 is repeated *verbatim*, with a significant addition (italicised below) in the statute of 1543 (section LIX). The king may

[4] BL, Cotton MS Vitellius C.1, fos. 39–44ᵛ; P. R. Roberts, 'A Breviat of the effectes devised for Wales, c. 1540–41', *Camden Miscellany*, XXVI, Camden 4th series, XIV (London, 1975), pp. 31–47.

[5] P. R. Roberts, 'The union with England and the identity of "Anglican" Wales', *Trans. Royal Historical Society*, 5th series, 22 (1972), pp. 52–8.

at all tymes hereafter from tyme to tyme chaunge, adde, alter, ordre, mynishe and reforme all maner of thinges afore rehearsed as to his moste excellent wisdoome and discreacion shal be thought convenient; *and also to make Lawes and Ordinances* for the Common wealthe and good quiet of his saide Domynion of Wales and his Subjects of the same, from tyme to tyme, at his Majesties pleasure . . .

This was notwithstanding anything to the contrary in the act 27 Henry VIII c. 26 or any other act; any such alteration or laws made by the king under his great seal were to be as valid as if made by authority of parliament.[6] This has been taken by historians and lawyers in the past to reflect a still cautious attitude towards the whole policy of pacifying the Welsh. It may well have been a precaution against the time when the policy, should it be judged unworkable, might have to be adjusted or reversed. But this does not explain why the king reserved larger legislative rights than were required for altering or annulling the details of the settlement. In the 'breviat' it made sense to confirm Henry's regality to modify an arrangement whereby judicial rights were delegated to the prince. When the ordinances were enacted in parliament, with their different provisions for the hierarchy of courts, the enabling clause was augmented to protect the king's rights to issue such ordinances in future. This was a perpetuation not merely of the various discretionary powers granted in the act of 1536, but of a general right to make laws for the dominion of Wales. It belonged to his prerogative yet the king had chosen on this occasion to exercise the right through parliament, and it would have for the future the sanction of statute law.

The fashion had already been set by Thomas Cromwell, in the case of the act for the court of augmentations and the act for the ordinances of Calais – both of 1536 – of preferring statute to ordinances or administrative orders where the choice plainly existed. That both these acts commenced as orders in council suggests that that body at first considered neither the erection of a court of record equipped with the king's seal nor the settlement of an outlying part of the realm to be a matter requiring the authority of parliament.[7] The erection of courts of common law was perhaps another matter, and this may have been the undeclared reason for introducing the Welsh settlement through parliament in the first place. Even if there was recent precedent for proceeding by statute in 1543 as in 1536, it is still remarkable that the king's rights were acknowledged by parliament in the case of Wales and preserved in such resounding terms in the formula of what is called in the *Lords Journal* the 'general proviso'. For the right to make laws and ordinances was different in

---

[6] *Statutes of the Realm*, III, p. 936. The bill received its three readings in the Lords on 24 and 26 Feb., and 30 April. On 1 May the 'provisio generalis pro billa Wallie' was read twice, the second time 'cui omnes proceres' (*sic*), which suggests unanimity reached after a discussion of its implications in which some misgivings may have been expressed. *Journals of the House of Lords*, I (1846), pp. 210, 227–8.

[7] Fitzwilliam to Lisle, 4 Nov., 1535: PRO, SP 3/3/69; G. R. Elton, 'The Tudor Revolution: a reply', *Past and Present*, 29 (1964) p. 41; *Statutes of the Realm*, III, pp. 569, 926.

kind, origin and purpose from the other Henrician instances of enabling clauses which it partially resembled. The acts for the conditional restraint of annates (1532), for canon law reform (1536), for creating new bishoprics (1540): these conferred on the king legislative rights of limited scope and duration.[8]

On the face of it, the 'general proviso' was a significant qualification of the union of laws in parliament as envisaged in the preamble to the act 27 Henry VIII, c. 26, but like that preamble it harked back to the Edwardian settlement of Gwynedd in 1284, the prototype for the political and administrative union that was now elaborated to embrace the whole of Wales. When they framed the 'general proviso' the draftsmen of 1543 evidently had before them the Statute of Rhuddlan, at the end of which Edward I affirmed:

Ita tamen quod quocienscumque, et quandocumque, et ubicumque nobis placuerit possimus praedita statuta, et eorum partes singulas declarare, interpretari, addere, sive diminuere, pro nostre libito voluntatis, et prout securitati nostrae et terrae nostrae predictae viderimus expedire.[9]

The connection between these provisos in the two pieces of legislation that enshrined respectively the Edwardian and the Henrician unions was noticed by Sir William Holdsworth. He remarked that in substance and form 'this so-called statute [of 1284] is an ordinance of the king with the advice of his nobles'. Edward's assumption of authority was an assertion of his rights over a conquered territory: as such Wales was subject to both laws made by the king and parliamentary legislation.[10] Holdsworth did not consider the legislative right to have been personal to Edward I: 'this power of the king would as a result of the Act [of 1543] have disappeared if this section (lix) had not preserved it'.

There was another dimension to its provenance in the 1280s, one that has not been appreciated by historians of English law. Edward I was deliberately appropriating to the crown, along with their lands, the legislative claims that the princes of Gwynedd had been arrogating to themselves in the course of the thirteenth century. After the conquest in 1282 Welsh laws and customs had been examined before the king and his council: Edward then proceeded (as is stated in the preamble to the 'Statute of Wales') to abolish some of them, allow and correct others and ordain new ones. Even before the final defeat of Llywelyn ap Gruffudd, the king had appointed commissioners to inquire into the Welsh legal system. In the winter of 1281 they had heard evidence to the effect that the prince of Wales claimed the right, in consultation with his council, to correct, enlarge or even abbreviate the law of Wales should it be

[8] 23 Henry VIII, c. 20; 27 Henry VIII, c. 15; 31 Henry VIII, c. 9: Ibid, pp. 385–8, 548, 728.
[9] 12 Edward I, *Stat. Wallie; Statutes of the Realm*, I (1810), pp. 55–68.
[10] W. S. Holdsworth, *A History of English Law* (7th edn., London, 1956) I, p. 124, n. 10.

found deficient. After exercising this right in making the settlement, Edward ensured that it became a permanent attribute of his sovereignty.[11]

It looks as if Henry VIII, conscious of this inheritance, was unwilling to surrender the legislative rights enjoyed by English kings – in theory at least – since 1284. These rights were now enlarged in scope to cover the whole of Wales where previously they had held good only in the royal lands. They were quite distinct from the king's authority under the act of proclamations, which applied to Wales as well as England. In the light of this it may be necessary at least to qualify Sir Geoffrey Elton's dictum, in his discussion of the significance of this latter act, that 'the Tudor crown neither could make law in its own right nor ever wished to acquire the power to do so'.[12] Constitutional lawyers and historians of the law have tended to view the act of 1539 in a different perspective, as an early precedent for the later modern practice of the delegation of legislative powers by parliament to the executive.[13] These powers have been labelled 'Henry VIII clauses' by the lawyers because of the two extraordinary instances dating from that reign. In finding the *locus classicus* of 'delegated legislation' in Henrician statutes, these authorities have in fact paid as much attention to the enabling clause in the act of 1543 for Wales as they have to the act 31 Henry VIII, c. 8. Sir Cecil Carr considered the provision for Wales 'of less notoriety and of narrower application' than that for proclamations, yet equally significant as anticipating more recent forms of law-making which endow administrative orders with statutory authority. In comparing the acts of 1539 and 1543, M. A. Sieghart concluded that the latter conferred on the king 'an even greater power of legislation by proclamation with regard to the laws of Wales'. For C. K. Allen the clause of 1543 was another 'famous and unorthodox' example of Henry's newly acquired power to act independently of parliament. Where Allen regarded the act for proclamations as 'a charter to absolutism', Carr believed that each successive delegation was a recognition of the supremacy of parliament.[14] By placing the act of 1539 in its proper historical setting, Elton has likewise been able to demonstrate the sovereignty of the king in parliament. In considering the constitutional significance of the 'general proviso' of 1543, we should see it

---

[11] 'Calendar of Welsh Rolls' in *Cal. Chancery Rolls, Various, 1277–1326*, II, *Welsh Rolls* (1912), pp. 191–211, esp. 199–200; T. Jones Pierce, 'The Law of Wales – the last phase', in his *Medieval Welsh Society*, ed. J. B. Smith (Cardiff, 1972), p. 377 & n. 26; R. R. Davies, 'Law and national identity in thirteenth-century Wales', *Welsh Society and Nationhood: Historical Essays Presented to Glanmor Williams* (Cardiff, 1984), ed. R. R. Davies, *et al.*, pp. 55–69.

[12] G. R. Elton, 'The rule of law in sixteenth-century England', *Studies in Tudor and Stuart Politics and Government*, I (Cambridge 1974), p. 274.

[13] In a series of acts passed since the local government act of 1888 (51 & 52 Victoria c. 41) ministers of the crown have been empowered by parliament to alter statutes by administrative order.

[14] C. K. Allen, *Law and Order: an Inquiry into the Nature and Scope of Delegated Legislation and Executive Powers in England* (London, 1945); C. T. Carr, *Delegated Legislation* (1921), pp. 48, 51; M. A. Sieghart, *Government by Decree: a Comparative Study of the History of the Ordinance in English and French Law* (London, 1950), p. 134.

not only in its immediate context but in relation to similar provisions made for Wales in the past, for as we have seen, the precedent itself had a history. What it reflected was parliament's recognition of the special relationship of the principality with the crown, a relationship that was not inaugurated or extinguished but preserved in 1543.

In the event Henry VIII did not use these special powers. The one significant addition to the settlement made in his reign – the provision for the payment of extraordinary expenses for Welsh M.P.s – was enacted in the next session of parliament, in February 1544, as 35 Henry VIII, c. 11. This complemented the provision for parliamentary elections of the act 27 Henry VIII, c. 26, and possibly resulted from the initiative of the new Welsh members who felt cheated of their fees and wages by negligent officers.[15] It may be that this use of statute was deemed necessary in respect of a feature of the settlement of 1536 that had no precedent in 1284. The special power in the 'general proviso' was, however, reserved for larger purposes than refinement of detail. In 1536 the principality had been enlarged rather than legislated out of existence as a territorial unit. The original measure of annexation, which dealt mainly with the shiring of the Marches, had been silent on the future of the principality as an apanage or province for a future prince. The birth in 1537 of the long-expected heir to the throne led to a radical reformulation, as the 'breviat' testifies, of the king's policy in Wales at the stage when the new system of courts was beginning to operate. The creation of a prince was traditionally by royal charter, and though the ceremony of investiture was according to custom, though not invariably, held in parliament, it was clear that in 'the effectes devised for Wales' the institution of the new Edwardian principality was cast in the form of a royal ordinance, not a statute. It is conceivable that the patrimony envisaged for Prince Edward had not been rejected outright in 1540–1, but was rather postponed until he was of maturer years. There were rumours in 1547, shortly before the king's death, that he was indeed to be created prince in the traditional way.[16] Had this happened and had Henry lived, the king's legislative right might well have been invoked on that or a subsequent occasion to institute a re-formed principality.

There was to be no other Tudor prince of Wales and no reason to redefine the constitutional status of Wales for the rest of the century. After 1543 the country was united within itself as never before, in the sense that internal divisions and conflicting jurisdictions had been eliminated in the interests of administrative uniformity. A separate identity could have been established for the twelve shires only within an institutional framework, such as that proposed in the scheme 1540–1, that would have described a frontier with the English shires. As it was, the council in the Marches survived, to administer the

---

[15] This much is suggested in the preamble to the act: *Statutes of the Realm*, III, pp. 969–70.

[16] *The Complete Peerage* (London, 1913 edn.), p. 444 and n.(b), citing, as a corrective to Grafton, F. Sandford, *A Genealogical History of the Kings of England* (London, 1677).

borderland as well as Wales, with the result that the boundary between the two countries was of little more than nominal significance in terms of jurisdiction. This served well enough one of the purposes of Tudor policy, which was assimilation; and yet the qualified nature of the resultant 'union' continued to be reflected in the statutory descriptions of the country. Acts of parliament named the 'principality and dominion' of Wales without pausing to define these entities, though they were understood to be interchangeable terms to describe the twelve shires. When the issue of a boundary with England was later raised, it was to be a matter of deciding the extent of the council's jurisdiction, of defining not so much the principality but the 'Marches' of Wales.

The king's commissioners at Ludlow emerged from the reorganisation of 1536–43 with a new role in supervising the administration of justice in Wales. Their governmental functions were defined by royal instructions while parliament passed occasional and piecemeal reforms for the Welsh courts.[17] The one Elizabethan measure that added significantly to the provisions of the Henrician settlement was the act of 1576 (18 Elizabeth, c. 8) for the making of additional justices of great sessions.[18] When attempts were made to alter the statute of 1543, the initiative was taken not by the crown or by the Welsh but on behalf of the inhabitants of the English border areas which remained under the jurisdiction of the council in Wales and the Marches. This movement was to be focused on the interpretation of the word 'Marches' in the statute 34 & 35 Henry VIII, c. 26, section III:

That there shal be and remaine a President and Counsaill in the saide Dominion and Principalitie of Wales and the Marches of the same.[19]

A dispute between the exchequer court of Chester and the council at Ludlow led in 1569 to the secession of the city and county, which successfully asserted their palatinate and civic liberties against what they represented as the council's encroachments.[20] This was later to be cited as a precedent by the disgruntled gentry of the shires of Shropshire, Hereford, Worcester and Gloucester in their petitions for exemption from conciliar jurisdiction. By the end of Elizabeth's reign this discontent had become a concerted campaign led by the common lawyers of the Westminster courts, who had their own

---

[17] 5 Eliz., c. 22: an act to fill up *juries de circumstantibus* lacking in Wales; 8 Eliz., c. 20: for repeal of a branch of an act of 1534 concerning trial of offences in Merioneth; 27 Eliz., c. 9: for reforming errors in fines and recoveries. Apart from the measure of 1562 for the translation of the bible and prayer book into Welsh and that of 1576 for extra justices, these were the only acts of parliament passed specifically for Wales in this reign. *Statutes of the Realm*, IV, pp. 454–7, 522, 715–17.

[18] See below, p. 124.

[19] *Statutes of the Realm*, III, p. 926.

[20] The opinion of C. J. Dyer, *et. al.*, 10 Feb. 1569, that the act of 1543 did not comprehend the city and county of Chester, was enrolled in chancery on 16 March. *CPR, 1566–69* (1964) no. 2676; G. Ormerod, *History of the County Palatine and City of Chester* (3 vols., 1882), I, pp. 127–9.

professional reasons for wishing to curtail the activities of the court at Ludlow. It was these lawyers who were probably behind the first parliamentary attempt to repeal section III of the act of 1543. A bill to this effect was read twice in the Lords on 21 January 1598 and committed, though it did not surface again before the session ended on 9 February.[21]

II

The attack was resumed by the Westminster lawyers early in James's reign.[22] It began with Fareley's case involving a procedural clash with king's bench and by 1604 had developed into a challenge, delivered by the attorney general, Sir Edward Coke, to the council's whole jurisdiction over the four shires. James referred the dispute to the privy council and the case presented for the council in the Marches has been preserved in a memorandum drafted by Francis Bacon for Robert Cecil late in 1604.[23] Among the official objections to the proposed exemption was that it would lead to the Welsh being again 'cantonised'. 'It will dissolve the union betwixt England and Wales, by breaking of their great traffic, their mutual alliances, and their equality of right.' Coke would have it that the word 'Marches' in section III of the act could not be understood to include the four shires, and a semantic debate ensued sustained by an array of rival precedents. From the outset the king regarded the request for exemption with hostility.[24] He told Cecil on 7 October 1604, that it would be to his dishonour if parliament 'should bandy that matter amongst them, before I first at my wits' end into it'. He resented that the common law should be used to contest the authority of the monarch and was concerned lest 'the country of Wales be not too justly grieved by dismembering them from their ancient neighbours'.[25] Neither James nor Cecil was able to prevent the issue being brought before parliament in 1606, when the initiative was gained by Sir Herbert Croft, M.P. for Herefordshire, and his allies, the members for the other English border shires.

A bill for the better explanation of 34 & 35 Henry VIII, c. 26, section III, was introduced into the Commons in February 1606 by Croft and John Hoskyns,

---

[21] Simonds D'Ewes, *The Journals of All the Parliaments during the Reign of Queen Elizabeth* (1682), p. 541.

[22] The history of the contest has already been well told and is outlined here only insofar as it impinges on the interests of Wales and the prince as identified in James's reign. Cf. P. Williams, 'The attack on the council in the Marches, 1603–42', *Trans. Honourable Society of Cymmrodorion* (1961), pt. I, pp. 1–22; R. E. Ham, 'The four shire controversy', *Welsh History Review*, 8 (1977), 386–99.

[23] J. Spedding *et al.*, eds., *The Works of Francis Bacon*, X: *Letters and Life*, III (1868), pp. 368–84.

[24] As long as the issue had remained one of conflicting jurisdiction, James had kept a judicious neutrality, as Dudley Carleton wrote to Ralph Winwood, 2 Jan. 1604: 'The Prerogative finds more friends among the Lords [of the Council], but the Judges and Attorneys plead hard for the Law. The King stands indifferent . . .' R. Winwood, *Memorials of Affairs of State* (3 vols., 1725), II, p. 44.

[25] HMC, Cal. of Salisbury MSS, XVI, (1933), p. 325.

burgess for Hereford.[26] The English shires, it was claimed, had not been part of the Marches since the act of 1536 and were not intended by either act to be subject to the council: the bill therefore set out to limit a 'usurped' jurisdiction. At its third reading the member for Caernarfonshire, Sir William Maurice, spoke against it, averring that the English shires had been included within the jurisdiction so that 'the President might have Englishmen to subdue the rudeness of the Welshmen, if they rebelled'.[27] This unpatriotic sentiment was the first recorded contribution by a Welshman to the series of parliamentary debates on the interpretation of various aspects of the act of 1543. After an initially hostile reception, the bill was passed by the Commons and on 13 March delivered to the Lords, where it was scrutinised by the defenders of the council. The case of the 'gentlemen opposers' was declared to be defective in law, logic and history, and some noteworthy political reasons were advanced for quashing the bill. To grant this exemption would be to 'give advantage of example to misinterpret all Statutes against direct meaning and usage'. The council had exercised its present authority before 1543: seven of the king's predecessors had sustained it even when they had no issue to create prince of Wales, 'and this to be donne now, when we have a Prince, the noblest that ever was ...!' The council's rule had done so much to assuage the old enmity between the two nations;[28] it was particularly mischievous to undermine this historic union at a time when another 'happie union of what hath been long severed and disunited' was being considered. None of these arguments (which may well have reflected common attitudes) deterred Croft, who reintroduced the bill, or another version of it, in the Commons in April. This was abandoned when James promised to institute reform himself: new instructions were prepared for the council, curtailing its authority, especially over the four shires, and the lord president, Lord Zouch, resigned in disgust.[29]

In 1607 the new instructions to the council under the presidency of Lord Eure confined the extraordinary criminal powers of the council to Wales, retaining for the English shires a civil jurisdiction in petty cases of debt and trespass and a commission of oyer and terminer. The common lawyers of Westminster alleged certain contradictions and ambiguities in the instructions; Eure submitted these to the privy council, and James agreed to refer

[26] PRO, SP 14/19/34 (draft bill), 35 (examination of the bill, endorsed 10 March 1606).

[27] *Commons Journals*, II, p. 281, cited P. Williams, 'The attack on the council in the Marches', p. 4. Though more tactfully put, this was one of the reasons urged against the bill by Salisbury: BL, Cotton MS Titus B 8, fo. 50.

[28] 'It will cast a generall skorne and contempt upon the Remainder of that aucthoritie left in that Court for hereafter, and make the Welshmen despised by the English, who are now by their common government holden in termes of love.' PRO, SP 14/19/35.

[29] *Commons Journals*, I, pp. 283, 296–7, 309; *Lords Journals*, II, pp. 394, 399, 406–7, 409; PRO, SP 14/19/53, 113; D. H. Willson, ed., *The Parliamentary Diary of Robert Bowyer, 1606–1607* (New York, 1971 reprint), pp. 49, 108, 115, 164.

them to a conference of the judges. Bacon, now solicitor general, was retained to argue the case for the council before the judges, against the advocacy of Sir Edward Coke and two sergeants, Harris and Hutton. Elaborating upon the points he had first raised in 1604, Bacon insisted that the legislators in 1543 had intended to continue the conciliar jurisdiction over the four shires. When the other side protested that usage was nothing against an act of parliament, Bacon riposted that it was permissible to appeal to usage to expound an act when it is doubtful. He went on, rather sententiously, to enunciate a principle:

Contemporanea interpretatis, whether it be of statute or Scripture or other author whatsoever, is of greatest credit. For to come 60 years after by subtilty of wit to expound a statute otherwise then the ages immediately succeeding did conceave it is *expositio contentiosa*, & not *naturalis* . . .[30]

This proved to be no empty formulation: although he seems to have lost the argument before the judges in 1608, Bacon's reconstruction of what happened in the settlement of Wales between 1536 and 1543 deserves our attention. Indeed there would be little point in reviewing these otherwise stale legal wranglings did they not contain, alongside a few spurious debating points, penetrating observations on the legislative intention in the Henrician parliaments. The lawyers had access to one document in particular which is no longer extant.

It was Sergeant Harris who introduced this into the discussion, and it was seized on by Bacon to advance his own case. As he put it, the statute 34 & 35 Henry VIII, c. 26 'was grounded upon a platform or preparative, of certain ordinances made by the King two years before, viz. 32' Henry VIII.[31] These ordinances were those authorised by the provision in the act 27 Henry VIII, c. 26 granting the king authority within a period of five years to erect new courts of record and to appoint justices in Wales. They were later reformulated as the act of 1543 but had evidently been promulgated by the king in council in 1540–1. We may envisage this instrument as an order in council cast in similar format to the 'breviat' (whose existence the Jacobean lawyers were not aware of). It was a later version of the same process of law-making by the king outside parliament, this time ratifying the existence of the council at Ludlow but confining its jurisdiction (so the lawyers agree in 1608) to the twelve shires. In respect of the authority for the council, Bacon admits a 'diversity of penning of that clause in the ordinance' and in the final statute. His explanation is that the earlier act of 1536 referred only to Wales, and so the word 'Marches' (which after the abolition of the marcher lordships could only refer to the English

---

[30] BL., Cotton MS, Vitellius C 1, fos. 180–95; Add. MSS no. 25, 244; National Library of Wales, Peniarth MS 408 D, fos. 14–47. J. Spedding, *Works of Francis Bacon*, VII: *Literary and Professional Works*, II (1861), pp. 569–611, esp. p. 598.

[31] Ibid, p. 600. This allusion to the document can be taken as independent confirmation of what can only otherwise be deduced from contemporary circumstantial evidence: see P. R. Roberts, 'A Breviat of the effectes devised for Wales', p. 33.

borderland) is omitted from the ordinances which grew out of it, but the act of 1543 embraced not only Wales 'but the commixted government and therefore the word *Marches* was put in'. The collating of the ordinance and the statute serves his cause best, Bacon claims, for 'marches' is not brought into section III of the latter by error or slip but advisedly. The absence of any allusion to 'Marches' in the title of the act, or in any of its other clauses, is easily explained. The border shires were brought within the council's purview 'first by the King or after by the parliament' not for their own sakes; rather it was 'for congruity's sake and for the good of Wales that that commixture was requisite', so that the Welsh and their immediate neighbours should have equal justice before the same tribunal. This was cogent reasoning and a commonsensical enough reading of what was no doubt intended but had been so inadequately expressed in the act.[32] To clinch his point, Bacon refers to the 'general proviso': 'there the word *Marches* is omitted, because it was not thought reasonable to invest the King with a power to alter the laws, which is the subjects' birthright, in any part of the realm of England'.[33] Hence for 'Marches' read 'the four English shires', *quod erat demonstrandum*. His reasoning again was plausible and, of course, it begged the question of the extent to which the Welsh themselves had been made equal before the common law of England. Bacon's adversaries contended that the four shires were in worse case than all other English shires in that they are subject to the discretionary judgment of the president and council of Wales: they were thus made part of Wales and deprived of the benefit of English law and justice.[34] To which the council's defenders replied that the statute of 1543 completed and did not inaugurate the union, so the English shires could not be reduced by this conjunction to Welsh laws, which had been abolished.[35]

Hitherto in the disputes there had been little sign that James considered Prince Henry's interests to be involved. The historical origin of the commissioners in the Marches as the prince's council had not been mentioned by Bacon in his brief of 1604, and as late as the summer of 1608 he was uncertain to what extent the king thought in such terms.[36] By the time he came to argue

---

[32] The subsidy act of 1540 refers to the council as established 'in the Marches of Wales, and the Shires thereunto adjoyning'. 32 Henry VIII, c. 50 (*Statutes of the Realm*, III, p. 812). No one cited this in the exchange before the judges as it is recorded (Spedding, *Works of Francis Bacon*, VII, p. 570) but clearly this was the phrasing that should have been used in 1543, and its absence shows the careless drafting involved in the conversion of the ordinances into the statute.

[33] Ibid, p. 588. Cf. also BL, Cotton MS Vitellius C 1, fo. 180; Add. MS 25, 244, fo. 80: reasons collected by Mr Law of the Middle Temple why the four border shires were not parcel of Wales or of the Marches. These included the 'special proviso' among those which 'cannot be construed to reach' to the English shires.

[34] On 8 Nov. 1608 J. Chamberlain reported to D. Carleton the king's conference with the judges: James would 'stretch his prerogative to the uttermost: the judges stand well yet to theyre tackling, but *finis coronat opus*. The fowre shires lately disioyned are now very like to be newly annexed to the iurisdiction of Wales . . .' SP 14/37/53.

[35] BL, Cotton MS Vitellius C 1, fo. 185.

[36] He confided in his *Commentarius Solutus* in July 1608 what he regarded as a challenge and an

before the judges he had presumably divined the king's thinking and had decided on the tack he would follow. In his glosses on the statute of 1543 he affirmed that one of Henry VIII's aims had been to emulate his predecessors' example in making 'a convenient dignity and state for his eldest (*sic*) son when he should be created Prince of Wales'. In the past the prince's household had been resident at Ludlow Castle or Tickenhill House, near Bewdley – that is, within the English border shires – where it was reasonable that the prince should exercise as much civil jurisdiction as he would in his principality or in his earldom of Chester.[37]

Bacon's advocacy did not move the judges, who reported their opinion on 3 February 1609. James would not allow it to be published, from which it was understood at the time to have been unfavourable to the council.[38] He stood on the dignity of his prerogative and retreated from compromise: in the new instructions issued in May 1609 the council's former authority was restored. Bacon received suitable reward for his services with his appointment, sometime after 1608, as the prince's solicitor general.[39] In raising the points about the prince's right and the 'general proviso', he had touched on aspects of the royal prerogative in Wales which were currently being explored by others in quite different contexts.

On St David's Day 1607, George Owen of Henllys, the Pembrokeshire antiquary, finished his tract on the history of the principality. His purpose was to urge the king to create his heir prince of Wales 'or of some other Principallitie . . . first to be erected or renewed againe by his Maiestie when it shall seeme best to his wisdome'. According to Owen, Edward, son of Henry VIII, had been formally entitled Prince of Wales.[40] In his *The Historie of Cambria, now called Wales* (1584), Dr David Powel had alleged that, because there had been no creation or investiture, Edward had been prince only under the general title of England. Owen is concerned to answer this claim, lest the reasoning be thought to be a bar to a renewal of the title. He insists that the union of Wales with England was effected by the Statute of Rhuddlan in 1284, that Henry VIII's acts merely endorsed this union, and that there must have been other reasons for not proceeding to a creation and an investiture in that reign.[41] The principality was subsumed in the crown not by the act 27 Henry VIII, c. 26, but by Edward's 'alteracion from the estate of Prince into his royall Soveraigntie upon the death of his father', and a dignity once drowned could be revived again.

opportunity: 'Memorandum, the poynt of the 4 shires and to think to settle a course in it; but to listen how the king is affected in respect of the prince, and to make use of my industry in it towards the prince.' J. Spedding, *Works of Francis Bacon*, XI, *Life and Letters*, IV (1868), p. 59.

[37] J. Spedding, *Works of Francis Bacon*, VII: *Literary and Professional Works*, II, p. 589.

[38] Ibid, pp. 580–1.

[39] Jonathan Marwel, *The Trials of Counsel: Francis Bacon in 1621* (Detroit, 1978), 220, p. 65.

[40] Owen cites Stowe's chronicle to the effect that Edward was created on 18 Oct. 1537, six days after his birth; but this could only have been a proclamation of his titles. For a corrective to Stowe and Grafton, see above, p. 117, n.16.   [41] Cardiff City Library MS 2.88, fos. 51–7.

Owen's manuscript treatise may or may not have reached the king, but renewed interest in the principality certainly dates from the summer of 1607, soon after Henry reached his teens. The officers of his household were among the first to alert Henry to his potential rights. Sir John Croke's promotion to be a justice of king's bench in June 1607 created a vacancy among the circuit judges in Wales, which Sir Thomas Stephens, the prince's attorney, believed ought to be in the thirteen-year-old Henry's gift:

What respect your Highness hath to the principality of Wales . . . which the kings of this realm have used to confer upon the Princes their eldest sons, is to yourself. But if you affect it, it may be expedient that such places as this be bestowed upon such as (being sufficient and fit for the place) shall be at your highness's service.

Stephens seems to be proposing himself for the position though he makes a modest disclaimer of his own 'sufficiency or desert'. An appointment was not made until the following May, when Sir George Snygge succeeded Croke as chief justice of great sessions for the Brecon circuit.[42] Before filling the vacancy the privy council hesitated about the instrument to be used, and referred to the judges the question of whether it should be letters patent or commission.

According to the act of 1543 (section IV) the justices of great sessions were to be appointed by letters patent *and* commissions.[43] In 1576 parliament authorised the appointment of a second justice in each circuit and Elizabeth and her successors were also enabled to appoint additional justices *ad hoc* by commissions of association. Before these provisions could be implemented the act itself (18 Elizabeth, c. 8) was found to be imperfectly drafted (perhaps because the instrument of appointing the second justice was not specified), and so the privy council had asked the law officers of the crown if the queen could use her prerogative to appoint justices.[44] Second justices were duly appointed to each circuit by letters patent in 1578–9, presumably by prerogative action, though not – as far as we can tell – by resort to the rights contained in the 'general proviso' of 1543. When James's privy council referred the case to the judges in 1608, it was possibly to decide whether the crown could appoint the first justice as well as associate justices by commission.[45] After consulting the acts of 1536 (27 Henry VIII, c. 26) and 1576, the judges concluded that justices in Wales were to be appointed by patent, not commission. Then the question was moved whether James could appoint by commission through an exercise of the regal right contained in the enabling

---

[42] Letter of June 1607: BL, Harley MS 7007, fo. 144; W. R. Williams, *The History of the Great Sessions in Wales 1542–1830* (Brecon, 1899), p. 131.

[43] In fact the first appointments had been made by patent, dated 28 June 1542. Ibid, pp. 13, 15; *Statutes of the Realm*, III, p. 926.

[44] *Acts of the Privy Council*, IX, p. 359.

[45] Croke had been chief justice, and not puisne or deputy justice of the Brecon circuit, and so the appointment did not come under the terms of the act of 1576.

clause of the act of 1543. The judges reasoned that this right could not be construed to apply to Henry VIII's successors, since there was nothing to that effect in the act, 'for as his wisdom and discretion, which they well knew, did not go in succession, so the power and great confidence which was annexed to them did not go in succession'. On the contrary, since 'what ensues upon this Act of the 34 H.8 concerning the uniting of Wales and England, and the subjection of them [viz. the Welsh] to the laws of England, none could divine', it was reasonable that Henry VIII during his lifetime might alter them. He did not do so in the event because the Welsh proved to be obedient and the settlement a success. It was never the intention to give the king and his successors a perpetual power, 'so that none of that country could be certain of his life, lands, goods, or liberty, or anything which he hath, and that would be of great servitude'.[46] The privy council seems to have accepted the judges' reasoning and acted on it: Snygge was duly appointed by letters patent (in the words of Coke's report) 'as others had before'.[47]

Both patents and commissions had to pass the great seal, so it is not immediately apparent why the privy council considered the issue important enough to refer to the judges, unless there was a political as distinct from a legal reason for preferring commissions. Justices of great sessions were *ex officio* members of the council in the Marches, but the case does not seem to bear directly on the dispute over that council's authority. The fact that the issue arose from this particular vacancy in the Welsh circuit, and not an earlier one in the reign, suggests a possible explanation. Stephens considered that judicial offices in Wales should lie within the prince's network of patronage, and his query may have raised more general questions. In the absence of the council's registers we cannot be sure, but the examination of the crown's right to appoint justices in Wales may have represented the privy council's first move to investigate the prerogatives of the principality against the time of Henry's investiture. Whatever the privy council's intentions, the prince's advisers were certainly engaged on such inquiries. Some time in 1608 Sir Thomas Challoner, the prince's governor, consulted Sir Robert Cotton about the traditional privileges of princes of Wales. Cotton was asked to find out, among other things, 'Whether any records are extant of commissions in Wales during the Prince's times, and whether his officers are named therein?'[48] The scheme of 1540–1, outlining the projected principality for Prince Edward, survives as an original manuscript among Cotton's collection of papers on the history of the prince's council in Wales.[49] It is conceivable that this was

[46] Edward Coke, *Twelfth Report*, p. 48: *English Reports*, LXXVII, *King's Bench Division*, VI (1907), 1328–9. I am grateful to Dr J. H. Baker for this reference. Cf. Coke's *Fourth Institutes* (1644), caps. 40, 240.
[47] W. R. Williams, *The History of the Great Sessions in Wales*, p. 131.
[48] Challoner to Cotton: Thomas Birch, *The Life of Henry, Prince of Wales* (1760), p. 203.
[49] On Cotton's own arrangement of his manuscripts, see Kevin Sharpe, *Sir Robert Cotton 1586–1631: History and Politics in Early Modern England* (Oxford, 1979), p. 68.

brought to the attention of Henry and his advisers in response to Challoner's request in 1608. The plan had been to endow Edward with full authority of justice 'and the gift of all offices ther, all process shal be made in the Princes name'.[50] A quasi-independent patrimony would hardly have accorded with James's conception of the unity of his kingdoms and might have reflected greater confidence in his elder son than he cared to express, so there would have been little political prospect for a revival of the scheme in its entirety. However, this had been the only occasion when the practical implications of the extension of the principality after the abolition of the marcher lordships had been worked out, and as such it could well have been one of the 'antient precedents' produced by Cotton in 1608. What Challoner had clearly appreciated was that a revived principality entailed a prince's council in Wales and that this touched the interests of members of Henry's household in London. This corollary of an impending investiture – the possible reconstitution of the king's commissioners in Wales and the Marches – was also drawn by others at this stage. In the summer of 1608, as we have seen, Bacon surmised that the prince's future dignity would be affected if the boundary of the council's authority were reduced, and in November he was arguing the point, through past analogy, before the judges.

The earliest evidence for an active interest displayed by Henry in his Welsh dignity dates from 1609, when he instigated searches without his father's prior knowledge. His comptroller in the duchy of Cornwall, Richard Cannock, produced a detailed report of the honours and revenues enjoyed by past princes.[51] This information was brought to James's attention by Henry's sergeant at law, Sir John Dodridge, in a manuscript version of the tract that was to be published in 1630 as *The History of the Ancient and Moderne Estate of the Principality of Wales, Dutchy of Cornwall and Earldome of Chester*.[52] In his preface addressed to James, Dodridge acknowledges Cannock's help and the encouragement of his patron, Lord Treasurer Buckhurst (who died 19 April 1608) in preparing his account, and begs the king's pardon for his boldness in tendering unsolicited advice. Dodridge explains the peculiar nature of a patrimony that is not an inheritance, for it is extinguished with the prince's accession to the throne or with his death and can never therefore be an apanage alienated from the crown. Henry VIII's annexation of Wales to England is praised for the peace and civility it brought to the Welsh and

---

[50] BL, Cotton MS Vitellius C 1, fo. 43^v: P. R. Roberts, 'A Breviat', p. 42.

[51] Cited, without source given, in Francis Jones, *The Princes and Principality of Wales* (Cardiff, 1969), p. 131.

[52] There are a number of near-contemporary copies of Dodridge's tract, one of them dated (rather improbably) as early as 1 Jan. 1604: Inner Temple, Petyt MS, vol. III, n. 9, fo. 205. Others include: BL Cotton MS Vitellius C 10, fos. 220–46; Harley 305, fos. 99–149; Lansdowne 1074, fos. 113 et seq; Sloane 3479, fos. 10–53. Stowe 1044, fos. 16–23, on the jurisdiction of justices itinerant in Wales, dated 1608, looks to be an early draft of one section of the tract.

'because in some respect it may serve as a proiect & president of some other union and anexacion by your Maiestie of as much or more consequence and importance'.[53] The tract traces the history of the government of Wales under the princes since the conquest of Wales, lists the officers with their fees and salaries, and adds a commentary on the provisions for justice in the act of 1543. A record of the revenues of the principality at the death of the Black Prince is contrasted with the survey made in the last year of Queen Elizabeth. There had been a decline in total income from £4681 to £1865. The king is advised to conduct a new survey before augmenting the revenues by act of parliament or some other means. By the end of the year 1609 James had agreed to Henry's request to confirm him in his title. It was decided to hold the investiture during the next session of parliament, which was to be approached to grant an annual contribution for his maintenance.[54]

III

Two clauses of the act of 1543 (34 & 35 Henry VIII, c. 26) had come under judicial scrutiny, for quite different reasons, in the year 1608. There is no indication that James took exception to the judges' opinion of Hilary 1608, or regarded it as diminishing his prerogative as he patently did the judges' opinion in respect of the council in the Marches. Both sets of opinions were to have political repercussions in parliament when it reassembled in 1610. It was in this session that the Welsh members first declared an interest in the interpretation of the 'second act of union' as it affected Wales itself. The attempt to repeal one 'branch' of the act was renewed in the Commons early in the session, to be followed soon after by a new request for the repeal of the other, though the relationship between the two manoeuvres is by no means simple and obvious.

When Croft and his allies resumed their parliamentary attack on the council in the Marches, their tactics took account of two new developments: the creation of the prince and the negotiation over the great contract. In his speech of 14 February, the third day of the session, Croft declared it to be the duty of 'every particular man to think of the grievances that most concern his Country'. Dealing with the objection that the exemption of the four shires

---

[53] Dodridge, *The History . . . of the Principality of Wales*, pp. 2, 5, 31 (cf. Cotton MS, Vitellius C, 10, fo. 238). He makes the point that the children of Henry VIII, Mary, Elizabeth and Edward, bore in turn, as heir apparent, the title of prince general, not prince of Wales. Camden claims that, though there was no creation or investiture in the reign, Henry's children were named princes of Wales in their turn. 'For, at that time, Wales was by authority of Parliament so annexed and united to the Kingdome of England, that both of them were governed under the same law.' William Camden, *Britannia* (1610 trans.), p. 683.

[54] HMC, *Cal., of Downshire MSS*, II, (1936) p. 211. According to the Venetian ambassador, Henry 'greatly desires' the title, the seat on the privy council that went with it, and the revenues of the principality. *Cal. State Papers, Venetian*, XI (1607–10), pars. 430, 837.

would be 'a derogation to the Prince, being now to be created', he suggested that the shires might submit to the Prince of Wales 'as President, no otherwise (sic)'.[55] He then moved that the grievance be referred to a committee with the same membership as that which had examined the bill of repeal in the second session of that parliament. In the Lords on the same day, and to a conference of both houses on the next, Salisbury reiterated James's message at the opening of the session, that the reasons for summoning parliament were to witness the creation of the prince and to supply the king's wants. In a leisurely disquisition on the history of the princes of Wales and their title to the earldom of Chester and the duchy of Cornwall, he insisted that 'parliament hath no essential power in the creation of princes . . . yet every one of those that have been made out of parliament hath been princes of infortunity'.[56] He then spoke pointedly that Henry's creation did not alter the king's prerogative in Wales: 'There hath the king a council established to determine causes, Westminster Hall is not troubled with those suits: yet *quoad potestatem* it is still the King's, though *quoad dignitatem* the Prince do have it.' This betokened an intention to re-form the commissioners in the Marches as the prince's council in name only. Clearly no more ambitious principality was envisioned for Henry beyond 'the title and territory by gift and creation' and the nominal headship of the council. Salisbury's message gave no comfort to the supporters of the cause of exemption and can be read as a rebuttal of Croft's suggestion of the previous day that Henry might be given a role in settling the dispute. The prince's creation was brought forward in parliament to enhance the king's case for financial aid and would not be allowed to serve any other political purpose there.[57]

In spite of Salisbury's strictures and James's discouraging speech to parliament on 21 March the Commons gave Croft a sympathetic hearing and insisted on including the four shires' petition among their general grievances. It was tacked on to the Commons' list, delivered to the Lords on 23 March, for inclusion in the great contract, with a request that what had been presented as a petition 'of right and justice' should be satisfied by the king 'as of grace'. It was again given a prominent place in the petition of temporal grievances presented to the king by the lower house on 7 July. James was asked to publish the opinion of the judges of November 1608 and to remove the four shires

---

55 *Commons Journals*, I, p. 193. This is the gloss put on the clerk's telegraphese notes by Spedding's fellow editor, D. D. Heath; J. Spedding, *et al.*, *The Works of Francis Bacon*, VII, p. 581, n. 2.

56 These were Richard II, Edward V, and Edward the son of Richard III. Francis Jones states that, historically, the investiture was 'a parliamentary occasion, a constitutional act': *The Princes and Principality of Wales*, p. 117.

57 E. Read Foster, ed., *Proceedings in Parliament 1610* (New Haven and London, 1966), I: *House of Lords*, p. 5; II, *House of Commons*, pp. 12–14, esp. n. 10. He expressed the hope that, for the sake of those doubters who might wonder why it was decided to create the prince in parliament, members attending the conference would report his remarks 'to men of inferior judgements because they do rather look upon the superficies than upon the inward causes'.

from the council's jurisdiction.[58] No progress was made in the bargaining on this front and in the interval of stalemate attention turned from one clause of the Henrician statute to another. Among the seven 'heads of ease' delivered by Richard Martin from the subcommittee of the committee of grievance on 16 July in preparation for a conference with the Lords was a petition that 'the clause of 34 H.8 giving the king power to make arbitrary law for Wales should be repealed'.[59]

Martin's is the only name associated with the petition, which reads like the joint composition of the Welsh M.P.s.[60] The immediate occasion for the suit was the great contract: the repeal of section LIX in the act 34 & 35 Henry VIII, c. 26 should be added to the measures of relief as a favour to the king's subjects in Wales. Since they did not experience purveyance and were subject to few tenures, the Welsh would otherwise receive little benefit from the contract, though they were willing to contribute to the payments for the good of the commonwealth as a whole. The petitioners' reading of the original purpose of the proviso shows the influence of the judges' opinion of Hilary 1608. The Henrician settlement enacted in 1543 was experimental, the rights conferred in the 'general proviso' reflected its provisional nature but were personal to Henry VIII. The 'newe government' had lasted successfully for 68 years and at no time had the rights been exercised. All subsequent alterations to the settlement had been made by act of parliament, except for the instructions issued to the council there, 'unto which the said subiectes in all dutie submytt themselves'.[61] In this way did the Welsh petitioners distance themselves from the discontent of the English border shires. They had discovered a complaint of more direct relevance to their constituencies. The retention on the statute book of the king's legislative right, vestigial but otiose, was represented by them as a grievance commensurate with feudal tenures and purveyances in England. In the atmosphere of distrust surrounding the recent abuse of proclamations, a suspicion had evidently been excited in the minds of the Welsh about a discretionary power which had never been used and which both judges and lawyers in the opinion and exchanges of 1608 had considered obsolete. Who raised the alarm? There is circumstantial evidence to suggest that the opponents of the council in the Commons in 1610, perhaps Croft or even Coke, if they did not suggest the anomaly as a grievance to the

---

[58] *Lords Journals*, II (1846), pp. 660–1; E. R. Foster, *Proceedings*, II, pp. 261–3; G. W. Prothero, *Select Statutes and other Constitutional Documents . . . Elizabeth I and James I* (Oxford, 1931), p. 294.

[59] In another version of the propositions this appeared as 'flaws in the statute of 28 (*sic*) Henry VIII for Wales may be taken away'. The source for Martin's propositions is suggested by Wallace Notestein, *The House of Commons 1604–1610* (New Haven and London, 1971), pp. 353–4 and n. 7.   [60] SP 14/55/54.

[61] 'The ordinances being then newlie established and the event thereof uncertain and doubtfull howe the people would conforme themselves to that newe government', parliament in its wisdom, 'careful to provide a remedie against all future inconveniences which upon that alteracion might suddenlie happen', had inserted the proviso in the act. SP 14/55/54.

Welsh members, at least encouraged them to pursue it.[62] They certainly tried to exploit the Welshmen's disquiet, once this had been voiced, for their own ends. When in the autumn of 1610 the 'gentlemen opposers' were urging Salisbury to change the instructions to the council, they elaborated upon the argument of their counsel of November 1608. If the four shires are included in the instructions to the council, they are also subject to the alteration of all their laws at the king's will and pleasure, 'which if they be, then are they likewise subject to that other mischife which even at this present enforceth the Welshmen to be sutors for grace to free themselves in that pointe as fearinge the danger of future times'.[63] These words echo those in the protest against the abuse of proclamations contained in the temporal grievances of the Commons. The fear of a future arbitrary power had not been expressed in the Welsh petition of 1610, though it was to be included in the versions presented in later parliaments.

If Croft, Coke and the other advocates of exemption ever used this ploy in the Commons in an effort to mobilize Welsh support in their agitation against the provisions of the 1543 act, they plainly did not succeed. The Welsh petition (in this parliament at least) was tactfully penned to avoid giving offence to the king. James, for his part, did not equate a theoretical right to make ordinances for Wales with his power to issue proclamations. Martin's propositions were added to the original petitions for the bargain with the king, whom Salisbury and three other councillors visited at Theobalds on the same day, 16 July. The Welsh petition was one of the few James was willing to concede. He recognised the Henrician clause to be a mark of conquest: the Welshmen's 'loyalty, Faith and Obedience was well known, and he would not leave a mark of separation upon them in point of Freedom'. The Commons were then given assurances on two related points. James 'wished that England and Wales might be all alike. He would not that any law should be altered by his letters patent.'[64] The support that the Welsh members had accorded the king's pet schemes for union of England and Scotland (early in the session of 1610 Sir William Maurice had tried to revive that unpopular cause in the Commons) was to receive its due reward.[65]

---

[62] Spedding and his fellow editors comment on the bill for repealing this clause as presented in parliament in 1614: '. . . there are some passages in some of the memoirs shewing it was, at any rate, sought to alarm [the Welsh] about this clause, which the advocates of the Council treated as obsolete'. J. Spedding, *The Works of Francis Bacon*, VII, p. 583, n. 1. One of these passages was doubtless the memorial to Salisbury quoted above (see next note); the others have not been traced.

[63] BL, Cotton MS Vitellius C 1, fo. 195: 'Memorial for Earl of Salisbury'; undated but from internal evidence it may be assigned to 1610, probably in the autumn, when the petitioners held some hope that the king might issue new instructions. See below, p. 131.

[64] John Pory to Winwood, 17 July 1610: R. Winwood, *Memorials of Affairs of State*, III, p. 193; E. R. Foster, *Proceedings*, II, p. 283.

[65] In 1607 Maurice had even proposed that James take the title of 'Emperor of Great Britain'. It was no less significant for the fate of their petition that Croft *et al.* had opposed the king's will in

On 18 July the Commons informed the Lords of their agreement to the sum of £200,000 per annum as parliament's contribution to the great contract. Even at this late stage the opponents of the council in the Marches tried to revive their supplication. The Speaker's observation, as recorded by the clerk of the Commons, 'that this is to repeal a Law that hath continued since 34 H.8' refers not to the Welsh petition but to Croft's renewed effort to have the four shires' grievance included in the contract. It looks as if he and his allies had seized on the king's willingness to repeal one section of the act of 1543 to press for the repeal of the other. Although the Commons were disposed to endorse the cause of exemption, they were resolved that it should not be to the prejudice of the main bargain and decided to await the king's answer before proceeding further.[66] Salisbury told the conference of the two houses on 21 July that, as for the council in Wales, 'the king keeps in his power yet unresolved'.[67] On this delicate issue James was not to be turned, and yet in the autumn he was understood to be prepared to concede that the four shires should be 'free, as borne to the liberty of the common law'.[68] While James prevaricated, negotiations over the agreed items of the bargain proceeded without any further reference to the council in the Marches, until they were finally abandoned early in November. When he asked for supply in the conventional way, the repeal of the 'general proviso' was one of the retributions offered in exchange for a grant. A disillusioned House of Commons failed to respond to the proposal and denied the king any further aid. Parliament was prorogued in December without any grievances being satisfied. One consequence was that the expenses for the prince's creation and for his endowment had to be met from the existing resources of the crown.[69] Henry himself bore some responsibility for this outcome. He was reported to covet the mastership of the court of wards as a princely perquisite; and his opposition to Salisbury's great contract contributed to the failure of the first parliamentary move to repeal the extraordinary clause in the act of 1543.[70]

Having failed to advance his cause in parliament, Croft turned to the court and the king's favourite, the earl of Somerset, who procured an audience for him in the autumn of 1613. James accused Croft of attempting to overthrow

the debates on the Scottish union. *Commons Journals*, I, 156; W. Notestein, *The House of Commons 1604–1610*, p. 256.

[66] *Commons Journals*, I. pp. 451–2. Foster confuses the two petitions in her editorial comment: E. R. Foster, *Proceedings*, pp. 286–7. Heinze also mixes up the bills introduced into parliament between 1605 and 1621 to repeal the two separate clauses of the act of 1543. Randolph W. Heinze, 'Proclamations and parliamentary protest, 1537–1610', in De Lloyd Guth and John McKenna, eds., *Tudor Rule and Revolution: Essays for G. R. Elton from his American Friends* (Cambridge, 1982), p. 242, n. 16.   [67] E. R. Foster, *Proceedings*, I, p. 163.

[68] J. Spedding, *The Works of Francis Bacon*, VII, p. 581: A. H. Dodd, 'Wales's parliamentary apprenticeship, 1536–1625', *Trans. Honourable Society of Cymmrodorion* (1942), pp. 33–4.

[69] Cf. Salisbury's speech of 14 Nov.; E. R. Foster, *Proceedings*, II, p. 330, n. 8.

[70] J. W. Williamson, *The Myth of the Conqueror: Prince Henry Stuart, a Study in Seventeenth Century Personation* (New York, 1978), p. 63, citing the separate testimonies of the Venetian ambassador and Walter Yonge. See above p. 127, n. 54.

the principality of Wales and the government there, and called him an oppressor who would haul his poor neighbours to London to answer for petty suits. All this emerges from Croft's later account in his letter to Somerset of 3 November 1613: he had no doubt been suitably awed in the royal presence, thought up his best answers afterwards and communicated them to the favourite. As they were meant to, the letter and petition duly reached the king, who scribbled his comments in the margins. And so we have in a single document an unusual exchange of views, conducted at a remove, between a sovereign and a recalcitrant subject.

Croft wrote that the king at the previous parliament had granted his special favour to the Welsh 'to vouchsafe to clere that doubte' arising from the act of 1543.[71] Against which James wrote: 'Quhat I now graunte to Wales was graunted long before to these shyres.' To the king's charge that he was impugning the principality, Croft reports that he had replied ('beseeching pardon in all humilitie') that the president and council were appointed by the king, whether there was prince or no, and he could not see how the inclusion of the four shires within the council's jurisdiction could be accounted in any way to concern the prince or principality. Since 1536 the principality had been inseparably united to the crown for ever and could not again be separated except by act of parliament. (James's marginal comment was: 'My sonne will not lyke this discourse.') Even if the English shires were also the Marches of Wales, which is the pretext for placing them under the government of the council, it still remained true that Edward III had ordained that all marcher lords were to be perpetually annexed to the crown and not to the principality. It followed from this that neither the four counties nor the Welsh shires newly created out of marchground in 1536 could be reputed part of the principality. Since 1354 (28 Edward III, c. 2) the creation of the prince of Wales had been but the gift of a title comparable to the creation as dukes, earls and barons of other subjects who bear their titles of places 'where perhaps they have not a foot of land and most commonly no authority'. The petition for exemption could not therefore be construed as an attack on a principality which former kings with the consent of parliament had thought fit to extinguish. When it had existed 'in the true nature of a principalitye' it had been considered to stir unnatural strife over its boundaries between Edward III and the Black Prince. James, confronted a second time with this lecture on the constitutional history of his dominions, noted sardonically '& so my soone cannot be Prince of Wales'. Charles, however, could and did become prince of Wales: the investiture was held at the palace of Whitehall on 4 November 1616, a less splendid ceremony than that for Henry if only because it was not held in the

---

[71] His power 'to chaunge theyr lawes, or to give them anew at his pleasure, which were an exceeding absoluteness of power in dede, and therefore how unhappie shall the people of those foure Englishe counties hold themselves if grace (conceived to be but justice) be refused to them'. SP 14/76/53.

time of parliament. The people of Wales rejoiced in their new prince, as did the inhabitants of 'your proper Meridian of Ludlow', in full expectation that he would take up residence there at the head of the council.[72] But for Charles, as for Henry before him the principality was to be an honorific affair; nothing was done about associating either of them with the council in the Marches. At no time did James conceive of the honour as a patrimony in the holding of which his sons might be fitted for kingship.[73]

IV

A bill for the repeal of the 'general proviso' was one of the bills of grace drawn up by the privy council to be ready if they were sued for by the Commons in the parliament of 1614. As such it was added to those matters 'of small moment and loss to his Majesty' that Sir Henry Neville urged on James to concede in exchange for supply and in fulfilment of promises made in 1610.[74] The bill of repeal was introduced into the Commons on 13 April, by whom is not recorded.[75] On its second reading on 18 April, Matthew Davies, burgess for Cardiff, treated the House to a lecture on the past of the British nation. Although conquered by Romans, Danes and Normans, Wales had not been absorbed into England until 1536. By 1543 Welsh members sat in the commons and 'sought Government by the Laws of England, before Government by a Justice', and were then granted the full apparatus of English local government. Davies was interpreting Henry VIII's original intention to have been ruled by justiciarship, but the Welsh M.P.s at the time had influenced a change of policy. He expressed gratitude to James for the act of grace 'for Release of his Power', but pointed out that the bill's title did not truly reflect its content and that it misrecited the original statute; and so he moved a commitment. Thomas Hitchcock, burgess for Bishop's Castle, introduced a sceptical note: if collated with the statute, the bill 'will appear to be a mere Shew, no Grace. The proviso, as penned in the copulative, cannot hurt them'. This was as much as to say that the original clause was hedged about with

[72] Daniel Powel, *The Love of Wales to their Soueraigne Prince* (London, 1616), epistle to Charles; F. Jones, *The Princes and Principality of Wales*, pp. 137–40.

[73] Neither prince received a charter granting him the land and revenues of the ancient Welsh estates. Each was assigned incomes from these, which had to be augmented by grants from crown lands. From the wealth of precedents for the creation of princes, James chose the example of Henry VII's second son, Henry, the last prince to have been formally created. It may have been no accident that this was also the only occasion on which the king had withheld the grant of the revenues of the old principality. HHL, Ellesmere MSS 1218–19; F. Jones, *The Princes*, p. 130.

[74] James said he was willing to cede anything that did not touch his prerogative in honour or profit. HMC, *Cal. of Hastings MSS*, IV, (1947), p. 241; D. H. Willson, *The Privy Councillors in the House of Commons, 1604–1629* (Oxford, 1958), p. 201.

[75] In the sixteenth century, bills of grace, written on parchment and bearing the sign manual, would have been introduced first into the Lords and passed without debate. Cf. M. A. R. Graves, *The Tudor Parliaments: Crown, Lords and Commons, 1485–1603* (London, 1985), p. 24.

sufficient qualification to prevent injury to the king's subjects of Wales. William Jones of Beaumaris spoke next, in much the same vein, to suggest that Davies was perhaps exaggerating the danger posed by the powers conferred in the act. Even so, he supported the repeal of the clause, while reminding the house that when it had been put to the question in the last parliament 'one moved (without the King's Privity) *quid vultis mihi dare?*' Who was thus cast in the role of Judas is not clear, unless it was an allusion to Salisbury's eagerness to reach a bargain with the Commons before first gaining James's approval for a surrender of his right. In 1543, Jones continued, parliament had granted Henry VIII a personal power 'only to alter the Form, not the Substance, of the Laws'. What he meant by this can only be conjectured, but conceivably it was that the king could decide which of the provisions of justice should continue in Wales, without altering the content of English common law. It is clear that this member read the clause in the same light as had the judges in Hilary 1608: the legislative right was limited to Henry VIII's lifetime. However, Jones goes further, to point out the 'Special Provision' (section LX in the statute) declaring that nothing in the act should be prejudicial to property rights. This was a more acute observation on the limitations on the king's right than was reflected in the judges' opinion, at least as this is reported by Coke.[76]

The bill was duly committed to all the knights and burgesses for Wales and all other Welsh members in the house, those for the English border shires, all the lawyers and the king's learned counsel, Sir Edwin Sandys, Richard Cannock, burgess for Liskeard and auditor to Prince Henry, and sundry others. In the debate of 18 May, during the second reading of a bill to prevent abuses in procuring process out of the Westminster courts, Matthew Davies seized the opportunity to complain that king's bench exceeded its authority by despatching such writs into Wales. He was thereby defending the jurisdiction of the council in Wales as well as that of the great sessions. When on 21 May the bill of repeal received its third reading, Sir Henry Townsend, representing Ludlow and from 1614 vice-president of the council there, wondered whether, 'if this Law stand, the Government in the Marches will be taken away'. He evidently believed that the king's right to issue instructions to his prerogative court was based on section LIX of the act of 1543. Both Jones and Davies spoke to disabuse him of this supposition, pointing out that the solicitor general 'had given allowance to it', that it was, after all, an official measure. Sir Edwin Sandys, who in 1610 had aligned himself with the cause for exemption of the four shires, claimed that parliament cannot give a liberty to the king to make laws, and so seemed to challenge the constitutional propriety of the original clause. There was altogether a perfunctoriness about the Commons' reception of the bill of grace which was duly read a third time in

---

[76] Section LXII also ensured that the Welsh system of partible inheritance should be finally supplanted by descent according to English common law. *Statutes of the Realm*, III, p. 937; *Commons Journals*, I, pp. 463, 468.

the Lords on 26 May, before the king dissolved parliament twelve days later.[77] Although it had been passed by the Commons, the bill of repeal had not escaped the general suspicion with which its members, a number of vociferous Welshmen foremost among them, greeted the king's bills of grace, tainted as they were by association with the undertakers.[78]

When in the parliament of 1621 the Commons took up some of the unfinished business of the assembly of 1614, the Welsh M.P.s petitioned the king in February for leave to reintroduce the bill for repeal presented in the previous two assemblies. They repeated their understanding of the legislative purpose of parliament in 1543, as given in the first petition of 1610, adding now their apprehension, perhaps induced by the delay in granting the request, lest the liberty left by the 'general proviso' to alter the laws and ordinances at pleasure 'might in succeedinge ages make them subject to uncertainty both of lawes & government'. Again, it was none of their intention to restrain or abridge the authority or the current instructions of the council in the Marches of Wales.[79] Sir Thomas Trevor, solicitor to the prince of Wales, brought the bill in with the king's blessing for its first reading on 6 March. At the second reading on 13 March, Sandys, qualifying his objection to the bill of grace at the previous assembly, declared that parliament had reposed great trust in Henry VIII but that the present bill did not recognise that the right had been limited to that king's lifetime. The logic of this argument, first enunciated by the judges in 1608, was that the right was defunct; James in agreeing to revoke it was behaving as if he were conceding an inherited right. When Sandys warned the house 'to have a caution', his meaning was clear – the bill of grace was an empty gesture.[80] The reasons for the repeal rehearsed in the bill bear out Sandys's point. It is declared that the laws already ordained and implemented for Wales are mostly consonant with English law and have brought the Welsh to obedience. After such a long interval of peace, any future innovation would be dangerous and the king wished to abolish distinctions between his subjects of England and Wales. Therefore, neither the king nor his heirs and successors will, by virtue of the clause to be abrogated, change any laws or customs or make new laws for Wales. Barnabe Gooch reported on the bill from committee on 27 April, with a proviso saving the authority of the council

---

[77] *Lords Journals*, II, pp. 706, 708.

[78] Fifteen or sixteen of the Welsh M.P.s in 1614 had served in 1610: A. H. Dodd, 'Wales's parliamentary apprenticeship, 1536–1625', *Trans. Honourable Society of Cymmrodorion* (1942), pp. 35–40.

[79] PRO, SP 14/119/128: a contemporary copy. Only eight of the members from Wales sitting in this parliament had served in 1614: A. H. Dodd, *loc. cit.*

[80] Sir John Glanville would have the committee check that 'no former law made, may be avoided' through the revocation of the clause. This was to assume that the legislative right had been used, which it had not. *Commons Journals*, I, pp. 529, 539, 551, 614–15, 661. The anonymous diarist for this parliament understood 'the kings had power to alter the laws . . . as it had been by proclamation and parliament'. *Commons Debates 1621*, ed. W. Notestein, F. H. J. Relf and H. Simpson (Yale, 1935), V, pp. 292–3.

in the Marches; they were then engrossed,[81] and produced for the third reading on 8 May. During these weeks the House was preoccupied with the more pressing business of the abuse of patents and monopolies, but of more immediate concern to Welsh interests were the bills restricting the importation of Irish cattle and regulating the trade in Welsh cottons. While all three Welsh measures were still being considered in the Commons, Sir Richard Wynn of Gwydir wrote to inform his father that if the Welsh members could ensure their passage, they would have 'done as much as they could desire for their country'.[82] Yet the Welsh members were out of sympathy with the growing voice of opposition to the crown, and the rival interests of the Shrewsbury drapers and the Welsh clothiers led one Shropshire M.P. to implore the Commons 'not to respect Wales so, as to prejudice England'.[83] On the issue of free trade in Welsh woollens, the Welsh M.P.s were at odds with their fellow members from the border shires,[84] but were supported by Coke. Prince Charles was present on most of the days when the bill of grace was debated in the Lords, where it was twice committed; on each occasion the proviso supplied by the Commons safeguarding the council's jurisdiction was amended.[85] On its return to the Commons on 10 December it fell casualty to the hostility generated by the Lords' rejection of the original bill of monopolies.[86]

In the parliament of 1624 the bill of repeal, with the proviso as penned in 1621, was reintroduced into the Commons on St David's day. This time, apart from any significance that may attach to the date there is no evidence that the Welsh members were the initiators or contributed to the debates on the bill. At its second reading on 6 March, Sir Edward Coke moved its committal, with a particular request 'for a clause in the End, that will concern four great Counties of England'. He objected to the existing proviso as it 'makes them to be within the Marches of Wales'. Sandys, for his part, was still exercised about the exact status of the discretionary power in the original statute. There was

[81] Ibid, IV, p. 265.

[82] Letter of 6 May [1621], misdated 1623, in J. Ballinger, ed., *Cal. of Wynn (of Gwydir) Papers* (1926), no. 1096a. Sir Richard was gentleman in ordinary in Prince Charles's household. The Irish cattle bill did not survive its committee stage. A. H. Dodd, 'Wales's parliamentary apprenticeship', pp. 57, 60.

[83] Ibid, p. 49.

[84] The bill for Welsh cloth was passed in this parliament, but did not become law until 1824. For its progress and the background to the conflict, see T. C. Mendenhall, *The Shrewsbury Drapers and the Welsh Wool Trade* (Oxford, 1953), pp. 163–89, 237–8.

[85] The readings were on 12 and 31 May, when the proviso was read twice and engrossed, followed by a long interval until 27 Nov., when the bill was recommitted. Charles was not present at its third reading on 10 Dec., when the bill was assented to and returned to the Commons, *Lords Journals*, III, pp. 119, 128, 146, 172, 186, 188. The draft bill with the new proviso and its variants is printed from the Lords MSS in *Commons Debates, 1621*, VII, pp. 110–12. It is included in error in the Petyt MSS list of bills [June 1621] sent up to the Lords but not passed there: Ibid, p. 301.

[86] Ibid, II, p. 508; A. H. Dodd, 'Wales's parliamentary apprenticeship', p. 56; R. Zaller, *The Parliament of 1621* (Berkeley, 1971), pp. 163–4.

'somewhat in this Bill to be tenderly looked into' in relation to 'more acts that put a personal trust in Henry VIII'. Nine Welsh members, four Welshmen serving for English constituencies, the knights and burgesses for the border shires, Coke and Sandys were put on the committee 'to have a clause'. On 12 March Sir Robert Harley, burgess for Radnor and an enemy of the council,[87] reported on the bill and clause 'without amendments' and they were duly engrossed. After the third reading on 17 March, however, there remained doubts to be resolved. Sir William Pitt, John Glanville and John Selden (M.P.s for Wareham, Plymouth and Lancaster respectively) were asked to take the 'paper book' with them and consult the parliament roll and the statutes at large for Henry VIII's reign. On the following day Selden reported that the enrolled act was 'as imperfect as the printed book, but the bill that passed rectifies it'. It looks as if what these searchers had done was to follow up Sandys's suggestion of comparing the legislative right authorised in 1543 with that granted in other Henrician statutes, as it might be the act of 1536 for Wales or the act of annates of 1532. In these latter they would have found that the king's right to suspend or amend either act within a fixed time was conditional on the decision being registered under the great seal *and* annexed to the parliament roll.[88] The 'general proviso', by contrast lacked not only a specific time limit but a stipulation that any alteration was to be certified on the parliament roll. That parliament had in the past authorised such a general delegation of its legislative right without insisting on this condition apparently baffled the members of 1624, and so they concluded that the clause was imperfectly drafted. At no time had it occurred to Sandys, Selden or Coke, or any of the other lawyers, to look for precedents earlier than the reign of Henry VIII. In their present predicament, they may have been reassured by the fact that the bill (like that presented in the previous parliament) bound the king's heirs and successors to the revocation of the offending clause: this at least served as a precaution to avoid misunderstanding about limitation in future.

Put to the question on 18 March, the bill 'passed for law' as far as the Commons were concerned. When the Lords scrutinised the bill on 14 April, new doubts arose which were put to a conference of both houses on the next day. Coke reported to the lower house on 20 April the objections of the Lords, led by the earl of Northampton, lord president of the council in Wales, 'that the proviso not as full now as the last parliament', since it made no direct mention of the council.[89] While the Commons prevaricated, Prince Charles acted as moderator with a proposal for another committee of both houses 'to reconcile all differences'. The house of lords, busied at this time with the

[87] P. Williams, 'The attack on the council in the Marches', p. 15.
[88] The act of proclamations continued in force until its repeal in the next reign, so it would not presumably have been included in the category of acts placing a 'special trust' in Henry VIII.
[89] Thomas Powell to Sir John Wynn, 28 Apr. 1624, expressing the hope that, despite Northampton's opposition, the bill of repeal will be passed. *Cal. Wynn (of Gwydir) Papers*, no. 1216.

impeachment of Lord Treasurer Middlesex, referred the bill to the judges, on whose behalf Mr Baron Bromley reported on 1 May, in the presence of the prince of Wales. They were unanimous in their opinion (with one exception 'and he not directly of the contrary opinion') that the jurisdiction of the council in the Marches of Wales, established by 'the residue' of the act 34 and 35 Henry VIII, c. 26, was not prejudiced by the bill as it stood, which 'only repealed this particular branch and no more'. This opinion was accordingly entered in the Lords' journal at the motion of the prince. And so with the interests of the council assured, the bill of grace was finally passed in the fourth parliamentary session since its first appearance.[90]

The abolition of differences between the king's subjects of Wales and England was taken one stage further with the revival of another bill left over from 1621, then moved by Sir James Perrot of Pembrokeshire. This sought to remove obsolete acts from the statute book in a more systematic way, among them fourteen of the penal laws passed against the Welsh by Henry IV's parliaments during the Glyndwr revolt. Effectively superseded by the Henrician legislation of 'union', these were now rescinded en bloc, and with the removal of hostile laws against them the Welsh came to enjoy the benefit extended to the Scots in 1607.[91] There is a sense, therefore, in which the union of laws promised to the Welsh in 1536 was achieved only in 1624. The Welsh members of the Jacobean parliaments did not respond with consistent or unanimous gratitude to the king's bill of grace. The original initiative in 1610 may or may not have been theirs, but they returned to the subject in successive sessions and the prize seemed to have gained in attraction the more elusive it became. Most of them were evidently persuaded that, now that their attention was drawn to it and so long as it remained on the statute book, the 'general proviso' cast a shadow across the union that had brought their countrymen equality before the laws of England. The continual postponement of the bill of grace had given the opponents of the council in the Marches tactical advantages they were quick to seize, but they failed to involve the Welsh in the campaign to repeal a far more vital clause in the act of 1543. When that campaign was resumed in the next reign, it was fuelled by complaints against the council from Welshmen who gave voice to new grievances.[92]

[90] Commons Journals, I, pp. 675, 739, 767, 771–2; Lords Journals, III, pp. 271, 273, 279, 304, 314, 336, 339.

[91] 21 James I, cc. 10, 28 section 11: Statutes of the Realm (1819), pp. 1219, 1239. W. Notestein, The House of Commons 1604–10, pp. 252–3; A. H. Dodd, 'Wales's parliamentary apprenticeship', pp. 46, 58–9.

[92] P. Williams, 'The attack on the council in the Marches', pp. 17–21; C. A. J. Skeel, The Council in the Marches of Wales (1904), pp. 156–63.

Robe and sword in the conquest of Ireland

BRENDAN BRADSHAW

HISTORIANS have recently discovered that the Tudor conquest of Ireland has an intellectual as well as a political history.[1] They are currently discovering that the one is no less problematical than the other. Over the past fifteen years a debate has developed about the mental world occupied by the Elizabethan *conquistadores*, and the debate has now come to focus on the best-known, as also the most notorious, of the political treatises generated by the conquest, Edmund Spenser's *A View of the Present State of Ireland*.[2] What follows is an attempt to address that debate. By situating Spenser's text in the context of the literature of the conquest it aims to illuminate the outlook that informs it as well as the ethos from which it emanated. The interpretative key will be found to lie in attitudes to law and government.

Something must be said before proceeding about the strategy of analysis that will be adopted towards the voluminous literature of which Spenser's treatise forms part. A previous exercise in comparative analysis adopted a schematic approach, attempting to relate *A View* thematically to the entire corpus of reform commentary generated in the final decades of the Elizabethan conquest and pursuing the survey into the era of consolidation under the Stuarts.[3] The purpose was to demonstrate that *A View* classically formulates the ideological paradigm which the New English colonists had

[1] The main contributions to the discussion of the mental world of the *conquistadores* are as follows in order of publication: D. B. Quinn, *The Elizabethans and the Irish* (Ithaca, 1966), Nicholas P. Canny, *The Elizabethan Conquest of Ireland* (Hassocks, 1976), ch. 6; Brendan Bradshaw, 'The Elizabethans and the Irish', in *Studies*, 66 (1977), 38–50; Idem, 'Sword, word and strategy in the reformation in Ireland', in *Historical Journal*, 21 (1978), 475–502; Nicholas P. Canny, 'Edmund Spenser and the development of an Anglo-Irish identity', in *The Yearbook of English Studies*, 13 (1983), 1–19; Ciarán Brady, 'Spenser's Irish crisis: humanism and experience in the 1590s', in *Past and Present*, no. 111 (May 1986); Brendan Bradshaw, 'Edmund Spenser on Justice and Mercy', in Tom Dunne, ed., *Historical Studies*, XIV (1987). Contributions to recent discussions of the mental worlds of the Anglo-Irish (Old English) colonial community and of the Gaelic Irish in the same period are not listed here.

[2] Canny, 'Edmund Spenser and Anglo-Irish identity', above n. 1; Brady, 'Spenser's Irish crisis', above n. 1; Bradshaw, 'Edmund Spenser on Justice and Mercy', above n. 1.

[3] Canny, ibid.

139

come to devise in order to conceptualise and legitimise the political order being created by the conquest. However brave the attempt and however perceptive, in some respects, the reading of Spenser's text that was offered, the exercise in comparative analysis can be seen to have foundered. In depicting the entire *genre* in the image of Spenser's treatise texts were ransacked for supporting evidence without regard for structure or form or substantial content or even at times for the *ipsissima verba*. No doubt the scale of the operation serves to excuse the employment of a juggernaut. The fact remains that the consequent distortion was no less than might have been expected.[4] Accordingly a more limited exercise is attempted here in the hope that in the end it will yield more secure interpretative dividends. It aims at depth rather than breadth of analysis. The proposal is to gain a comparative perspective on Spenser's treatise by approaching it in the context of an examination in turn of two other major tracts devoted to analysing and prescribing for the Irish malady, both of them, like Spenser's, the work of an English humanist intellectual who wrote on the basis of first-hand experience of Ireland in the course of the fateful decade from 1586 in which a mounting Irish crisis erupted into the last and the greatest of the Tudor rebellions.[5] The interest of the comparison, it will emerge, lies in the differences as much as in the similarities of approach displayed by the authors.

I

Sir William Herbert's *Croftus sive de Hibernia Liber* recommends itself as a benchmark for the purpose of the exercise. First, in format it provides a good example of the conventional 'book on the state of Ireland' as devised in the Elizabethan period. Secondly, and more importantly, the evidence forges interesting links between the author and Spenser. At the intellectual level there is direct evidence of Herbert's association with the Sidney circle, of which Spenser was such a distinguished member;[6] and there is the fact, in any

---

[4] Some of the inadequacies of Canny's analysis have already been pointed out in Brady, 'Spenser's Irish crisis', above n. 1. However, the criticisms occur in the context of a reading of *A View* which is in turn unsatisfactory. Brady argues that Spenser's analysis of the Irish problem and his solution for it are each representative of a different colonial viewpoint, viewpoints which are incompatible. The analysis follows conventional humanist (i.e. rational) lines. The solution follows the draconian approach urged by military hardliners. In Brady's presentation Spenser stands condemned of bad faith since the humanist analysis is intended merely to provide a veneer of reason and moral justification for the hardline solution. Contrary to Brady's understanding, the reading proposed here argues that Spenser's analysis was not conventional but novel. The novelty pertained to the particular kind of ethnographic analysis which he introduced and to his adoption of a Machiavellian criterion of political morality. On these twin scaffolds Spenser was able to construct a rationale that was perfectly consistent with his hardline solution, see below pp. 271–83.

[5] The political history of the crisis had been analysed in Hiram Morgan, 'The Outbreak of the Nine Years War: Ulster in Irish Politics, 1583–95', Cambridge Ph.D, 1987.

[6] Q.v. *Dictionary of National Biography, s.v.*

case, that his writings reflect the combination of evangelical high-mindedness and literary grace that marked the group. At another level it seems pertinent to note the physical proximity of the two in Ireland, as near neighbours in the Munster plantation, even though Spenser arrived seven years earlier than Herbert, in 1587.[7] Thirdly, and plausibly against that background, a 'striking similarity' is claimed to exist between Herbert's treatise and that of Spenser. Indeed, *Croftus* is cited as providing 'the most convincing evidence that Spenser's *View* was a representative statement [of the New English colonial viewpoint]'.[8] Fourthly, however, such claims have been made on the basis of a cursory summary of the content of Herbert's treatise. It seems that a more extended account might be in order, all the more so because Herbert's humanist latinity serves to render his discussion less than readily accessible.[9] It is proposed to launch this exercise in comparative analysis, therefore, by following the argument that Herbert offers in some detail over the fifty-six pages of the printed text.

Despite its apparent irrelevance, the paean to wisdom that occupies the first seven pages of the *praefatio ad lectorem* is not to be dismissed as a rhetorical flourish. It establishes the frame of reference which the work is to employ. In this connection a significant tension can be observed between the disquisition on ancient philosophy with which the paean opens and the disparagement of human knowledge by comparison with revealed truth with which it concludes. Like all evangelical humanists from Melanchthon onward Herbert had a theoretical difficulty in bridging the gap, opened up by Luther, between reason and revelation.[10] In practice, as was usually the case, he adopted the Erasmian synthesis and resorted to the classical authors without inhibition as founts of moral wisdom.[11] Thus, in the course of the substantive discussion, he constantly seeks guidance from the classical masters, especially from the two humanist sages, Plato and Cicero, and from the history of hellenistic civilisation. More importantly, the central argument is advanced by means of a political analysis based on the categories of classical moral philosophy. The important point, for the purpose of comparison with Spenser's treatise, is that Herbert looks to humanist wisdom to provide him with the conceptual tools for analysing the Irish problem. The rest of the preface (pp. 8–12) is centred on a touching tribute to Herbert's kinsman, Sir James Croft, who, as Herbert explains, governed Ireland before he was even born – in 1551–3 to be precise – and with whom he had often discussed Irish affairs on returning to England

---

[7] See my 'Sword, word and strategy', above n. 1, pp. 486–7.

[8] Canny, 'Edmund Spenser and Anglo-Irish identity', above n. 1, pp. 10–11.

[9] The treatise was not published until the nineteenth century, W. E. Buckley, ed., *Croftus sive de Hibernia Liber* (Roxburghe Club, III, London, 1887). References are to this edition.

[10] See for instance Carl E. Maxcey, *Bona Opera: The Doctrine in Philip Melanchton* (Chicago, 1980) *passim*.

[11] Bradshaw, 'The Christian humanism of Erasmus', in *The Journal of Theological Studies*, n. s. 33 (1982), 411–47.

from Munster.[12] Here also, though in quite a different way, the preface has important implications for the substantive discussion. These are contained in Herbert's modest attribution (p. 8) to his conversations with Croft of whatever merits the treatise might be deemed to possess and in his delicate acknowledgement of this by the inclusion of Croft's name in the title. This coy gesture of familial piety takes on a wider political significance when it is related to the fact that Croft, at the time of writing, was not just a superannuated Irish lord deputy but an influential politician with access to the inner recesses of Elizabethan government, most especially as an adviser on Irish affairs.[13] Against that background *Croftus sive de Hibernia Liber* may be looked to for an insight not only into the mentality of a highly civilised Elizabethan colonist resident in Munster in the 1580s and 1590s but also for an insight into the analyses of the intractable Irish problem circulating among policy-makers in England at a crucial period of decision.

Proceeding to the exposition proper, a brief introductory section (pp. 12–15) treats, according to the convention, of the natural history and topography of the island and of its inhabitants. It was used by Herbert to take him with all speed to the heart of his matter. This was done by manipulating the customary lore to elaborate two arguments. One was the by now familiar trope of colonial promotional literature which extolled Ireland as a land of promise, especially in virtue of its under-exploited natural resources: a prize, according to Herbert, to be compared to Sicily when acquired by ancient Rome (p. 14). The second consisted in drawing an optimistic lesson from a melancholy paradox, frequently reiterated in the literature of reform, which concerned the ease with which Ireland could be conquered, but the difficulty of bringing it to obedience. Alluding summarily to the pre-Norman colonisation of the island and singling out the 'auspicious entry' of Henry II and the addition of the Irish diadem to the English crown by Henry VIII in 1541, Herbert emphasises the frequency with which Ireland had been subjected in past times and urged that the prize was available now, as never before, for the taking.[14] This brings him to the essence of his thesis which is that the present crisis – 'these floods of evil by which Ireland for so long agitated, might have been at length overcome' [hi malorum gurgites ... a quibus Hibernia diu agitata eversa demum fuisset atque obruta (p. 16)] – also offered the opportunity of a lasting settlement, provided that the sources of the evil were recognised and remedied. Thus the discussion is brought in double-quick time to the subject with which Herbert is preoccupied, and around which the voluminous literature of commonwealth commentary had developed since the opening decades of the century, namely, 'the causes of the evil state of Ireland and the remedies

[12] Q.v. 'Sir James Croft' in *Dictionary of National Biography*.
[13] As n. 10; Canny, *Elizabethan Conquest*, p. 120.
[14] On this last episode see my *The Irish Constitutional Revolution of the Sixteenth Century* (Cambridge, 1979), pp. 231–8.

thereof.[15] However, before engaging with that central issue, he devotes a preliminary four pages (pp. 16–19) to disposing of the stock objection that the best interests of England lie in leaving the island unreformed. That discussion must be passed over here except to note two features of it of special relevance to present interests. One is the way the objection draws from Herbert indignant appeals to the conventional humanist political morality which enjoined reform of the commonwealth as the primary task of government.[16] The second is his invocation, by way of clinching the argument, of the example of that famous hero Henry VIII who had spurned such vain and frivolous calculation in undertaking the reformation of Wales (p. 19). Herbert's treatment of this episode is of special interest because he indicates, in so many words, that the reform of Wales – as part of the Cromwellian revolution in government of the 1530s – is his model for the reform of Ireland half a century later.[17] What he envisages is the establishment of a unilateral framework of government, incorporating the semi-autonomous lordships of the Irishry, and exactly replicating the English system: '[thus] under one king, one law, one equitable, prudent and merciful government they might be made citizens, under different sceptres [i.e. the English and the Irish], of one happy and flourishing commonwealth' [ut sub uno rege, una lege, una equabili, prudenti et clementi administratione, sub variis sceptris unius felicissimae ac florentis-simae reipublicae cives efficerentur (p. 19)]. Fundamental differences between this conception and that of Edmund Spenser will emerge as the substantive discussion unfolds. Before proceeding to that discussion, however, one omission from Herbert's introduction deserves a moment's notice, as it serves to foreshadow these differences. This is the absence of the conventional antiquarian excursus on the origins and characteristics of the native inhabitants. It must be inferred that Herbert did not consider these matters relevant to his purpose as he hurried on from a description of the island itself to an account of the advent of the Anglo-Normans. Not so for Spenser, however, who dwells long on these matters to develop a sophisticated and, for all that, spurious ethnography of the native race, on the basis of which he then proceeds to argue for his stark final solution of the Irish problem.

The substantive discussion is taken up on page 20 and occupies the

---

[15] For the *genre* in the earlier period see Bradshaw, n. 12, pp. 36–48. For discussions of the literature in the later Tudor period see D. B. Quinn, ed., 'Edward Walshe's "Conjectures concerning the state of Ireland"', *Irish Historical Studies*, 5 (1946–7). Nicholas P. Canny, 'Rowland White's "Discors touching Ireland", c. 1569', in *Irish Historical Studies*, 20 (1977), 439–63; Brendan Bradshaw, 'A Treatise for the Reformation of Ireland', in *The Irish Jurist*, 16 (n. s. 1981), 299–315.

[16] Recent accounts of the movement in England are in G. R. Elton, *Reform and Reformation* (London, 1977), cc. 1, 3; J. A. Guy and Alistair Fox, *Reassessing the Henrician Age* (London, 1986) Maria Dowling, *Humanism in the Age of Henry VIII* (London, 1986) cf. my 'The Tudor commonwealth: reform and revision', in *Historical Journal*, 22 (1979), 455–76.

[17] P. R. Roberts, 'The "Acts of Union" and the Tudor Settlement of Wales', Cambridge Ph.D, 1966; Elton, above n. 14, pp. 203–5.

remaining 36 pages. It is divided into three parts comprising, according to the well-worn medical metaphor which Herbert employs (p. 16), a diagnosis of the ailments of the body politic, a prescription of remedies, and the provision of safeguards and antidotes to prevent a recurrence of the illness. Before reviewing all of this in its specific content, Herbert's general approach must first be noted since this serves to point up once more the emerging contrast with Spenser's treatise and to bring the issue of law and government to the centre of the discussion. In a word, the perspective which Herbert brings to bear is the political one. His understanding of the Irish problem derives from a study of the political history of the medieval lordship, the lessons of which are elucidated by recourse to a formal analysis according to the modes of classical philosophy. Likewise, his scheme of reform is devised as a political strategy in reliance upon the resources of civil government, specifically upon the resources of the English political system which, as Herbert believes, had been developed to a peculiarly high pitch of effectiveness. Spenser's perception, in contrast, as already indicated, is profoundly informed by ethnology which leads him both to discard a political–historical analysis of the Irish crisis, in favour of a culturally grounded one, and to renounce, with drastic consequences, Herbert's confidence in the English political system as an agent of civility in Ireland. The nub of the problem of reformation lay, therefore, in the effectiveness of law and civil government in the reformation of a barbarous people.

Against that background it is possible, at last, to turn to Herbert's diagnosis. This is hung on an account of the original acquisition of Ireland by the English crown (pp. 20–6) which enables Herbert to inculcate two lessons. The first does not detain him long and need not detain us either. He is concerned to emphasise the ease with which the conquest was achieved and the manner of its accomplishment. The point here is the employment of a 'minimum force' strategy: the way for conquest was cleared by war-like colonial adventurers but in fact the conquest itself was the work of Henry II, in the course of a six-month sojourn in 1172, to whom the vast majority of the Irishry 'offered themselves . . . and submitted to his power and authority' [Illorum qui se regi dediderant, eiusque potestati et authoritati se suaque commiserant: hi numero et multitudine ceteros longe superarunt (p. 20)]. The second lesson relates to the destabilisation of the settlement, to which Herbert devotes considerably more attention (some $5\frac{1}{2}$ pages). In this connection, it must be remembered, he is providing an explanation of the contemporary crisis and, in that way, anticipating his own proposals for a solution. Here it must suffice to single out the features that bear most directly on these latter purposes. It is noteworthy, then, that although the discussion begins with the diplomatic suggestion that the causes of instability are to be sought in the behaviour of the two communities of the island – the native Irish and the colonial one – it soon emerges that the fundamental problem lies in the faulty polity established by

Henry II. Three mistakes were made by 'that most prudent prince' (p. 22). One was the failure to establish an 'administration', by which is meant, as Herbert elaborates in detail, the administrative system of government developed in England. A second was the failure to establish a civil society by the abolition of native Irish laws and customs, the establishment of defensible towns, and the development of a nucleus of viable English colonies. The third was to entrust military defence to garrisons of mercenary soldiers instead of to the colonists supplemented by some modest military assistance. It is hardly necessary to draw attention to the polemic which is implicit in all of this on behalf of a politic and civil approach to reformation. The polemic is sustained in Herbert's discussion of the contribution of the two communities to destabilising the settlement. This he does in the course of tracing the historical disintegration of the lordship which he explains in terms of specific kinds of politically disruptive conduct, ascribing it variously to the native Irish – calumny, sedition, rebellion (p. 20) – and to the colonists – faction, sedition, tyranny (pp. 23–6) – the net result of which was to breed hatred and contempt for the crown's government. In characterising the disruptive conduct of the two communities in these terms Herbert believes that he has diagnosed the specific causes of instability within the lordship and that he has placed himself, accordingly, in a position to prescribe specific remedies. It is significant therefore, that he does not relate these disruptive patterns of behaviour to the cultural characteristics of the Irishry or to innate racial dispositions. The implications of the absence of this ethnographic dimension will become clear in considering the remedies which he proposes.

Having uncovered the causes of the disease through a study of history Herbert now (p. 27) turns to philosophy to reveal to him their nature and to provide him with remedies. Inverting the order of the historical analysis he deals first with the types of politically disruptive behaviour that he has just identified, discussing each in turn (pp. 27–33). The main relevance of this discussion to present purposes is that it reveals Herbert's firm option for civil policy – statecraft, as it would later be called – as an alternative to military force to counteract political subversion. An illuminating comparison in this regard is provided by his treatment of popular sedition (pp. 28–9), since Spenser deals with the same problem in a well-known passage in Book v of the *Faerie Queene*. Herbert's strategy is to isolate the 'stirrers and leaders' of such movements, for 'the cause and origin of every furore belong to authors, the rest become wild by contagion' [nam multitudo omnis, sicut more, per se immobilis est, et multitudinem Aeoli isti exitant, et causa atque origo omnis furoris penes autores est, reliqui contagione insaniunt (p. 28)]. Accordingly he proposes a programme of counter-espionage: propaganda to coax away the popular following; the exploitation of divided interests; bribery to detach susceptible lieutenants; the offer of a general pardon; ultimately the assassination of the ringleaders. Spenser's treatment, in contrast, is devoted to demonstrating the ineffectualness of civil government (in the person of Artegall) when confronted by popular protest and the necessity, therefore, for deploying punitive force (in the person of Talus) without restraint of law to crush the threat to order.[18] The implications of this comparison for approaches to the problem of Irish disorder need hardly be stressed. However, it also has wider intellectual implications, which sharpen our perception of the contrasting outlooks of Herbert and Spenser. The former's confidence in civil policy as a strategy against political subversion serves to place his treatise in a rationalist tradition of political reflection whereas Spenser, as will be clear, stands squarely in the voluntarist tradition which looks to power and to coercive authority as the foundations of good government. It remains to add a word about the conception of statecraft revealed in these pages. The Machiavellian resonance of Herbert's strategy for dealing with popular sedition is no coincidence. In fact, as the discussion proceeds, he repeatedly acknowledges his debt to 'that notable Italian'.[19] Nevertheless, he also takes care to reject Machiavellian political morality, insisting that statecraft must be made to serve the moral purposes ascribed to politics in the classical philosophical tradition, i.e. the profit and interest of the commonwealth. Indeed, that is precisely the possibility he seeks to demonstrate while, in the process, manifesting the conventional disapprobation of oppressive and tyrannous government. In all of this he reflects the characteristic humanist aspiration towards a rigorously rational and yet moral approach to politics.[20]

On page 34 Herbert turns from the politically disruptive behaviour of the two communities in Ireland to consider the 'defect of the political administration' which he had noted in the original settlement. And he turns in search of a remedy from statecraft to polity (*politicum*). As may be guessed from his description of the malady, the remedy is not far to seek. Invoking Plato's definition of polity as 'the discipline and rule, the nurse and custodian of conduct by which men are formed either to wicked or honest life' he affirms that 'no form of administration or polity can be imagined more illustrious, more excellent or more suited to Ireland' than the English one [Politia est disciplina et regula, nutrix et custos eorum morum quibus homines varie sive ad turpem sive ad honestam vitam informantur. . .Nulla vero administrationis aut politiae forma illustrior aut praestantior aut Hiberniae accommodatior excongitari potest, quam ea qua Anglia ad summam perfectionem eximiamque felicitatem adducta est atque evecta (p. 34)]. Accordingly he devotes two pages (pp. 34–5) to outlining its main elements – its central institutions, its judicial machinery and its system of local government – and to

---

[18] *Faerie Queen*, v. ii. 29–54.
[19] On the reception of Machiavelli in England see Felix Raab, *The English Face of Machiavelli* (London, 1964); J. G. A. Pocock, *The Machiavellian Moment* (Princeton, 1975), chs. X–XII.
[20] On northern humanism see Quentin Skinner, *The Foundations of Modern Political Thought* (Cambridge, 1978), I, chs. 8, 9.

proposing a scheme to bring the Irish polity into exact conformity with the English one. With a view to the latter two principal proposals are made: one for the establishment of regional councils in Munster and Ulster as a means of providing the central administration with an effective presence in the remote parts; the other for the extension of the shire system from the colonial area into the semi-autonomous lordships, and in this way replicating the English system of local government throughout the island. The effect of these two measures would be to transform Ireland's political constitution into an exact model of the English one, already possessing, as it did, the central English political institutions of administration, judiciary and parliament, as a heritage from the medieval lordship. Thus, Herbert concludes, Ireland might be 'restored and brought back to a perfect form of public administration and polity' [Sic et in Hibernia faciendum, priusquam ad perfectam publicae administrationis et politiae formam redigi possit et reduci' (p. 35)]. The interest of the scheme lies in the fact that it entails nothing more than the implementation in a systematic and comprehensive way of a policy already being advanced tentatively and piecemeal since mid-century.[21] It reflects, accordingly, a fundamental tenet of the conventional wisdom which concluded from the manifest excellence of English law and government to its effectiveness as an instrument for bringing the Irish to civility – a tenet which Herbert believed had already been verified in the reformation of Wales. As we shall see, it is precisely this logic that Spenser questions and by doing so arrives at an entirely more radical understanding of what the reformation of Ireland entailed.

Meanwhile Herbert proceeds to consider the strategy for implementing his scheme. In doing so he brings the discussion to the major practical issue raised by the diverging approaches of Spenser and himself. Reverting to a perennial debate he raises the question (p. 35) whether the extension of crown government is to be achieved by force of arms or by the consent of the local communities. He responds by choosing a *via media*. Appealing to the authority of Machiavelli he emphasises that the magistrate must possess the capacity to enforce his will. He then asks how the magistrate is to be provided with such a capacity in Ireland. This is his cue to introduce his strategy for a civil reformation and to unfold the third of his remedies for the Irish malady. His answer is, again following Machiavelli, by establishing a nucleus of viable colonies.[22] The importance which Herbert attaches to this proposal is indicated by the space he allots to considering it (pp. 35–42). Here it must suffice to single out three significant features of the treatment which provide

---

[21] On the piecemeal extension of Tudor government in Ireland see Ciarán Brady, 'Court, castle and country: the framework of government in Tudor Ireland', in Brady and Raymond Gillespie, eds., *Natives and Newcomers* (Dublin, 1986), pp. 22–49.

[22] This section is lifted more or less *verbatim* from *The Prince*, ch. III on the subject of 'composite principalities' – an incidental confirmation that Herbert envisages scattered settlements among the native population, not a radical re-ordering of land-ownership as Spenser plans.

points of comparison with Spenser's proposals. The first is the preclusion of a military solution by means of a mercenary army distributed in garrisons: this, Herbert argues, would prove inordinately costly and would cause widespread alienation.[23] The second, a corollary to the first, is the insistence (p. 37) that the opportunity already existed for a civil reformation – without a preliminary military conquest – by proceeding to colonise territories forfeited to the crown by recent rebellions in Munster, Leinster and Connacht, and by co-ordinating such a scheme with the colonial venture of the earl of Essex on crown lands in Ulster. The third is Herbert's provision for extirpating the native socio-political system. In a long discussion (pp. 37–42) of measures to prevent the destabilisation of the new settlement in the manner of the original one, Herbert insists on the need for the immediate and total abolition of 'Irish customs and public institutions' – though not, as later appears, of the Irish language. Adhering to the dynamic, Platonic concept of polity, he holds that the maintenance of native socio-political forms would not only frustrate the effectiveness of English law and government in reforming the Irishry but would also serve, as history showed, to corrupt the colonists. Herbert's insistence on this point has special interest because of a passage (p. 41) which, for once, seems to anticipate Spenser in envisaging drastic military action to overcome obdurate resistance. There is, however, a crucial difference. Herbert brings himself to contemplate such a prospect only as a possible last resort for the sake of securing a civil reformation already in progress whereas Spenser's ethnological analysis, as we shall see, leads him to insist upon a drastic military campaign as a necessary preliminary to a civil reformation. The difference serves to illustrate the search for the *via media* between the extremes of coercion and conciliation which is the hallmark of Herbert's strategy.

Three further pages (pp. 42–5) are devoted to remedying a final defect of Ireland's medieval polity, 'hatred and contempt of the chief magistrates and the public administration'. That discussion need not detain us except to note the way in which it serves to demonstrate the consistency with which Herbert applies the principles of political humanism to the Irish problem. His remedy in this instance reflects a discussion that was a commonplace of humanist political writings, as to whether it is better for the ruler to be feared or loved, a discussion invariably resolved in favour of love and then expanded to show that the ruler's means of eliciting love is virtue.[24] Accordingly, these pages are given over largely to a discussion of political justice and personal virtue as necessary attributes of those responsible for conducting government in

---

[23] For Machiavelli's hostility to mercenaries see *The Prince*, ch. XII. Cf. Quentin Skinner, *The Foundations of Modern Political Thought*, I, pp. 163–4. Skinner's remarks on p. 200 do not take account of humanist colonial literature as developed in Ireland.

[24] A classic exposition of the theme is Desiderius Erasmus, *Education of a Christian Prince*, ch. 2. Cf. Skinner, *Foundations*, I, pp. 228–36.

Ireland. All that need be noted further about that discussion is the appearance once more of the *via media* as a key element in Herbert's thought, on this occasion in the form of a *caveat* against the extreme of rigour which breeds hatred for government, and of indulgence which brings government into contempt: the cardinal virtue for the magistrate is prudent moderation.

Herbert has now elaborated over some nineteen pages four remedies for the evil state of Ireland: statecraft to counter political subversion; the extension of English government on a unilateral basis to remedy Ireland's defective public administration; a refurbished colonial settlement to re-establish the crown's power; just and virtuous magistrates to gain respect for government in place of hatred and contempt. At the same time he has been conducting, in effect, a re-run of the original conquest, supplying what was omitted with fatal consequences by Henry II. In that respect, however, only two of the three flaws noted at the outset have been repaired: the defective polity and the unstable colonial settlement. The third, the failure to establish a civil society, is repaired in Herbert's concluding pages (pp. 46–55) in the context of a discussion of the antidotes and safeguards that are necessary to prevent the conquest from being undermined. These latter constitute a programme of social engineering designed to 'incline to virtue and probity of spirit and to weaken the dishonesty and wickedness of men' [Praecipuum vero Hiberniae antidotum duabus in rebus consistit, in animorum ad virtutem et probitatem inclinatione, et in virum ad improbitatem et nequitiam enervatione (p. 46)]. The specific content here, as elsewhere, is not strikingly original even though interesting variations on familiar themes occur. Much attention is devoted to the promotion of religion and education as means of strengthening moral virtue (pp. 46–50) – a university is proposed for Limerick to serve Munster as well as one at Dublin.[25] Side by side with these, somewhat unusually, Herbert emphasises the role of public justice as a persuasive rather than as a coercive moral pedagogue, and he proposes various ways of exploiting its possibilities in this regard, e.g. the public honouring of exemplary conduct and of the officers of justice (p. 51), exhortations *ad rem* on the occasion of judicial sessions (p. 52), etc. In turning to deal with the nefarious influences within society that incline men towards evil, Herbert's major preoccupation is the traditional Gaelic life-style: earlier arguments about its countervailing influence against the civilising processes of English law and government are reiterated, and a counter-strategy is proposed, combining the resources of statute and statecraft (pp. 52–4). To this is added a veritable rag-bag of familiar devices which are summarily listed and given a general, if rather dismissive, benediction as 'very useful' (p. 54): they run the gamut from

[25] Unfortunately the recent authoritative history of Trinity College Dublin has little to say about the long prehistory that culminated in the foundation of Trinity from the endowments of the dissolved religious orders, R. B. McDowell and D. A. Webb, *Trinity College Dublin, 1592–1952* (Cambridge, 1982).

the construction of cities in pastoral Gaelic Ireland to the domiciling of Gaelic noblemen at the English court.[26] A final proposal is given more extensive treatment and rounds off the section with a graceful peroration. It proposes a transformation of popular culture by the purveyance of 'sacred hymns and songs in praise of virtue' in the (Irish) vernacular so that 'they [the Irish] may be soothed by this sweet music, that they may celebrate the divine majesty with harp and lute and may be delighted with Doric and Phrygian harmony of which the one disposes to modesty and calm, the other incites to piety and divine contemplation' [ut suavi hac musica demulceantur, divinum numen in psalerio et cythara celebrent, et Dorica atque Phyrigia harmonia delectentur, quarum altera ad modestiam et affectum sedationem suadet, altera ad pietatem divinamque contemplationem hortatur et incidat ... (p. 54)].

The programme of social engineering, directed towards the creation of a civil society schooled in virtue, united in submission to a common law and government, devoted to the pursuit of peace, provides the final plank in Herbert's scheme for the reformation of Ireland. Its implications for his colonial outlook and for the purposes of comparison with Spenser remain to be considered. Conveniently, as it happens, when Herbert's social programme is examined with these concerns in view, it is found to confirm a pattern of thought that has gradually emerged in the earlier discussion. In reviewing the intellectual and ideological content of the social programme, therefore, an opportunity is offered to delineate the conceptual framework of Herbert's treatise as this has emerged laboriously and piecemeal in the analysis so far. Three key concepts of the social programme may be singled out in this connection. One is philosophical–anthropological in character. It expresses a rational conviction about the capacity of the mind to move the will, on which subject, revealingly, Plato is much invoked at this point: hence, religious evangelisation and catechesis figure as a means towards a civil reformation rather than, as in the protestant view, as a sequel to it (pp. 46–7); hence, the attention devoted to the scheme for the universities (pp. 48–50); hence, finally, to illustrate the point from a negative angle, Herbert's perception that the threat posed by the Gaelic order resides primarily in the Gaelic *literati*, the bardic caste, rather than in socio-cultural institutions, e.g. nomadic pastoralism (pp. 51, 54). All of this reflects an intellectual stance already evident in Herbert's opening paean to wisdom and serves, therefore, to locate him philosophically in the mainstream of Christian Platonism.[27] At the same time it is noteworthy that this approach to civil reform provides in every instance a point of contrast with the scheme of Spenser, a contrast which can now be seen to be conditioned fundamentally by a philosophical–anthropo-

[26] Brady distorts Herbert's thought by singling out transplantation as a feature of his scheme on the basis of a reference to it in this list, 'Spenser's Irish crisis', above n. 1, p. 24.
[27] W. K. G. Guthrie, *A History of Greek Philosophy* (Cambridge, 1969), III, pp. 450–73; idem (Cambridge, 1975), IV, pp. 213–35; Bradshaw, 'Christian humanism of Erasmus', above n. 11.

logical conception. The second conceptual scaffold is ideological. In the social programme it manifests itself in the form of a predilection for civil and political strategies, implemented by means of law and 'policy', as against coercive military methods. The same civil and political bias was noted earlier in Herbert's formula for reconquest, and earlier still, from a different angle, in his initial analysis of the Irish problem. Two other manifestations of the same cast of thought help to identify its intellectual provenance: the polemic against mercenaries and garrisons, and the espousal of a morally purified Machiavellian statecraft. Thus, an ideological profile emerges characterised by a deep commitment to civilian and political values, a deep antipathy towards mercenary standing armies, and an enthusiasm for Machiavellian statecraft, reconciled, however, with conventional humanist morality. These, in short, are the unmistakable features of contemporary civic or republican humanism.[28] It remains to note once more the contrast which Spenser's programme provides on the same emotive issues, a contrast which serves, therefore, to demarcate an ideological frontier between the two, reinforcing the philosophical frontier earlier noted. The third conceptual frame of Herbert's social programme takes the form of a moral perception, namely, that virtue must be sought in the middle way between extremes, in accordance with the Aristotelian maxim. The social programme provides a neat illustration here in the antidote which it offers to the baneful influence of 'wanton and turbulent spirits': eschewing 'tyrannous force' and 'sophistical persuasions' alike, Herbert contrives, nevertheless, to combine both in moderation by means of a strategy based on statute and statecraft (pp. 52–4). Here, as elsewhere, the social policy serves to illustrate a concept that has moulded Herbert's approach throughout the treatise, strikingly, as noted at the time in devising a strategy of political conquest. In relating the principle in this instance to the contemporary intellectual context, one later application holds special interest – significantly the concluding sequence of the entire treatise. Here Herbert turns finally to the question of power, raising it in the specific context of the lord deputy's authority (p. 55). By way of answer he manipulates a characteristically Neoplatonic cosmic analogy to uncharacteristic effect, not to provide a unitary–hierarchical model of political order but a model based on checks and balances: thus, he urges, as the moon and the stars moderate the excessive energies of the sun, so parliament and the laws function to moderate the power of the lord deputy. Herbert's treatise is rounded off, therefore, with an affirmation of political moderation as an inherent element in the English system of polity, an affirmation which serves to set him squarely in the mainstream of the English constitutional tradition.[29] It is a measure of his commitment to the constitutional tradition that this affirmation was made in the face of an escalating Irish crisis. And that commitment provides a final

---

[28] Pocock, *Machiavellian Moment*, pp. 333–400.
[29] Robert Eccleshall, *Order and Reason in Politics* (Oxford, 1978), pp. 47–75, 97–125.

revealing contrast with the treatise of Spenser which, as we shall see, is concerned to affirm quite a different perception of political morality.

In the light of the foregoing explication of Herbert's text the exercise in comparative analysis envisaged at the outset may now proceed – and with all the more speed for the time spent in establishing the benchmark. Using *Croftus* as a basis of comparison the intention now is to scrutinise two other contemporary contributions to the literature of Irish reform and in this way to gain a comparative perspective on Spenser's treatise, specifically on the claim that it constitutes the classic statement of the ideology of the emerging New English colonial community. Before proceeding to the analysis, however, it may be useful to describe in summary form the nature of the benchmark that has been provided. First, then, *Croftus sive de Hibernia Liber* reflects the quest for a rational, political and moderate solution to the Irish problem. Second, informing these qualities and providing the intellectual framework within which they operate the treatise reflects the thought of three major intellectual traditions: Platonic rational philosophy, the political thought of Florentine civic humanism and the constitutional ideas developed within the English tradition of political reflection. Thirdly, embodying the mind and the traditions of thought in a historical author, Herbert emerges from his text as an Elizabethan humanist in the classic Erasmian mould – committed to social and religious reform by rational means, i.e. education and civil policy – and as a member of the Tudor ruling elite with a characteristic predilection for English political institutions and for the ideals of moderate constitutional government which the English system supposedly enshrined.

II

An instructive route from Herbert's text to that of Spenser is provided by Richard Beacon's *Solon His Follie*, published in Oxford in 1594. Interestingly, from the comparative viewpoint, his experience of Ireland was gained as a legal official of the crown in Munster where his sojourn overlapped with that of Spenser and Herbert.[30] Interestingly also, for comparative purposes, his treatise bears the same strong imprint of literary humanism as that of Herbert: it is presented in dialogue form and by means of an elaborate metaphor referring to the reform by Athens of her satellite territory, Salamania.[31] These circumstantial similarities lead one to anticipate a common perspective, and, indeed, on first approach, Beacon's discussion seems to share the same ground as that of Herbert. He begins, as Herbert does, by making out a case for an immediate and general reformation, pitching his argument more directly than the latter against the policy of gradual and 'particular' (i.e. limited

---

[30] Richard Beacon, *Solon His Follie* (Oxford, 1594) (*STC* 1653). The biographical details are in the text.

[31] The metaphor pivots on the account of the recovery of the island of Salamis for Athens by the statesman and sage Solon. The title alludes to the story.

and *ad hoc*) reformation on which the crown was half-heartedly engaged.[32] More significantly, when he proceeds to elaborate his scheme of reform he displays the same political and civilian cast of thought noted in Herbert. The fundamental conception of both is of the inhabitants of Ireland reduced to civility through the instrumentality of English law and government. Accordingly Beacon plans, like Herbert, for the extension of the English political system unilaterally throughout the island, and proposes to that end the creation of regional presidencies and the shiring of the Gaelic territories – on which he echoes Herbert's invocation of the precedent of Wales.[33] Again, in discussing strategies of enforcement, he focuses on the resources of civil government and, in this connection, like Herbert, gives special prominence to the Machiavellian motifs of 'policy' or statecraft and of colonies as the necessary alternative to military garrisons.[34] Finally, to draw agreement from silence, Beacon shows as little interest as Herbert in the possible implications of ethnography for the Irish problem, omitting, like the latter, to speak of the racial origins or characteristics of the native race.

Yet, despite the appearance of a shared outlook which this conveys, the views of Beacon and Herbert on the reformation of Ireland sharply diverge. The differences between them quickly emerge when Beacon's scheme is set in the context of the total thought pattern earlier discerned in Herbert's treatise. The effect is to highlight a conflict of values of dramatic practical import. The conflict hinges partly on what Beacon leaves out. Here comparison reveals that two of the three conceptual pivots of Herbert's treatise are missing from Beacon's scheme. One is the Platonic understanding of reason, with all that it implies about intellectual formation as the key to political and social reform: Beacon provides no paean to wisdom and the university project is not even mentioned in his scheme. The second is Aristotelian moderation, with its corollary, in Herbert's conception, of the notion of government as bound by constitutional constraints. The contrast in this case is doubly revealing for it brings Beacon's radical alternative to the fore. This is the notion of severe justice to which he resorts as the key to effective government with the same persistent regularity as Herbert resorts to reason and moderation. And Beacon's insistence on the application of this principle, even in defiance of the due processes of law – hence his vindication of the draconian regime of Richard Bingham in Connacht – provides a measure of the distance thus placed between the approaches of the two.[35] Further light is thrown on

---

[32] Above p. 147.

[33] On this see Beacon's description of his scheme of general reformation, *Solon*, pp. 57–65, especially 60–5; also Beacon's remedy for overmighty subjects, ibid, pp. 78–85. The example of the reform of Wales is invoked on p. 83.

[34] On statecraft see Beacon, *Solon*, pp. 11, 26–8, 32. On colonies as preferable to garrisons see pp. 105–11.

[35] The theme of severe justice as the key to good government is reiterated throughout the treatise. Bingham's peremptory justice is defended on pp. 7–8, 16.

these divergent outlooks by means of another contrast. This relates to the ideological affinities of the two treatises in the context of contemporary currents of reform thought in England. Set in this context, as already noted, the preoccupations and affirmations of Herbert's treatise serve to place it in a classic Erasmian humanist mould.[36] When Beacon's text is approached with the same question on view it is found to bear the marks of a more specifically religious reforming ethos. Two features are especially relevant in this connection. One is the apocalyptic and providential categories that intrude into the discussion, especially in a lengthy disquisition on the rise and fall of nations: by contrast, Herbert refers to God's providential decrees only to relegate them to the domain of inscrutable mystery. The second is the association of Irish reform with a call for the establishment of a protective protestant international alliance: a subject on which Herbert is totally silent.[37] These preoccupations, placed in the context of Beacon's affirmation of severe justice, provide a readily recognisable ideological pattern: an apocalyptic and providential world view, a vision of England as part of a 'protestant international', a radically rigorist conception of political justice, these are the hallmarks of late Elizabethan puritanism.[38] It is now clear, therefore that the divergent approaches of Beacon and Herbert to the reformation of Ireland reflect a radical tension discernible in the reformation movement in England as between an outlook derived from early sixteenth-century Erasmian humanism and the outlook of stern unbending Calvinism.

While emphasising these contrasts, it is necessary, nevertheless, for the purposes of comparative analysis, to bear in mind the common ground noted at the outset. From a comparative perspective, therefore, it seems proper to assign the treatises of Herbert and Beacon to a common generic category on the basis of their shared civilian reform strategies. Their contrasting formulations are then assigned to the different sub-categories of moderate humanism and radical puritanism within the same generic category of civilian reform strategies. The value of this classification is that it provides a way of measuring the 'something else again' which Spenser's scheme represents by assigning it to a different generic category of reform treatises.

III

Offered for publication in 1596 – but, significantly, declined a licence – *A View of the Present State of Ireland* shares two features with its immediate pre-

---

[36] Above pp. 141, 154.

[37] The theme is introduced in the context of a discussion of change/decline, Beacon, *Solon*, pp. 70–3. Cf. Herbert, *Croftus*, p. 27.

[38] Richard Bauckham, *Tudor Apocalypse* (Abingdon, 1970); Jan Albert Dop, *Eliza's Knights* (Albasserdam: Remak, 1981).

decessors.[39] It seeks to persuade the crown to undertake a major initiative in Ireland – a general reformation. And in doing so it follows the conventional tripartite organisation of such treatises into sections analysing the problem, proposing a strategy for solving it and elaborating a programme of political and social reform designed to prevent subsequent deterioration. These two features apart, Spenser's treatment differs in every significant respect, though to a greater or lesser extent, from the treatises of Herbert and Beacon. Even in presentation it offers less of a parade of literary humanism than either *Croftus* or *Solon*. True, it adopts the dialogue form, but the tone is different: it opens *in media res*, without introductory flourish, and the prolonged discussion that follows is of a pattern: undeviating, unadorned, unpedantic, shorn of classical references except where they contribute substantially to the argument. The style is well suited to the matter, as from the outset Spenser sets about subverting the basic principles of the civilian position and constructing a rationale for a radical alternative.

The diagnosis of the Irish malady which Spenser provides hangs, like those of Herbert and Beacon, upon the paradox that the advancement of the polity in England and the deterioration of the polity in Ireland occurred under the same system of law and government. However, the paradox is differently explained, and the difference is crucial, since, of course, the diagnosis is intended to imply the cure for the disease. Where, therefore, Herbert and Beacon situate their explanations in specific historical circumstances, in the failure to extend the English political system throughout the whole of the island in the aftermath of the conquest, Spenser situates his explanation in the context of a disquisition on political science. The strategy of the argument is to replace the philosophical notion of a political constitution, as a perfectly ordered and universally valid system of government, with a more contingent and relativised conception, and then to bring that more sceptical notion to bear in attributing the evil state of Ireland to the inherent limitations of English polity. His exposition focuses on three variable factors which, he argues, circumscribe all arrangements for the ordering of political societies: time, the passage of which alters the conditions for which the system was framed; racial type, which reflects different psychological dispositions, basically as between civil (peace-loving) and barbaric (warlike) societies, each of which requires a different mode of government; political circumstance, which may be such as to render civil government inoperable altogether, specifically, Spenser argues, the circumstance of popular rebellion.[40] Deploying these explanatory strategies over more than ninety pages of the printed text Spenser proceeds to account for the concurrent reformation of England and the

---

[39] I have used the earlier and more easily accessible modern edn., W. C. Renwick, ed., *A View of the Present State of Ireland* (Oxford, 1970).

[40] The themes are introduced in the opening discussion of law, *A View*, pp. 3–20.

deformation of Ireland under the same political system. Despite the interest of the exposition our attention here must be confined to noting the way in which it functions to achieve Spenser's ulterior purpose, i.e. the demolition of the rationale on which the civilian approach to reform was based and the construction of a rationale for his radical alternative. In brief, this is done by exploiting the same three explanatory strategies. By means of the first Spenser is able to reject the cherished aspiration of Herbert and Beacon towards a restoration of the original civil conquest: time, Spenser argues, in effect, rendered such a conception anachronistic – altered times require a new conquest.[41] By appeal to the second he is able to remove the central plank in the civilian strategy of reform, i.e. the reduction of the Irish to obedience by means of English law and government; the barbaric character of Irish society, Spenser argues in his lengthy ethnographic disquisition, renders the Irish ungovernable by the processes of English civil polity – Irish reform calls for the creation of an Irish polity *sui generis*.[42] The third enables Spenser to counter the civilian polemic against the deployment of a mercenary army: the rebellious condition of Ireland – by reason of Irish character and Irish history – precludes the deployment of civilian instruments of government without the prior use of the military sword to secure and maintain social order.[43] In addition to this three-pronged assault on the civilian position, a fourth argument developed by Spenser in the course of the long opening section adds a necessary moral dimension to his radical rationale. Here, in line with his subversion of the idealised, philosophical conception of political constitutions, he seeks to emphasise the contingent and relative nature of political justice. Highlighting the practical impediments in the way of dispensing legal justice in accordance with an absolute and universally valid form, he invokes as a criterion instead public necessity and the interests of the commonwealth – thus identifying himself with the Machiavellian tradition in precisely that aspect which Herbert had indignantly repudiated.[44] By means of these four intellectual constructs, therefore, Spenser is able to manipulate his analysis of the causes of the evil state of Ireland to provide a rationale for his notorious 'final solution' which he now proceeds to unfold in the tones of a messenger of light and, indeed, of mercy.

Two features of the solution outlined in *A View of the Present State of Ireland* need to be emphasised in the light of current interpretations. One is the stark contrast which it provides with Herbert's scheme; this because the two have been supposed to correspond so closely, indeed, as to provide the clinching evidence for the existence of a common colonial viewpoint. The other is the logical coherence of the solution with the preceding exposition of the

---

[41] E.g. *A View*, pp. 3, 67ff.
[42] The argument is developed mainly in *A View*, pp. 4–62.   [43] *A View*, pp. 12–13.
[44] The discussion develops around the notion of *Jus Politicum*, *A View*, p. 21f. For Herbert's rejection of Machiavellian morality see above p. 146.

problem; this because, alternatively, Spenser has been accused of using a 'conventional humanist' analysis of the problem as a smoke-screen behind which to advance an intemperate and ill-considered remedy – reflecting nothing more rational, in fact, than the knee-jerk reaction of the militant hard men.[45] Neither suggestion is found to have any substance when the contents of Spenser's scheme are set in the context of the present comparative analysis. Spenser's scheme, in line with the remedies of Herbert and Beacon, is based upon the perception that the source of the present problem lies in the failure of the original conquest. However, as his understanding of that failure differs fundamentally from theirs so does his approach to a solution. Whereas Herbert and Beacon proceed to plan for the consolidation of a conquest that had been left with that final stage uncompleted, Spenser starts from the perception that the original conquest had been misconceived in any case. The barbarous Irish could not be reduced to submission by political means. Accordingly their subjugation needed to be undertaken afresh and in a different way. His strategy for a new conquest is elaborated in the second section of the treatise and is the source from which the notoriety of his general scheme mainly derives. The strategy has two objectives. The ultimate aim is what he calls a 'reformation of the realm' by which he means the creation of a new socio-political order. This primarily entails a massive project of trans-plantation in which rebellious septs are to be uprooted from their traditional territories and resettled in modest, dispersed holdings as sub-tenants of colonial landowners.[46] Meanwhile, however, he anticipates widespread native resistance and he provides against it by proposing as his immediate objective a war of conquest. The reduction of the Irish by the sword, Spenser insists, is a necessary preliminary to any programme of political reform 'for it is vain to prescribe laws where no man careth for keeping them, nor feareth the danger for breaking them'.[47] Accordingly most of the section is devoted to planning in detail a horrific military strategy whereby the septs – men, women and children – are to be pinned into their territories by garrisons of mercenaries and reduced either to submission or extinction by a combination of relentless military attrition and scorched-earth tactics.[48] This, then, is Spenser's re-run of the medieval conquest: a massive project of transplantation designed to create a new socio-political order, preceded by a ruthless military campaign designed to subdue the warlike dispositions of the Irish.

It remains to draw out the implications of the scheme for the comparative analysis to which this essay is devoted and, in the process, to engage with the recent historiography. First, to emphasise the contrast, the Spenserian

---

[45] For the charge of incoherence see Brady, 'Spenser's Irish crisis', above n. 1, pp. 33–41. Brady fails to distinguish between the argument in conception and in execution. My intention here is to demonstrate the conceptual coherence of Spenser's argument. Flaws in execution seem to me entirely explicable in terms of the scale and range of the work. Spenser was an amateur in most of the areas touched on. He was working without assistance and at a time of great stress.

[46] *A View*, pp. 93–4.   [47] Ibid, p. 95.   [48] Ibid, pp. 95–120.

strategy of reconquest has no parallel in the schemes of Herbert and Beacon. True, both moot the possibility of a military campaign to coerce submission. But they do so in a way that highlights the contrast. The prospect is contemplated only fleetingly, as a possible last resort, and neither displays a willingness to plan for the contingency.[49] This could hardly be more at variance with the approach of Spenser who regards a war of conquest as the first necessary step in the programme of reformation, and devotes almost the entire middle section of his treatise to planning it. Conversely, the first necessary step envisaged by Herbert and Beacon – and planned for by them with similar care and attention to detail – is the extension of civil government on the English model to the disobedient Irishry and the establishment of a nucleus of civilian colonies to provide an infrastructure of power, this latter expressly as an alternative to military garrisons.[50] The contrast thus highlighted is of fundamental significance. It provides, in fact, a litmus whereby the colonial ideology of Spenser may be distinguished from that of the civilians, Herbert and Beacon, namely, the place assigned to the military sword in the reformation of the body politic. It must be emphasised, to pass to the second historiographical misconception, that Spenser's militarism is to be referred to an intellectually grounded ideology, not to a psychological reflex prompted by the mounting Irish crisis. Whatever his exasperated frustration, his radical solution emerged, for better or for worse, as the logical dictate of a sophisticated analysis of the problem. His thesis, with its built-in assault on the fundamental assumptions of the civilians, scarcely needs to be rehearsed here yet again. Suffice it to note that Spenser places a summary statement of it by way of apologia at the head of the exposition of his conquest strategy.[51]

However, it remains to comment on one aspect of the apologia there presented as it seems to indicate a shift in Spenser's position in a significant respect. Surprisingly, having earlier invoked the Machiavellian criterion of political necessity in order to liberate the state from the constraints of absolute justice, Spenser now enunciates a principle that seems to trammel the state once more. Considering the policy to be adopted towards obnoxious elements in Irish society he indignantly rejects the possibility of simple extermination. On the contrary, he insists that the royal sword may be wielded with justice only when it is directed to a reformative end; the extirpation of evil but the reformation of people must be the aim, 'for evil people by good ordinance and government may be made good'.[52] It seems proper to emphasise, if only to ensure that Spenser incurs no more than the obloquy he deserves, that at this crucial juncture he affirms a notion of justice that indicates reformation rather than retribution to be his aim. It may be added that this reformative conception is, indeed, basic to his approach to the Irish problem. Its importance is

[49] Above p. 148. A reference in similar vein comes at the conclusion of *Solon*, p. 113.
[50] Above pp. 147–8, 153.
[51] For the apologia see Spenser, *A View*, p. 93.   [52] Ibid, p. 95.

reflected not only in its pivotal location in the present text – at the point where the discussion passes from a consideration of the problem to its solution – but also in the fact that the same affirmation is found at a crucial juncture in Book v of the *Faerie Queene* where the moral issue raised by Irish reform is more fully addressed.[53] On the other hand, it must be emphasised that affirmation of the moral principle of reformative justice does not imply a repudiation of the Machiavellian principle of political necessity. Rather, as the details of the scheme of conquest lamentably demonstrate, what is involved is an adaptation of the principle of necessity to the task in hand. Thus Spenser seeks to provide that the war of conquest will be prosecuted only against dissenters and that subsequently execution will fall only on those who continue to dissent from his scheme. Extirpation in both cases becomes a just necessity as the excision of irremediably corrupted elements for the sake of restoring the body politic as a whole to health. Thus, having assimilated the humanist political morality of reform to the Machiavellian morality of the needs of the state, Spenser can virtuously contemplate the perpetration of carnage on a scale to match the hard men's thirst for retribution. That is the major moral achievement of part II of *A View of the Present State of Ireland*.[54]

In the third part of the treatise Spenser proceeds to outline a programme of political and social reform directed to the construction of a stable commonwealth in the aftermath of conquest. A brief review of this final aspect of Spenser's treatise will serve to complete the comparative analysis offered here and, in the process, to demonstrate once more, against current historiographical interpretations, both the inner coherence of Spenser's scheme and the contrast which it provides with that of the civilians. Conveniently, in both these respects, Spenser's first contention is that the army of conquest must remain on as a garrisoned standing army in order to provide the coercive power necessary to carry through the programme of reform. Thereafter, when the reformation is securely established, he is reluctantly prepared to allow some scaling down of the military establishment but advises against it.[55] The question is then raised about the nature of the political reformation that is to be implemented. Here Spenser seems to backtrack. Having argued that constitutions must be adapted to the character of the people – not vice-versa – and having argued in particular that the English civil constitution did not meet the needs of barbaric Irish society, he now proposes to retain the English political system instead of devising a new constitution. However, he hotly denies the charge of inconsistency; and correctly so for two reasons. First, as he points out, he must take account of the fact that post-conquest Irish society

---

[53] *Faerie Queene*, V, x. 2.
[54] *A View*, pp. 98–102, 122–3. Brady finds here an example of intellectual incoherence. It seems to me that he has overlooked Spenser's emphasis on the irreformability of the victims, demonstrated by their refusal to comply. Cf. Spenser's defence of Lord Grey, *A View*, p. 106.
[55] *A View*, pp. 125–31, 140.

will be mixed, containing an elite of new English colonists, formed under the English constitution and unwilling to be governed by any other.[56] Second, in any case, what he proposes is not an exact replica of the English system but a radically modified version of it. Some of the most cherished constitutional rights of the English subject are to be rescinded under a programme of particular reformation – most notably trial by jury.[57] An especially intensive system of community policing called tithing is to reinforce the ordinary machinery of local government – an institution, Spenser emphasises, of barbaric Anglo-Saxon provenance, not of the Norman civil polity.[58] Meanwhile, special provisions are to be made for controlling the Anglo-Irish nobility, partly by means of the system of bonds and recognisances *ad terrorem*, exploited in England by Henry VII, and partly by an investigation of legal titles directed towards a substantial reduction in their land-holdings and a revival of their feudal obligations to the crown.[59] Buttressed in these ways, and operating in the favourable conditions created by the military conquest, Spenser believes that the English political system will be capable of reversing the downward spiral of degeneration that resulted from its adoption as the constitution of the medieval Lordship: whereas then 'the fewer [colonists] followed the more [native Irish]', now 'the better [colonists] shall go foremost and the worst [native Irish] shall follow'.[60] The happy outcome notwithstanding, the significant point in the context of a comparative analysis is the contrast between Spenser's 'make-do' adaptation of the English system and its unqualified adoption by Herbert and Beacon as the perfect form of government for Ireland.[61] The underlying ideological conflict here reflected is pointed up by a final aspect of Spenser's discussion of political reform: his resounding silence on the subject of that new, much acclaimed, resource of civilian government, statecraft – a silence all the more resounding for the fact that Machiavelli is the only contemporary author cited in the treatise.[62]

Turning, however, to a review of Spenser's programme of social reform, a degree of correspondence with the earlier treatises emerges, at last, in two important areas. These must now, finally, be set in perspective. One relates to social stability, in pursuit of which Spenser elaborates a scheme along the same lines as Beacon: tight socio-economic stratification, the elimination of idleness, and, above all, the administration of severe justice.[63] Agreement in such an important area is of course, highly revealing but its significance is

---

[56] Ibid, p. 141.

[57] For the details of the particular reformation Spenser refers the reader to the specific items of the existing constitution that were singled out in part I of the treatise as unsuited to Irish conditions, *A View*, pp. 143, 21–36.
[58] Ibid, pp. 143–5, 152–5.
[59] Ibid, pp. 146–51.
[60] Ibid, p. 152.
[61] Above pp. 12–13, 22.
[62] The reference occurs in the concluding passage of the treatise, *A View*, p. 167. The enthusiasm for statecraft of Herbert and Beacon is noted above, pp. 145–6, 153.
[63] See, for instance, *A View*, pp. 9–10, 151–4.

somewhat complex. On the one hand, it points to a common element in the ideological profiles of Spenser and Beacon, namely a deep commitment to social discipline, an attitude peculiarly characteristic of the reforming ethos of puritanism. On the other hand, it will now be abundantly clear that this common ground has been approached by Spenser and Beacon from two quite different directions. Affinity on this issue does not, therefore, provide a basis for postulating a common colonial viewpoint. All the more is this the case because the basis of Beacon's agreement with Spenser constitutes precisely the basis of his disagreement with Herbert; so much, once again, for the alleged common viewpoint of the Munster neighbours, Spenser and Herbert.[64] Nevertheless, the second area of correspondence that comparison brings to light raises the possibility of an affinity between these two in one respect at least. As the final item on his agenda and the effective conclusion of his substantive discussion, Spenser presents his scheme for a religious reformation. In a much-quoted passage he deprecates the use of violence for the purposes of religious reform and pleads for a religious campaign by means of evangelisation, education and the example of holy living.[65] In this respect, in any case, it would seem, Spenser and Herbert find themselves in agreement. Not so. Their difference does not concern the methods whereby religious reform is to be achieved but the conditions under which it is to be pursued. In this regard Herbert adopts the classic humanist viewpoint: inner religious conversion is envisaged as a means towards outward social docility; consequently religious reform is pursued as a precondition of social harmony. Spenser, in contrast, adopts the orthodox protestant viewpoint: the effective preaching of the Word is dependent upon pre-existing social harmony procured by means of the secular sword.[66] Accordingly, he is quite explicit that the Irish may be evangelised only after the purifying experience of conquest and reformation earlier described – and to the extent, of course, that they survive the experience.[67] Against that background, Spenser, appealing for a campaign of religious reform by persuasion, suggests the image of Esau stealing the clothes of Jacob – as was more often than not the case in Ireland – to the confusion of latter-day Isaacs.

To complete this examination of Spenser's treatise an attempt must be made, as in the previous two cases, to set it within an ideological context. In this regard, certain features of Spenser's approach that bear the signature of English puritanism have already been noted. Further evidence of a puritan provenance is provided by Spenser's appeal to the Foxean historical scheme in attributing the state of the contemporary Irish church to the corrupting influence of popery, introduced by St Patrick and Palladius at the first conversion of the island.[68] However, the clinching evidence is provided, of

---

[64] Above, p. 140–1.   [65] *A View*, p. 162.

[66] Bradshaw, 'Sword, word and strategy', above n. 1.

[67] *A View*, p. 86.   [68] Ibid, pp. 84–5.

course, by the darkly protestant theology of justice elaborated in Book v of the *Faerie Queene*, which was composed concurrently with *A View of the Present State of Ireland*, and, as the poem itself indicates, addressed to the moral issue raised by Irish reform.[69] In locating Spenser's treatise securely in this way in the context of the Elizabethan puritan movement the question arises of accounting for the difference in approach between himself and Beacon whose treatise has also been identified with the same ethos. The answer lies in a development only now coming under the attention of historians: the emergence in the 1580s of a group of radical young courtiers and intellectuals, led by Sir Philip Sidney, with the earl of Leicester in the role of godfather, who strove to combine the ideals of protestantism and neo-chivalry, and to put military arms at the service of social renewal, the protestant cause, and the greater glory of England.[70] This, as is well known, was the group to which Spenser was linked by ties of patronage, friendship, and ideological affinity. The present study may serve, therefore, to throw some light on the ideology of the Sidney circle from a direction that is seldom regarded but is, nonetheless, central.

Some remarks on the implications of this study for the general questions raised at the outset may serve to provide a somewhat graceless peroration. The results of the comparative analysis offered here must cast doubt on the existence of a colonial consensus among the New English of Elizabethan Ireland. Certainly Edmund Spenser's *A View of the Present State of Ireland* cannot now be regarded as the classic expression of such a viewpoint – which can only be to the benefit of the historical reputation of the colonists. In the short run, in any case, it would seem preferable methodologically to explore the tensions within the colonial ethos rather than search for a dubious consensus. It is only in the light of the tensions that a more basic agreement, if such existed, can be perceived. Furthermore, it must now be clear that the intellectual history of the colony cannot be understood in isolation from the intellectual history of the metropolis. Recent studies of the former have proceeded on the basis that the colonists' response to the Irish experience can be – and ought to be – understood by reference to the content of that experience alone. On the contrary, this study has sought to demonstrate that perceptions of the Irish reality were conditioned by attitudes and values, philosophies and world-views, acquired in the course of an English upbringing. *Quidquid recipitur de modo recipientis recipitur*: the psychological insight of the adage of scholastic epistemology is verified by the radically different responses reflected in the three treatises examined here to the same traumatic experience.

[69] See my 'Edmund Spenser on Justice and Mercy', above n. 1.
[70] Jan Albert Dop, *Eliza's Knights*; John Goua, ed., *The Prose Works of Fulke Greville* (Oxford, 1986).

The principal secretaries in the reign of Edward VI: reflections on their office and archive

C. S. KNIGHTON

IN 1974 with the encouragement of Professor Elton, I began to prepare a new calendar of the State Papers, Domestic for the reign of Edward VI. These papers, which constitute the kernel of the surviving archive of the principal secretaries, were among the first Record Office papers to be described in print; but the calendar edited by Robert Lemon in 1856 and which covered the years 1547 to 1580 offered only very brief treatment of the contents of the eighteen volumes of letters and papers which make up the domestic series for Edward's reign: manuscripts were generally identified in a few lines of description often taken verbatim from the endorsement of the originals.[1] It was soon recognised that such a modest method was inadequate, and subsequent volumes have presented more extended summaries. One consequence of the comparatively meagre calendaring of the SP 10 series has been that the original manuscripts have been much more frequently consulted than would otherwise have been necessary, with the inevitable result that their physical condition has seriously deteriorated; this was a major consideration in commissioning a new and comprehensive calendar to replace Lemon's early work. Although it was decided not to incorporate any material not included in the original calendar,[2] the opportunity has been taken to reflect modern evaluation of the dating and authorship of some of the manuscripts – the unsurprising consequence of more than a century of research since the first calendar was published. Some papers have indeed proved not to belong to the reign of Edward VI at all.[3] Many official papers of the principal secretaries have, of course, found their way into private collections, including those now in the British Library – perhaps rather more than the relatively unimportant

---

[1] *Calendar of State Papers, Domestic Series, of the reigns of Edward VI, Mary, Elizabeth, preserved in the State Paper Department of Her Majesty's Public Record Office*, 1 (1547–80), ed. R. Lemon (1856), hereafter *CSPD*.

[2] *CSPD* included relevant documents from SP 9 (Grants of Arms), SP 11 (State Papers, Domestic, Mary) and SP 38 (Dockets for Warrants).

[3] [PRO] SP 10/18, nos. 20 (now SP 16/523, no. 119), 38, 41, 43 (now MPF/161).

items noted as having strayed from the secretarial office of Henry VIII's day.[4] This had become recognised as an abuse by the time of Elizabeth I, when the practice of her father's reign was recalled as having been more orderly, papers being kept at Westminster rather than in the secretaries' private custody.[5] Conversely the Record Office papers now include much which bears solely on the private affairs of the principal secretaries – in particular, William Cecil. Nevertheless the domestic state papers remain a central source for the constitutional and administrative history of this as of any other reign, and have particular relevance to the history of the secretariat by which they were generated.

The development and expansion of the office of principal secretary has long been accepted as, in Professor Elton's words, 'a commonplace of the administrative history of the sixteenth and seventeenth centuries'. Although the principal (that is, as opposed to the Latin and French) secretaries did not become known as 'secretaries of state' until the end of the sixteenth century, Elton accepted this anachronism to describe the status of Thomas Cromwell.[6] The standard modern account of the office of secretary of state remains that of F. M. G. Evans, written in 1923. As her title indicated, the author was concerned primarily to consider the secretaryship from 1558 onwards (to 1680); but her first two chapters treat in some detail of the medieval origins and early Tudor enlargement of the office, and she recognised the particular interest for the secretaryship occasioned by the minority of Edward VI.[7] A work now over sixty years old inevitably calls for some revision in the light of more recent studies. Dr Evans was misled by incorrect dating in the old *Calendar of State Papers, Domestic*, where Secretary Petre's 'Orders and regulations for the despatch of public business' was assigned to February 1547, to suggest that Petre may have played a more important part in the power struggle of the early months of the reign than he actually did. We know now, thanks to Petre's biographer, that this document belongs to the last year of the reign.[8] Dr Evans was also deceived in claiming that William Cecil was composing memoranda of conciliar business while yet in Protector Somerset's private service; but the item cited in support of this view has since been found to be of later date, and has to be considered with several similar pieces composed when Cecil was principal secretary under the duke of Northumber-

[4] S. R. Gammon, *Statesman and Schemer: William, First Lord Paget, Tudor Minister* (Newton Abbot, 1973), p. 67.

[5] Robert Beale, 'A treatise of the office of a councellor and principal secretarie' (1592), printed in C. Read, *Mr Secretary Walsingham and the Policy of Queen Elizabeth* (Oxford, 1925), I, p. 437.

[6] G. R. Elton, *The Tudor Revolution in Government: Administrative Changes in the Reign of Henry VIII* (Cambridge, 1953), pp. 126, 302–3.

[7] F. M. G. Evans, *The Principal Secretary of State* (Manchester, 1923), pp. 1–42.

[8] Ibid, p. 38. F. G. Emmison, 'A plan of Edward VI and Secretary Petre for reorganising the privy council's work, 1552–53', *Bulletin of the Institute of Historical Research*, 31 (1958), 203–10, concerning SP 10/1, no. 15.

land's rule.[9] Dr S. R. Gammon may also have been led astray by the mis-dating of Petre's 'Orders and regulations', which he used as evidence for secretarial procedure during the last years of Henry VIII's reign.[10]

Gammon's work on Sir William Paget, along with the biographies of Petre by Emmison, Sir Thomas Smith by Dewar and Cecil by Conyers Read, have variously treated the careers of their subjects as principal secretaries in the reign of Edward VI, to which should be added the recent biographies of these men and of Sir John Cheke in the History of Parliament volumes.[11] But for none of the Edwardine secretaries has there been a study so detailed as that given by Elton for Cromwell's secretaryship. All the authorities agree that while between 1526 and 1540 there are indications of the advancing status and importance of the secretaryship, it was always its informal and undefined character (never limited by patent of appointment) which allowed Cromwell and his successors to enlarge the secretarial function into a prime ministry. During Edward's reign the secretaries continued to have an influence out of proportion to their official standing. On great public occasions, such as Henry VIII's funeral and his son's coronation, they might have no special place;[12] but in the council chamber, though notionally junior to the other lords, the custom by which they therefore spoke first allowed them to present the government's case.[13] They were vitally important channels of communication to and from the council and the chief ministers, and within the council itself. They had comprehensive responsibility in all areas of government business, from high policy to personal patronage: in the same letter Bishop Hooper could urge Secretary Cecil to redress a wide range of perceived ills in the commonwealth, while also seeking a royal licence to eat flesh on fish days.[14] In Henry VIII's time it had been common for a letter to the king to be enclosed in a covering note to the secretary, to be passed on only with the latter's approval.[15] I can find no precise example of this in the Edwardine papers, but it was quite usual even for privy councillors to write to the secretary rather than directly to Somerset or Northumberland; here, for example, the earl of Arundel writes to Petre concerning the appointment of a justice of oyer and terminer:

I thought good to wryeth this myche vnto yow bycasse I haue syns or departure from my lordes grace hard this myche, prayeing yow to revelle the same vnto him and to none

[9] Evans, *Principal Secretary*, p. 39. W. K. Jordan, *Edward VI: the Threshold of Power: the Dominance of the Duke of Northumberland* (London, 1970), p. 441, n. 4, concerning SP 10/5, no. 24.
[10] Gammon, *Statesman and Schemer*, pp. 68–9.
[11] F. G. Emmison, *Tudor Secretary: Sir William Petre at Court and Home* (London, 1961). M. Dewar, *Sir Thomas Smith: a Tudor Intellectual in Office* (London, 1964). C. Read, *Mr Secretary Cecil and Queen Elizabeth* (London, 1955, paperback edn. 1965). *The House of Commons, 1509–1558*, ed. S. T. Bindoff (History of Parliament Trust, 3 vols., 1982), I, pp. 603–6 (Cecil), 626–30 (Cheke), III, 42–6 (Paget), 92–6 (Petre), 338–40 (Smith), hereafter *HPT*.
[12] SP 10/1, nos. 9, 17.
[13] D. E. Hoak, *The King's Council in the Reign of Edward VI* (Cambridge, 1976), p. 126.
[14] SP 10/13, no. 3.　　　　　　　　　　　　[15] Gammon, *Statesman and Schemer*, p. 60.

other. Also thynkyng this mater meter to be openyd by you my frend then by myne owne letters vnto his grace, I trust you therwith.[16]

Elton opined that Cromwell's successors as secretary were less concerned than he had been with financial affairs – noting that Lord Burghley moved to the treasury for this purpose.[17] The Edwardine secretaries were not, however, without responsibilities in this area. Secretary Smith engaged in detailed correspondence about the coinage, taxation and other fiscal measures; he was also directly involved in payment of wages to messengers, mercenaries and others in the king's service.[18] Several papers in Cecil's hand witness to his efforts to reduce royal expenditure and debts, and he has been seen as instrumental in the financial reforms begun in 1552.[19]

During Edward's reign the post-Cromwellian division of the secretaryship was generally followed – though with a period of almost a year in which there was a single secretary and the last few weeks of the reign when there were three. Of the six individuals who held office in this period the three Sir Williams, Paget, Petre and Cecil, were administrators of the first rank, while Sir Thomas Smith, Dr Nicholas Wotton and Sir John Cheke were men whose celebrity rests in accomplishments other than their custody of Edward VI's signet. Paget and Petre retained the posts they had enjoyed since 1543 and 1544 respectively; Petre was to do so throughout the reign, while his original colleague was succeeded in turn by Smith, Wotton and Cecil, Cheke being the supernumerary added in 1552. All six men were graduates, which placed them at least in the intellectual leadership of Edward VI's privy council, a body which became progressively *less* educated in the course of the reign.[20] Their social and cultural backgrounds were broadly similar, and all save Wotton the diplomat had administrative and parliamentary experience. In fact the specifically foreign and diplomatic training which had been so important in the rise of the secretaryship seems of less significance among Edward's secretaries. Paget was, in a way, the last of this line, Wotton a throwback. Cecil never served overseas, and was to be criticised for devoting his attention to parliamentary business rather than foreign affairs.[21]

There was initially a distinction made between Paget and Petre by the terms of Henry VIII's will. Paget was named there as one of the sixteen executors who were to be *ex officio* privy councillors to the new king, but Petre was merely appointed one of twelve 'assistant' councillors. This disparity was underlined by Petre's omission from financial bequests made by the old king to all other

---

[16] SP 10/7, no. 44.   [17] Elton, *Tudor Revolution*, p. 299.

[18] SP 10/7, nos. 38, 38(1), 39; 8, no. 68. SP 38/1, fols. 1ᵛ, 3, 3ᵛ, 5, 5ᵛ, 7. Cf. Dewar, *Sir Thomas Smith*, p. 49.

[19] SP 10/15, no. 42. Hatfield House, Cecil Papers, 151/44, 46. G. R. Elton, *Reform and Reformation: England 1509–1558* (London, 1977), p. 358.

[20] Hoak, *King's Council*, p. 85.

[21] Evans, *Principal Secretary*, p. 28. Elton, *Tudor Revolution*, p. 32. *HPT*, I, pp. 604–5.

executors and assistants. It has been suggested that this is evidence of some antipathy to Petre, perhaps on religious grounds, on the part of Henry VIII.[22] Petre was at least rewarded with an annuity of £100 as high steward of the bishop of Winchester's lands, part of the several grants of largesse which, if we are to believe Paget, were extracted from Henry VIII in the last months of his life.[23] But is there any significance in the fact that Paget did not use this opportunity to secure for his fellow secretary full compensation for the omission in the will, which had awarded £200 to the other assistants? Did Paget perhaps envisage that in the new reign he might be the sole minister secretary in the Cromwellian mould, with Petre relegated to a decidedly inferior status? It was observed by Professor Elton that the original division of the secretaryship in 1540 was occasioned by the need for one secretary to be in attendance on the king, the other on the often absent chief minister.[24] Such requirements were soon to be made redundant upon Cromwell's fall, and in the new reign quite different circumstances obtained; it must have been evident that there would be no job for a permanent secretary in Edward VI's nursery. The hugger-mugger activities which followed upon Henry VIII's eventual death, with Paget and the earl of Hertford plotting in feverish secret the shape of the new regime, strongly suggest that Paget, whose experience in government and diplomacy was probably the greatest in the new privy council, deliberately sought for himself the position at the protector's right hand which he was indeed to enjoy at the outset of the reign. He was later to recall that as Henry VIII lay dead Hertford had promised to follow his advice more than that of any other.[25] In the early months of the reign it was soon realised that Paget had secured considerable influence with the new ruler; it was to him that questions of public order and patronage were addressed, and he was responsible for measures taken to inform the country and the world of the new regime.[26] Paget's omission from the list of new peers has caused some surprise, including that of his biographer; it may be that he saw that his greatest potential for political power lay, for the immediate future, in retention of the secretaryship – that place of uncertain and therefore multifarious responsibility which was nevertheless still considered incompatible with the dignity of a peerage.[27] In the event it was to be Cecil who would exercise the secretaryship in much the way that Cromwell had done.[28] More immediately, both secretaries surrendered their seals on February 13 and had them returned by the king. A month later, when the Seymour–Paget machinations

[22] Emmison, *Tudor Secretary*, pp. 65–6.
[23] SP 10/1, no. 11. See H. Miller, 'Henry VIII's unwritten will: grants of lands and honours in 1547' in *Wealth and Power in Tudor England: Essays Presented to S. T. Bindoff,* ed. E. W. Ives, R. J. Knecht and J. J. Scarisbrick (London, 1978), pp. 87–105.
[24] Elton, *Tudor Revolution*, p. 314.   [25] SP 10/8, no. 4.
[26] SP 10/1, nos. 5, 8. Gammon, *Statesman and Schemer*, pp. 130–1.
[27] Gammon, *Statesman and Schemer*, p. 58. Cf. Elton, *Tudor Revolution*, pp. 120–1.
[28] Elton, *Tudor Revolution*, pp. 354–5.

had succeeded in establishing the protectorate and abandoning the conciliar arrangements envisaged in Henry VIII's will, Secretary Petre was re-admitted to the privy council along with some of the other 'assistants'.

It may be that by this stage Paget had decided that he did not after all wish to continue with the considerable burdens of the secretaryship and felt – probably unwisely – that his position was sufficiently secure to allow him to assume the more dignified and less onerous posts of comptroller of the household and chancellor of the duchy of Lancaster. So from June 1547 until the following April Petre was left as sole secretary. During this period his functions were to some extent upstaged by the activities of Smith and Cecil, neither yet of the privy council, who were effectively political secretaries to the duke of Somerset. Smith's elevation to the vacant principal secretaryship (and with it a place in the privy council) in April 1548 did, as Professor Elton observed, regularise his position.[29] Even so Smith, and to a lesser extent Petre, would act essentially as secretaries to the protector rather than to the king or council; perhaps this was inevitable in view of the king's minority and Somerset's assumption of vice-regal powers. But the secretaries were also used to subvert the role of the privy council; state papers were surrendered to the protector's own servants, who engaged in the management of affairs by-passing the established routines of the council.[30] The fiction that the principal secretaries were the king's personal servants could still be used to effect; when the London councillors during the 1549 coup wrote to the king they pointedly referred to the semi-captive Petre as 'your highness secretarye'.[31]

The coup cost Smith his secretaryship.[32] His replacement, Wotton, has of the Edwardine secretaries left least mark in the office. There seems a certain inevitability in his replacement, in September 1551, by the rising star of William Cecil. Letters he received after his appointment was announced indicate much satisfaction but little surprise on the part of his friends such as the duchess of Suffolk, Lord Stourton, Sir Edward North, Sir John Thynne and Thomas Parry. Of these Thynne was the most fulsome in his congratulations ('Being as glad as any frende you have this day lyvinge that ye be so placed as ye are, I shall desire you to make reconinge of my small friendship as fere as my power may extend, which shalbe redy during my lief when ye shall like to use it'); like the other correspondents Thynne took the opportunity to press home his current suits. Duchess Catherine offered what is presumably an oblique witticism on the pecuniary advantage which Cecil stood to enjoy ('Shale I call you so scell now you be master cecretore showes you if you wyll not have it so for tel you deny it I wole call you so').[33] Having managed more adeptly than Smith to dissociate himself from Somerset's disgrace, Cecil

---

[29] Elton, *Reform and Reformation*, p. 338. But Smith's secretaryship was not, as here suggested, immediate upon Paget's elevation.

[30] Hoak, *King's Council*, pp. 115–16.   [31] SP 10/9, no. 17.

[32] Dewar, *Sir Thomas Smith*, p. 3.   [33] SP 10/10, nos. 25, 27, 28, 29, 32, 33.

seems soon to have attached himself to the earl of Warwick's household and to have served the new ruler in much the same capacity as he had the old before being elevated to the principal secretaryship. More papers survive from his tenure of the office than from those of his colleagues; in part this may be accidental, in part it is certainly a result of the deliberate destruction of papers of the protectorate on the eve of Somerset's fall.[34] We should therefore be cautious in concluding from the archives which survive that Cecil involved himself in wider concerns and wielded greater influence than did the other secretaries of the time.

Northumberland's rule was characterised by a much stricter adherence to the procedures of conciliar government than had been practised during the protectorate. The function of the secretaryship in relation to the council seems equally to have become more regular and orderly. Of special importance in interpreting the secretaries' as also the council's working are the forty-one drafts of business agenda and suits which belong to the period of Northumberland's government, and which Dr Hoak has examined in some detail. Most of these papers are found in the state papers, domestic, but were often widely mis-dated by the original editor. It has since been possible to assign more certain dates to many of these items.[35] In only one instance have I taken issue with Dr Hoak's judgment: an item which he ascribed to 1553 by comparison with a Hatfield paper said to be dated April 29 of that year. My own examination of the Hatfield MS suggests that the year date (of the endorsement) is insufficiently clear, while the matters it deals with, along with those of the Public Record Office document, belong in greater likelihood to the spring of 1552, along with several other agenda which treat of similar topics.[36] A constant problem with such papers, as Dr Hoak pointed out, is that individual suits and matters of business were not infrequently raised before the privy council on repeated occasions over several months. We have no means of knowing whether the papers we have are those which the secretaries actually took with them to the council board and which therefore contained the actual agenda for particular meetings. This is particularly apparent from Cecil's papers, of which two small notebooks are preserved in the state papers.[37] These present a jumble of names and subjects, Cecil's personal affairs interspersed with matters of state. Although set out in columns, the same items recur over and over again in many places. Clearly such notebooks were of the type later to be recommended to prospective secretaries – to be

[34] D. E. Hoak, 'Rehabilitating the Duke of Northumberland: politics and political control, 1549–53' in *The Mid-Tudor Polity, c. 1540–1560*, ed. J. Loach and R. Tittler (London, 1980), pp. 34–5.

[35] Hoak, *King's Council*, pp. 28–33.

[36] SP 10/13, no. 79. Hatfield, Cecil Papers, 151/98. D. E. Hoak, 'The King's Council in the reign of Edward VI' (unpublished Ph.D dissertation, University of Cambridge, 1971), p. 45 n. 2.

[37] SP 10/5, no. 24; 14, no. 53.

kept always at hand for jotting down matters as they came to mind.[38] These books contain material recorded over many months, and it is impossible, indeed without purpose, to seek to associate the memoranda they contain with specific meetings of the council. Interpretation of these particular documents is not helped by Cecil's extreme economy of expression, his fondness for initials, and the fashion by which entries were scribbled together so that it is often impossible to determine whether neighbouring words and abbreviations are connected or not. Entries are also sometimes obscure: it took some time to discover that the entry 'Ragged staff' was a reference to allegations that the duke of Northumberland had set up his own mint with the familiar Warwick device on the coins. Some unlikely adjacent entries prove to be related: 'the goldsmythes wiffe/marches of wales' concerns Florence, widow of Edmund Pees, goldsmith of London, who had petitioned the council of the marches; but 'Sir Ingram Percy' is surely an error for 'Sir Ingram Clifford', while 'Charta variosa' is one of several curiosities which have eluded interpreta-tion.[39] Even the more careful Edwardine memoranda lack the precision familiar to those who have read Cromwell's papers, and do not exhibit the orderliness which would be of professional concern to secretaries later in the century, when public matters were to be set out before private suits.[40] By contrast the Edwardine papers present a jostling of public, private, domestic and foreign affairs.

The survival among the Edwardine State Papers of fair copies of council out-letters, to some of which have been added facsimiles of the councillors' signatures, has been seen as a significant sophistication of administrative and archival method.[41] Some such letters carry the original signatures, and for these further or alternative explanations may be suggested. Circular letters to sheriffs, justices and 'special men in every shire' were most probably mass-produced in the secretaries' office, signed by such councillors as were available, and held for despatch against check lists. We see such lists being requisitioned in a business paper of March 1553:

A note of the names of certen gentlemen in Somerset, Glocester, Devon, Wales, Worcester, Hereforde and Chesshier for amassing horsemen and footmen to be always in readiness or service in Ireland

to which Cecil added 'ordered' and 'the like for Callice'.[42] Several of these lists have been preserved among the state papers, generally drawn up for some military or taxation purposes, but with the common feature of arrangement by county. The order in which the names of individuals occur under these county heads has been found to correspond very closely to that in which gentlemen

---

[38] 'Nicholas Faunt's Discourse touching the office of principal secretary of estate &c. 1592', ed. C. Hughes, *English Historical Review*, 20 (1905), p. 503.

[39] SP 10/5, no. 24. *Acts of the Privy Council of England*, n. s., ed. J. R. Dasent (32 vols., 1890–1907), III, pp. 375, 377, 462, 464.   [40] Beale, 'Treatise', p. 424.

[41] Hoak, *King's Council*, pp. 23, 157.   [42] Hatfield, Cecil Papers, 201/109.

are named in the commissions of the peace; such resemblance is particularly close in lists of July 1548 (naming those to stay at home in case of invasion) and July 1549 (naming those sent for to come to Windsor). This may account for the frequent appearance of individuals under more than one county in the check lists, since it was quite common for commissions of the peace to be held in several counties.[43] If, then, circular letters were drawn up by reference to lists which had themselves some basis in the county commissions, it is possible to understand why more copies were produced and even signed than proved to be necessary, with one example being retained for the files. Similar explanations, coupled with more obvious political reasons, may be offered for the survival of several signed copies of letters from Somerset directed to the commissioners for enclosures in the last months of his rule.[44] It may be noted that, as Paget observed in 1550 (and as recalled by Robert Beale at the end of the century) the secretaries were responsible for overseeing the work of the council clerks in making up the register and securing for it (so also, presumably, for the out-letters) signatures of the councillors:

The clearke having charge of the counsaill booke shall . . . the next daye following at the furst meeting presenting the same by the secretary (who shall furst consydre wether the entrey be made accordingly) to the boorde the counsaill shall the furst thing theye do signe the book of entrees, leaving space for the counsailors absent to entre theyre names whenne they cum.

The secretary also had 'the keeping of all lettres, minutes of lettres to and from the king for the counsaill, instruccions and suche other writinges as shalbe treated vpon by the counsaill'; but because councillors' signatures might be made retrospectively they cannot therefore be used to establish the presence of particular councillors at specific meetings of the board.[45]

That Northumberland's government was more orderly than that of his predecessor and has left a more complete record of its proceedings does not in itself prove that it was more efficient, let alone morally superior. The satisfying dichotomy of the good duke and the bad remains a powerful image. Thirty years ago Conyers Read could still write that of Edward VI's councillors 'Somerset was the only one who enjoyed the affection of the English at large – Warwick was without doubt the most resolute, the most unscrupulous and self seeking.'[46] Professor Jordan's substantial volumes did little to alter that general view. It has only been in the last few years that Somerset's claim to be the father of social democracy has been seriously challenged. And as with Somerset's benevolence, so with Northumberland's iniquity – a trend which

---

[43] The lists are (i) SP 10/2, no. 1, (ii) SP 10/2, no. 29, (iii) SP 10/4, no. 12(1), (iv) SP 10/5, no. 17, (v) SP 10/8, no. 2, (vi) SP 10/18, no. 44; *Calendar of Patent Rolls, Edward VI*, I, pp. 80–92.
[44] SP 10/8, nos. 11–20, 25–9.
[45] BL, Egerton MS 2603, fos. 33–4. Printed in 'The Letters of William, Lord Paget of Beaudesert, 1547–1563', ed. B. L. Beer and S. M. Jack, *Camden Miscellany* XXV (Camden Society, 4th series, XIII, 1974), pp. 98–100. Beale, 'Treatise', p. 425. Cf. Hoak, *King's Council*, pp. 13–14, 23–5.   [46] Read, *Secretary Cecil*, p. 46.

Professor Elton encouraged with the hope that the 'soberer' view of Somerset may 'yet lead to a revised view of Northumberland'.[47] The extensive correspondence between Northumberland and Cecil, much of which is contained in the state papers, lends weight to the case for a more sympathetic assessment of the duke's personality and political style. These letters are well enough known and were used by Jordan to illustrate what appears to be Northumberland's increasing weariness and disillusionment with public life towards the end of his career.[48] It seems most improbable that the views he expressed in closest confidence to Cecil were no more than a ruse to conceal carefully premeditated treason. The view that in 1549 the then earl of Warwick was probably not playing a 'deep game', but was driven by political necessity from one expedient to another, seems equally valid as an account of his actions in 1553, when the controlling factor was the uncertain state of the king's health. Northumberland's own illnesses may have been the cause of much of the melancholy which he directed to Cecil in letters of 1552 and 1553. It is now recognised that his emphasis on conciliar rule and his concern to eschew primacy of place were genuine enough. It is of course true that the unhappy experience of the protectorate and his own lack of any royal kinship dissuaded him from any aspiration he may have had (until, maybe, the last few weeks of the reign) for supreme personal power. He seems to have been content to use Cecil as his agent in dealings with the other councillors, writing to him with great frequency – sometimes when he admitted there was nothing worthy of immediate mention to the council; at other times to add a point he had overlooked when they met.[49] He would, on occasion, express frustration that matters could not be settled by the councillors but were referred to him – in one letter to Cecil 'marveling not a little that a pon the comyng of the L. chancelor this matter of the proclamation colde not haue byn depeched according to soche deuise as was thereupon talkyd of and and fully concludyd but that my sayd L. chancelor hath sought me and travelyd the stretes a fote only to speke with me who can shew him no more than others than were fyrste privy before me.' On another occasion he wrote, again to Cecil, in response to a letter from Lord Willoughby about his remaining at Calais: 'I perceue he hath wrytten to no more but to me at least for anything that I can here, whereat as I do not a lyttel mervell the matter being of suche moment so wold I be glad that in thaunswer yt would please my lordes to haue consideracion that he and others may knowe that those weightie officeds ys ruled by the hole bourd.'[50] He was notably concerned that slanders against his person should be debated without his involvement, while counselling impartial and lenient treatment of

[47] W. K. Jordan, *Edward VI: the Young King: the Protectorship of the Duke of Somerset* (London, 1968), and *Edward VI: the Threshold of Power*. Elton, *Reform and Reformation*, p. 353. See also Hoak, *King's Council* and M. L. Bush, *The Government Policy of Protector Somerset* (London, 1975).
[48] Jordan, *Edward VI: the Threshold of Power*, pp. 496–8.
[49] Hatfield, Cecil Papers, 151/40, 58.   [50] SP 10/10, no. 30; 15, no. 12.

those who had criticised him or otherwise offended. Of Somerset's agent William Cornish he told Cecil: 'In case his offence hathe rather happenyd for the zeale towardes hys master then apon anny malicious mynde or intent, he may the better be born with the rather seinge he hathe byn well ponished all reddye.' Concerning a reported slander against his brother and himself he wrote: 'But be caus the matter as yt semyth tocheth noon other of the councell but my brother and me I haue refusyd to here yt referring thorder thereof to the rest of my lordes.' And when one John Borroughe accused the duke of meddling with the king's coffers Cecil was advised that slander could be mitigated by good breeding and a protestant conscience: 'And for that I do understand the sayde berer ys of a good hous and nat so motche in defaut as others, and a yonge man of a talle personage and peraduenture suffyciently ponyshed by this long imprisonment, I shall desyre you to be means to the rest of my lordes to spare him from the pyllery and other publike ponishmentes for I truste with godes grace he wyll amend. His brothere as I am enformyd ys of the best sorte for fauering the kinges godly procedinges and hathe no heyre but this yonge man.' Clemency was also urged for one accused of theft: 'but beinge of so good hous yt were pity but he shold be repreued'.[51] In more important affairs Northumberland allowed Cecil a remarkable degree of influence with the king and the rest of the privy council. When in July 1551 Peter Vannes, the ambassador in Venice, wrote proposing a marriage between the son of the duke of Ferrara and one of the king's sisters, Northumberland passed on the letter to Cecil with instructions to open the matter with the king, and 'when you haue shewyd the sayde lettre to the kinges maistie and yf his highnes like the matter you may therin worke with the rest of my lordes as to theyr wysdomes shall seme mete'. At the end of the same year, when consideration was being given to the despatch of ambassadors to the French and Imperial courts, Northumberland responded to Cecil's nomination of his brother and son-in-law by again asking the secretary 'to be meane to the reste of my lordes to be so moche there good lordes as to gyve theym theyr fauorable instructions'.[52] Sixteenth-century dignitaries did not often complain about the extent of their travelling attendance; but Northumberland, about to embark on a progress, told Cecil he would visit the latter's father in Lincolnshire but 'will nat trouble no frendes house of myne otherwys in this journey, my trayne ys so great, and wilbe, whether I will or not'.[53]

For a supposedly black-hearted tyrant Northumberland could command an endearingly whimsical turn of phrase – returning to Cecil 'a mass of matters . . . without having gathered much fruit', and he had a refreshing antipathy to the impossible Knox.[54] He showed dignified grief at the death of his daughter-in-law, Lady Ambrose Dudley;[55] and, *pace* Professor Elton, he did

---

[51] SP 10/14, no. 31; 15, nos. 3, 39, 50, 60.
[52] SP 10/14, no. 50; 15, no. 74. Cf. Hoak, 'Rehabilitating the Duke of Northumberland', p. 40.
[53] SP 10/14, no. 34.   [54] SP 10/15, no. 66.   [55] SP 10/15, nos. 37, 38.

refer to the death of his father Edmund Dudley, Henry VII's too faithful servant, and asserted that like him he had worked for king and country rather than his own advancement:

And tho my pore father, who after his master was gon suffered dethe for doinge his masters comandement, who was the wysest prince of the worlde lyvinge in thos dayes, and yet coulde not his comandement be my fathers discardg after he was departyd this lyffe, so for my parte withe all earnestnes and duty I will serue without fear, sekinge nothinge but the true glorye of god, and his highnes suertye.[56]

This might be taken as a conventional gesture of self-denigration; more telling was his complaint at having worked long in the evenings when others had gone to their amusements:

And yet so long as helthe wolde give me leave I dyd as syldome fayle myne attendaunce as any others did, yee and with soche helthe as when others went to thyre suppers and pastymes after theyr travayle I went to bedd, with a carefull hart and a weryed bodye, and yet a broode no man skarsly hadd any good opynyon of me.[57]

Writing on occasion to both secretaries – though more usually it was to Cecil or to Petre in Cecil's absence – Northumberland commented that all the council were well appointed save himself, and lamented that he felt himself to be deficient in the qualities which the position demanded:

His maiesties choyse of counsellors ys in my opynuon very well apoynted all save my selffe, who nether hath understandinge nor wytt mete for the association nor body apt to render his duty any wayes as the wyll and hart desireth. And as yt ys a most great grief to me to think yt, so I cannot but lament yt that yt ys my chauce to occupy a rome in this commonwele mete for a man of moche wytt and gravite.[58]

The overall impression of these letters to the secretary is of a man wearied by personal and political misfortune. What the recipient made of it all we cannot tell, for it is a one-sided correspondence. But he cannot have been unaware of the crucial position he enjoyed as confidant and agent of the duke, whose frequent absences from the council board served to strengthen the influence of the principal secretary there and in the administration generally.

The final change in the secretaryship during Edward VI's reign was the appointment of Sir John Cheke, the king's tutor, to be secretary in addition to Petre and Cecil on 2 June 1553. This was at a time when Cecil was absent from court indulging in a bout of real or diplomatic sickness. It was once supposed that this move was intended as a warning to Cecil that his position was in jeopardy; but Conyers Read argued that it was improbable that in such a case Cecil's close friend and brother-in-law would be chosen to replace him. He preferred the reported view of the Imperial ambassador that it was Petre whom Cheke was to replace. Petre's biographer has supported the suggestion

---

[56] SP 10/15, no. 66. Cf. Elton, *Reform and Reformation*, p. 353.
[57] SP 10/18, no. 2.　　　　　　　　　　[58] Hatfield, Cecil Papers, 151/53.

that he had sought to retire.[59] But Petre remained active as secretary; a memorandum partly in his hand is dated June 3, the day after Cheke's admission to the privy council as third secretary; another, of June 11, is drafted jointly by Petre and Cecil.[60] It has recently been suggested that Cheke's close association with the king was the cause of his appointment:[61] but by this stage the king was mortally ill, and the move cannot be credibly linked to the efforts which earlier had been made to introduce the king to conciliar and government business. It might be thought to have more sinister implication, and to be in line with Northumberland's efforts to win over the king's closest personal attendants.[62] But we now know that Cheke had been marked out as secretary in January 1553 when he received a writ of assistance to the House of Lords in this capacity for the parliament which was to assemble in the following March.[63] At this time there can be no question of Cecil or Petre being replaced; in January Northumberland was in his most regular and intimate correspondence with Cecil, while Petre was engaged in the drafting of his new rules for conciliar and secretarial procedure, which do not convey any suggestion of being drawn up for the guidance of an imminent successor.[64] It remains unclear why Cheke did not take up his secretarial post until June; but his appointment cannot now be seen as an aspect of Northumberland's designs on the subversion of the succession.

The introduction of a third secretary was indeed a 'short-lived reform'.[65] The main impression offered by the history of the principal secretaryship during Edward VI's reign would seem to be the convenience and durability of the dual occupancy of the office which Thomas Cromwell had first moulded into the chief instrument of government. The secretaries played a vital part in sustaining the administration in the difficult years of Edward's reign, and in doing so ensured that their own office would remain 'the binding force of the state'.[66]

[59] Read, *Secretary Cecil*, pp. 92–3. Emmison, *Tudor Secretary*, pp. 106–7.
[60] SP 10/18, nos. 27, 28.
[61] Hoak, 'Rehabilitating the Duke of Northumberland', p. 44.
[62] See D. E. Hoak, 'The King's Privy Chamber, 1547–1553' in *Tudor Rule and Revolution: Essays for G. R. Elton from his American Friends*, ed. D. J. Guth and J. W. McKenna (Cambridge, 1982), pp. 87–108.
[63] *HPT*, I, p. 629.   [64] SP 10/18, nos. 1, 2, 3, 4, 6, 8, 9, 10, 11; I, no. 15.
[65] Elton, *Reform and Reformation*, p. 355.   [66] Evans, *Principal Secretary*, p. 31.

Philip II and the government of England

DAVID LOADES

WHEN Philip landed at Southampton on 20 July 1554, neither his status nor his functions in England were defined to his own satisfaction, nor, indeed, clearly defined at all. The position of king consort was unprecedented and unknown to English law, so that the statements contained in the marriage treaty which had admitted him to a share in the government of the realm were the result of *ad hoc* political negotiations, and not of any clearly perceived principles. Moreover, these negotiations had not been carried out by Philip himself, but by the agents of his father, the emperor Charles V. Charles had been primarily concerned to secure for his son a prestigious match which would strengthen his hand in northern Europe generally, and in the Netherlands particularly.[1] Consequently he had not scrupled to accept conditions imposed by the English negotiators which might severely restrict his son's effectiveness in domestic affairs. The English, for their part, had started from a position of deep mistrust, being well aware of the strength of opposition to the marriage at all levels within England, from the council down – and Charles was also well aware of this background to their demands. One of the factors which had fuelled English apprehensions had been the well-known Habsburg proclivity for 'conquest by marriage'. Another had been legal doubts about the exact nature of the queen's own authority. A ruling queen was also a novelty, and although there was no Salic law in England, there were common lawyers who were prepared to argue that Mary had only a 'woman's estate' in the realm. That is, by analogy with the law of real property, that the kingdom would pass on her marriage to her husband in full ownership, and would remain vested in him during his natural life, irrespective of whether she was alive or dead.[2] The prevailing view was that the royal office was unique, and that the laws of real property did not apply, but enough doubt remained to require a statutory pronouncement in April 1554:

---

[1] For a full discussion of the emperor's motivation in this negotiation, see my *Reign of Mary Tudor*, pp. 112–14.

[2] 'He hath power likewise over his wife's estate; and if she hath a fee, he gaineth a freehold in her right . . .' Giles Jacob, *A New Law Dictionary* (London, 1773), Baron et Feme, IV.

Be it declared and enacted by thaucthorititie of this present parliament that the law of this realm is and ever hath bene and ought to be understanded that the Kingly or Royall Office of the realm and all dignities Prerogatives Royall ... thereunto annexed and belonging, being invested in either Male or Female, are and be and ought to be as fully wholly absolutely and entirely deemed judged accepted invested and taken in thone as in thother ...[3]

These same doubts had produced in the marriage treaty, in January 1554, a clear and unequivocal statement to the effect that, should there be no issue of the marriage, Philip's interest in the realm would terminate with Mary's death.[4]

As if this insecurity of tenure was not enough, the emperor was also prepared to concede on his son's behalf

... that he shall not promote, admit, or receive to any office, administration or benefice in the said realm of England and the dominions thereunto belonging any stranger or person not born under the dominion and subjection of the said most noble lady, Queen of England ...

and

That the said noble Prince shall receive and admit into the service of his household and court gentlemen and yeomen of England in convenient number, and them as his proper subjects shall esteem entertain and nourish ...

When he discovered the terms of the treaty, Philip was indignant and considered abandoning the match. In the event he contented himself with a secret disclaimer, but his own advisers wasted no opportunity of persuading him that neither his honour nor his interests had been well served.[5] On 16 February Philip had written to Simon Renard, his father's ambassador in England, in an apparently co-operative mood:

When I arrive I shall have to accept the services of natives in order to show them that I mean to trust myself to them, and favour them as much as if I were an Englishman born ...[6]

but Spanish indignation, both against the English and against the emperor's negotiators, continued to be high throughout the long months of preparation. In one respect the situation was even more unsatisfactory than Philip realised, because he seems to have believed that he had been proclaimed king in England after the ratification of the marriage treaty by parliament. He styled himself 'Philippus Rex' in a series of innocuous letters of greeting which his harbinger the marquis of Las Navas brought over in June for members of the English council; and he was also styled king of England in a papal brief

---

[3] Statute 1 Mary st. 3 cap. 1 *Statutes of the Realm*, IV, p. 222.
[4] '... in case that no children being left, the most noble lady the Queen doth die before him, the said Lord Prince shall not challenge unto him any right at all in the said kingdom ...', P. L. Hughes and J. F. Larkin, *Tudor Royal Proclamations*, II, p. 25.
[5] *Calendar of State Papers, Spanish*, XII, pp. 4–6.   [6] *Cal. Sp.*, XII, pp. 103–5.

directed by Julius III to Cardinal Reginald Pole in the same month. Renard would not allow Las Navas to deliver his letters,[7] and the papal brief was later judged invalid, because the highest style to which Philip was entitled on his arrival in England was that by which he was referred to in the treaty – prince of Spain. In order to protect his son's dignity and enable him to marry Mary as an equal, Charles invested him with the kingdom of the two Sicilies between his arrival and his nuptials, but the English were meticulously insistent that his English title depended upon the queen, and it was only after the wedding in Winchester cathedral on 25 July that they were jointly proclaimed

King and Queen of England, France, Naples, Jerusalem and Ireland, Defenders of the Faith; Princes of Spain and Sicily; Archdukes of Austria; Dukes of Milan, Burgundy and Brabant; Counts of Habsburg, Flanders and Tyrol.[8]

Even when the full protection of the treason laws was belatedly extended to him by parliament in January 1555, it was reiterated that this applied only 'during the term of the said marriage', and implied no extended authority unless the queen should die leaving an heir under age.[9]

It was in an attempt to circumvent this limited interpretation of his position that Philip sought a coronation in England. At first the attempt was low-key, representing the matter as little more than a courtesy, but, as with the question of the queen's authority, there were English lawyers who were willing to take advantage of the lack of legal certainty to magnify it out of proportion. Renard picked up their opinions, and writing to the emperor in November 1554 he declared

... in England the coronation stands for a true and lawful confirmation of title and means much more than in other realms ...[10]

There seems to have been no foundation for this view, because the processes of consecration and acclamation, which tended to support it, were counteracted by the coronation oath, which in Philip's case would certainty have included a reaffirmation of the marriage treaty. Nevertheless the king himself seems to have felt that it represented a loophole worthy of exploration, and began to press the matter behind the scenes during the third parliament, in December 1554 and January 1555. He got nowhere, because his interest immediately aroused suspicion, and the opponents of such a move succeeded in associating it with possible involvement in 'the King's war' against the French – a commitment which the marriage treaty had specifically rejected.[11]

---

[7] Philip had apparently been misinformed by Antonio de Guaras, a Spaniard in Mary's service. E. H. Harbison, *Rival Ambassadors at the Court of Queen Mary*, pp. 188–9.

[8] Hughes and Larkin, *Tudor Royal Proclamations*, II, pp. 45–6.

[9] 'That if any person or persons after the first day of February next to come, during the marriage between the King and the Queenes Majesties, doo compass ... etc.' Statute 1 & 2 Philip and Mary cap. 10; *Statutes of the Realm*, IV, p. 255.

[10] 23 November 1554, *Cal. Sp.*, XIII, p. 101.

[11] '... that the realm of England by occasion of this matrimony shall not directly or indirectly be

As long as it appeared likely that Mary would bear a child (and she was believed to be pregnant from September 1554) the coronation was in any case a secondary consideration; but with the failure of that hope in the summer of 1555 it became the only faint possibility for Philip to obtain any independent authority in England, or any interest in the kingdom at Mary's death. Consequently, from September 1555, when he arrived in the Netherlands, until at least April 1556 he tried by a variety of methods to persuade Mary to have him crowned. She replied with excuses; there was strenuous opposition which she could not overcome in his absence; the parliament would never consent.[12] He in turn then professed his unwillingness to return without a coronation and the prospect of more authority. Each was holding out on the other. Mary, with the emperor's support, was trying to use the coronation as an inducement to Philip to go back to England. He was probably using its non-fulfilment as an excuse to stay where he was, thinking that he would also lose face if he returned with his conditions unsatisfied. The consent of parliament was a red herring, as he belatedly discovered, because no matter what rights parliament may have exercised in the event of a disputed succession, the question of a coronation had never been referred to it. By the summer of 1556 the issue survived mainly as raw material for anti-Spanish propagandists and agitators in England – an aspect of the Black Legend. '... ther woold be Vc, ye & more than Vc that woold dye in this quarrell that no stranger should have the Crown'.[13]

Philip was baffled at every turn in his search for an effective role in English government, and it is easy to conclude that this was the inevitable consequence of English hostility, and of the way in which the marriage treaty had been negotiated. In fact, however, the reasons appear to have been rather more subtle, and to have depended at least as much upon the attitudes of both the royal partners as upon the circumstances in which they found themselves. One curious feature of the marriage settlement was that Philip, unlike the queens of recent English kings, was granted no personal patrimony within England, and therefore had absolutely no English money of his own, nor any means of rewarding his English servants and adherents except by drawing on his

entangled with the war that now is betwixt the most victorious Emperor the said Lord Prince's father and Henry the French king.' See also, Loades, *Reign of Mary*, pp. 223–4.

[12] There is little direct evidence for these exchanges, which were reported by the Venetian ambassador in Brussels, Federigo Badoer, but they are consistent with reports which were circulating in England at the same time. *Calendar of State Papers, Venetian*, VI, pp. 227, 253.

[13] From a statement by William Hinnes (one of the Dudley conspirators), 30 March 1556. PRO, SP 11/7/46. Objection to the coronation was the main inspiration behind the Dudley conspiracy, as well as behind such tracts as *The copye of a letter* (STC 3480), *A warnynge for Englande* (STC 10024), and *A supplycacyon to the Queenes Majestie* (STC 17562). Foreign observers believed that Philip's coronation would be one of the main items of business in the parliament of 1555, and Dr Jennifer Loach, in her recent study of Mary's parliaments, takes that possibility seriously. I formerly shared that view, but now believe that parliament would only have become involved if there had been a plan to make specific additions to Philip's authority by statute. J. Loach, *Parliament and the Crown in the Reign of Mary Tudor*, pp. 130–1.

Spanish revenues. His name was formally joined with that of the queen in the granting of normal English patents, but the extent to which he influenced Mary, or the English council, in the distribution of this patronage is largely a matter of conjecture.[14] Only in one respect is the evidence somewhat firmer, and that is the consistent manner in which he interceded for, and secured the release and pardon of, political offenders. The most obvious example of this is provided by the fortunes of the Dudley brothers, the sons of the executed and attainted duke of Northumberland. Their widowed mother, Jane, and their brother-in-law Sir Henry Sidney had been endeavouring to outflank Mary's indignation since Sidney had accompanied the earl of Bedford to Spain in the spring of 1554. By the autumn they had been befriended by such powerful Spaniards as the duke of Medina Celi and Don Diego de Mendoza, and the duchess was again received at court. It was uphill work and her eldest son, the earl of Warwick, was already mortally sick when he was released on 18 October. His death was too much for his mother, who took to her own bed, and died on 22 January 1555, 'beseeching' her Spanish friends 'for God's sake to continue . . . good lords to my sons in their needs, and my trust is that God will requite it them'.[15] On the very day of her death Ambrose, Henry and Robert were released from the Tower, along with their uncle, Sir Andrew, Sir James Croftes, Sir Nicholas Throgmorton, Sir Edward Warner and a number of others who had been involved in the Wyatt rising twelve months earlier.[16] The role of Philip and his courtiers in this clemency is confirmed by the fact that Ambrose and Robert immediately became involved in one of the king's Anglo-Spanish tournaments, by the comments of Venetian observers, and by the pensions shortly after awarded to Croftes and Cuthbert Vaughn.

Philip was anxious to recruit 'serviceable men', particularly soldiers, and was probably behind the pardons subsequently granted to Sir Peter Carew, Peter Killigrew, and a number of others who were to serve in the St Quentin campaign of 1557, or in the navy during the last two years of the reign. These men were grateful to the king, and regarded him in a sense as their patron, but none was received into Mary's favour, or allowed anywhere near the court. The Dudleys were pardoned, and received modest annuities, or small grants of land;[17] Sir William Winter recovered his office as surveyor of the navy;[18] but there was apparently little else which Philip could do, apart from

---

[14] Several important commissions, such as those for the sale of church lands, were reissued in August 1554, bearing Philip's name, and a few petitions were addressed to him alone, but there is no evidence at all to suggest that Philip was actively promoting the interests of any court group.

[15] A. Collins, ed., *Letters and Memorials of State* (1746) I, p. 34.

[16] J. Foxe, *Acts and Monuments of the English Martyrs*, ed. S. R. Cattley and G. Townsend, VI, p. 587.

[17] *Calendar of the Patent Rolls, Philip and Mary*, II, pp. 43, 71, 98 (Sir Andrew); II, p. 150 and III, p. 535 (Ambrose); II, p. 159 (Robert) etc.

[18] T. Glasgow, Jnr., 'The maturing of Naval Administration, 1556–1564', *Mariner's Mirror*, 56 (1970).

employing them in war, or granting them a pension out of his own revenues. These pensions, indeed, constituted a major element in the patronage which he was willing to dispense, and their political purpose is obvious, but they remained outside the normal patronage structure, and were akin to the inducements which any powerful monarch would have offered to subjects of a friendly but foreign crown. In March 1554, about two months after the marriage treaty was signed, and as a part of the customary lubrication of diplomacy, Renard had distributed gold chains and cash gifts to a total of 4950 crowns, or about £1235.[19] The recipients had mostly been minor courtiers or gentlemen servants although some more important figures such as Sir John Gage (the lord chamberlain) and Sir John Bridges had also been included. Pensions had probably been under discussion since the previous autumn, but their actual granting had to await Philip's arrival, lest the source of the largesse should be mis-identified. Someone, probably Renard, drew up a list for his guidance shortly before his landing, suggesting specific annuities of between 600 and 2000 crowns for twenty-one named noblemen and councillors, together with unspecified rewards for a number of others, including Susan Clarencius and Frideswide Strelly 'the queen's chief ladies'.[20] Philip deliberated for about a month, and then on 23 August issued patents to twenty-one pensioners.[21] His grants followed the suggested list closely, but by no means exactly, being perhaps less concerned to reward past services than to ensure future ones.

Both lists were headed by the earls of Arundel, Derby, Shrewsbury and Pembroke, each with 2000 crowns (or £500) per annum;[22] both lists also assigned 1000 crowns to the earls of Bedford and Sussex, Lord Howard of Effingham, Lord Clinton, Sir William Petre, Sir Robert Rochester and Sir Henry Jerningham. However, the suggestions for similar grants to the earl of Worcester, Lord Grey, Lord Dacre and Lord Wentworth were not followed up. In their places appeared the marquis of Winchester, the earl of Huntingdon and Sir Thomas Cheyney. Sir John Gage, Sir Francis Englefield, Sir Richard Southwell, and Secretary John Bourne all received less than suggested, and Sir Thomas Wharton was added, at 300 crowns. The two biggest discrepancies however, related to the major political antagonists of the reign, Lord Paget and the chancellor, Stephen Gardiner. The original list had referred to the need to reward Paget, but had suggested no pension, while

---

[19] *Cal. Sp.*, XII, p. 158, 15 March 1554. A second and shorter list containing some of the same names, and some others, was drawn up in July 1554 and headed 'a list of persons to whom chains are to be given'. This second distribution may have been connected with the weddding.

[20] *Cal. Sp.*, XII, pp. 315–16.

[21] Archivo General de Simancas, CMC la E, Legajo 1184 contains the originals of all these patents (in Latin), signed by the recipients.

[22] *Cal. Sp.*, XII, p. 315. AGS, CMC la E, 1184, fos. 51–64. These were 'crowns English' counted at four to the pound. Some of Orbea's accounts were made up in crowns, some in pounds sterling, and some in marevedis.

describing the chancellor as 'reserved for some pension or benefice'. In the event Gardiner received nothing, while Paget was allocated an annuity of 1500 crowns, one of the highest awarded.[23] Considering that Gardiner had dominated the council since April 1554, and Paget, although no longer in disgrace, was still distinctly out of favour with the queen, these discrepancies were significant. Paget became very much Philip's man, and assiduously cultivated the relationship without much reference to Mary.[24] When Gardiner died in November 1555, the king wanted to promote his protégé to the chancellorship, but Mary demurred, preferring the innocuous Nicholas Heath, archbishop of York. Instead Paget became lord privy seal – the only major political preferment which can be ascribed directly to Philip's influence. But his failure to obtain the chancellorship is an interesting comment upon the queen's supposed subservience to her husband's wishes. Philip added only modestly to this original pension list after 1554. Sir Anthony Browne seems to have been granted 500 crowns a year when he was created Viscount Montague, and possibly in compensation for his summary and unexplained dismissal as the king's master of the horse.[25] The others whose names had appeared by 1558 were Lord Hastings, Sir Henry Sidney, Sir James Croftes, Sir John Brende, Francis English, Thomas Barton, Edward Randolf, Francis Basset and Anthony Kempe.[26] The last two had originally been appointed to the king's privy chamber as interpreters, and seem to have been pensioned when they were replaced by men of lower social status; the rest were mainly soldiers.

The original pension list represented an annual commitment of 22,600 crowns (£5600) per annum, which had risen by 1558 to about 27,000. The first instalments had been backdated to 1 April 1554, and had been paid up to the end of December on the day of grant.[27] Thereafter they were paid regularly by 'tercios', or four-monthly periods, down to the end of 1556. By that time Philip was in grievous financial difficulties, and some pensioners began to be disappointed. At the end of 1558 when Dominico de Orbea, the teserero general, took stock of the situation he found that some – such as the earls of Derby and Shrewsbury, were owed for two full years; others – such as Arundel, Pembroke and Winchester, for eighteen months; only a few were as fortunate as Lord William Howard, who was twelve months in arrears.[28] The total debt on pensions by that time was 45,462 crowns, or £11,365. When

---

[23] AGS, CMC la E, 1184; also Estado Inglaterra, Legajo 811, fo. 121.

[24] As a Venetian observer commented, it was from the king that 'all favours shown to him proceed, nor does he fail to seek them by all means and with all his might'. *Calendar of State Papers, Venetian*, VI, pp. 415–16.

[25] AGS, E 811, fo. 121. Browne's dismissal was much resented by the English, and Renard found himself being blamed by the Spaniards for his alleged shortcomings. *Cal. Sp.*, XIII, pp. 49, 58. He was created Viscount Montague on 2 Sept. PRO, SP 11/4/21.

[26] AGS, E 811, fo. 124.

[27] AGS, CMC la E, 1184, fo. 64. The original receipts (in Spanish) signed by the recipients are unfoliated. [28] AGS, E 811, fo. 124.

Mary was clearly dying, on 14 November 1558, the conde de Feria, Philip's personal envoy, called upon Elizabeth to assure her that his master had instructed all his English pensioners and servants to place themselves at her disposal. Her response took him aback:

... she said that she would like to know who these and the other servants were, in order to decide whether it was right or not that they should be receiving money from your majesty ...[29]

The princess clearly had unexpectedly scrupulous views on the subject of undivided allegiance, and when Orbea finally discharged his English account in April and May 1559, Philip does not appear to have attempted to keep a foothold in English politics by that means.[30] His pensioners represented a substantial investment, and must be seen as a serious attempt to establish his influence; but it is hard to assess what returns he actually received. At the end of the reign Feria reported sourly that the English nobility were '... all as ungrateful to your majesty as if they had never received anything from your hands'; but by then they had little to gain from gratitude, and as Feria admitted, they greeted him 'like one who bears bulls from a dead Pope'.[31]

Earlier on there were hints and suggestions of a 'king's party' within the council, working to increase his share in the government, and even to arrange his coronation. The earls of Arundel, Derby, Shrewsbury and Pembroke were addressed in this connection in a clandestine pamphlet by John Bradford, urging them of the dangers of giving the crown over to a 'stranger prince'.[32] Lord Paget was in a special sense the king's man, and when he visited the emperor's court in March 1556 he endeavoured to claim the chief credit for promoting Philip's interest.[33] However, it is very difficult to see what he, or any of the other pensioners, actually achieved in that direction, and not certain that they made any real effort. Paget supported the call for war against France in March 1557, and may eventually have provoked it.[34] Pembroke and some of the other nobles also welcomed the onset of hostilities, and served the king capably but briefly in the St Quentin campaign. Apart from that, they seem to have done little to earn their pensions. Significantly, none were major recipients of the queen's own patronage, and apart from his role in securing the pardon of political malefactors, there is very little evidence that Philip influenced his wife's policy in that connection. A handful of clerical promo-

[29] M. J. Rodriguez-Salgado and S. Adams, eds., 'The Count of Feria's despatch to Philip II of 14 November 1558', Camden Miscellany, XXVIII (1984), p. 332.
[30] In the despatch quoted above, Feria made it clear that in his opinion Philip should pension the principal ministers of the new regime as quickly as possible. Ibid, p. 336.
[31] 'The Count of Feria's despatch . . .', p. 329.
[32] The copye of a letter sent by J. Bradforthe to the erles of Arundel, Debie, Shrewsbury and Penbroke (1556) (STC 3480).
[33] Badoer to the Doge and Senate, 26 April 1556. Cal. Ven., VI, p. 419.
[34] For a discussion of this point, see Loades, Mary Tudor, pp. 365-7.

tions and commercial concessions were granted to the king's Spanish servants, but there was nothing to compensate for his lack of direct control over English land and offices.[35] Debarred by the treaty from bringing Spanish officials or ministers into English government, he would employ no Englishmen in any of his other dominions, except as soldiers and no Englishman received any honour or estate outside the realm. The pensions which he distributed were by no means trivial, but they could not on their own sustain the pattern of service and obligation which normally rested upon a wide variety of patronage and 'good lordship'.

The only other Englishmen who were specifically bound to Philip were the members of his household.[36] These had all been chosen for him before he arrived, and although there are a number of discrepancies between the list drawn up in June 1554 and that appearing in Orbea's accounts for 1558, only a few can be attributed, even by inference, to the king's direct intervention. The lord chamberlain, Sir John Williams, served throughout the reign and Sir John Huddlestone the vice-chamberlain until his death in 1557. Originally there were seven *chamberlones*, or gentlemen of the privy chamber, all the sons of major English peers. Three of these had gone by 1558. Lord Maltravers (the only Spanish speaker among them) had died in Brussels in June 1556, on embassy to the king of the Romans;[37] the earl of Surrey had succeeded to his grandfather's dukedom in August 1554, and had withdrawn at that point. There is no obvious explanation for the disappearance of Lord Herbert, and Lord Fitzwalter continued on the list, in spite of having become both earl of Sussex and lord deputy of Ireland in 1557. Of the three gentlemen 'aids' of the chamber, originally appointed for their skill in languages, two, Kempe and Basset had by 1558 been transferred to the list of pensioners, as we have seen. The third, Richard Shelly, was still in the household as *gentil hombre de la boca*. In their place six men described specifically as interpreters had been appointed, none of whom featured in the original household.[38] Unlike the 'aids', these men ranked only one place above the grooms and pages, and so were probably classed as yeomen rather than gentlemen. The reason for this change can only be inferred, but probably indicates that there was little need for interpreters in close proximity to the king, because he dealt with his English household and councillors through Spanish intermediaries rather than English ones. The king spoke no English, and understood very little, so

---

[35] E.g. two Regius chairs in Oxford to Pedro de Soto and Juan de Villagarcia, a monopoly to Gomes de Navarette to make and sell 'Spanish leather' for ten years, and a licence to Pedro Deprado to buy 100 dickers of leather within two years. *CPR* II, p. 286, III, p. 182.

[36] They were specifically sworn to Philip's service in June 1554. *Acts of the Privy Council*, VI, p. 31.

[37] The original list of June 1554 is printed in *Cal. Sp.*, XII, p. 297. For the list as it had evolved by 1558, see AGS, E 811, fo. 122. On Maltravers, see V. Gibbs, ed., *The Complete Peerage of England* by G. E. Cockayne, *sub* Arundel.

[38] Thomas Dennis, Robert Moffat, Peter Gage, John Brett, Thomas 'Vol' and John 'Panon'. AGS, E 81, fo. 122.

there is no question of his having dispensed with the 'aids' because he had no need of them.

The remaining twenty-four gentlemen servants of 1554, classed as cup-bearers, carvers, sewers, gentlemen ushers, gentlemen waiters, sewers of the chamber and harbingers, appear in the later accounts as *gentil hombres de la boca, gentil hombres de la casa, castilleros, panatiers, apostendores* and *huxiers de saleta*.[39] Seventeen of the twenty-four served throughout, and thirteen new names were added, bringing the total of gentlemen in Philip's service to thirty by 1558. In addition there were eleven grooms and pages, the interpreters, and a guard of one hundred yeomen archers, four of whom died in the course of the reign. The principal officers and *chamberlones* were paid 400 crowns a year, the *gentil hombres de la boca* 300, the *gentil hombres de la casa* 280, the *castilleros* 138 and the yeomen of the guard 95 – or £24, the same as the queen's guard.[40] By contrast the *panatiers* appear to have received a mere honorarium of 45 crowns a year – hardly worth a gentleman's having by the standards of the time. The total bill for this household came to about £6000 per annum, and they seem to have been paid regularly at four-monthly intervals until April 1557, when payments were suspended as they had been four months earlier to most of the pensioners. By the end of 1558 20 months were owing,[41] and most of these debts were discharged, along with the outstanding pensions, by Orbea's agent in London, Francisco de Lixalde, early in 1559.[42] Only the archers were exempted from this freeze, continuing to receive their money regularly through George Brodyman, the keeper of the queen's privy purse, until August 1558. In their case only one 'tercio' was owing at the end of the year.[43]

How much service this household actually performed in return for its wages is not very clear. When Philip first arrived there was a major quarrel because he brought a complete Spanish household with him.[44] He had been expected to come with a modest noble entourage, and to bring his own chapel and stable staff, but no more. It took almost four months of acrimony to resolve this dilemma and work out a rough division of responsibility. There is no record of just how this was done, but to judge from the complaints of both sides the king used Spaniards almost exclusively in his privy chamber, while leaving his English servants to perform outer chamber and ceremonial duties.[45] Once

---

[39] AGS, E 811, fos. 119–22.

[40] Ibid; PRO, E 101/428/9.

[41] In March 1558 the debts owed to the pensioners 'and to the Chamberlains and serving gentlemen and other servants for wages for one year ending 30th. April next' came to £8814. *Cal. Sp.*, XIII, p. 373. By the end of 1558 this had risen to £11,365, AGS, E 811, fo. 124.

[42] Ibid, fo. 127.

[43] PRO, E 101/428/9; AGS, E 811, fo. 128.

[44] Loades, *Mary Tudor*, pp. 211–15.

[45] The Spaniards complained that they were unable to wait on their king, and that the duke of Alva was not allowed to bear his wand of office, as majordomo. *Tres Cartas de lo sucedido en el viaje de Su Alteza a Inglaterra* (La Sociedad de Bibliofilos Españoles, 1877) Primera Carta. The English complained that they had no access to the king, and the Spaniards would not attempt to communicate with them. *Cal. Sp.*, XIII, pp. 45, 50.

this pattern had been established, by November 1554, it probably continued unchanged during the rest of Philip's residence. Apart from a small group of *chamberlones* who accompanied him to Brussels in September 1555, and stayed a few weeks, the household was stood down at his departure.[46] A year later it was reconvened in expectation of his return, but this turned out to be a false alarm, and it was not until March 1557 that Philip again had need of his English servants. In July of the same year the household was again disbanded, this time finally, and by the time they were discharged in 1559 its members had drawn four and a half years wages for some fifteen months of service. On the other hand, none had received any provision at the king's hands apart from their wages, and neither side had any particular reason to feel pleased with their bargain. Almost as soon as he arrived in England Ruy Gomez, Philip's secretary, was complaining sourly that his master was having to pay for two full households 'without any help from the queen',[47] but this was not entirely true because the king was also provided with a household 'below stairs' which was effectively an augmentation of the main royal household, and paid through the countinghouse. Ninety-two named individuals representing twenty-two different service departments were ordered to Southampton to attend upon Philip when he arrived.[48] This establishment seems to have been modelled upon the consort's household provided for earlier queens, except that the lord steward, treasurer and controller were identical with those of the main household. Since Philip was to spend only a few days apart from Mary during his residence in England, these servants can have had little sense of separate identity.[49] The senior officer, John Dodge, clerk of the greencloth, was assigned a wage of £44 6s 8d, but only five others were similarly treated. The vast majority, irrespective of whether they were described as clerk, yeoman, groom or page, were paid either £2 13s 4d or £2 0s 0d, which probably represents the supplements which they received for this particular duty. Their normal duties would have been performed in the appropriate departments of the court, where they represented an increase of almost fifty per cent on the normal establishment, and may have helped to account for the steep rise in Mary's housekeeping costs during the second year of her reign.[50] It seems unlikely that the king himself would have been particularly aware of them, and he did not reward them himself, either individually or collectively.

Mary apparently wished her husband to play a prominent role in the

---

[46] On 18 December 1555 the select council wrote to the king recommending that Lord Williams (Philip's chamberlain) should be allowed a table at court during the king's absence. The reply is not recorded. PRO, SP 11/6/78.

[47] Ruy Gomez to Eraso, 27 July 1554. *Cal. Sp.*, XIII, p. 2.

[48] *Cal. Sp.*, XIII, pp. 298–9.

[49] While he was digesting his disappointment over the failure of Mary's pregnancy, Philip left her for a few days and spent the nights of 4 to 12 August 1555 at Windsor and Oatlands. *Cal. Sp.*, XIII, p. 444.

[50] To over £75,000, according to one set of accounts. BL, Lansdowne MS, 4, fo. 19.

government of the realm, and both the emperor and his own servants expected no less. On 27 July 1554 the privy council decided to keep a minute of all its business in either Latin or Spanish for the king's guidance, and it was generally expected that his arrival would mean substantial changes in the domestic balance of power.[51] However, very little happened. One anonymous Spaniard declared that neither the king nor the queen had any authority in this God-forsaken land where '. . . the councillors govern and are lords of the kingdom . . .' but that was hardly an informed judgment.[52] Paget, Pembroke and Arundel were more regular in their attendance at the council after mid-August, and the influence of Simon Renard was eclipsed, but there is very little evidence of Philip concerning himself with English affairs. He continued to consult with his own councillors particularly Alva, Feria and Olivares, about other business, but he was never at ease with the English council. The problem was partly linguistic. Philip was not at home in any language other than Spanish, although he understood both French and Latin, and consequently always worked through an interpreter. He was also profoundly ignorant of English law and customs and was strongly influenced by his secretary, Ruy Gomez.[53] Gomez was as ignorant of England as the king, and spread rumours that Philip wished to leave England, not to return until he was permitted to act 'as befits their king and sovereign Lord'. Such indiscretions were seized upon by Antoine de Noailles, the French ambassador, and considerably impeded the development of a good working relationship with the English council. The services of a Spanish-speaking English secretary were available to the king in the person of Bernard Hampton, one of the clerks to the council,[54] but never seem to have been employed and Philip's will to tackle the intricacies of English affairs must be in serious doubt.

In one respect, however, his energy and commitment at this time cannot be questioned. Within a few weeks of his arrival in England, he had taken a firm initiative to break the deadlock in negotiations for reconciliation with the papacy. It must be remembered that Philip had his own reasons for wishing to bring this about as speedily as possible, reasons which had much to do with Habsburg influence in the Curia and very little to do with England.[55] Nevertheless he was quick to appreciate the strength of aristocratic feelings about the secularised church lands, and it was he, through his own envoy in Rome, Don Manrique de Lara, who finally persuaded Julius III to cut the church's losses over these lands. It was he also who used the persuasive powers of Simon Renard to force the reluctant Reginald Pole into accepting

---

[51] *Acts of the Privy Council*, v, p. 53. *Mary Tudor*, pp. 135–7. Gardiner was particularly apprehensive. [52] *Mary Tudor*, p. 214.

[53] Ruy Gomez de Silva, a Portuguese who was high in Philip's confidence. It was he who misinformed Don Fernando Enriquez, the Admiral of Castile about the king's position in England, and almost caused a relief expedition to be fitted out. *Cal. Sp.*, XIII, p. 47.

[54] Hampton was granted an annuity of 40 marks in April 1555 'for his daily pains in writing the Queen's Spanish letters'. *Cal. Pat.*, II, p. 72. [55] *Mary Tudor*, pp. 218–22.

this situation, and agreeing to issue a general dispensation.[56] Between October 1554 and January 1555 Philip spent much time with the English councillors, preparing the strategy whereby the crucial legislation was steered through parliament. He appeared three times in the House of Lords along with Mary, and played a prominent part in welcoming Cardinal Pole on his return.[57] He had pledged his personal credit on the satisfactory nature of the new papal brief, which reached Pole only days before he was due to meet parliament on 28 November, and was duly vindicated. Philip and Mary did not see eye to eye on the question of church lands. During discussions over Christmas, Mary made it clear that she agreed with Pole, and did not accept that the 'possessioners' had any title to the church lands, save that conferred by the papal dispensation.[58] Philip, who had the strongest reasons for not wishing the deal to fail, seems to have sided consistently with the lay aristocracy, and may well have been responsible for the bull *Praeclara*, published on 20 June 1555, which settled the legal issue by canonically extinguishing the former religious houses.[59] Outside England the reconciliation was generally regarded as a personal triumph for the king, and *Il Felicissimo ritorno del regno d'Inghilterra alla catholice unione* was typical of many tracts produced in celebration.[60]

However, the close working relationship which Philip seems to have developed with Paget and his allies over this issue was not continued into normal business. This may have been because he failed to reduce the size of the council as he wished. The evidence for this is circumstantial and second hand, but observers such as the Venetian Giacomo Soranzo, who listed the most influential councillors in the autumn of 1554 as Gardiner, Paget, Arundel and Petre, also commented upon the king's failure to create a 'select council'.[61] The alleged reason was that Gardiner feared isolation in such a body, because of the likely predominance of Paget and his allies, but if such was the case, the unspoken comment must have been that Mary supported Gardiner, because the chancellor alone could hardly have thwarted the king's wishes in such a matter. The signs of Philip's influence in government during

---

[56] *Cal. Sp.*, XIII, pp. 63–4. The emperor left these negotiations entirely in Philip's hands, probably on account of his poor health.

[57] Philip attended the opening of parliament on 12 November, Pole's address to both houses on the 28th, and the final assent to legislation. Pole arrived from Gravesend by water on the 24th. *Diary of Henry Marchyn* (Camden Society, 1847), pp. 74–6.

[58] *Mary Tudor*, pp. 327–8; Letter and postscript by Alvise Priuli, 22 and 24 December 1554. BL., Add. MS 41557.

[59] M. C. Knowles, *The Religious Orders in England*, III, p. 423. By the summer of 1555 Philip's influence in the Curia had been much reduced by the election of Pope Paul IV, but this may well have been a measure formally approved by Julius III before his death in March. Such a delay would not have been unusual in papal bureaucracy.

[60] Published in Rome on 1 December 1554 (allegedly – but presumably later because the events which it describes took place on 28 November). Mary also attributed the success of the negotiation 'largely . . . to the wise guidance of my said Lord'. *Cal. Sp.*, XIII, p. 117.

[61] *Cal. Ven.*, V, pp. 532–63.

the latter part of his residence, from January to July 1555 are largely negative. Open quarrels between councillors, of the kind which loom so large in ambassadorial reports of the first year of the reign, and reappear from 1556 onward, are scarcely mentioned during this period, except by Noailles who had his own axe to grind. On 11 June Giovanni Michieli reported that the king played no part in the government, but he may have derived that opinion from Philip's Spanish servants rather than by direct observation.[62] The early summer was dominated by nervous anticipation of Mary's confinement, with many rumours as to what Philip, or the emperor, would do if she should miscarry. In fact the king seems to have had no plan for action once a rather half-hearted attempt to marry off Elizabeth had failed. The eventual failure of the queen's 'pregnancy', however, stirred him into action. His father had been talking of handing over power in the Netherlands for several months, and once the religious settlement in England was complete only the uncertainty of Mary's condition had kept him in England. By the end of July he was making active preparations to leave, and these included formally establishing the council of state which he had so long hankered after. This was to consist of Gardiner, Thirlby, Paget, Arundel, Pembroke, Winchester, Rochester, Petre and Pole. Either the chancellor's long opposition had been circumvented, or the queen was too exhausted and despondent to continue her support, because Rochester was his only consistent supporter within this group.[63] In early August the king was actively involved in preparations for the planned parliament, and his energy and application during this month attracted much favourable comment.

When he departed for Brussels on 27 August, no one knew quite what to expect. He left the bulk of his Spanish household behind, including its master, Don Diego de Acevedo, and spoke of returning for the parliament. However, on 15 October he wrote both to the council and the parliament, excusing his absence, and exhorting them to their accustomed diligence and loyalty.[64] Throughout the ensuing negotiations over his coronation, he also kept up a steady correspondence with the English council over routine business. At the end of December they sent him a lengthy memorandum of business transacted, to which he responded with praise and encouragement in early February.[65] At about the same time there was a disagreement over his titles, because Philip wished to place his newly acquired crown of Spain above that of England, and he sent Figueroa across to consult them. On 16 March he

---

[62] *Cal. Ven.*, VI, p. 106. A month later the same writer was declaring that 'with the king's departure, all busines will cease'. Ibid, p. 173.

[63] BL, Cotton MS Titus B. 2, fo. 160. Gardiner's health was beginning to fail by this time, and his attitude to Philip is the subject of a vigorous controversy centring on the authorship of the so-called 'Machiavellian treatise', *A Discourse on the coming of the English and Normans to Britain* which was presented to the king after his death. P. S. Donaldson, *A Machiavellian Treatise by Stephen Gardiner*, and D. Fenlon in the *Historical Journal*, 19 (1976).

[64] PRO, SP 11/6/28.   [65] PRO, SP 11/6/82 and SP 11/7/5.

acknowledged receipt of the pardon for Sir Peter Carew, which he must have requested. Sometimes his reactions were astonishingly quick. In Ghent on 13 September 1556 he replied to a council letter of the 10th, but usually the interval was between a fortnight and a month.[66] The same type of business constantly recurred; piracy by the English against the Flemings, the interests of German or Italian merchants in England, the security of Calais. Beneath the polite expressions of regard and satisfaction there was clearly tension, as the king consistently favoured his Flemish or Spanish subjects against the commercial interests of the English, and even backed the Portuguese and the Hanseatic League against the merchant adventurers, whom he regarded as a bunch of heretics.[67] Of interest in English domestic affairs there is very little sign, and it seems likely that by the summer of 1556 the 'select council' existed only for Philip's benefit, since there is no other sign of it acting apart from the privy council proper.[68] Meanwhile the quarrels, subdued during the king's residence and permanently changed by Gardiner's death in November 1555, were flourishing again, and one of Mary's numerous pleas for her husband's return spoke eloquently of the need for his 'firm hand'.

The whole pattern of Philip's involvement with England, and particularly after the failure of his dynastic hopes, indicates that he saw it primarily as a base and a source of supply for his perpetual struggle against France. He had been particularly incensed by the clause in the marriage treaty which had rejected involvement in that war, and later angered by his failure to obtain any financial support. Only in one respect had he succeeded, and that was when the English council recommenced its shipbuilding programme in the autumn of 1555, laying down two new warships in response to his promptings and demands.[69] In the year ending December 1555 some £120,000 was dispensed on the navy, and in January 1556 a series of orders was issued to improve the efficiency of the admiralty, directing Lord William Howard to take musters of seamen and to arrange the 'wise placing of the ships for ready service'. In July of the same year the effectiveness of these measures was demonstrated when the queen's ships scored a rare and notable victory over an Anglo-French pirate fleet.[70] By the end of 1556 the pressure for war was building up. In December the earl of Pembroke was sent to Calais; in early January the French commenced hostilities in Flanders, and an 'ordinary' of £14,000 a year was allocated to the English fleet. At the same time the English council was

---

[66] PRO, SP 11/9/30 and SP 11/9/28.

[67] *Mary Tudor*, pp. 379–80. On heresies among the merchant adventurers, see Philip's letter of 30 September 1556. PRO, SP 11/9/34.

[68] The surviving correspondence peters out in December 1556, when the king's return was again expected, but the distinction between the 'select council' or 'council of state' and the main privy council, clearly intended in Philip's scheme, seems to have disappeared in the early part of the year. *Mary Tudor*, pp. 257–8.

[69] The 'Philip and Mary' and the 'Mary Rose'; Glasgow, 'The maturing of Naval Administration', p. 6 and n.

[70] Michieli to the Doge and Senate. *Cal. Ven.*, VI, p. 536.

totally unco-operative, advising the queen emphatically against war 'where necessitie of defence shall not require the same',[71] and the king's neglect of his English interests began to show to his disadvantage. Paget certainly, and Pembroke probably, supported Mary in her attempts to come to his assistance, but they would probably have failed without Philip's personal intervention. In the event it took about a month of intense pressure, plus the curious episode of Thomas Stafford's raid on Scarborough, to break down the council's resistance. Philip got his declaration of war, and the use of the English fleet. He also got an expeditionary force of 7000 men, but no money. Honour was satisfied, but little else. The English served for four months, and cost him some £48,000, which may have pleased the military aristocracy, and aroused expectations of more rewarding service to come, but did little to convince Philip of the value of such assistance.[72] England and Spain remained allies in war for the remainder of the reign, but relations steadily deteriorated. After Philip's second and final departure in July 1557 regular correspondence with the select council was not resumed, and what was by then a fiction seems to have been finally abandoned. By the early part of 1558, after the recriminations surrounding the fall of Calais, Feria reported that all those members of the English council (and he specifically mentioned Lord Paget) who had hitherto been willing to support and promote the king's interests had abandoned all efforts to do so.[73] The English aristocracy seem to have concluded that there was no more honour and profit to be gained by serving Philip in war than by serving him in peace.

In spite of his early enthusiasm to obtain the title, Philip made very little effort to project himself as king of England, and seems to have had no sense of his own image. On 18 August 1554 he shared with Mary a magnificent entry into London, in which various attempts were made to give him an English identity, but no record suggests that he made any favourable, or noticeable, response. One pageant, borrowed from that which had greeted Catherine of Aragon in 1501, displayed a genealogical tree tracing his descent from John of Gaunt. Another, of Corineus Britannus and Gogmagog on London bridge bore the grandiloquent verse

> Teque putant omnes missum divinitus urbi,
> Cuius mens, studium, vox, virtus atque voluntas
> Gaudet, et in clari consentit amore Philippi.[74]

---

[71] BL, Cotton MS Titus C 7, fo. 199.
[72] For the commissions, warrants and accounts for this campaign, see BL, Stowe MS 571, fos. 77–132. *Mary Tudor*, pp. 370–3; C. S. L. Davies, 'England and the French war, 1557–9' in J. Loach and R. Tittler, eds., *The Mid-Tudor Polity* (London, 1980).
[73] Feria to Philip, 22 February, 1558. *Cal. Sp.*, XIII, pp. 361–2.
[74] *Chronicle of Queen Jane and Queen Mary*, ed. J. G. Nichols (Camden Society, 1850), p. 146. The idea that Philip was no stranger, but a rightful heir of the Plantagenets, was used on a number of occasions, notably in the 'Discourse on the coming of the English ...', and in John Christopherson's *An exhortation to all menne to take hede and beware of rebellion* (1554) sig. M. v.

Sympathetic observers who recorded the spectacle, such as the author of *Le Solenne et felice intrata*, saw signs of warmth and affection in the crowds who witnessed these scenes,[75] but the type of reciprocal gesture which the English expected of their sovereigns was not forthcoming. When he did attempt to put on a show of his own, three months later, the attempt misfired badly. The *juego de canas* was a purely Spanish spectacle, and was too tame for the pugilistic English, in spite of the splendid costumes and the king's personal appearance. Henry Machyn's unenthusiastic response was typical

(The xxv day of November) the wyche was Sonday, at afternone, the Kyngs grace and my lord (Fitzwalter) and divers Spaneards dyd ryd in divers colas, the Kyng in red . . . and with targets and canes in ther hand, herlyng of rods on at anodur . . .[76]

This time Philip got the message, and on 18 December staged and took part in, an orthodox foot tournament '. . . a greet tryhumph . . . by the king and dyvers lordes both English-men and Spaneards in goodly harnes' as the same observer noted.[77] Over the next four months several such spectacles were provided, which represented a genuine effort to please at least the English aristocracy. On 12 February a 'cane play' was staged in honour of the wedding of Lord Strange, one of his *chamberlones*, and on 20 April at the nuptials of the favoured Lord Fitzwalter '. . . his Majesty in person, as a mark of greater honour (took) part with many other gentlemen in a tournay on foot . . .'.[78] Full-scale tournaments were also staged on 23 January, when the list of Anglo-Spanish Defenders was headed by the Dudley brothers (released from the Tower only the day before) and on 25 March in the great tilt yard at Westminster. This latter was a grand event, almost in the style of Henry VIII

. . . ther was as gret justes as youe have seen . . . the chalyngers was a Spaneard and ser George Haward; and all ther men and ther horsses trymmed in whyt, and then cam the Kyng and a grete mene all in bluw . . . and ther was broken ii hondred stayffes and a-boyff.[79]

'By such demonstrations', the Venetian observed 'he from day to day gains the goodwill of all . . .'. Unfortunately for Philip, this was not true. Such welcome as he received always depended upon English affection for Mary, and it was typical of the king's limitations that the obvious opportunity to involve her in these displays as the object of courtly love devotion, in the manner of the later Accession Day tilts was not taken. Philip was not indifferent to magnificence,

---

[75] As also did Giovanni di Stroppiana, an envoy of the duke of Savoy. *Cal. Sp.*, XIII, p. 81.

[76] Machyn, *Diary*, p. 76. Even Philip's Spanish advisers recognised this effort as a mistake.

[77] Ibid, p. 79.

[78] *Cal. Ven.*, VI, p. 58. Machyn records several other 'combats' of a similar nature in which the king did not take part.

[79] Machyn, pp. 80, 84. On these jousts see also S. Anglo, 'Financial and heraldic records of English tournaments', *Journal of the Society of Archivists*, 2 (1962), 192; and R. C. McCoy, 'From the Tower to the tiltyard; Robert Dudley's return to glory', *Historical Journal*, 27 (1984), 425. The 'challenge' for the January tournament is in College of Arms MS 6.

as the records of court festivities during his residence indicate,[80] but he had little or no sense of how it might be used in an English setting.

As king of England there is no doubt that Philip was a failure, but the reasons were not as straightforward as is sometimes assumed. Neither English xenophobia nor the marriage treaty in themselves prevented him from getting a grip upon the government of the country. Inevitably, his priorities were elsewhere, and that deprived him of the necessary consistency and commitment, but he did not lose interest in ruling England until his main hopes had been frustrated. His investment of time and money was considerable, and the treatment of his English pensioners and household generous. But two factors were critical; he lacked any sense of how to present himself, and he lacked English patronage. The former was his own fault, but the latter was Mary's. If the queen was as anxious to shift the burden of government onto her husband as she professed to be, it is hard to see why she did not give him a personal estate in England, or help him to build up his aristocratic connection by using her own patronage. She was not conspicuously mean in rewarding her own favourites.[81] The evidence also suggests that when Mary was really determined about something – such as her marriage or the reconciliation – no amount of conciliar opposition would deter her. And this was even more the case when Philip was also present – as over war with France. So we must conclude that, whatever may have been said at the time or since, the queen was not anxious to step aside and let Philip take over. She certainly wanted him, but on her own terms – just as he wanted her on his own terms. The questions of his coronation and of the promotion of Lord Paget are pointers in the same direction. Since Mary was not noticeably sensitive to the wishes of her subjects, however forcefully expressed, this was probably a sign of her basic Tudor temperament. Of course the Spaniards blamed the English council for their master's dishonour – but no Tudor council really had that power.

When Mary made her will in March 1558, she wrote in her own hand

And I do humbly beseeche my said most dearest lorde and husband to accepte of my bequeste and to keep for a memory of me one jewell . . . sent unto me by the Count d'Egmont . . . and also one other table dyamond which his Majesty sent unto me by the Marques de las Navas . . .[82]

but when she died in November, Philip instructed that all her jewels should be handed over to her successor.

[80] A. Feuillerat, *Documents Relating to the Office of the Revels* (Louvain, 1908–14), I, xiv. etc. although, as Sydney Anglo pointed out (*Spectacle Pageantry and Early Tudor Policy*, pp. 340–2) these entertainments were not very expensive by Henrician standards, they were described as 'Great masks' and 'goodly revels' by contemporaries, e.g. '. . . on Sunday night at Court there was a brave maskery of cloth of gold and silver, the maskers dressed as mariners . . .', Francis Yaxley to Sir William Cecil, 12 October, 1554; BL, Lansdowne MS 3, fo. 92.

[81] *Mary Tudor*, pp. 89–100.

[82] BL, Harley MS 6949. Printed in J. M. Stone, *The History of Mary I* (London, 1901), pp. 507–17.

Sin and society: the northern high commission and the northern gentry in the reign of Elizabeth I

CLAIRE CROSS

The act books of church courts are among the more strikingly repulsive of all the relics of the past – written in cramped and hurried hand, in very abbreviated and technical Latin, often preserved (if that is the right word) in fairly noisome conditions, ill-sorted and mostly unlisted, unindexed and sometimes broken in pieces. Cause papers, where they exist, are likely to be found in total confusion and with no guide to their contents... Only young scholars, still enthusiastic, physically strong, and possessed of a sound digestion, are advised to tackle these materials. On the other hand, they offer a most promising field of research because they illumine the history of church and people in ways that no other source can. They take one to the realities. This is because of the wide range of cases that came before these courts, and because that range touched the human being so very near his personal centre.[1]

LITTLE HAS CHANGED in the nineteen years since Professor Elton wrote these words, and, their custody apart, all his strictures apply to the sixteenth-century ecclesiastical court records of the province of York. Yet, as he rightly maintains, these documents give an insight into the mores of a society not obtainable elsewhere. Unlike the southern province which lost the records of its chief prerogative court on the outbreak of the civil war, York has retained a long run of high commission act books, to all intents and purposes complete for the reign of Elizabeth.[2] This essay concentrates on

[1] G. R. Elton, *England 1200–1640* (London, 1969), pp. 104–5.
[2] In his two as yet unpublished theses, which I am grateful to have been allowed to read, 'The admininstrative character of the Ecclesiastical Commission for the Province of York, 1561–1586', (Oxford B.Litt 1960) and 'The Ecclesiastical Commission for the Province of York, 1561–1641', (Oxford D.Phil 1965), in an article, 'The Significance of the Ecclesiastical Commission at York', *Northern History*, 2 (1967), pp. 27–44 and in his introduction to his edition of R. G. Usher, *The Rise and Fall of the High Commission* (Oxford, 1968), Dr P. Tyler has pioneered the work on the northern high commission. Dr R. A. Marchant through his monograph *The Church Under the Law: Justice, Administration and Discipline in the Diocese of York, 1560–1640* (Cambridge, 1969), has made it possible to place the high commission in the context of the traditional northern ecclesiastical courts, while in his *Puritans and the Church Courts in the Diocese of York, 1560–1642* (London, 1960), he has made much use of the high commission records for evidence of northern protestantism. Similarly in *Post Reformation Catholicism in East*

merely one aspect of the work of the high commission, its attempt to impose a moral discipline on the northern gentry in the second half of the sixteenth century. Being drawn from a single source the evidence at best can only provide a partial impression of a very varied society and inevitably highlights gentry licentiousness: nonetheless, as the animadversions of contemporaries of the stature of Archbishop Sandys and Lady Margaret Hoby demonstrate, such an interpretation may not fall entirely wide of the mark.[3]

From time immemorial the ecclesiastical authorities in the north had been trying to gain obedience to the moral laws from the gentry as from all other sectors of the clergy and laity and on the accession of Elizabeth they could have recourse to a whole hierarchy of church courts before which offenders might be arraigned. Clerics and churchwardens were expected to present gentlepeople along with all other wrong doers at the archidiaconal and episcopal visitations. Except for a solitary court book of 1598 for the archdeaconry of York which contains two cases relating to gentry husbands and wives living apart, the archidiaconal records have disappeared, but those for the episcopal visitations have survived and these indicate that the old procedure was still functioning to some extent, albeit imperfectly. About fifty gentlepeople were cited at the episcopal visitations of the reign, a minority of whom eventually surfaced in the high commission court.[4] Cases too serious for summary punishment by episcopal officials, however, in the normal course of events went not to the high commission but to the archbishop's court of chancery. That court's act books have been examined for a sample decade between 1580 and 1590, and during this period five gentry cases have come to light, all concerned with fornication, adultery or clandestine marriages, in itself a very small number of gentry morals cases though not quite so insignificant when extrapolated for the reign as a whole.[5] At the very least they suggest that the growth of the court of high commission did not bring about a total decline in the use of the subordinate courts even when lawyers had to deal with some of the most influential members of local society. Although matters may have altered in the Laudian period, in the sixteenth century the high commission never established a monopoly over the supervision of gentry

Yorkshire, 1558–1790 (East Yorkshire Local History Society, 1960), *The Catholic Recusants of the West Riding of Yorkshire, 1558–1790* (Proceedings of the Leeds Philosophical and Literary Society, X, pt. VI, 1963), *Northern Catholics: the Catholic Recusants of the North Riding of Yorkshire, 1558–1790* (London, 1966), and in *Catholic Recusancy in the City of York, 1558–1790* (Catholic Record Society, 1970), Mr J. C. H. Aveling has searched the high commission act books exhaustively for information on northern catholicism. I am greatly indebted to the work of all of these three scholars.

[3] J. T. Cliffe, *The Yorkshire Gentry from the Reformation to the Civil War* (London, 1969), p. 246; D. M. Meads, ed., *Diary of Lady Margaret Hoby* (London, 1930), pp. 269–72.

[4] Borthwick [Institute of Historical Research, York] Y V/ CB 1 fos. 16, 60; the figure of gentry citations is based on V 1567–8 CB 1–2; V 1575 CB 1–2; V 1578 CB 1–3; V 1582 CB 1; V 1586 CB 1; V 1590 CB 1–3; V 1594 CB 1; V 1595 CB 1–3; V 1600 CB 1–2.

[5] Borthwick Chanc. AB 11, 1579–85 and Chanc. AB 12, 1585–95.

morals: an analysis of its records in consequence can give no more than an approximate account of the offences committed by the gentry in the north.

The Elizabethan act books of the northern high commission yield at the very minimum 120 cases relating to gentry morals, and this figure is certainly an underestimate. Because of the summary nature of the records and the pressure under which the scribes were working (they often seem to have been taking down proceedings verbatim), the social status of the defendants has on occasions been omitted and in some instances so few details of the case supplied that it has not proved possible to classify the offence. Nevertheless, despite the very real limitations of the evidence, it still seems clear that around a quarter of the gentry morals cases heard before the high commission concerned the validity of marriages, a further quarter or so marriage breakdowns and almost all the rest fornication or adultery, with only a tiny handful of cases referring to defamation or slander.[6]

In its treatment of morals cases the northern high commission seems to have been at its most conservative, modelling its procedure and record keeping upon the old ecclesiastical courts, particularly upon the court of chancery. The laws governing these types of offences had come through the period of reformation crisis virtually intact and this held true even for the laws on marriage. In spite of repeated attempts, Elizabethan churchmen failed to achieve a reform of the old canon law and as a result the lawyers went on trying to enforce medieval laws in no way tempered to the needs of sixteenth-century society, some of which seem to have borne particularly hard upon the gentry. In order to uphold their social position, for them marriage had to be substantially, if not primarily, a property transaction. The church's teaching that present consent at a betrothal constituted an unbreakable contract might consequently threaten the realisation of parental ambitions: the examination of such contracts which could bar an alternative marriage, or even invalidate a marriage already solemnised, occupied a considerable amount of the Elizabethan ecclesiastical lawyers' attention as it had done that of their medieval predecessors, and their verdicts, unsurprisingly, adhered closely to precedents set in the past.[7] When, for example, William Tattersall in 1583 made a promise to marry Mary, the under-age daughter of a York gentleman, Richard Bell, in the doorway of a house in Coney Street without her father's knowledge or consent, the high commissioners did not declare the contract invalid, as the father seemed to have hoped they would do. Instead, after sending the young man to prison for a few days for his disorderly behaviour, they bound him over not to associate with Mary for three years and then not to

---

[6] Borthwick HC AB 1–14, 1562–1603; because of the problems over identifying gentry cases in the act books precise percentages of the types of cases have not been attempted since these would have given an unwarranted impression of accuracy. In all quotations the spelling has been modernised.

[7] R. H. Helmholz, *Marriage Litigation in Medieval England* (Cambridge, 1974), pp. 25–7.

proceed with the marriage until he had accumulated goods clear of all debt (and up to a maximum of 200 marks) equal to what her father might bestow upon his daughter.[8]

Other gentlemen shared Bell's frustration when a youthful exchange of vows stood in the way of their family's advancement. In 1571 the banns had actually been read for the marriage of Alexander Palmes, gentleman, of Otley, and Margaret Pulleyn when Nicholas Morden, alleging a pre-contract, with her relatives' connivance came to Otley to carry Margaret away. She for her part confirmed that she had plighted her troth to Morden and claimed to have been detained by force by the Palmes.[9] In this case the commissioners' decision has not come down, though they usually insisted on the fulfilment of a prior contract as in 1580 when they directed Leonard Reresby, gentleman, to marry before the next sitting of the president of the council in the north Mistress Bevet, a widow, to whom he had promised marriage four years previously.[10] Furthermore they habitually prohibited the performance of a marriage while investigations into pre-contract were in train, though not always with success as in 1598 when Richard Skrimsher, a Staffordshire gentleman, found himself before the court for marrying Mary Willinson of Kirby Wiske when proceedings in a cause of matrimony brought by Susan More of York were still pending.[11]

While lay people showed much reluctance to accept the church's teaching that a verbal promise on its own established an unbreakable contract, laity and clergy alike believed that once sexual relations had taken place between the parties then neither the man nor the woman could marry another in their partner's lifetime. The commissioners seem to have thought that this principle applied even in a case of child molestation in which Philip Pulleyn had raped Jane, the daughter of Leonard Foster, gentleman. In 1587 the court prohibited Foster from arranging a marriage for Jane with any other man than Pulleyn so long as the hearing lasted, while at the same time ordering Pulleyn to do penance in St Michael le Belfrey and on the Pavement on York on market day with a paper on his head to inform bystanders that his punishment had been imposed 'for polluting a girl of eleven years of age'.[12]

The chief issue of contention between the gentry and the ecclesiastical judges when it came to pronouncing upon the validity of betrothals and clandestine marriages was that of social disparagement. This emerged very clearly in 1562 when, alleging pre-contract, William Dabridgecourt challenged the marriage of Lady Alice Sutton to Sir Nicholas Fairfax. In the ensuing claims and counterclaims the defence brought forward the information that Lady Alice enjoyed an income in moveable goods of £200 a year whereas Dabridgecourt, being neither a knight, an esquire, nor a knight's son,

[8] Borthwick HC AB 10, fos. 182–3.
[9] Borthwick HC AB 6, fos. 126–43; HC CP 1571/2.　　　[10] Borthwick HC AB 10, fo. 64.
[11] Borthwick HC AB 13, fos. 191, 197.　　　[12] Borthwick HC AB 11, fos. 104, 106, 109.

possessed an annual income of under 10 marks in land and less than 40 marks in goods, an impediment which ought to have had no bearing on the ultimate decision.[13] This particular case does not seem to have reached the high commission, but in 1572 a rather similar one affecting a gentleman's social aspirations did command a hearing. Then the commissioners went so far as to imprison John Lascye in York castle for forcibly preventing his thirty-four year old daughter from co-habiting with Francis Ashbourne, the son of Christopher Ashbourne, vicar of Halifax. The fact that a lawful marriage had been solemnised and that Elizabeth and Francis were 'man and wife before God' did not stop Lascye from arguing that 'he thinketh that by the queen's majesty's injunctions the [said] Francis being within orders, cannot marry his said daughter against his will, being her father'. Obviously Lascye could not stomach his daughter marrying a minister, even though this particular cleric by 1570 had graduated a Master of Arts from Cambridge. The commissioners referred the case to the archbishop's court of audience for a final judgment: perhaps Francis Ashbourne's succession in 1573 to the vicarage of Halifax, one of the wealthiest livings in the whole of the north of England, may have gone far to persuade his unwilling father-in-law to accept the status quo.[14] Other contentious marriages they certainly confirmed. In 1577, despite the opposition of Richard Aldebroughe, gentleman, the bridegroom's father, they pronounced in favour of the marriage of William Aldebroughe and Anne, daughter of Arthur Kay, deceased.[15] Richard Rishworth of Bolling Hall, Bradford similarly failed to overturn his daughter's irregular marriage in 1581 after Frances Rishworth had pledged herself to Thomas Wentworth, esquire, before witnesses in a private house in Normanton without banns, dispensation or consent of parents. The commissioners showed no hesitation in recognising the marriage before going on to consign the irate father for five days to the Kidcote until the archbishop intervened to authorise his release.[16] As with the disputed marriage of Ralph Conyers and Katherine Brakenbury in 1564 and that of Richard and Mary Burton of Methley in 1590 the court was clearly continuing the medieval practice of maintaining marriages however irregular the circumstances of the contract or ensuing ceremony.[17]

The northern gentry, however, discovered to their cost that the high commissioners, again following medieval precedents, always felt far more inclined to uphold a marriage than permit a separation, even though the marriage might seem insupportable to the parties concerned. Many more cases involving marital disputes came before the court than for pre-contract or clandestine marriage and it may well be that the convention of arranged marriages among the gentry led to an abnormal degree of marriage break-

---

[13] Borthwick CP G 1059; CP G 3511.
[14] Borthwick HC AB 7, fos. 50, 66–7, 75, 77, 79; J. and J. A. Venn, *Alumni Cantabrigienses*, Pt I, vol. 1 (Cambridge, 1922), p. 43. [15] Borthwick HC AB 9, fo. 99.
[16] Borthwick HC AB 10, fo. 126. [17] Borthwick HC AB 1, fo. 164; AB 11, fo. 304.

downs, though, of course, such breakdowns would have been far more visible among the upper reaches of society than among the populace at large where a husband could much more easily simply abandon his wife and disappear without trace. The commissioners, despite the odds, could look to some fairly positive achievements as marriage guidance counsellors. Their immediate reaction, when learning that a couple had separated illegally, was to attempt to resolve the quarrel. To this intent in October 1571 they ordered Richard Danyell, esquire, of Daresbury in Cheshire to cohabit with his wife Ellen, and Sir Thomas Venables to set aside his concubine and return to his wife, and at least in the latter case had the satisfaction of receiving a certificate that Sir Thomas and Lady Maud had come back together.[18] Again, in 1578 Gilbert Moreton and Marmaduke Ealand who had both separated from their wives without permission produced evidence of renewed cohabitation and had their cases dismissed.[19] The commissioners had considerably less success in 1582 with Ralph Lawson, a gentleman of county Durham who in the first instance, as an inhabitant of the palatinate, refused even to acknowledge the jurisdiction of the court. This hurdle surmounted, the archbishop himself tried to effect a reconciliation between Lawson and his wife, Jane, who had absented herself from his company, but the composition, if it occurred, did not last and in 1583 the court allowed Jane a judicial separation together with alimony from her husband's estate.[20]

The case of Sir Oswald and Lady Anne Wilstrop illustrates the lengths to which the commissioners would go to reinstate a marriage. In 1573 they instructed Lady Wilstrop to go back to her husband thirty-two years after she had been allowed a legal separation by the privy council. Understandably, Lady Wilstrop objected, maintaining that so many years had elapsed since they parted that she and her husband had become 'as it were strangers' and, no less cogently, that as she and Sir Oswald had both passed their seventieth year there remained little danger of unclean life or sin to either of them from living apart. Unmoved by these arguments, the commissioners sent Lady Anne to York castle for a time for her continuing disobedience, subsequently relaxing her confinement to house imprisonment in Micklegate.[21] Their efforts to bring together Sir Roland and Lady Ursula Stanley met with an equally resounding rebuff. As early as 1561 Lady Ursula had brought a suit against her husband in the chancery court alleging that Sir Roland, having tired of his middle-aged wife, had trumped up a charge of adultery in order to put her aside, and so ill-treated her physically that she went in fear of her life. Exactly ten years later both parties appeared before the high commission on a charge of living apart. As Lawson had done, Sir Roland at first, as a denizen of the

[18] Borthwick HC AB 6, fo. 75; HC AB 9, fos. 106, 108, 148.
[19] Borthwick HC AB 9, fos. 164, 180, 200, 207.
[20] Borthwick HC AB 10, fos. 151, 171–2, 175, 177, 219.
[21] Borthwick HC AB 5, fo. 253; HC AB 6, fos. 122, 124; HC AB 7, fos. 72, 90–1, 98–9.

palatinate of Chester, attempted to deny the court's authority and like him suffered a few days' imprisonment in York castle until he changed his mind, but despite the co-operation of the bishop of Chester the marriage itself seems to have been past saving.[22]

In some other cases the commissioners seem to have been more ready to admit defeat earlier in the process and to allow the parties to live apart until such time as God should move their minds to come together once more, in the meanwhile ensuring that the estranged husband made an adequate financial provision for his wife. They granted Anne Calverley, for example, permission in 1575 to set up her own household at Eccleshall in Staffordshire with alimony of £5 a year and a moiety of a lease from her husband's estate.[23] Three years later they allowed John Ratcliffe of Guisborough to live away from his wife on the understanding that she should receive £10 annual maintenance and John Nettleton to do the same provided that he contributed 20 marks each year to his wife Jane.[24]

Cruelty was the usual reason for a wife's seeking a separation from her husband, often associated with his adultery and open flaunting of his mistress, as happened with Sir Roland and Lady Stanley. Gentlewomen, however, by no means invariably figured as the innocent parties in these cases. In 1579 Thomas Yowart brought a suit for divorce from his wife Anne, almost certainly on the grounds of her misconduct.[25] Another gentleman, John Skyers, refused to take back his wife Mary in 1597 because, as he said, there were others she liked better than him. The high commissioners bound over one of Skyers's rivals in his wife's affections, Richard Ellis, not to associate with Mary in the future, though they still countenanced the parties living apart and decreed that Mary should be paid £12 (later increased to £16) by her husband.[26]

In none of these separations, of course, could the husband or wife obtain freedom to re-marry in their partner's lifetime. In the sixteenth century the court of high commission never once annulled a gentry marriage on the grounds of impotence though it did grant a divorce because a marriage had taken place within the prohibited degrees, ironically when the parties desperately wanted to stay together. In 1562 the commissioners pronounced the marriage of Thomas Standish of Heapey, Lancashire, incestuous, having discovered that Standish had married his deceased wife's sister, Margaret: Standish was fined for the offence and made to enter into a bond to abstain from Margaret's company. Undeterred, he reappeared in the high commission ten years later accused of continuing to live with his pretended wife.[27]

[22] Borthwick CP G 975a; HC AB 6, fos. 79, 108, 204, 205.
[23] Borthwick HC AB 8, fo. 146.
[24] Borthwick HC AB 9, fo. 146; HC AB 9, fo. 154.   [25] Borthwick HC AB 9, fo. 234.
[26] Borthwick HC AB 13, fos. 107, 125, 140, 155; HC AB 14, fo. 214.
[27] Borthwick HC AB 1, fos. 34–5; HC AB 6, fo. 160; HC AB 7, fo. 121.

Normally it seems that the church's canons prevented the solemnisation of marriages within the prohibited degrees, though they did not dispel the desire for such marriages. Thomas Paslewe, for instance, in 1579 was forced by the high commission to do penance for co-habiting with his deceased brother's wife.[28] The commissioners in 1590 punished William Stable of Chapeltown, Leeds, 'according to the ecclesiastical laws of the realm' for having had carnal knowledge of Elizabeth Rawden, his late wife's brother's daughter, and getting her with child, while in 1596 they fined George Ellis, gentleman, £20 and ordered him to do penance for having lived incestuously with Frances Greaves, his late wife's sister.[29]

Whenever possible the commissioners opposed the granting of legal separations because of the opportunities such separations gave to the parties to establish illicit alternative unions. Even as matters stood by far the largest number of gentry morals cases to come before the high commission related to fornication or adultery. Despite the fact that uncomplicated cases of this nature could either have been dealt with summarily at the hearings which resulted from the archidiaconal and episcopal visitations or more formally in the archbishop's court of chancery, many nevertheless appeared in the high commission court. Gentlemen, no less than other heads of households lower in the social scale, frequently formed liaisons with household servants and many had to answer to the high commission on this account. In the summer of 1575 Thomas Bulmer had been presented at the episcopal visitation for having had a child in his wife's lifetime by his housekeeper, Anne Mason: in October of the same year he was called before the high commission and sent briefly to the Kidcote until he entered into a bond to perform public penance for his offence.[30] In 1575, also, the commissioners gaoled Francis Neville, esquire, of Barnby Dun, 'being married to the Lady Brandon yet living', for adultery with his servant Isabel Langstaffe and dispatched Isabel to a different prison, but neither incarceration nor bonds produced the desired effect for in 1577 Neville was found still to be alienated from his wife and to be co-habiting with Isabel.[31] William Dawtry, gentleman, of Full Sutton received rather more lenient treatment from the commissioners who, since he had expressed penitence for his adultery with his housekeeper, Maud Sutton, and for getting her with child, permitted him to commute his public penance to a fine of 20 nobles.[32]

Perhaps the rationale behind bringing routine cases of this kind before so august a court as the high commission lies in the long duration of some of the offences. Lawrence Tetloe, for example, in 1571 was charged with having kept a whore for twenty years, with maintaining like gentlemen the divers

[28] Borthwick HC AB 9, fos. 208, 222.
[29] Borthwick HC AB 11, fos. 236, 237; HC AB 13, fos. 12, 14, 15.
[30] Borthwick V 1575 CB 1, fo. 86; HC AB 8, fos. 133, 149, 164.
[31] Borthwick HC AB 8, fos. 98, 115, 121; HC AB 9, fos. 95, 148.
[32] Borthwick HC AB 11, fos. 170, 176; HC CP 1588/9.

children he had had by her and with disinheriting his legitimate children.[33] By 1589 John Fryston's adultery had been going on for six years. The ecclesiastical authorities had previously commanded him to part from Margery Sheppard of Normanton, but he had refused and as a consequence of his disobedience spent three months in York castle in addition to having to pay a £200 fine, reduced on appeal to £40: for her offence Margery had to face six months in the Kidcote.[34] Unions such as these were clearly more than passing affairs, as the long-running case of Roger Beckwith demonstrates particularly well. Beckwith of Thorpe by Selby, accused of incontinence with his servant Alice Petty in 1578, wilfully disregarded the high commissioners' injunction not to associate with her further and continued to keep her in his house. When he then failed to find compurgators to clear his name, the commissioners with some justification sent him to the castle. During his imprisonment he began divorce proceedings against his wife, Elizabeth Beckwith alias Chomley, from whom he had separated and who, it emerged from another case, had had one or more children in adultery since leaving her husband. Beckwith must have known that he would have been free to marry again only if the commissioners deemed his first marriage to have been invalid. Nevertheless with everything against him and before the case had reached a conclusion he gambled on its outcome and in a clandestine ceremony married Alice on St Mary's day 1580. Incensed by this defiance, the commissioners ordered him to do double penance in the churches of Selby, Cawood and Brayton, relenting a little subsequently and allowing him to substitute for penance at Cawood and Brayton a £50 fine to be spent partly on the local poor and partly on providing copies of Foxe's *Acts and Monuments* in each of the three parishes. Alice they similarly subjected to both imprisonment and penance while William Scorer, the cleric who had had the temerity to perform the marriage, was also forced to undergo the humiliation of a public confession.[35] The case demonstrates very aptly one gentleman's frustration at his powerlessness to overthrow a first marriage in order to enter upon a second.

Northern gentlemen were not battling alone in the second half of the sixteenth century against the constraints of life-long marriage; very interestingly some gentlewomen were also openly challenging the church's decrees. In 1575 William Webster, gentleman, initiated a case against his wife, Anne, because of her adultery with a certain John Dickinson. The court had gone so far as convicting and punishing John but not of sentencing Anne when the suit came to an abrupt end on Webster's death. Casting caution to the winds, Anne thereupon at once married Dickinson at four in the morning with no banns called. The commissioners replied by sending her a close prisoner to the lower

---

[33] Borthwick HC AB 6, fo. 81.
[34] Borthwick HC AB 11, fos. 224–5; HC AB 12, fo. 10; HC CP 1588/9.
[35] Borthwick HC AB 9, fos. 161, 190, 201, 219, 278; HC AB 10, fos. 101, 107, 112, 122, 123, 124, 127–8, 129, 130.

Kidcote as a convicted adulteress.[36] Elizabeth Rasing, widow, a gentlewoman on New Malton, similarly spent a period in the castle in 1578 on suspicion of adultery with John Mason.[37] All too material evidence in the form of an illegitimate child prevented another gentry widow in 1597 from even contesting her adultery. Elizabeth, the late wife of Thomas Leigh, had begun her association with Edward Middleton of Middleton Hall, so she claimed, to gain his advice over her son's inheritance; they became lovers and Middleton got her with child. For so blatantly abusing his trust the high commission sentenced Middleton to public penance in Kirkby Lonsdale and to a £100 fine.[38]

Judith Barwicke, the wife of Thomas Barwicke of Arthington Nunnery near Leeds, while still in the married state showed a comparable lack of respect for social convention. For a time she seems to have lived harmoniously with her husband and they had a child before they all moved at Easter 1574 to the house of Thomas Cranmer, the son of the archbishop, at Kirkstall Abbey. Barwicke then went off to London on business, unwisely leaving Judith with Cranmer, and when he returned she refused either to cohabit with him or to go back to their house at Arthington. Suspecting her to be pregnant by Cranmer, Archbishop Sandys had Judith sequestered to the house of John Dean where she still contrived to meet her lover. That supervision proving totally ineffective, Judith moved to Thomas Haldesworth's house in Halifax and from there Cranmer carried her back to Kirkstall where they continued their affair until the high commission intervened yet again to break up the illicit menage.[39] In 1588 in a rather similar case the commissioners called to account Alice Lister, wife of George Lister, gentleman, on a charge of adultery with Leonard Simondson who had abandoned his own wife for her sake.[40] Three years later they ordered Anne Samson, the wife of John Samson, gentleman, to abstain from the company of Mr Anthony Morton.[41] In 1597 they required both mistress Mary Gower, widow, of Stittenham and John Milburne, gentleman, of Henderskelfe to enter into separate bonds not to associate with each other in future, imposing upon Milburne in addition a £20 fine.[42]

By 1600 Milburne cannot have had much reputation to lose, for much earlier in his career he had been involved in a different affair which resulted in the most savage penalty ever inflicted by the court upon a lady in a morals case in the whole course of the reign. In 1570 he enticed Pascall Atkinson away from her possibly much older husband, Thomas Atkinson, M.A., rector of Bulmer and prebendary of Stillington. Atkinson began proceedings in the

[36] Borthwick HC AB 8, fo. 161.
[37] Borthwick HC AB 9, fo. 127.   [38] Borthwick HC AB 13, fo. 133; HC CP 1597/8.
[39] Borthwick HC CP 1575/1; HC AB 8, fo. 175; HC AB 9, fos. 29, 43; J. Ridley, *Thomas Cranmer* (Oxford, 1962), pp. 152–3.
[40] Borthwick HC AB 11, fo. 159; HC AB 12, fo. 16.
[41] Borthwick HC AB 12, fos. 22, 39, 57, 63.   [42] Borthwick HC AB 13, fos. 77, 78, 92, 235.

high commission in consideration of her conduct, and the commissioners not only allowed him a divorce but also sentenced Pascall to imprisonment in the Kidcote, to public carting around York and finally to banishment from the city. The wronged husband must subsequently have relented a little towards his wife for when he came to die the following year he left her some small bequests in his will.[43]

Married northern gentlewomen were in no way unique in their failure to conduct themselves chastely: their unmarried sisters, too, did not escape ecclesiastical censure on the same issue. In addition to the occasional, usually anonymous gentlewoman with child reported as being harboured in remote parts of the region at episcopal visitations, some single gentlewomen also appeared for examination before the high commission.[44] In 1581 Katherine Savill, daughter of Thomas Savill, gentleman, of Welburn in the North Riding was presented for already having had one child in fornication with Christopher Warren, and of then being with child by another.[45] Twenty years later the commissioners dispatched Elizabeth Pudsey, who had recently given birth to an illegitimate child at Penistone of which Thomas Weldon, gentleman, was the father, to her uncle, Mr George Pudsey, in Warwickshire, imprisoning Weldon for a time in York castle for perjury for denying the offence.[46] Clearly both before and after marriage these gentlewomen felt able to behave with surprising freedom.

The degree to which this licence might extend is illustrated by a quite extraordinary case of wife-leasing which caused considerable consternation in the high commission. In the spring of 1598 Charles Barnby, having conceived 'a good affection and liking to ... Frances Nelson' offered her husband William Nelson of Drax in the West Riding an annuity of £20 to 'have the use of the body of the said Frances'. Nelson responded favourably and the parties signed and sealed a formal legal agreement. On her side Frances scarcely fitted the role of a hapless dupe of male manipulation. As disillusioned with her husband as he with her, she had already been named by the Drax churchwardens for adultery with William Babthorpe, gentleman, for which, having failed purgation, Babthorpe had eventually done penance in his parish church. By 1598 she seems to have been more than ready to pass on her favours elsewhere. A difficulty, nonetheless, arose when the time came for Nelson to fulfil his side of the bargain because of Barnby's imprisonment for recusancy in York castle. Nothing daunted, Nelson approached the gaoler's wife, Mistress Readhead, promising her six yards of serge and an elne of lawn if she would introduce Frances into the castle. Mistress Readhead complied,

Borthwick HC AB 5, fos. 148, 149, 189; HC AB 9, fo. 39; York Minster Library D & C Prob. Reg. 5, fos. 65–6.
[44] Borthwick V 1578 CB 3, fo. 22; V 1590 CB 3, fo. 86; V 1595–6 CB 1, fo. 138, CB 3, fo. 170; V 1600 CB 1, fo. 112.
[45] Borthwick HC AB 10, fos. 145, 147.   [46] Borthwick HC AB 14, fos. 146, 173, 174.

sent her horse to fetch Frances from the country, and, on the pretext of inviting her to a wedding feast, brought her into the prison. Once there Frances lost no time in seeking out Barnby's chamber where, as Nelson had planned, Mrs Readhead discovered them in bed, and, to make the offence doubly sure, locked them together in the same room overnight. Only at this juncture did the scheme begin to go awry when Barnby laid before Mrs Readhead an even more tempting bribe of a tuft taffeta gown and a figured kirtle if she would give an undertaking 'to conceal the said fault'. The matter indeed might never have been discovered had a local mercer not refused the gaoler's wife her goods on account of Barnby's poor credit, so bringing her in anger to reveal all to the high commission ten or twelve days after the offence had happened. Understandably affronted by a drama which had been enacted under their very noses, the commissioners ordered Frances to perform a public penance for her adultery in the York church of All Saints, Pavement on the Sunday preceding St Andrew's day before Mr Harwood, the city lecturer, delivered his sermon, forced her co-offender, Barnby, to make confession of his guilt on a scaffold in the castle yard at a time of maximum publicity when the assizes were being held, and decreed that Mary Readhead should subsequently stand in the same place with a paper proclaiming her 'a bawd' fixed about her head. The chief protagonist, William Nelson they pronounced 'guilty of the crime of lenociny or bawdry in the highest degree, and decreed him to be punished for his said offence in such manner and form and at such time and place as should afterward be declared and described in a schedule made for the same purpose'.[47]

The readiness of certain members of the northern gentry to defy the church's laws in this way and tolerate highly irregular behaviour apparently on occasions extended even to incest. In practice the high commission did distinguish irregular sexual unions between relatives by marriage from those between blood relations, castigating the latter as a 'detestable, odious, grievous and damnable' offence.[48] Two possible cases of incest among the northern gentry emerged at episcopal visitations: in 1567 the bishop's officers heard charges against Robert Yoward of Minthorpe, gentleman, for having had a child by one of his daughters when estranged from his wife, while much later, in 1600, Anthony Morton, gentleman, of Haworth was presented for having got his daughter, Elizabeth, with child four or five years previously and then for subsequently marrying her to Robert Thornhill of Misterton, a charge which he ultimately had to answer before the high commission.[49]

The most notorious case of suspected incest within the northern gentry,

[47] Borthwick HC AB 13, fos. 212, 214, 226, 236, 237, 239–40, 248, 252, 276, 277; J. C. H. Aveling, *Catholic Recusancy in the City of York*, pp. 64–5.

[48] Borthwick HC AB 12, fo. 226.

[49] Borthwick V 1567–8 CB 1, fos. 126–7; CB 2, fos. 17, 58; V 1600 CB 2, fo. 26; HC AB 14, fo. 76.

however, occurred not between different generations but between siblings. In 1572, having previously been convented before the bishop of Chester to no avail, Anthony Huddleston of Millom Castle in Cumberland appeared before the high commissioners in York on the charge of living incestuously with his sister Anne, wife of Ralph Latus. Despite repeated admonitions, Huddleston persistently refused to evict his sister from Millom Castle where she had set up her household with him apart from her husband or to cohabit with his own wife. The high commission in consequence prohibited him from returning to Cumberland and confined him to his estates in Yorkshire and County Durham for several years until the privy council intervened to secure his greater liberty.[50]

The privy council evidently regarded the Huddleston case with less disapprobation than the high commission and the possibility arises that some of these accusations of incest and other charges of immorality may have been maliciously inspired. Given the readiness of both men and women from lower levels of northern society to have recourse to church courts for redress for defamation and sexual slander in the early modern period, it is rather surprising that no more explicit cases of this kind concerning the gentry surface in the high commission records.[51] In fact in only one instance in Elizabeth's reign did a member of the gentry come before the court to seek redress. John Oburn, in 1590, in an attempt to sabotage marriage negotiations between a widow, Mistress Jane Washington and Henry Brabyn's son, set on foot rumours that he had had carnal knowledge of Jane himself, which his brother, the vicar of Walton in Cheshire, passed on in a letter. Jane appealed to the high commission to clear her name with the result that they not only imprisoned Oburn for a time in the castle but also imposed upon him the very substantial fine of £200.[52]

The two other cases of vexatious slander heard by the high commission in which the northern gentry appeared concerned the reputation not of the laity but the clergy. In 1590 Robert Blackwood, parson of Kirton in Nottinghamshire, accused John Huddlestone, his gentleman parishioner, of defamation by calling him a 'whoreson, drunken slave' and his wife a 'Scottish quean', saying he would make Blackwood 'beg his meat with a pair of bones, and his wife her bread in a wallet', adding later that 'his preaching is naught, for that his life made it worth nothing. And that the roaring of an ox in the top of an ash tree is better than all the preaching that he can preach'.[53]

The Tankard family, perhaps like Huddlestone motivated by a disagreement over tithe, mounted an altogether more sinister attack upon their

[50] Borthwick HC AB 6, fos. 147, 161–2, 184; HC AB 7, fos. 92–3, 169, 183–4; HC CP 1572/2; J. R. Dasent, ed., *Acts of the Privy Council*, VII, (London, 1894), pp. 114, 146.
[51] J. A. Sharpe, *Defamation and Sexual Slander in Early Modern England: the Church Courts at York* (Borthwick Paper 58, York, 1980).   [52] Borthwick HC AB 11, fos. 303, 306, 319.
[53] Borthwick HC AB 1590/13; HC AB 11, fos. 239, 243.

incumbent when in 1584 they got the churchwardens of Hornby to present the rector, Anthony Watson, on a charge of fathering the child to which William Tankard's wife had recently given birth. On the refusal of the archdeacon of Cleveland to entertain the accusation the churchwardens appealed to the high commission, and Elizabeth Tankard made a dramatic appearance in court with the baby in her arms which she swore was the rector's child. Suspecting her honesty the commissioners sent her to the castle and eventually extracted a scarcely credible account of the family's nefarious activities. Her husband and father-in-law, so Elizabeth alleged, had forced her under extreme duress, to attribute the paternity of the child to the rector, knowing all along the assertion to be untrue. By recording her confession in the chancery act book the commissioners retrospectively did their best to vindicate Watson's good name. The Tankards were far from being the only consummate liars among the gentry: clearly the danger to their souls of even accidental perjury which so much exercised the consciences of presbyterian ministers carried little weight with certain unregenerate members of northern society.[54]

Throughout Elizabeth's reign, however, the chief function of the high commission remained the enforcement of religious uniformity, not the oversight of lay morality which occupied only a relatively small part of the court's attention. While aggrieved laymen did not scruple to revile the 'archbishop and his associates' in the commission as 'devilish tyrants', in reality they seem to have treated errant gentlepeople comparatively leniently.[55] In marked contrast to the Laudian period when the commission imposed a punitive fine of £1000 for incest committed by Edward Paler, esquire, of Thoraldby and his niece, in the sixteenth century the highest recorded fine exacted from a gentleman in a morals case was £100.[56] Probably the court's power to imprison, which it seems to have used with increasing frequency during the period, constituted a considerably greater deterrent for most gentlemen than moderate fines. Nevertheless, too much should not be claimed for the court's control over the gentry: it certainly did not exert the sort of godly discipline many zealous ministers were demanding. For their part, in their capacity as property owners, northern gentlemen needed the system of church courts just as much as did the clergy. While only somewhat over a hundred cases concerning gentry morals came before the high commission over the entire course of the reign, gentlemen themselves in one year alone initiated between forty and fifty-five actions in the consistory court, probably chiefly to uphold their rights to church presentations and tithe.[57] For

[54] Borthwick HC AB 10, fos. 270, 291; HC AB 11, fo. 24: Chanc. AB 11, fo. 306; A. Peel and L. H. Carlson, eds., *Cartwrightiana* (London, 1951), pp. 28–30.

[55] Borthwick HC AB 7, fo. 75.

[56] J. Raine, ed., *The Fabric Rolls of York Minster* (Surtees Society, xxxv, 1859), p. 319.

[57] This figure has been calculated for the sample year 1580–1, Borthwick Con. AB 38, fos. 1–223; D. M. Gransby, 'Tithe Disputes in the Diocese of York. 1540–1639' (York M. Phil 1968).

protestant gentlemen, at least, the surveillance of the high commission may have seemed a small price to pay for the assistance they received from the lower ecclesiastical courts. In addition, as in the past, traditional penalties could still be circumvented and money could buy exemption from public shame. In 1590, for example, the vicar of Weaverham in Cheshire, Edward Shawcross, had to answer an accusation of taking 'bribes or sums of money for certifying false penances'.[58] A year earlier in a synodical sermon delivered before the clergy of the Nottingham archdeaconry the rector of Cromwell had caused great offence by addressing the Southwell prebendaries as 'Masters of Sodom' and by 'charging them publicly forth of the pulpit . . . with commutation of penance and taking money for the same which they put in their own purses.'[59] The northern high commission in the latter half of the sixteenth century may well have tightened its grip a little over gentry morals, and certainly called some gentlemen and women to account for their sinful behaviour, but many from lower reaches of society must in their hearts have agreed with the complaint of the Hull lecturer, Griffith Briskin, that 'there is defect in magistrates in punishing poor men, and in bearing with rich offenders'.[60]

[58] Borthwick V 1590 CB 2, fos. 78–9.   [59] Borthwick HC AB 11, fo. 172.
[60] Borthwick HC AB 10, fo. 100.

The crown, the gentry and London:
the enforcement of proclamation, 1596–1640

FELICITY HEAL

ON 20 JUNE 1632 Charles I issued a proclamation 'commanding the Gentry to keepe their Residence at their Mansions in the Countrey, and forbidding them to make their habitations in London, and places adjoyning'. The document gave voice to several concerns about the growth of London: the city was becoming difficult to govern, was increasingly vulnerable to dearth and disease and was intolerably burdened by the cost of maintaining the poor, including those who followed the rich into town. But the influx of gentry also denuded the localities, depriving them of their natural rulers, those who had customarily 'served the King in severall places according to their Degrees and Rankes'. In consequence the poor were left unrelieved by hospitality, uncontrolled by good discipline and without adequate employment. Finally, the removal of the gentry to town was alleged to have adverse economic consequences, encouraging the consumption of luxury imports 'from Forraigne parts, to the enriching of other Nations, and unnecessary consumption of a great part of the Treasure of this Realm'. The remedy for these ills was the return of the gentry to their native seats, and the Caroline government did not hesitate to order all those not holding office in the council or royal household back into the country. An exception was made for periods of the law-terms, for the transaction of essential business 'so as they doe not by pretence thereof remove their families, but leave the same to continue in the Countrey, and keep their houses and Hospitality. . .'. Command was supported by the threat of action against delinquents: any found in default of the proclamation, according to returns made by the ward constables and churchwardens of London and Middlesex, faced the possibility of prosecution in star chamber.[1]

The 1632 proclamation is the culmination of a series of orders by which successive governments sought to counteract the attractive force which the capital possessed for the ruling classes. Between 1596 and 1640 seventeen

[1] *Stuart Royal Proclamations: vol. II, The Royal Proclamations of Charles I, 1625–1640*, ed. J. F. Larkin (Oxford, 1983), pp. 350–3.

proclamations were addressed wholly or in part to the problem, and these were supported by an impressive array of conciliar letters, charges to the assize judges in star chamber and royal speeches.[2] Both in time and in structure these activities obviously relate to those other regulations which Professor Barnes has aptly described as 'the ambitious program of late Tudor and early Stuart "strict and strait governance"', such as the restriction on building within London, or the control of enclosure.[3] A 'commonweal' rhetoric informs the pronouncements of governments on all these issues, affording them a coherent ideology even when the immediate catalysts for action were obvious economic crisis or the needs of defence. Also coherent is the choice of agency to enforce the royal will: the regular use of the flexible weapon of proclamation in preference to parliamentary action.[4] Allied to this is a confidence in the capacity of government to achieve difficult feats of social engineering by the exercise of fiat and without much consultation of those most directly affected, the members of the political nation. It may be valuable to follow Professor Barnes in describing these aspirations as absolutist, though with the caveat that no developed theory of absolutism is likely to have informed the actions of these regimes.[5] The language of authority could also serve to conceal the various specific intentions moving the crown to action: intentions which it is the purpose of this essay to uncover and analyse.

Even the rhetorical structure of the edicts removing the gentry from London offers insight into the varying intentions of government. The diplomatic form of the proclamations has a long pre-history in the Tudor orders requiring the gentry to return to their shires in time of military emergency or internal disturbance. Such orders are usually terse and direct: in 1545 for example M.P.s and others congregated in London for parliament were instructed to leave for their counties 'as well for the putting themselves in order for their defence and annoyance of our enemies . . . as for service to be done to his majesty, touching his subsidy and other affairs'.[6] In many respects the proclamation of November 1596 reiterates these earlier orders, emphasising the obligation of the gentry to reside in their counties and to provide for their defence.[7] But the 1596 document is a composite order, designed in

---

[2] *Tudor Royal Proclamations*, ed. J. F. Larkin and P. L. Hughes (3 vols., New Haven, Conn., 1969), III, pp. 169–72; *Stuart Royal Proclamations: vol. I, James I, 1603–1625*, ed. J. F. Larkin and P. L. Hughes (Oxford, 1973), pp. 21–2, 44–5, 186–8, 323–4, 356–8, 369–70, 561–5, 572–4, 608–9; *Stuart Royal Proclamations*, II, pp. 112–13, 170–2, 292–6, 350–3, 516–19, 708–10.

[3] T. G. Barnes, 'The prerogative and environmental control of London building in the early seventeenth century: the lost opportunity', *Californian Law Review*, 58 (1970), pp. 1340–1.

[4] Ibid, pp. 1343–7. There is no evidence that the issue of the gentry and London was raised in parliament in this period. However, in 1597 related issues of dearth and hospitality were introduced into the Commons in a bill that may have been part of Robert Cecil's legislative programme. HMC *Hatfield MSS*, VII, p. 497; S. D'Ewes, *Journals of All the parliaments during the Reign of Queen Elizabeth* (1682), p. 591.

[5] Barnes, 'The prerogative and environmental control of London building', p. 1342.

[6] *Tudor Royal Proclamations*, I, p. 362.

[7] Ibid, III, pp. 169–72. For other early orders see I, pp. 228, 478.

response to the combined dangers of invasion and dearth, and this conjunction of threatening circumstances stimulated Elizabeth's government to produce a more thorough critique of gentry behaviour than that found in the earlier records. In particular the crown argued that there was a change in behaviour patterns which threatened to undermine the traditional modes of preserving order. The gentry were alleged to be leaving the countryside so that they might 'with covetous minds live in London and about the city privately. . .'. Tone as well as substance obviously derives from a moral vocabulary common in Tudor reflections on society, but there is novelty in its application to the problem of the growth of the capital.

After 1596 the Elizabethan government employed this proclamation, but did not choose either to reinforce it with parliamentary action or to introduce further refinements to its initial order. James, in contrast, was profligate with his use of this weapon, issuing no less than ten proclamations directed against London residence. The majority were concentrated into two periods between 1614 and 1617, and between 1622 and 1624.[8] In his early formulations James appears dependent on Elizabethan precedent, even repeating the 1596 order verbatim in 1608. The only obvious distinction from the earlier document is that the needs of defence were no longer given as a major reason for the gentry to return to their counties. From 1614 onwards, however, new themes and an elaborated rhetoric begin to inform the proclamations. For the first time wives and families are mentioned as particularly likely to be resident in town, and the Christmas season is singled out as the most important time for gentry to be active in their own localities. The 1615 order goes further, and is so distinctively phrased that, even without Bacon's note to this effect on the warrant, we might wish to identify it as a piece of royal polemic.[9] The problem of hospitality has now become the alleged focus of governmental anxiety, the proclamation lamenting that the natural rulers of England 'doe rather fall to a more private and delicate course of life, after the manner of foreine Countreys'. In consequence of such change, it continued, the realm no longer experienced 'that mutuall comfort betweene the Nobles and Gentlemen, and the inferiour sort of Commons' which had been its unique heritage.[10] After such powerful language it is somewhat disappointing to find that the enforcing clauses add little to the earlier orders.

This distinctive rhetorical performance must be set alongside another in the subsequent year when James made the removal of the gentry one of the cornerstones of his star chamber speech.[11] Complaining that his will had not been regarded, or at best that it had only been taken as applying to the Christmas season, the king once again lauded the good old English custom of

---

[8] The pattern is as follows: May 1603, July 1603, July 1608, October 1614, December 1615, April 1617, November 1622, December 1622, March 1623, October 1624.

[9] PRO, C 82/1862/11. [10] *Stuart Royal Proclamations*, I, pp. 356–7.

[11] James I, *Workes*, ed. James Montagu (1616), p. 567.

hospitality. In vivid language he denounced the creeping Italian fashion in which country residence was despised and the gentry were 'dwelling all in the Citie', depopulating their own counties and ensuring that soon 'England will onely be London'. Instead he argued for balance in the commonwealth, for a restoration of previous norms, so that 'as every fish lives in his own place, some in the fresh, some in the salt, some in the mud; so let everyone live in his own place, some at Court, some in the Citie, some in the Countrey'. Here we are faced with an articulated concern for social harmony which proceeds far beyond the simple orders of the sixteenth century and which is clearly intended by the king to introduce permanent change in the habits of the gentry. But to ensure that the rhetoric could be translated more immediately into action we find the later Jacobean proclamations concentrating on the expulsion of the gentry specifically at the festal seasons, notably Christmas, which the king had noted as the most appropriate moment for the practice of hospitality.

The group of orders concentrated in the years between 1622 and 1624 mark a retreat from the elaborate language of James's earlier statements and instead address themselves far more systematically to the problem of enforcement, insisting peremptorily that the king would brook no opposition to his will.[12] The only issue to be given more critical comment is that of the role of women in the growth of the London season. As the second of the 1622 pair of proclamations expressed it, the habit of bringing families to London was 'an innovation and abuse lately crept in, and growne frequent'. James gave full rein to his misogynist sentiment on the matter in a poem of the same year:

> You women that doe London love so well
> whome scarce a proclamacon can expell
> and to be kept in fashion fine and gaye
> Care not what fines there honest husbands pay.
> You dreame on nought but vizitts maskes and toyes
> And thinke the cuntrey contributes noe ioyes. . .[13]

In this case rhetoric seems to have been matched by some action. When the countess of Lincoln petitioned to be allowed to stay in town for the winter of 1624 she was told by her royal master that 'the countrey is the most fitting place for the ladies to live in, in the absence of their Lords' and that she must retire and keep her hospitality there.[14]

The Caroline orders continued to follow the general directions established in the previous reign, although Charles did not attempt to rival his father's

[12] See, for example, the proclamation of October 1624, in which James reiterates his 'constant and setled resolution' to return the gentry to the country, and his intention that all who flout his will 'may feele the severitie of Our justice'. *Stuart Royal Proclamations*, I, p. 608.

[13] James I, *Poems*, ed. J. Craigie (2 vols., Scot. Text Soc., 3rd series XII, XXVI, Edinburgh, 1955–8), II, p. 178. There were also rumours in 1622 that James had written two pamphlets against London residence: *The Court and Times of James I*, ed. R. F. Williams (2 vols., 1849), II, p. 364.

[14] *Calendar of State Papers Domestic: James I, 1623–5*, p. 378.

habit of constantly reiterating commands. During the first years of his reign three proclamations were issued, most of them deliberately emphasising continuity with the past in government policy.[15] There are several references to the actions of the king's 'deare Father of blessed memory deceased', and in 1630 the memory of Elizabeth was also invoked, though without the pious preamble. The language of the proclamations refers back to hospitality and the obligations of the gentry, especially to the importance of country residence during the Christmas season. But in one sense it is modified: far greater emphasis is placed on the problems of London 'overburthened with Inhabitants and resiants', a theme that had previously been aired principally in conciliar letters.[16] Thus we return to the 1632 document from which this essay began: the genesis of the diverse anxieties raised in its preamble can now be more plainly discerned. Shared concerns for local governance, for adequate defence measures in the shires, for proper measures to regulate food supply in time of dearth intersected with a growing preoccupation with the expansion of London. By 1632 the language of proclamation suggests that the latter may have superseded the former group at the centre of governmental attention.

If quantity could be taken as a legitimate measure of importance, we would be forced to conclude that endeavours to force the gentry out of London ranked high among the interests of late Tudor and early Stuart governments. However, earnestness of intent must be measured by other indices, most obviously by the determination with which the proclamations were enforced. Three periods of serious enforcement can be identified: the first lasted from 1595 to about 1601, the second from 1622 to 1624 and the third from 1632 to about 1636. Between these bursts of governmental energy lie years when rhetorical pronouncements were scarcely matched by any serious attempt to render the royal will effective. In the years of serious enforcement we may further distinguish two types of activity: verbal reinforcement of proclamation, and the pursuit of individual delinquents. To the Elizabethan regime must go the credit for developing a method of rendering the general commands of the queen immediately urgent for the local gentry. In 1595, a year before the promulgation of our first proclamation, the lord keeper had deliberately revived the practice of issuing a general charge to the assize judges before they began their circuits, they in turn being obliged to impart the substance of the charge to their local audiences.[17] Since the occasion for the giving of the general charge was highly public, and involved a large gentle and noble audience attending in the star chamber, the crown was also enabled to convey

---

[15] November 1626, November 1627, September 1630.
[16] *Acts of the Privy Council: 1601–4*, pp. 47–8.
[17] John Hawarde, *Les Reportes del Cases in Camera Stellata*, ed. W. P. Baildon (1894), p. 20. On assize charges in general see J. S. Cockburn, *A History of English Assizes, 1558–1714* (Cambridge, 1972), pp. 67–9.

directly to members of the political nation its concern for justice and good governance. The 1595 charge urged all office-holders to return to their country houses 'there to maintain hospitality'.[18] In a series of later charges for 1596, 1598 and 1599 there was a sustained effort to exhort J.P.s to perform their duties in the localities and to remove themselves from London.[19] These 'ordinary' charges were afforced by the famous speech made by the lord keeper after the uncovering of the Essex conspiracy, in which the most important secondary theme was the queen's earnest wish 'that all Justices of Peace will resort and drawe themselves to the contrye, and to keepe hospitalitye there, and not to runne to London and keepe no hospitalitie at all'.[20]

The pursuit of delinquents was initiated a few months after the issue of the proclamation. On 25 December 1596 the council wrote to the lord mayor of London requiring him to search out offenders and to certify their names.[21] The lord mayor duly set in train an enquiry to discover gentlemen still in the city, and to record their lodging-places, county of origin and length of stay. Aldermen were enjoined to organise their ward-constables to provide the relevant details with the utmost rapidity.[22] It should come as no surprise to discover that the ward-constables failed to produce the information. City government was experiencing greater difficulties in the 1590s than for several decades previously and by the early months of 1597 the burden of governmental demands for information and action temporarily defeated the mayor.[23] In February of that year he wrote to the aldermen lamenting the collapse of his authority. No less than five important precepts directed to him by the council had not been enacted and the conciliar letter of the previous December was singled out as the most prominent of these.[24] Perhaps for our purposes, however, it is more interesting to observe that for a time the government persisted in pursuing the harassed mayor: on no less than three occasions he was informed that the queen was 'greevously offended, towardes me and other the Magistrates and governors of this citie'.[25] It is impossible to judge whether their persistence was rewarded, since no returns survive for this date among the state papers, but it appears that routines for the collection of information were established and were employed again in 1601 and in the second half of James's reign.[26] By 1601 it was already recognised that the lord mayor had to coordinate his efforts with those of the Middlesex J.P.s if delinquents were not to avoid expulsion merely by removing themselves from the city to Westminster.[27]

The ultimate test of the earnestness of royal intent would have been the

[18] Les Reportes del Cases, p. 20.   [19] Ibid, pp. 56, 102, 326.   [20] Folger Lib., v^b. 142, fo. 49.
[21] APC: 1596–7, p. 381.   [22] Guildhall RO, Journal of Common Council, 24, fo. 174^v.
[23] N. Brett-James, The Growth of Stuart London (London and Middx. Arch. Soc., 1935), pp. 75ff.
[24] Guildhall RO, Journal of Common Council, 24, fo. 198.
[25] Ibid, fo. 191^v; Remembrancia v, no. 180.   [26] APC: 1601–4, pp. 47–8. PRO, SP 14/134/86.
[27] Guildhall RO, Remembrancia v, no. 205.

prosecution of offenders in star chamber by the attorney-general. It seems that in the 1590s only one case was brought before the court under the enforcement clauses of the proclamation, and that does not directly concern London residence, but relates to Richard Maudley, gent., who was an inhabitant of Bristol.[28] The details of the case cannot be recovered, since the original papers are missing, perhaps removed by Attorney-General Noy for use as precedents in the much broader prosecution of 1632.[29] However, we do know that the case was pursued to a conclusion and Maudley fined the substantial sum of £250.[30] The choice of a west country case for prosecution tells us something about the priorities of Elizabeth's government in these years, for Maudley was probably in default of that part of the proclamation that required subjects in the maritime counties to return to their homes in order to ensure the proper defence of their shires.[31] In 1596 conciliar letters certainly concentrated on defence and there was a specific order to the western gentry to leave London 'her Majestie being advertysed of the preparacions of the King of Spaine to attempt invasion on some parte of this realme. . .'[32]

The earnestness of purpose displayed by the late Elizabethan government was not really matched by that of its successor. James's early proclamations had highly non-specific enforcement clauses, and there is no evidence before 1615 of any pursuit of offenders. The loss of the privy council registers for these years makes it difficult to assert with confidence that nothing was done, but other sources such as the London records are silent for the period as well. Occasionally the lord keeper still referred to the problem of London in his charges: in 1608, for example, he instructed the lord mayor to take note of those gentry who 'lurke aboute the towne' and the judges to provide returns of those not keeping hospitality in their country residences.[33] Yet among the five charges available for the period of Bacon's lord keepership, exactly the period when the king's pronouncements on the subject became so hyperbolic, only that for Trinity 1617 even mentions the subject.[34] It certainly does not seem that the threat to remove persistent offenders from the commission of peace, which was incorporated into the 1615 proclamation, was put into effect.[35]

Some explanation for the loss of momentum is no doubt to be found in the general laxity of Jacobean government. But an interesting series of documents associated with the 1617 proclamation suggests that there were also divided counsels on the importance and efficacy of royal initiatives in this area. When

---

[28] Harvard Law School MS 1128, fo. 71ᵛ. I owe this reference to the kindness of Professor Clive Holmes.

[29] Evidence for the careful quest for precedent in 1632 is also to be found in the lord keeper's charge to the judges: *Report of Cases in the Courts of Star Chamber and High Commission*, ed. S. R. Gardiner (Camden Soc., 1886), pp. 176–80.

[30] *Estreats of Fines in Star Chamber*, PRO listing by T. G. Barnes (available in the PRO).

[31] *Tudor Royal Proclamations*, III, p. 172.

[32] HMC, *Hatfield MSS*, VI, pp. 546–7.   [33] *Les Reportes del Cases*, p. 368.

[34] *The Works of Francis Bacon*, ed. J. Spedding (14 vols., 1857–74), VI, pp. 211–12.

[35] *Stuart Royal Proclamations*, I, p. 357.

Francis Bacon prepared the drafts of the two previous proclamations he duly annotated the bills, offering the king a brief resumé of their contents.[36] In 1615 his phraseology makes abundantly clear the king's own involvement: the bill contained 'yor Matie proclamacon signifying yor dislike of the aboade of Noblemen. . .'. Two years later Bacon demonstrated that behind these careful words there lay doubts about the wisdom of his royal master. Early that year James left on his visit to Scotland, having agreed with the privy council that one of the documents they should publish in his absence would be yet another order against London residence.[37] On 27 March Secretary Winwood sent a general business letter to Secretary Lake, who was travelling with the king, in which he casually mentioned that the council felt it unnecessary to publish the proclamation since 'the Londiners already say *Magna civitas magna solitudo*'.[38] Three days later Bacon added the explanation that the city was already so dead in the absence of the court and after the end of the law term that no purpose would be served by the order, though he promised to add the issue to his Trinity term charge. James begged to differ. The receipt of the two letters produced two dramatic outbursts of royal temper: the council were roundly abused for neglecting his will, and Lake hastened to tell the lord keeper that the document must be dispatched forthwith.[39] Dispatched of course it was, and Bacon also followed the king's will in including the expulsion order in his next charge.[40] Yet the tone of that charge only serves to confirm that he thought James ill-advised: the version recorded in Harleian MS 1576, and confirmed in another source, notes a comment that is flippant to the point of disrespect to the royal will. Having ordered the gentry into the country, Bacon added, 'But as farre as I see, the cittie wantes not, it is so settled. But this were more fitt at Christmasse, then now, when Gentlemen should show their hospitalitie in the Contrie, for now I thinke the smell of London will drive them farre enough.'[41] In the lord keeper's own official version of the speech he wisely chose to exclude this particular passage .

Bacon's doubts about the wisdom of James's policy may help to explain the disjunction between the rhetoric of the proclamations, at its most powerful during his years of ascendancy, and effective enforcement, which seems to post-date his fall. Unfortunately, the charges of his successor Bishop Williams cannot be traced, but under his guise of dean of Westminster he certainly pursued the delinquent gentry with some energy. In November 1622 the king signalled very clearly that he meant to have his latest proclamation obeyed, and the machinery for investigating defaulters was put in motion with great rapidity. The lord mayor, for example, received a letter 'under his highnes hand and signett' on 20 December and had the returns of many of the ward-

---

[36] PRO, C 82/1846/4; C 82/1862/11.   [37] PRO, SP 14/91/2.

[38] PRO, SP 14/90/143.   [39] *Works of Francis Bacon*, VI, pp. 160–1, 161–2; PRO SP 14/91/10.

[40] *Works of Francis Bacon*, VI, pp. 211–12.

[41] BL, Harleian MS 1576, fo. 154. Inner Temple, MS Barrington 16, fo. 58ᵛ. I owe this reference to the kindness of Professor Clive Holmes.

constables at his disposal within two or three days.[42] Bishop Williams, giving the J.P.s under his jurisdiction a few days longer, nevertheless made clear the urgency of their task. 'Herein', he wrote, 'yow are to omitte no vigilance, as being a Service especiallie [at this point he first put *recommended* and then crossed it through and substituted *commaunded*] by his Maiestie.'[43] And on this occasion we have the proof that the system worked in the form of returns from the Middlesex J.P.s, including the presentment of one Mr John Pym, lodging at Boswell House in St Clement's parish.[44] Since the king so evidently intended to make his will effective a small number of individuals began to seek dispensation from expulsion, accompanying their petitions with appropriate medical certificates.[45]

The weeks before Christmas also witnessed the most extraordinary exodus of families from London. On 3 January the Rev. Joseph Mead received a report that 7000 families had removed themselves from the metropolis, taking with them their 1400 coaches.[46] The particular numbers should no doubt be treated with scepticism, but there is plenty of corroborating evidence for the upheaval in Chamberlain's letters, and in those of some of the resident ambassadors.[47] John Taylor, the water-poet, in his attack on the fashion for coaches, observed that it was a great relief to see the streets of London cleared of the vehicles 'although myselfe, with many thousands more were much impoverished and hindered of our livings. . .'.[48] In January 1623 John Coke, one of the masters of requests, was advised by his London agent that he could now have his choice of houses in St Martin's Lane at very good rates since 'the two proclamations have so emptied the City and the suburbs'.[49] But already by mid-January the newsletter writers were remarking the return of the gentry, who complained bitterly about their enforced exile.[50] The returnees were premature: on this occasion James was determined to reinforce the sharp lesson he had taught. At the end of February 1623 a further enquiry was instituted, and as soon as the law term ended the gentry found themselves on the move once more, an experience, as Chamberlain commented sardonically that 'is nothing pleasing to all; but least of all to the women'.[51] This double assault seems, in the short term, to have concentrated the minds of some gentlemen on their obligation to be out of London in the vacations. In November 1623 the countess of Bedford expressed her surprise that Lady Bacon and her husband had been such 'punctual observers of the comandement [which] empties this towne'.[52]

[42] Guildhall RO, Journal of Common Council, 32, fo. 112ᵛ.   [43] PRO, SP 14/134/86.
[44] Ibid.   [45] *Cal. St. Pap. Dom.: James I, 1619–23*, pp. 464, 467.
[46] *Court and Times of James I*, II, p. 353.
[47] Ibid, p. 358. *Cal. St. Pap. Ven.: 1621–23*, pp. 530, 584.
[48] John Taylor, 'The World Runnes on Wheels', in *Works* (1630), p. 238.
[49] HMC, *Cowper MSS*, I, p. 358.
[50] *Court and Times of James I*, p. 358.   [51] Ibid, p. 383.
[52] *Private Correspondence of Lady Jane Cornwallis*, ed. Lord Braybrooke (1842), pp. 84–5.

John Holles, first earl of Clare, is an interesting example of a noble who responded to the governmental pressures of the 1620s, though not necessarily in a way which James would have approved. By the beginning of the decade he was effectively excluded from court influence, having suffered imprisonment for his rash support of his patron Somerset, and having been worsted in a major conflict with Sir Edward Coke and the duke of Buckingham in 1619.[53] He therefore considered it prudent to observe the letter of the law whenever possible since 'sum must be exemplary' and the proclamations might be applied with particular rigour when a man had enemies and 'neither bedd-chamber, councelorship, office, nor state employment to shelter him'.[54] In the early Caroline period Holles did indeed leave London solemnly each Christmas, driven away 'as Adam was out of Paradise', but always calculating his return at the earliest possible moment when the law term lent a legitimacy to his movements.[55] Early in 1623, however, the general situation was so uncertain that Holles was doubtful if it was prudent to come up to town even after the beginning of the term, so stringent were the conditions imposed by the proclamation, and throughout January and February 1623 his correspondence is full of allusions to the problem. His fear seems to have been genuine enough, though it was associated with some prudential sense of the wisdom of being away from London at a time when his landlady, Lady Lennox, wanted him to engage in the irksome task of removing his property and finding other accommodation.[56] James had generously provided Holles with an excuse for delay, but a man who had had 'the honor to have dwelt in the Fleet 4 tymes', and who still had Edward Coke bent on revenge against him, had ample reason to fear the instruments of prerogative government.

James's last years saw no repetition of the mass exodus of 1622–3, though some attempt to enforce the proclamations continued until the end of 1624.[57] By then dispensations from the obligation to retire to the country had become one of the routine pieces of patronage available to leading members of the court. The countess of Bedford thought the precipitate departure of Lady Bacon foolish because with warning she could readily have obtained a licence for her to remain in town.[58] Despite Holles's fears, no active campaign of prosecution followed the king's intervention: the only star chamber case brought under the proclamations was a promoted cause, almost certainly a malicious prosecution, in which a minor Essex gentleman was charged with having moved into his nearest market town.[59] It would, however, be mistaken to conclude that the Jacobean regime ceased to have any interest in the problem after 1623. For example, when one Henry Atkinson tried to obtain a

---

[53] *Letters of John Holles 1587–1637*, ed. P. R. Seddon (2 vols., Thoroton Soc., Record Series, XXXIV–V, 1979, 1983), I, Introduction.
[54] Ibid, II, p. 265. Letter dated 23 January, 1623.
[55] Ibid, II, pp. 341, 375.   [56] Ibid, II, p. 265.
[57] *Cal. St. Pap. Ven.: 1623–5*, pp. 166, 481. *APC: 1623–5*, pp. 127, 383.
[58] *Correspondence of Lady Cornwallis*, p. 85.   [59] PRO, STAC 8/32/2.

licence to stay in London at the end of 1624 because of his wife's ill-health, the council claimed that 'they are very sparing to give way to suitors in this kind', though they would endeavour to persuade the king of the worthiness of the case.[60]

The early Caroline years mark a further retreat from this policy of enforcement: the government no doubt being too deeply engaged in the logistics of warfare to trouble itself about the behaviour of the gentry. The habit of seeking dispensations to remain in town over Christmas continued, though only a handful survive, and there is little sign that the king was prepared to act on his high-sounding threat 'to take a strict and severe accompt' of those who did not obey his orders.[61] Some charges to the judges mention a return to the country, but others are silent on the issue, notably those for 1626 and 1628.[62] The first sign of more positive governmental initiative comes from a report by Sir Thomas Barrington on the lord keeper's charge of November 1628, heard by many M.P.s in London for parliament. Coventry spoke on various themes including innovations in religion and then 'gave a charge to all gentlemen to repaire into the countrye, to keepe up hospitallytie. . .'.[63] In the next two years the Caroline government had plenty more critical problems to preoccupy it, and it was only in mid-1631 that the lord keeper really returned to the attack. Then he told the gentry that 'they had had many warnings; but the last should bee by a proclamation. . .'.[64] This time the minister had engaged in legal research and was equipped to cite precedents of similar orders fixing the residence of office-holders and others. The next year, the day after the issue of the major proclamation, Coventry again addressed the judges, defending government action with precedents commencing with an order to protect the Cinque Ports of 23 Edward I.[65] Although the lord keeper spoke for the king and council we should probably see Charles himself as playing an active role in the enforcement of this policy: in 1634 a letter-writer was moved to comment 'the King is verie zealous in the prosecusion of his proclamation against towne dwellers, and therefore hath often charged his Atturney to prosecute agaynst them'.[66]

This comment immediately underlines the contrast between the campaign of 1632 to 1636 and those undertaken by the Elizabethan and Jacobean governments. The mechanisms for the investigation of delinquents remained much as before: in some cases the constables and J.P.s were pressed to give more detail in their returns, but the basic data assembled for the government

---

[60] *APC: 1623–25*, p. 383.

[61] *Cal. St. Pap. Dom.: Charles I, 1625–6*, p. 504; *1627–8*, p. 477.

[62] BL, Add. MS 34324; Add. MS 48057, fos. 105–6. The latter charge is printed in T. G. Barnes, 'A charge to the judges of assize, 1627–8', *Huntingdon Library Quarterly*, 24 (1960/61).

[63] *Barrington Family Letters, 1628–32*, ed. A. Searle (Camden Soc., 4th series, XXVIII, 1983), p. 39.

[64] PRO, C 115/M35/8384. I owe this reference to the kindness of Dr Kevin Sharpe who first drew my attention to the important 1630s newsletters in Chancery Masters Exhibits.

[65] *Star Chamber Cases*, pp. 178–80.   [66] PRO, C 115/M36/8439.

in two great surveys in 1632/3 and 1634/5 was of a kind similar to that supplied to James.[67] The contrast lies in the determination of the Caroline government to prosecute offenders, a determination which it manifested before the first survey was initiated in the show trial of William Palmer.[68] Palmer was charged by Attorney-General Noy with remaining in town in contravention of the proclamation when he possessed substantial estates in both Somerset and Sussex. The case aroused intense interest: there are few newsletters or series of personal correspondence from London at the end of 1632 that fail to mention it.[69] Palmer was fined £1000, much to the amazement of the writers, none of whom appear to have been aware that the fine was later reduced to the more reasonable figure of £25.[70] By then, presumably, Palmer had served his purpose, and the gentry had been left in no doubt of government determination. There is an excellent example of their response in the *Autobiography* of Sir Simonds D'Ewes, who was living in Islington in the early years of the decade.[71] D'Ewes confessed that he had been a little startled by the summer proclamation, but, after consulting with Coventry and with one of the justices of king's bench, he was persuaded he was safe. He therefore ordered his year's provisions and settled down to enjoy a winter of research in town. However, the outcome of the Palmer case forced him to decide 'for a remove, being much troubled not only with my separation from records, but with my wife's being great with child'. Ironically his move came too late to prevent him being listed as an offender, and appearing on the attorney-general's schedule of those to be subpoenaed in star chamber early the next year.[72]

The full story of the prosecutions threatened by the government in 1633 and again in 1635 deserves a paper of its own. The bald statistics are intriguing enough: in February 1633 248 men and women were subpoenaed, two years later 180, a few individuals being threatened twice.[73] The cases did not run their course and it must be presumed that the individuals concerned compounded for their offence.[74] Many of those charged in 1633 were careful to acquire dispensations from the provisions of the proclamation thereafter. An

---

[67] Bodleian Library, Bankes Papers, Calendar.

[68] The full proceedings in the Palmer case are in Harvard Law School MS 1128, fos. 71ᵛ-2.

[69] PRO, C 115/M35/8416; M35/8417; *The Knyvett Letters, 1620-44*, ed. B. Schofield (Norf. Rec. Soc. xx (1949), p. 78; *The Court and Times of Charles I*, ed. T. Birch (2 vols., 1848), II, p. 192.

[70] PRO, SP 16/232/43.

[71] Simonds D'Ewes, *Autobiography and Correspondence*, ed. J. O. Halliwell (2 vols, 1845), II, p. 78.

[72] Inner Temple Library, Petyt MS 538/43, fo. 181ᵛ. I owe this reference to the kindness of Professor Clive Holmes.

[73] Ibid, fos. 178-82ᵛ. J. Rushworth, *Historical Collections* (8 vols., 1680-1701), II, pp. 288-93. For a discussion of the results of the returns see L. Stone, 'The residential development of the west end of London in the seventeenth century', in *After the Reformation; Essays in Honour of Jack Hexter*, ed. B. Halament (Manchester, 1980), pp. 175-6.

[74] The presumption that the cases were not pursued derives from the absence of fines in the star chamber, and from the lack of contemporary comment.

active trade in such dispensations is recorded in the Bankes papers, where 238 warrants are noted as issued between 1632 and 1640.[75] No doubt a financial interest stimulated this trade, as part of those profits of justice which Professor Barnes has described as being 'virtually limitless' for the Caroline regime.[76] Nevertheless it is difficult to correlate all this energy with pure fiscalism; both Charles and his servants do seem for a time to have been concerned to render the governmental will effective for ideological as well as financial reasons. In October 1634, when Attorney-General Bankes was planning the second general prosecution, it was reported that he 'doth first peruse all the Answeres of all those against whom Atturney Noy exhibited bills into the Star Chamber: that so by knowing their former pretences, he may fortifey this proclamaton against the like excuses thereafter'.[77] Amendments to the procedures for the pursuit of delinquents were still being discussed energetically in 1636 and only in the next year do the routines of enforcement appear divorced from any real enthusiasm for the success of the policy.[78]

Although these intermittent periods of energetic investigation and prosecution are testimony to the seriousness of intent of all three regimes, we are still left with some unanswered questions about the objectives underlying all this activity. A series of objectives are, of course, articulated in the proclamations, and it would be unwise to assume that these do not represent a substantial part of true governmental intention. E. M. Leonard long ago pointed out the close connection between periods of dearth and the pressure which was brought to bear on the gentry to leave London.[79] 1596, 1608, 1621–3 and 1630–2 were all years of harvest failure and the crown's anxiety about the regulation of supply provided one obvious reason for its enthusiasm. In 1621–3, when the Jacobean government made dearth one of the prime focuses of its proclamation rhetoric, the newsletter writers accepted that concern about the state of the countryside did much to explain the pronouncements.[80] Likewise the needs of defence under Elizabeth, concern for the exercise of royal authority in the localities and worries about the dramatic growth of the city and suburbs, were all substantive issues which served to stimulate the flow of proclamations.[81] The romantic nostalgia which James and Charles displayed for a good old world of English hospitality is of a rather different order. In James's case we seem to be confronted with an individual, not to say idiosyncratic, conviction that there really had been an English past in which rural society had displayed that open bonhomie which he so valued in his own periods of

---

[75] Bodleian Library, Bankes Papers 38/29.
[76] Barnes, 'Prerogative and environmental control', p. 1351.
[77] PRO, C 115/M36/8437.
[78] PRO, SP 16/319/92; PC 2/48/431. The privy council order of December 1637 does not seem to have been followed by active measures of enforcement.
[79] E. M. Leonard, *The Early History of English Poor Relief* (Cambridge, 1900), pp. 144–7.
[80] *Cal. St. Pap. Dom.: James I, 1619–23*, p. 483. *Cal. St. Pap. Ven.: 1621–23*, p. 530.
[81] Brett-James, *Stuart London*, pp. 75ff.

retirement from the court.[82] He also sought to articulate what his son made fully explicit, that order and harmony in the social universe were as dependent on everyone observing their correct geographical place as on the due observance of place within the hierarchy. For Charles, surrounded by a court culture which idealised the countryside as a place of social integration, London with its 'spleen' which sucked the life-blood from this organic system, was an obvious focus for regulatory action.[83] In themselves such visions of social harmony might not have been sufficient to stir these governments to action. However, in combination with appropriate catalysts such as dearth or the desire in the early 1630s to render the personal rule effective, they became powerful stimuli and justifications for regulation.

As the policy of removing the gentry came to be enforced more and more rigorously from 1622 onwards, letter-writers and ambassadors were inevitably led to speculate on the *real* intentions of the government and showed an understandable reluctance to take its stated objectives at face value. The Venetian ambassadors, perhaps mindful of their home regime, were eager to link the expulsions with a desire to stifle political debate.[84] It is true that the proclamation of 1622 did coincide with a moment of intense speculation on the prince's marriage, while that of the subsequent March appeared in the immediate aftermath of the revelation of the Madrid adventure. Two years later one ambassador suggested that the 1624 proclamation had as its main objective the dispersal of members of parliament still in London after the end of the session.[85] It is impossible wholly to counter these speculations, but as a prime explanation for James's actions they do not convince. The court, that centre and focus of most political rumour and intrigue, remained untouched by the proclamations, and there is no explicit comment in the English sources that political control was the objective of the king and his ministers. The other possibility mooted by the ambassadors was that the crown was acting for fiscal reasons. As already suggested, it is likely that Charles derived some financial benefit from the judicial proceedings against defaulters. However, this does not mean that it is sensible to echo the Venetian ambassador who in 1632 explained that the enforcement of this and other proclamations was undertaken solely because it resulted 'in the flow of cash into the Royal Chamber, the exiguity of which . . . makes them resort to every means in order to obtain money'.[86] The policy of expelling the gentry from London no doubt came to dovetail very neatly with other revenue-raising devices employed in the early

---

[82] Leonard, *Poor Relief*, p. 146, cites the comment attributed to James that a country gentleman in the country was like a ship in a river, which looked very big.

[83] See, for example, Fanshawe's poem in praise of the 1630 proclamation: *Oxford Book of Sevententh-Century Verse*, ed. H. J. C. Grierson and G. Bullough (Oxford, 1934), pp. 448–52. K. V. Sharpe, 'Cavalier Critic? The Ethics and Politics of Thomas Carew's Poetry', *Politics of Discourse* ed. K. V. Sharpe and S. W. Zwicker (Berkeley, 1987) pp. 117–46.

[84] *Cal. St. Pap. Ven.: 1621–3*, pp. 530, 538, 584.

[85] *Cal. St. Pap. Ven.: 1623–5*, p. 486.   [86] *Cal. St. Pap. Ven.; 1632–6*, p. 38.

1630s but the ideology of the Caroline regime seems to provide a more convincing explanation for its actions than the desire to turn a profit.

Whatever the motives of governments, their actions were deliberately directed against the immediate self-interest of the gentry, and as such risked political hostility from men of influence. One is compelled to enquire whether the risk was worthwhile; that is to say whether the crown was able to achieve its objectives and whether the cost was justified. We have already noted the visible success achieved by the Jacobean and Caroline regimes: men did remove from London in great numbers, even if they subsequently returned.[87] In a narrow sense the will of the crown was enforced: in a slightly broader perspective the ruling classes may have been reminded that they could not colonise the city with complete security. How much difference was made to the growth of the West End, of the London season, or of the habit of semi-permanent settlement in town, is very questionable. After about 1636 the Caroline regime seems to be acknowledging that regulation, rather than removal, was the appropriate policy, and the physical expansion of gentry London was permitted to continue.[88] It is even more questionable if governmental action achieved its desired ends in the localities: although the short-term needs of defence were partially met by the return of the gentry, local government and the poor were not obvious beneficiaries. When the great exodus from London occurred in 1622 it had, as Chamberlain pointed out, the opposite effect to that which James wished. 'It falls out', he commented, 'that the commandment did little good, but rather hurt; for being driven to make their provision in haste, the markets rose so in all places that they came to, that the poor, instead of relief, found their burden heavier.'[89] It is difficult to escape the conclusion that, at times, the Jacobean and Caroline regimes, unlike the more pragmatic Elizabethan one, were using proclamation as a way of demonstrating that they could control the landed elite when they so desired.

This prompts the final question about the value of the exercise: if the achievements were temporary, limited and uncertain, were they bought at too high a price? Professor Barnes praises the parallel restrictions on building in London, despite the political tensions they caused, as the first serious English attempt at town-planning, sound in assumptions if not always in methods of enforcement.[90] It is difficult to return so enthusiastic a verdict on the expulsion of the gentry. Under Elizabeth it was perhaps acceptable as part of the shared concern for the defence of the realm. Under James it provoked much complaint among the elite, though no evidence of any general revolt. The risks became manifest under Charles when the expulsions were inevit-

---

[87] See, for example, Chamberlain's comment to Carleton that the 1624 proclamation almost 'beggared' the town: *Cal. St. Pap. Dom.: James I, 1624–6*, p. 360.

[88] Brett-James, *Stuart London*, pp. 114–17. The detailed returns for the 1630s provide very interesting evidence of the pattern of gentry residence.

[89] *Court and Times of James I*, p. 358.

[90] Barnes, 'Prerogative and environmental control', p. 1334.

ably linked to the broader threat posed to men of property and substance by the strictness of the regime. The lord keeper and attorney-general in the early 1630s both had to address themselves to the precedents which permitted the crown to force its subjects to change their place of residence. D'Ewes expressed much surprise that Noy, 'being accounted a great lawyer', should remove mens' liberty to live where they would within the kingdom.[91] Other commentators confined themselves to expressions of surprise that the proclamations were so strictly enforced, but there are hints in the prosecution records that the government's rights over residence were being questioned in gentry circles.[92] It is scarcely an accident that some years after this particular policy of straight and strict governance had been allowed to fall into desuetude, article 28 of the Grand Remonstrance challenged the right of the crown to restrain 'the liberties of the subjects in their habitation, trades and other interests'.[93]

When the expulsion of the gentry is set against the major political issues of the early seventeenth century it inevitably appears as small beer. There is even a farcical quality about the gyrations of the elite as they calculated the pleasures of continuing residence in town against the pains of royal disapproval. But the rhetoric which three monarchs and their advisers expended on the problem, and their intermittent determination to construct machinery of enforcement to render their will effective, should alert us to the value of these royal proclamations. In retrospect James and Charles look all too like their distinguished predecessor Canute, unable to keep back the rising flood of urban residence. In the context of the early seventeenth century, however, their actions do appear to be directed with some effectiveness to the reassertion of traditional values of governance and social control in the localities. These values *were* threatened by the relatively novel fashion of general London residence, and the arbitrariness of specific governmental action should not disguise from us the basic sense of its assumptions. All that the crown lacked was the power to engage the elite in a shared vision of the dangers of London and of the joys of the countryside.

[91] D'Ewes, *Autobiography*, II, p. 78.

[92] The attorney-general made it part of his 1635 charge against the violators of the proclamation that they 'have had several meetings, and therein advised and consulted in what manner ...' they might best obstruct the royal will: Rushworth, *Historical Collection*, II, pp. 292–3.

[93] *Constitutional Documents of the Puritan Revolution, 1625–1660*, ed. S. R. Gardiner (Oxford, 1889), p. 212.

Taxation and the political limits of the Tudor state

ROGER SCHOFIELD

TAXATION occupies a sensitive position in the nexus of constitutional, political, and social relationships, for it is through taxation that economic resources are mobilised for political ends. Societies not only differ in the ends which they deem proper to be attained by taxation, but are also constrained in the kinds of tax they can levy by the nature of their economic resources and by their level of administrative skill. Moreover, since taxes entail compulsion, the ways in which they are authorised and organised are essentially political matters. A study of taxation, therefore, should throw light not only on the social and economic characteristics of a society, but also on its political and administrative structure and its constitutional concepts of obligation and consent.[1]

The Tudor period furnishes a particularly interesting episode in the history of taxation in England for it was under Henry VIII that taxation based on the direct assessment of the wealth of each individual was revived, after having been abandoned as unworkable in the fourteenth century.[2] Direct assessment was to be abandoned again in the mid-seventeenth century after decades of complaint over evasion and under-assessment, and would not be revived again until the very end of the eighteenth century.[3] In the long run, therefore, the Tudor experiment in taxation failed, but an examination of that experiment, and of the timing and causes of its failure, may throw some light on the changing political limits of the Tudor state.

[1] For a path-breaking attempt to relate changes in taxation to social, political and economic developments in early modern Europe, see R. Goldscheid, 'A sociological approach to problems of public finance', in R. A. Musgrave and A. T. Peacock, eds., *Classics in the Theory of Public Finance* (London, 1958), pp. 203–13.

[2] Directly assessed taxes in the middle ages are discussed in J. F. Willard, *Parliamentary Taxes on Personal Property, 1290–1334* (Cambridge, MA, 1934). For the sporadic and unsatisfactory character of directly assessed subsidies granted between 1334 and 1485 see R. S. Schofield, 'Parliamentary lay taxation, 1485–1547' [hereafter cited as 'PLT'] (Unpublished Ph.D dissertation, University of Cambridge, 1963), pp. 160–1.

[3] There were two further, short-lived, attempts at direct assessment of incomes: in 1670–1 and 1689–98. Taxation practice in the late seventeenth and eighteenth centuries is summarised in W. Kennedy, *English Taxation 1640–1799: an Essay on Policy and Opinion* (London, 1913 [reprinted 1964]), pp. 38–50.

227

In Tudor England taxation was levied within an agreed theory of public finance which reflected conventional constitutional notions about the rights and duties of king, parliament and people. The king, as chief magistrate of the realm, was charged with the provision of defence and justice. Accordingly, the crown should be endowed with sufficient regular revenues, ideally in the form of income from landed estates, to enable it to meet both the ordinary expenses of government, and immediate emergencies such as rebellion or invasion. However, it was evident that prolonged military campaigns were in practice too expensive to be met from any surpluses accumulated on the ordinary account. Constitutional theory, therefore, matched the duty of the king to defend the realm with a reciprocal duty on the part of his subjects to grant him financial aid in providing for this defence. By the later fifteenth century it was generally accepted that a gracious aid, fulfilling this obligation, could only be asked for in parliament, where the crown had to demonstrate the existence of a state of emergency threatening the safety of the realm, and where it was the commons which determined the size of the grant.[4]

In theory, therefore, national taxes were expected to be episodic rather than permanent. They could be levied only with the consent of parliament, though parliament could not withhold consent if the crown's claim that a state of emergency existed were correct. In practice, and with few exceptions, both crown and parliament in the Tudor period respected these reciprocal obligations. The case for taxation was made in parliament largely in terms of military necessity, or of financial need directly arising from past military expenditures, as in the case of the Antwerp debt.[5] The commons debated the size of the sum to be granted, occasionally disagreeing with the crown's military plans, as in their opposition to Henry VIII's plans to invade France in 1512, but they did not deny the crown taxation in a state of emergency.[6]

The crown, on its side, did not attempt to levy general taxation without

---

[4] The classic exposition of late medieval doctrine is in J. Fortescue, *De dominio regali et politico*, ed. by Lord Clermont (London, 1869), pp. 449–65. The most recent discussion of these issues is in J. D. Alsop, 'The theory and practice of Tudor taxation', *English Historical Review*, 97 (1982), 1–30.

[5] The question of how far the case for taxation contained in the preambles to the subsidy acts, especially those of 1534 and 1543, was widened to include ordinary expenditure has been keenly debated, since it was first raised in Schofield, 'PLT', pp. 24–30. The latest contribution to the debate is Alsop, 'Tudor taxation'.

[6] Parliamentary opposition under Henry VII and Henry VIII is discussed in Schofield, 'PLT', pp. 31–41. Later in the century the Commons deliberately delayed readings of the subsidy acts in 1566, 1589 and 1601, during debates on the succession, on the reform of abuses in purveyance and the exchequer, and on monopolies, respectively. J. E. Neale, *Elizabeth I and her Parliaments, 1559–1581* (London, 1953), pp. 136–9, 143, 166, 168–9 (1566); J. E. Neale, *Elizabeth and her Parliaments, 1584–1601* (London, 1957), pp. 206–15 (1589), 352–67 (1601). For the precise timing of events see *Commons Journals*, I, entries for 2 October 1566 to 2 January 1567, 7 February to 23 March 1589, and 24 October to 19 December 1601. The lack of Commons Journals and diaries makes it difficult to detect whether similar tactics were used in the early Tudor period.

securing parliamentary approval. Apparent exceptions, such as the notorious 'forced loans' and benevolences turn out on closer inspection to underpin the principle of parliamentary consent.[7] First, the loans were not taxes; they were repaid, usually within a year, from the revenue accruing from parliamentary taxation.[8] Second, both loans, and benevolences which were not repaid, were raised only in times of military emergency, and from a very restricted and wealthy section of the population, the size of the payments being negotiated on an individual basis. Moreover, the crown took great care to justify the necessity for loans and benevolence in precisely the same terms of national emergency as were used in justifying the necessity of taxation in parliament, and used persuasion, not compulsion, to secure compliance.[9] Third, when the crown needed to enforce the payment of an agreed sum by way of a benevolence, or to renege on an agreement to repay a loan, it obtained parliamentary sanction in the form of a special statute.[10] Finally, the Amicable Grant of 1525, which was the only occasion on which the crown attempted to levy a compulsory benevolence from a wide section of the population at standard rates, provoked universal, uncompromising, and successful opposition on the constitutional ground that it was 'not by an ordre of the law' and its promoter, Wolsey, was held to be a 'subversor of the Lawes and Libertie of England'.[11] Far from superseding parliamentary grants, loans and benevolences, respectively, were devices for anticipating, or supplementing, the collection of duly authorised taxes from a small number of wealthy subjects.[12] They were necessary because military exigencies could not wait upon the lengthy process of the summons of parliament, the passage of legislation, and

[7] For the late medieval period see G. L. Harris, 'Aids, loans and benevolences', *Historical Journal*, 6 (1963), 1–19.

[8] See, for example, the *pro forma* letter inviting contributions to the 1497 loan and specifying the date of repayment. PRO, SC 1/51/116. Repayments are recorded in the exchequer tellers' book. PRO, E 405/79. For a later sixteenth-century example, see the terms of the privy seal loan of 1570 in PRO, E 407/16, fos. 16–18. Repayment from the exchequer was ordered within the year, as promised in the privy seal letter. Dietz, *English Public Finance*, pp. 25–6.

[9] Examples of instructions to commissioners levying loans and benevolences as to how to justify them and secure individual consent can be found in W. H. Nicholas, *Proceedings of the Privy Council* (7 vols., London, 1834–7), V, pp. 418–21 (1491 benevolence); *LP* xvii 194 (1542 loan); *LP* xx (2) 6, App. 4, s. 2 (1545 benevolence).

[10] The benevolence of 1491 was written off by 11 Henry VII c. 10, the loan of 1522 by 21 Henry VIII c. 25, the loan of 1542 by 35 Henry VIII c. 12, and the benevolence of 1545 by 37 Henry VIII c. 25. In addition Mary's loan of 1556 was not repaid by Elizabeth, nor did she repay the loan of 1597. Dietz, *English Public Finance*, p. 81.

[11] Accounts of the attempt to raise the Amicable Grant and the hostility it aroused can be found in R. Holinshed, *Chronicles*, ed. by H. Ellis (6 vols., London, 1807–8), III, pp. 684–6, and in E. Hall, *Chronicle* (London, 1809), pp. 694–9. The quotations are from Ibid, p. 696. Correspondence between hard-pressed commissioners and Wolsey, commenting on the nature of the opposition are calendared in *LP*, iv 1235, 1243, 1260, 1263, 1266–7, 1272, 1295, 1311, 1319, 1321, 1323, 1329–30, 1332, 1343, 1345, App. 39.

[12] Special arrangements were also made for the speedy assessment and payment of parliamentary subsidies amongst a wide group of rich taxpayers in 1523 and 1545. Schofield, 'PLT', pp. 312–15.

the setting into operation of the whole complex machinery of Tudor taxation.[13]

The manner in which taxes were authorised testifies to a mutual understanding of the constitutional position, and to a practical political co-operation between the crown and parliament in Tudor England. However, granting taxes in a time of emergency was one thing, ensuring that individual subjects actually paid in accordance with their ability to contribute to the defence of the realm was quite another. It is the latter issue which forms the principal focus of this paper. In order to investigate the efficacy of taxation under the Tudors, we shall need to examine the nature of the taxes granted by parliament, and the degree to which they were properly assessed and collected.

The taxes granted by Tudor parliaments were of two distinct types: the fifteenth and tenth, and the directly assessed subsidy. As figure 1 shows, both forms of tax were granted throughout the Tudor period. The fifteenth and tenth was a simple tax of fixed yield, levied on communities rather than individuals. When parliament granted a fifteenth and tenth each vill and urban ward in the country had to pay a sum of money which had been fixed in 1334 and little altered thereafter; how the sum to be raised was to be apportioned amongst individuals was left to each community to decide. The yield of the tax was, therefore, predictable, and by the Tudor period it amounted to about £30,000.[14]

In one respect this predictability was an advantage: the crown knew how much it was getting, and the commons knew both how much they were giving and what the social and geographical incidence of the tax would be. On the other hand, not only was a fixed-yield tax of diminishing utility in an age of mounting inflation,[15] but the geographical distribution of wealth had changed markedly since 1334,[16] so that by the sixteenth century some areas and social groups were relatively overburdened by the tax, while others were not contributing in due proportion to their means. Clearly, in order to tap the wealth of the country more effectively a new form of taxation had to be devised, which was based on a direct assessment of the current wealth of each individual.

---

[13] The subsidy acts usually set a final date for payment of tax monies into the exchequer from four to eleven months after the passage of the subsidy bill through parliament. For early Tudor taxes, see Schofield, 'PLT', pp. 308–11. For taxes granted after 1574 compare the payments dates in the statutes cited in table 2, below, and the final dates of parliamentary session in the Commons Journals.

[14] The assessment, collection, and yield of the fifteenth and tenth are discussed in Schofield, 'PLT', pp. 60–136, 156–9. Changes in the local quotas after 1334 were mainly exemptions for religious houses, and reductions for vills experiencing natural distasters. Ibid, pp. 137–56.

[15] By 1601–10 the price of a basket of consumables had increased by a factor of 5.27 over its average price level for the period 1450–99. Comparable indices of industrial prices and agricultural wages had risen 2.56 and 2.19 times, respectively. D. M. Palliser, The Age of Elizabeth: England under the Later Tudors, 1547–1603 (London, 1983), table 5.2, p. 141.

[16] R. S. Schofield, 'The geographical distribution of wealth in England, 1334–1649', Economic History Review, 18 (1965), 483–510.

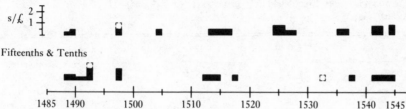

Figure 1   Incidence of direct taxation under the Tudors

Note: The vertical scale indicates the severity of the rates in force, with a fifteenth and tenth made equivalent to a subsidy rate of 6d in the pound.
Dashed boxes indicate taxes granted, but never levied.
A = levied on aliens only.
Sources: See tables 1 and 2.

In 1485 the omens for the success of such an enterprise were far from auspicious. Directly assessed taxes had only been levied occasionally during the fifteenth century; they were regarded with suspicion by parliament and were singularly unsuccessful as sources of revenue to the crown.[17] Initially the Tudors fared no better: when parliament granted the first directly assessed subsidy in 1489 the tax was hedged around with restrictions and declared not to be a precedent. The subsidy was a conspicuous failure; designed to yield £75,000 it was sabotaged by collusive under-valuation and produced only about £20,000.[18]

However, the goal of direct assessment was not abandoned; in 1497 and 1504 an ingenious compromise was adopted by which direct assessment by crown commissioners was used to re-apportion amongst individuals the global sums traditionally contributed to the fifteenth and tenth by each county.[19] Then in a burst of legislative activity between 1512 and 1515, four subsidy acts

---

[17] Schofield, 'PLT', pp. 160–2.   [18] Ibid, pp. 166–80.   [19] Ibid, pp. 180–98.

Table 1. *Yields of taxes**

Fifteenths and tenths: Fixed yield of c. £30,000 (1537: £36,000)
Lay subsidies:

	£'000		£'000
1488	1	1556	68
1489	c.24	1557	77
1497	31	1558	134
1504	31	1559–60	137
1513	33	1563–4	150
1514	50	1567–8	87
1515	45	1571–2	117
1516	44	1576–7	115
1524	73	1581–2	110
1525	65	1585–6	106
1526	6	1588–9	105
1527	9	1590–1	103
1535	22	1592–3	97
1536	23	1594	95
1541	47	1595	91
1542	48	1596–7	87
1544	77	1599	83
1545	57	1600	81
1546('43)	55	1601	?
1546('45)	110	1602	76
1547	97	1602–3	76
1549	54	1603–4	67
1550	47	1604–5	67
1551	40		
1552	43		

Note: * All figures are net sums payable to the crown after assessment, and have been rounded to the nearest thousand pounds.
Sources: 1485–1547: Schofield, 'PLT', table 40, col. 5, facing p. 416 [1489; ibid, p. 178, and PRO, E 101/413/2/1]. 1549–1605: F. C. Dietz, *English Government Finance 1485–1558* (Urbana, Illinois, 1921), p. 226, and *English Public Finance 1558–1641* (New York, 1932), pp. 392–3.

were passed which abandoned the safeguard of fixed county yields and developed an elaborate administrative apparatus for the assessment and collection of taxes directly from individuals. The subsidy act of 1523 redrafted some of the clauses; thereafter all subsequent acts embodied the principles evolved between 1512 and 1515, and in most cases they repeated the 1523 codification *verbatim.*[20] It is not known who was responsible for this considerable political and administrative achievement in transforming the basis of

---

[20] Ibid, pp. 198–218. For later Tudor subsidy acts, see the references in table 2. The only significant departure from the codification of the act of 1523 is the act of 1534. The clauses in this act lack precision, being particularly defective when dealing with the procedure of assessment. They were not repeated. Ibid, p. 215.

taxation; but the formative acts were devised during the early years of Wolsey's influence in the Council, and they were drafted by John Hales, reader in Gray's Inn in 1514, and baron of the exchequer from 1522 until his death in 1539.[21]

From the 1510s the directly assessed subsidy became the standard form of taxation granted by parliament, usually in conjunction with the fifteenth and tenth. As befitted their constitutional status as extraordinary revenues, the frequency and timing of the taxes reflected the occurrence of the exigencies of defence finance. Figure 1 shows that the incidence of taxation was sporadic over much of the Tudor period, but in the 1540s and 1550s, and in the last twenty years of Elizabeth I's reign, taxes were granted in almost every parliament and levied in almost every year.[22]

The directly assessed subsidy, therefore, became an important item in the Tudor fiscal repertoire. But it was also strikingly ambitious in its scope, posing formidable problems of administration and enforcement. When parliament granted a subsidy every adult in the country, with the exception of married women whose legal personalities were incorporated in those of their husbands, had to be assessed under two heads. These were the net value of annual incomes, and the capital value of moveable possessions, including debts owing to the taxpayer, but excluding debts owed and personal clothing.[23]

In practice the number of people who were liable to taxation was considerably reduced by the existence of minimum exemption limits below which no tax was payable. These varied from tax to tax, as is clear from table 2. Since wealth was unevenly distributed in Tudor England, the exemption limits ensured that a far from negligible proportion of the population escaped taxation altogether. For example, in 1524–5 when the minimum exemption limits were set at low levels ($£1$ for annual incomes and $£2$ for moveable goods and wages), about 10 per cent of the rural population in one hundred in Norfolk was too poor to be taxed, while comparable proportions for towns were substantially higher at about a third for Exeter and Leicester, and 47 per cent for Coventry.[24] At the other extreme, when exemption limits were set very high, as in the case of taxes levied between 1526 and 1542, only the very

---

[21] Ibid, pp. 198–212. This John Hales is to be distinguished from his namesake, the social critic once believed to be the author of the 'Discourse of the Common Weal' [1549].

[22] The role of taxation as a reason for the summons of early Tudor parliaments is discussed in Schofield, 'PLT', pp. 15–23.

[23] This account of the assessment clauses in the subsidy acts is based on a fuller discussion in 'PLT', pp. 238–79.

[24] J. Sheail, 'The distribution of taxable population and wealth in England during the early sixteenth century', *Transactions of the Institute of British Geographers*, 55 (1977), p. 14. Sheail quotes a figure of 37 per cent for Coventry. The figure of 47 per cent in the text has been obtained by relating the 840 persons assessed to the subsidy (PRO, E 179/192/125) to the revised total of 1584 households in Coventry in 1523, calculated by C. Phythian-Adams, *Desolation of a City: Coventry and the Urban Crisis of the Late Middle Ages* (Cambridge, 1979), pp. 188–90, 301.

Table 2. *Directly assessed subsidies: minimum assessments and rates of payment*

Years levied		Subsidy act
1489	Annual incomes 2s/£; goods 20d per 10 marks (Commoners only)	*Rotuli Parliamentorum*, VI, 420–4
1497	County quotas apportioned according to local assessment of wealth	12 Henry VII c. 13
1504	County quotas apportioned according to local assessment of wealth	19 Henry VII c. 32
1513	Flat payment according to assessment category Annual incomes: from 1s for £2–9, up to £2 13s 4d for £800 and above. Goods: from 2s for £2–9, up to £2 for £40 and above. Social status: from 30s for a knight to £6 13s 4d for a duke.	4 Henry VIII c. 19

	Annual incomes		Goods		Wages		
	min.	rate	min.	rate	min.	rate	
1514	£1	6d	£2	6d	£1	6d[1]	5 Henry VIII c. 17
1515 } 1516	as 1514 except no poll payment (note 1)						6 Henry VIII c. 26 7 Henry VIII c. 9
1524–5	£1	1s 0d	£2 £20	6d 1s 0d	£2	4d[2]	
1526	£50	1s 0d	–	–			14 & 15 Henry VIII c. 16
1527	–	–	£50	1s 0d			
1535–6	£20	6d	£20	6d			26 Henry VIII c. 19
1541–2	£20	1s 0d	£20[3]	6d			32 Henry VIII c. 50
1544–6[4]	£1	4d	£1	2d			
	£5	8d	£5	4d			34 & 35 Henry VIII c. 27
	£10	1s 0d	£10	8d			
1546–7	£1[5]	2s 0d	£5	8d			
			£10	1s 0d			37 Henry VIII c. 25
			£20	1s 4d			
1549–51	–	–	£10	1s 6d[6]			2 & 3 Edward VI c. 36
1552	as in 1549–51						3 & 4 Edward VI c. 23
1556–7	as in 1546–7						2 & 3 Philip and Mary c. 23
1558	£1	4s 0d	£5	2s 8d			4 & 5 Philip and Mary c. 11
1559	£1	2s 8d	£5	1s 8d			
1560	£1	1s 4d	£5	1s 0d			1 Elizabeth I c. 21
1563	£1	2s 8d	£3	1s 8d			
1564	£1	1s 4d	£3	1s 0d			5 Elizabeth I c. 31
1567	£1	1s 6d	£3	1s 0d			8 Elizebeth I c. 18
1568	£1	1s 6d	£3	10d			

Table 2 (*cont.*)

1571–2					13 Elizabeth I c. 27
1576–7					18 Elizabeth I c. 23
1581–2					23 Elizabeth I c. 15
1585–6	as in 1563–4				27 Elizabeth I c. 29
1588–9					29 Elizabeth I c. 8
1590–1					
1592–3					31 Elizabeth I c. 15
1594–5	£ 1	4s 0d	£ 3	2s 8d	35 Elizabeth I c. 13
1596–7	as in 1563–4				
1599–1601	£ 1	4s 0d	£ 3	2s 8d	39 Elizabeth I c. 27
1602	£ 1	4s 0d	£ 3	2s 8d	
1602–3					
1603–4	as in 1563–4				43 Elizabeth I c. 18
1604–5					

1 Only wages received 'by the yere' were taxed. All aged fifteen years and above, not otherwise liable to tax, paid a poll of 4d.
2 Flat payment.
3 Minimum assessment for aliens was £1.
4 In 1545 and 1546 half-rates were charged, except on annual incomes above £10 and goods above £20.
5 £2 minimum for annual wages received by servants.
6 All aged twelve and above, not otherwise liable to tax paid a poll of 8d.

From 1513 aliens often had different minimum assessment limits; and were charged at special rates, often double the normal rates. If not otherwise liable, they paid a poll of 4d (8d: 1515–25, 1549–52; 2d: 1568; none in 1535–6, 1546–7).

From 1556 all wage earners were exempt from taxation under the heading of annual incomes, except royal servants earning more than £5 a year.

rich were liable and the vast majority of the population escaped taxation altogether.[25]

In general, the subsidies were more restricted in incidence than the fifteenth and tenth, to which quite poor people contributed in several communities.[26] The unequal distribution of wealth in Tudor England also meant that even amongst those who were taxed, the greater part of the tax

[25] For example, in the West Riding of Yorkshire in 1545, when the minimum exemption limits were £1 for both lands and goods, 75 per cent of an estimated 20,000 households were assessed for the subsidy. However, in the following year, when the exemption limit on goods was raised to £5, only 23 per cent were assessed. If the exemption limits in that year had been as high as £20 for both annual income and goods, as for the subsidies of 1535–6 and 1541–2, less than 2 per cent of the households would have been taxed. R. B. Smith, *Land and Politics in the England of Henry VIII: the West Riding of Yorkshire, 1530–1546* (Oxford, 1970), pp. 109–10.

[26] Local assessment practice for the fifteenth and tenth is discussed in Schofield, 'PLT', pp. 88–102. Dietz's statement that the tax 'passes over the landless population entirely' (*English Government Finance*, p. 14) is erroneous. In the mid-1550s the crown certainly thought that the fifteenth and tenth fell on the poor, telling the subsidy commissioners that it had foreborne to ask parliament for a fifteenth and tenth 'bycause we wold spare the poorer sorte of our said subiectes'. The document is undated, but internal evidence points to late 1555. BL, Add. MS 48018, fos. 155^v–7^r.

revenues were contributed by relatively few very rich people.[27] Moreover, as can be seen in table 2, progressive rates of tax were in force in 1524–5, and between 1544 and 1557, thereby further increasing the proportional burden on the rich.

Table 2 also shows that the early Tudor acts experimented extensively with different tax rates, which became standardised in the late sixteenth century. In principle each person was to be assessed on each category of wealth, but only paid tax on the category which produced the highest tax charge. In practice, however, the rates of tax payable on each category were always set so that only those with very large incomes from lands or fees would pay tax under that head. For the rest of the population the tax payable on moveable possessions would normally amount to the greater sum, and it is not at all surprising that the overwhelming majority of Tudor tax payments were in fact based on assessments of the value of moveable goods.[28]

In the absence of any permanent bureaucracy the administration of the subsidies was entrusted to county commissioners, who were appointed afresh under letters patent each time a subsidy was levied. In practice the commissioners, who were drawn from the same social stratum as the justices of the peace, subdivided the county so that responsibility for the implementation of the subsidy acts rested with the social leaders of each locality. The commissioners were responsible for appointing assessors and collectors, for supervising the accuracy of the assessments, and for certifying to the exchequer the assessments and the individual sums to be collected so that the collectors could be called to account.[29]

The assessors were to be two or more local inhabitants or officers, who were to be charged on oath to

... truely inquire ... of the best and most value and substaunce of every persone ... wythout concelment favor love affeccion dred fere and malice.[30]

The commissioners were to scrutinise the valuations made by the assessors and amend them as they thought fit. To this end they were empowered both to interrogate the assessors and to summon individuals to be examined on oath

[27] For example, in Lavenham, Suffolk, 35 rich taxpayers contributed about £170, and 164 poorer taxpayers contributed only £9. Sheail, 'Distribution of taxable population and wealth', p. 121.

[28] In 1525 in the hundred of Earsham, Norfolk, of those not assessed on wages, only 8 per cent of taxpayers were assessed on annual incomes and 92 per cent on goods. Assuming a net yield of 5 per cent from land (20-years' purchase), the tax rates in force for most subsidies meant that only those with lands worth more than 13 times the value of their moveable goods would have had an income high enough to be taxed under that head.

[29] For a fuller discussion of the appointment of commissioners and their responsibilities, see Schofield, 'PLT', pp. 219–38. Being nominated a commissioner brought power and prestige, and members of the county elite tried to ensure that they were included on the subsidy commission. See, for example, I. H. Jeayes, ed., *The Letters of Philip Gawdy of West Harling, Norfolk 1579–1616* (London, 1906), pp. 82, 89, 93–4, 116, 125–6.

[30] The quotation is from the act for the subsidy of 1516, 6 Henry VIII, c. 26, s. 6.

about their wealth. An individual also had the right to appear before the commissioners to challenge an assessment on oath. The commissioners' decision was final; the tax charges on the assessment that they certified to the exchequer, and copied to the collectors, had to be paid.[31]

The Tudor subsidies, therefore, were intended to reflect the current value of the wealth of every adult whether in the form of incomes or moveable goods, and responsibility for ensuring that this was the case rested squarely on the shoulders of the commissioners. So wide-ranging and complex a form of taxation posed a severe challenge to the Tudor polity. Could that society, in which literacy was far from universal, mobilise sufficient administrative skills to ensure the efficient assessment and collection of taxes from hundreds of thousands of taxpayers scattered throughout the realm?[32] And was there sufficient political commitment to the national interest amongst the leading social classes, from whose ranks the commissioners were drawn, to ensure that the assessments certified to the exchequer really were based on the true substance and value of every taxpayer?

The first of these questions can be answered clearly in the affirmative. The exchequer records contain thousands of lists of individual assessments, and hundreds of particulars of account, which constitute impressive testimony of the ability of Tudor society to administer the assessment and collection of taxes on a massive scale.[33] Moreover, in the early Tudor period at least, despite delays of several months beyond the final date for the collection of the taxes, all but an insignificant fraction of the sum due for each subsidy was ultimately paid to the crown.[34] In principle the crown should have been able to enforce prompt payment through the writs of distraint and attachment against the collectors that were issued by the exchequer. But in practice, at least in the early Tudor period, the sheriffs often protected the collectors by failing to distrain their goods or arrest them, claiming that they were indigent and not to be found. Although the enforcement of the collection of the subsidies was

---

[31] For further details of the theory and practice of assessment and collection of the subsidies, see Schofield, 'PLT', pp. 238–308. For two rare surviving examples of local assessment documents, see Bodleian Library, Henley Borough Records, A XIII, 3 (draft assessment list, probably 1545); North (Wroxton) MSS, a 1, fos. 28ᵛ–37ʳ (commissioners' notes, Cambs, 1549).

[32] D. Cressy, *Literacy and the Social Order: Reading and Writing in Tudor and Stuart England* (Cambridge, 1980), especially pp. 157–67, 176–7.

[33] Local assessment documents can be found primarily in class E 179, and particulars of account in class E 101, at the PRO.

[34] The proportions of the tax due that were unpaid were usually under 1 per cent. Schofield, 'PLT', pp. 429–30, and table 40, facing p. 416. Before 1540 less than 10 per cent of the tax due reached the exchequer before the statutory payment date, a third within a month, three-quarters within 6 months, and almost all within a year. Taxes were collected much quicker in the mid-1540s. Schofield, 'PLT', table 41, facing p. 432. From scattered evidence it would appear that a similarly brisk pace was still being achieved in 1558; but that in the 1580s the delays in payment were about the same as had been the case before 1540. PRO, SP 11/13, fos. 112–13; SP 12/150, no. 68; SP 12/185, no. 31.

effective in the end, local loyalties and collusion between collectors and sheriffs could make that enforcement a long drawn-out process.[35]

How far the provisions of the subsidy acts concerning assessment were enforced is more problematical. On this issue the Tudor subsidies have certainly had a bad press, for historians have had little difficulty in finding contemporary comments alleging substantial, and widespread, undervaluation.[36] Perhaps the most celebrated example is Sir Walter Raleigh's statement in the 1601 parliament that 'our estates that be 30l or 40l in the Queen's Books, are not the hundred part of our wealth'.[37] However, almost all of the comments in this genre date from the second half of the reign of Elizabeth; it is much more difficult to find contemporary allegations of serious undervaluation earlier in the Tudor period, though it is true that the period lacks the detailed records of parliamentary debates, which provided so much of the later evidence of publicly acknowledged undervaluation.[38] Apart from an improbable allegation by the French ambassador in 1541,[39] there are two indications of official suspicion of undervaluation earlier in the century: remarks to this effect in Cromwell's remembrances in connection with the subsidies of 1535–6,[40] and Wolsey's threat in 1516 that the mayor and aldermen of London were 'to be sworn of and vppon the true value of their substaunce within the sum of C markes'.[41]

The most systematic continuing source of comment on the adequacy of the subsidy assessments in the period is the correspondence from the crown, or privy council, to the subsidy commissioners, of which several examples have survived, beginning in 1524. In that year, after the individual assessments had been received in the exchequer, the crown informed the commissioners in some parts of the country that in some cases the individual assessments appeared to have been made erroneously 'partely by inadvertance and

---

[35] For a detailed discussion of the nature and efficacy of exchequer writs and processes against individuals, collectors and sheriffs in the early Tudor period, see Schofield, 'PLT', pp. 450–62.

[36] For a recent example, see Palliser, *Age of Elizabeth*, pp. 109–10.

[37] S. d'Ewes, *The Journals of all the Parliaments During the Reign of Queen Elizabeth* (London, 1682), p. 633; facsimile reprint (Shannon, 1973).

[38] D'Ewes also reports that Mildmay admitted in the 1576 parliament that under-assessment was common. Ibid, p. 246. By 1587 Mildmay was claiming in parliament that the assessment practice was so lax that 'not the sixth part of that which is given ... doth come to her Majesty's coffers'. Parliamentary diary cited in Neale, *Elizabeth and her Parliaments*, II, p. 168. Undervaluation was frequently mentioned in the debates on the subsidy in the 1593 and 1601 parliaments. D'Ewes, *Journals*, pp. 477–94, 629–33.

[39] Marillac reported that the subsidy commissioners for London were accused of disobeying royal commands by making assessments that were too low, and were threatened by punishment as traitors. Whereupon the mayor and magistrates allegedly begged for mercy and promised to pay at double rates. *LP*, xvi 223.

[40] 'Concernyng the Subsidy with the remedy for the deceit used therein'. *LP* xiii (1) 187.

[41] Corporation of London RO, Repertory, III, fo. 116.

misexposicion of the said act and partely percaas by favour', and instructed the commissioners to revise them.[42]

Thereafter, correspondence was usually confined to letters accompanying the subsidy commission, in which the crown encouraged the commissioners to be diligent in discharging their duties. It was only in the late 1550s that these letters show that the crown was aware of serious and systematic undervaluation, and evidently suspected that the rot was beginning at the top.[43] Writing in 1558 to the subsidy commissioners the queen enjoined them first to assess themselves

. . . according to the juste valewe of your landes or goodes with out the whiche ye cannot haue auctorie [sic] to call earnestly vpon others to do the same.[44]

In a parallel letter to an inner group of trusted commissioners of exceptionally high status the queen admitted that the assessments of commissioners had been 'farre vnder the Some of that they all knowe you have whiche wee haue heretofore felt to our grete losse'.[45]

During Elizabeth's reign the privy council continued to reproach the commissioners for favouring themselves and their friends, and accused them of a growing catalogue of malpractices, all of which undermined the accuracy of the assessments and the yield of the subsidies to the crown. In 1576 the council accused the commissioners of conniving in a general bias in the assessments in favour of the rich whereby

. . . heretofore persons of very great possessions and wealthe haue ben assessed at very meane sommes, and persons of the meaner sorte haue ben enhanced to paye after the vttermost value of their substance. . .[46]

In 1593 this accusation was made publicly by the lord keeper in an address to parliament, in which he claimed that the queen herself attributed the low yield of the subsidy to the fact that

. . . the wealthier sort of men turn this charge upon the weaker, and upon those of worst ability, for that one dischargeth himself, and the other is not able to satisfie what he is charged withal.[47]

By 1589 the council had apparently abandoned the notion that the assess-

---

[42] From a signet letter to the commissioners for Wiltshire, dated 26 February 1524. PRO, SP 1/30, fo. 141. For an example of a certificate containing revised assessments, dated 26 May 1524, see PRO, E 1789/133/117.

[43] For examples of earlier letters from the crown to commissioners with no mention of undervaluation see Guildford M[uniment] R[oom], Loseley MSS, 1484 (1541): Bodleian, North (Wroxton) MSS, a 1, fos. 27ᵛ–28ʳ (1549).

[44] Guildford MR, Loseley MSS, 1488/1. Copies of the text can be found in PRO, SP 12/4, fos. 96–97ᵛ, and in BL, Add. MSS 48018, fo. 151 (Beale's precedent book).

[45] Guildford MR, Loseley MSS 1488/2; PRO, SP 12/4, fos. 98–9ᵛ; BL, Add. MSS 48018, fo. 151.

[46] SP 12/107, fo. 97–8ᵛ.   [47] D'Ewes, *Journals*, p. 458.

ments should be realistic valuations of the wealth of individual taxpayers, assuring the commissioners that

... although we meane not herby to have anie men of wealth assessed comparablie to their livinges, but with some mediocrity according to their callinges.[48]

By 1601 the extent of the retreat from any expectation that the assessment provisions of the subsidy acts would be implemented was painfully clear:

... for allthoughe her Majestie dothe not expect from yow that accordinge to the purporte of this guifte and graunte from the high Courte of Parliament all men shalbe taxed at their iust and true valewes eiether of their landes or goodes nevertheles ... there ought good regard to be had to assess men in some farr better proporcion then heretofore hathe bene done.[49]

Indeed by the 1590s the degree of undervaluation had become so notorious that the council was reduced to attempting to ensure that justices of the peace were at least assessed at the minimum statutory qualification for office ($£20$ income from lands) by threatening to put anyone assessed at a lower sum out of the commission.[50] Finally, in 1598 the privy council complained of a further abuse, namely that in some parishes a few poor persons were assessed 'and the whole paryshe dothe contrybute to the payment of the same'.[51] Forty years later this was described as normal assessment practice in a Yorkshire village.[52]

Thus the council's correspondence with the commissioners confirms the allegations of contemporary commentators that substantial undervaluation was rife in the later years of Elizabeth's reign. If these sources can be taken at face value, undervaluation would appear to have been unremarkable earlier in the Tudor period, and only to have become sufficiently serious to be worthy of comment some time in the middle of the century. However, arguments *ex silentio* are notoriously unsafe; a proper answer to the question of the adequacy of the enforcement of the assessment clauses in the Tudor subsidy acts requires a direct check of the accuracy of the subsidy assessments against independent valuations of taxpayers' wealth.

Helen Miller has already made such a check for the peerage.[53] Peers were assessed on a national basis by a special commission, so their assessments should not have been affected by the undervaluation arising from the local

[48] *A[cts of the] P[rivy] C[ouncil]*, XVII, pp. 423–5.
[49] From a letter from the privy council to the Northants. subsidy commissioners in December 1601, transcribed in J. Wake, ed., *Musters, Beacons, Subsidies, etc. in the County of Northampton, A.D. 1586–1623* (Northampton Record Society, III, 1926), pp. 81–3.
[50] Letter from the privy council to the subsidy commissioners, 9 July 1593. *APC*, XXIV, p. 378. On 2 December 1593 the privy council wrote to the lord keeper instructing him to put out of the commission of the peace all who refused to be assessed at $£20$ in annual incomes. *APC*, XXIV, p. 514. [51] *APC*, XXVIII, pp. 625–7.
[52] *Rural economy in Yorkshire in 1641, being the farming and account books of Henry Best of Elmswold in the East Riding in the county of York* (Surtees Society, 33, 1887), pp. 186–9.
[53] Helen Miller, 'Subsidy assessments of the peerage in the sixteenth century', *Bulletin of the Institute of Historical Research*, 28 (1955), 15–34.

collusion amongst the commissioners complained of by the crown and privy council. Yet despite substantial inflation, the average assessment of the peers fell from £800–900 in Henry VIII's reign to reach about £300 in the late 1580s, at which level it remained for the rest of Elizabeth's reign.[54] A significant feature of this decline was a drastic reduction in the assessments of the richest peers: in Henry VIII's reign the highest annual incomes were about £3000, while from the 1580s they were a little over £1000. Indeed from the late 1580s only two peers were assessed at more than £1000 (only one from 1593), yet almost a third of the peers were assessed at this level in the years before 1560.[55]

The annual incomes of the peers, therefore, would seem to have been ludicrously undervalued in the later sixteenth century, and this inference is confirmed in those cases in which the subsidy assessments can be compared with independent evidence. For example, the earl of Oxford was independently estimated as worth £12,000 per annum in the 1570s, yet he was assessed at £1000 in the subsidies of 1571 and 1576, £200 in 1581 and £100 thereafter.[56] On the other hand, when the subsidy assessments of the peers made in the reign of Henry VIII were checked against independent evidence, they were found to be reasonably accurate.[57] In the case of the peerage, therefore, there appears to have been a marked decline in the rigour with which the clauses of the subsidy acts regarding assessment were enforced. But the peerage constituted a very small minority of taxpayers, subject to special assessment procedures. Before we can make any general statements about the enforcement of the subsidy acts, we need to discover whether other taxpayers were also tolerably accurately assessed in Henry VIII's reign, and whether they too succeeded in getting their assessments reduced to a fraction of their true worth by the final decades of the century.

In order to test the accuracy of the subsidy assessments, we need to find independent valuations of individuals' incomes, or wealth. For the comparison to be fair, the independent valuations should have been made within a short period of time of the subsidy assessments, and they should provide sufficient detail to enable a comparable tax assessment to be made, taking account of the assessment rules in the subsidy acts. For example, the tax on annual incomes was on the 'clear yearly value', so charges such as management expenses, annuities payable to others, and the wages of deputies in office need to be identified and excluded.[58] And in the case of goods, items such as

---

[54] Ibid, 18.   [55] Ibid.   [56] Ibid, 24, n. 1.

[57] Ibid, 24–31. Despite finding two cases of under-assessment 'on a considerable scale', Miller concludes 'it seems clear that subsidy assessments of the peerage in the reign of Henry VIII were more than mere formal assessments; that considerable efforts were made by the subsidy commissioners to reach a genuine assessment; and that on the whole they were not unsuccessful.' Ibid, 30–1.

[58] Although after 1540 the subsidy acts no longer specified 'clear' yearly values, it seems likely that it was standard sixteenth-century practice in assessing annual incomes to take net, rather than gross, values. Schofield, 'PLT', pp. 238–41.

personal clothing and debts owed by the taxpayer were exempt and thus need to be identified, so that the valuation can be adjusted accordingly.[59] These are demanding conditions; but two sources were found which, though far from ideal, provided information in sufficient detail to enable a comparison with the subsidy assessments to be made. They were the engrossed feodaries' surveys kept by the court of wards and liveries, for annual incomes; and probate inventories, for moveable goods.

The feodaries' surveys contain valuations of all the estates of persons dying seized of any parcel of land held by knight service in chief of the crown, and the engrossed accounts consolidate valuations from several counties as a matter of convenient record for the court.[60] The documents not only list the income yields of the estates, but note enfeoffments to use, as well as annuities and other charges on the revenues. Although the surveys cover landed income in exceptional detail, the values contained in the surveys are not necessarily correct. In principle the feodaries were supposed to make an independent, and more realistic, valuation of lands than the suspiciously low figures certified by the escheators, but it is far from clear how far they achieved that aim.[61] Moreover, since the feodaries confined their attention to lands, omitting incomes from other sources such as fees and offices, their surveys do not provide a full record of the clear yearly value of the annual incomes of the deceased. Thus in comparing the subsidy assessments with the feodaries' surveys it is important to bear in mind that although the latter offer an independent estimate of annual incomes, the information they provide is both stylised and incomplete.

The books of engrossed surveys were searched for individuals who had died a reasonable interval after being assessed for a subsidy, and whose assessment had survived amongst the records of the exchequer. Forty-nine cases were found spanning the years 1524 to 1560.[62] In ten cases the feodaries' surveys produced clear yearly values which were less than the subsidy assessments. Since this outcome probably indicates that the individuals concerned had substantial incomes from sources other than land, these cases have been disregarded. Amongst the remaining thirty-nine cases, which included four

---

[59] The categories of goods liable to assessment are discussed in Schofield, 'PLT', pp. 241–3.

[60] For a discussion of the jurisdiction of the courts of wards and liveries and of the activities of the feodaries, see H. E. Bell, *An Introduction to the History and Records of the Courts of Wards and Liveries* (Cambridge, 1953), especially pp. 1–4, 40–2, 54–6, 76–9. The engrossed accounts are in PRO, Wards 9.

[61] In a few cases where it is possible to compare the valuations returned by the feodaries and escheators for the same estate, Bell finds that at the end of Elizabeth's reign the feodaries' valuations were 5–25 per cent higher than those of the escheators. *Courts of Wards and Liveries*, pp. 56. However, Smith finds little to choose between the valuations of the two officials in the West Riding in the period 1520–79. *Land and Politics*, pp. 274–5.

[62] The feodaries' valuations were taken from PRO, Wards 9/129, 131, 135, 137–8, 579; and matching subsidy assessments from PRO, E 179.

knights and three peers, a clear pattern emerged. First, amongst the thirty-three cases dating from Henry VIII's reign the subsidy assessments showed no tendency towards any greater or lesser accuracy during the course of the reign: at all dates they were spread fairly evenly across a range of between forty-seven and ninety-six per cent of the landed income as assessed by the feodaries.[63] On average the subsidy assessments of these rich landowners were about two-thirds (68 per cent) of the independent valuations. In principle the absence of any information in the feodaries' surveys about annual incomes from sources other than land results in too low a target valuation, and so gives the subsidy assessments an unfair advantage in the comparison. In practice, however, this is unlikely to have been a serious source of error, since for most members of the social class investigated here land provided the overwhelming bulk of annual incomes assessable under the subsidy acts. In Henry VIII's reign, therefore, the subsidy assessments on annual incomes would appear to have been tolerably realistic, a far cry from the openly acknowledged farce they had become towards the end of Elizabeth's reign.

Second, among the remaining six cases dating from the years 1556 to 1560, the level of assessment was clearly inferior, ranging from 25 to 51 per cent of the independent valuations.[64] The average subsidy assessment was only 38 per cent of the survey valuation, much lower than the 68 per cent achieved under Henry VIII. Although six cases may appear to be rather few on which to base any conclusion, the contrast with the thirty-three Henrician cases is so great that the quality of assessment may be presumed to have worsened markedly after Henry VIII's death.[65]

Fortunately, the independent valuations of taxpayers' goods contained in the probate inventories have survived in greater numbers, and so provide a better basis for investigating changes in the accuracy of assessment over time. Inventories of the goods of deceased persons were required by canon law, and by the statute of 21 Henry VIII c. 5, as a safeguard against fraud on the part of executors and administrators.[66] Moreover, it was in the interests of the latter to have the inventory made because their liability to meet the legacies and debts of the deceased was limited to the value of the inventory.[67] However, by the same token, it was in the interest of executors and administrators to obtain

---

[63] Except for two cases in the mid-1540s in which the subsidy assessments were 29 and 30 per cent of the feodaries' valuations, respectively.

[64] The subsidies levied between 1549 and 1552 were assessed only on goods. See table 2.

[65] The probability that the difference between the distributions of the individual results obtained in the two periods could have arisen merely by chance is less than 1 in 50 (2 per cent). A Kolmogorov-Smirnov, two-sample, 1-tailed test with chi-square approximation yielded a value of p between 0.01 and 0.02. This test is clearly explained in S. Siegel, *Nonparametric Statistics for the Behavioral Sciences* (Tokyo, 1956), pp. 127–36.

[66] Sixteenth-century canon and statute law on the subject is conveniently summarised in H. Swinburne, *Brief Treatise of Testamentes and Last Willes* (London, 1590), fos. 217^v–221^r.

[67] Ibid, fos. 220^v–221^r.

as low a valuation as possible; and it was to prevent this that 21 Henry VIII c. 5, s. 2 required them to make the inventory in the presence of at least two creditors or beneficiaries of the estate, if any, otherwise in the presence of two honest persons, preferably next-of-kin. According to this section of the act the inventory was to contain 'all the goodes catells wares marchaundyses as well movable as nott movable whatsoever' of the deceased. Furthermore, the church courts required the goods of the deceased to

be particularly valued and praised by some honest and skilfull persons, to be the iust value thereof in their iudgements and consciences, that is to say, at such price as the same may be solde for at that time.[68]

In principle, therefore, probate inventories should provide a fair valuation of a person's goods in current prices. The position with regard to debts was more complicated: canon law required debts owing to the deceased to be included in the inventory, but not debts owed by the deceased. However, it was in the interests of executors or administrators to include them, since that registered a debt on the estate and limited their liability.[69] Provided the inventories specify all debts, and provided they give enough detail for tax-exempt categories such as personal clothing, and non-moveable goods such as crops in the fields, to be indentified, they would appear to furnish a basis for comparison with the subsidy assessments on moveable goods.

There can, of course, be no guarantee either that inventories were complete or that the valuations were realistic. While some inventories were immensely detailed, others, generally those of poor people, were summary in the extreme. There is little evidence on the reliability of the valuations, though it is encouraging that an investigation of probate values of grain in East Anglian inventories in the period 1660–1735 found that they were only fifteen per cent below current market prices, and fluctuated closely in sympathy with them.[70] As in the case of the feodaries' surveys, it must be remembered that the subsidy assessments are being compared with valuations which are independent, but not necessarily accurate.

A search was made of diocesan record offices to locate all inventories made a few months after a subsidy assessment, and for which there was a matching subsidy assessment for the individual concerned amongst the records of the exchequer. The search was confined to the period before 1575, and the conditions of access prevailing in the archives at the time of the search, together with the ravages of time since the sixteenth century, combined to limit both the temporal and the geographical coverage of the investigation.[71]

[68] Ibid, fo. 220^r.
[69] Ibid, fo. 218^v.
[70] M. Overton, 'Estimating crop yields from probate inventories: an example from East Anglia', 1585–1735', Journal of Economic History, 39 (1979), 373.
[71] The data were collected in 1963–6.

In the event only 580 cases could be found in which a direct comparison could be made between a probate valuation and a recent subsidy assessment.[72]

The data are drawn from twenty-one counties and cover the period from 1524 to 1578. However, as table 3 shows, the cases are very unevenly distributed across time and space. Only twenty cases were available before 1543, compared with 307 for the last five years of Henry VIII's reign, 121 for Edward and Mary, and 132 for the first half of Elizabeth's reign. Lincolnshire provides almost a third of all the cases, and Warwickshire and Worcestershire a further third.

Table 3. *Probate inventory/subsidy assessment comparisons: number of cases by area and period*[1]

	Period							
Area	1524–42	1543–5	1546–7	1549–56	1559–68	1571–2	Total	(%)
Yorks(13)/Lancs(7)	2	5	3	4	*1*	5	20	(3)
Staffs(46)/Salop(10)	6	22	17	9	*1*	*1*	56	(10)
Derbs(32)/Notts(3)	*0*	21	5	6	*0*	3	35	(60)
Lincs	8	**77**	**45**	*18*	8	**28**	184	(32)
Leics(33)/Rutland(1)/ Cambs(2) Suffolk(2) Essex(1)	2	12	11	5	*1*	8	39	(7)
Warwks(79)/Worcs(35)	*0*	**38**	28	17	**16**	15	114	(20)
Berks(43)/Wilts(8)/ Bucks(2)	2	*2*	16	15	13	5	53	(9)
Hants	*0*	*0*	5	**47**	*0*	**27**	79	(14)
All	20	177	130	121	40	92	580	(100)
(%)	(3)	(31)	(22)	(21)	(7)	(16)	(100)	

Note

1 Figures which are less than half the frequency that would be expected with a uniform distribution across time and space are printed in *italic* type; figures which are more than double the expected frequency are printed in **bold** type.

Sources
Subsidy assessments: PRO, E 179.
Probate inventories, loose or filed with original wills and administrations, usually unnumbered, from the following repositories and courts:
Yorks   Borthwick Institute, York: Dean and Chapter of York; Dean of York.
Leeds City Libraries Dept: Archdeaconry of Richmond (Eastern Deaneries).

---

[72] In a further 683 cases there was no entry in the subsidy assessment list for the vill of residence of an individual whose probate inventory had been recovered. Because it is uncertain whether the individuals concerned were absent from the vill, or were present and assessed at a figure below the exemption limit, these cases were omitted from the main investigation. The analysis was repeated including them with the subsidy assessments arbitrarily set to 10 shillings below the appropriate exemption limits. The results were close to those of the main investigation, and the few differences of any consequence will be reported below.

Notes to Table 3 (*cont.*)

Lancs — Lancashire County RO, Preston: Chester Consistory; Archdeaconry of Richmond (Western Deaneries).

Salop
Staffs } Lichfield Joint RO: Lichfield Consistory.
Derbs

Notts — P. A. Kennedy, ed., *Nottinghamshire Household Inventories* (Thoroton Society Record Series, XXII, 1962).

Lincs — Lincolnshire Archives Office, Lincoln: Lincoln Consistory.

Leics — Leicestershire County RO: Archdeaconry of Leicester.

Rutland } PRO: Prerogative Court of
Essex } Canterbury.

Cambs — University Library, Cambridge: Chancellor of Cambridge University.

Suffolk — Suffolk RO, Ipswich: Archdeaconry of Suffolk.

Warwks } Worcestershire County RO: Worcester Consistory.
Worcs

Berks — Bodleian Library, Oxford: Archdeaconry of Berks.

Wilts — Wiltshire County RO, Trowbridge: Archdeaconry of Sarum.

Bucks — Buckinghamshire County RO, Aylesbury: Archdeaconry of Buckingham.

Hants — Hampshire County RO, Winchester: Winchester Consistory, and unclassified wills.

These counties, together with Staffordshire, Derbyshire, Leicestershire, Berkshire and Hampshire contribute 531 (92 per cent) of the cases. The remaining 49 come from a further 13, mainly neighbouring, counties; consequently, large tracts of the country are entirely unrepresented. One reason why only 580 cases could be found is that inventories were accepted only if the appraisal was within a reasonable time of the subsidy assessment. In the event, the average interval between the two valuations was 4.8 months; in a quarter of the cases it was under 4 months, and in three-quarters less than 7 months (see table 4).[73]

A comparison of probate valuations and subsidy assessments on the scale attempted here is bound to be subject to some error. First, the documents were linked on the basis of matching names, and in the case of common names it is possible that documents relating to two separate individuals have been improperly linked and compared.[74] Second, the fact that the two valuations were not drawn up at the same time, means that some of the discrepancies in wealth may have been genuine, though we may well be suspicious if the subsidy valuation is always the lower of the two. Third, the summary nature of some of the inventories, and the uncertainty over the degree to which they reveal the true debt position of individuals, will in some cases have defeated the attempt to apply the subsidy assessment rules to the information on wealth

---

[73] In a few cases in which the date of the subsidy assessment was missing, the interval was arbitrarily set to the average figure.

[74] If two individuals were found with the same name in the subsidy assessment, even if in adjacent vills, the case was discarded.

Table 4. *Intervals between subsidy assessments and probate valuations*

Months	No.	Per cent	Cumulative per cent
Under 1	22	3.8	3.8
1	40	6.9	10.7
2	46	7.9	18.6
3	59	10.2	28.8
4	146	25.2	54.0
5	54	9.3	63.3
6	67	11.6	74.8
7	55	9.5	84.3
8	35	6.0	90.3
9	24	4.1	94.5
10	15	2.6	97.1
11	17	2.9	100.0
Total	580	100.0	

Sources: see table 3.

contained in the inventory.[75] Thus a comparison of the valuations in the two sets of documents can only be an approximate exercise. But so too must have been the original subsidy assessments, for it is unlikely that the assessors would have had either the time, or the courage, to make a full visual appraisal of everyone's moveable possessions, as at the making of a probate inventory, and some items, such as debts, would have been invisible to them.

In the circumstances, therefore, it is scarcely surprising that the outcome of the comparison is that the subsidy assessments on goods comprised a much lower percentage of the probate valuations than did the assessments on lands of the valuations in the feodaries' surveys. Even after deducting from the inventories those items which were not liable to be taxed, notably personal clothing and crops in the field, the subsidy assessments averaged only 30 per cent of the probate valuations, compared to the overall figure of 63 per cent for annual incomes. This result may partly reflect the greater difficulty in making a fair comparison between the sources in the case of moveable goods, but it is likely that the task of assessing annual incomes was intrinsically less prone to error. A high proportion of annual income was derived from land, and since land was visible and its value per acre usually a matter of local knowledge, the

---

[75] Debts were sometimes noted on the will rather than on the inventory. Unfortunately many inventories lacked an accompanying will. Two further problems are the variable degree with which apparel was specified in the inventories, and the seasonal cycle of crops. Where the subsidy assessment was before the harvest and the probate valuation after it, crops in the barn were deducted. However, when both valuations were after the harvest no correction was made for the consumption of crops in the intervening interval.

subsidy assessors would probably have been able to make a reasonable estimate of its net annual value.

Although on average the subsidy assessments amounted to only 30 per cent of the matching probate valuation, there is a considerable variation around this figure with individual subsidy assessments ranging from 2 to 100 per cent of the probate valuations. Table 5 shows that most of the subsidy assessments (nearly 60 per cent) lay in a range of 10 to 40 per cent of the probate valuations. However, 17 per cent of the assessments were apparently highly deficient, at less than 10 per cent of the matching probate valuation, while at the other extreme 16 per cent of the assessments amounted to between 50 and 100 per cent of the probate valuations.

Was this variation from case to case wholly fortuitous, reflecting individual circumstances which we can no longer recover? Or do the data contain patterns of variation which will enable us to identify the factors which were systematically associated with the accuracy of assessment under the subsidy acts? There are six factors whose influence on the accuracy of the assessments can be tested on the data. First there are two factors which may have intervened to complicate the comparison between the probate valuations and the subsidy assessments. They are variations in the interval of time that elapsed between the valuation and the assessment, and variations in the complexity and visibility of the wealth to be assessed. A second pair of factors relate to aspects of the assessment process. Since the number of individuals eligible for assessment varied considerably from subsidy to subsidy according to the minimum exemption limits in force, we can use variations in the latter to investigate whether the accuracy of the assessments was affected by the magnitude of the administrative burden imposed on the assessors and the commissioners. We can also take into account the wealth of the taxpayers to test whether the commissioners were guilty of systematically favouring the rich with more lenient assessments than they allowed the poor, as alleged by the Elizabethan privy council. Finally, we can examine whether there were any systematic variations in the patterns of underassessment over time or across space. Did the commissioners in some parts of the country consistently implement the subsidy acts with greater rigour than their counterparts elsewhere? And did the accuracy of the subsidy assessment of moveable goods decline substantially during the Tudor period, as was the case with assessments of annual incomes?

Since there are several possible factors which could have influenced the accuracy of each subsidy assessment, we shall need to find a way of estimating the relative importance of each factor net of the effect of the others. This is important, because some of the factors are interconnected in ways which make it difficult to disentangle their separate effects, and which may lead us into drawing false conclusions. For example, table 3 shows that the geographical distribution of the data for some of the subsidies, notably those levied before

Table 5. *Subsidy assessments as percentage of probate valuations*

Percentage of probate valuation	No.	Per cent of cases
Under 10	96	16.6
10–9	155	26.7
20–9	121	20.9
30–9	69	11.9
40–9	44	7.6
50–9	29	5.0
60–9	21	3.6
70–9	10	1.7
80–9	11	1.9
90–9	4	0.7
100–	20	3.4
Total	580	100.0

Sources: see table 3.

1543 and between 1559 and 1568, was most unusual. Conversely, the data for some of the areas, notably Hampshire and Staffordshire/Salop, were drawn far more heavily from some periods than others. If we were simply to tabulate the accuracy of the assessments by period, we would not know whether any patterns we found reflected genuine changes over time, or whether they were spurious, having been produced by changes in the mix of areas, which themselves differed in the accuracy of the assessments. And if we were to tabulate by area, we should be in the same dilemma: the geographical patterns might be genuine, or merely reflect the fact that the data for each area were drawn unevenly from time periods which differed in the accuracy of the assessments.

Thus, in seeking to explain the variation in the accuracy of the subsidy assessments we need to find a form of analysis which takes account of the interconnections between the various explanatory factors, such as time–period and area, and corrects for the unavoidable unevenness in the historical data. There are several ways of achieving this result by statistical methods, and table 6 reports the results of a technique known as multiple classification analysis.[76] This form of analysis estimates the magnitude of the *independent* influence of each of the six explanatory factors outlined above, eliminating the

---

[76] Expressed formally, the problem is one of multivariate analysis of variance with unbalanced data. The analysis was performed using the ANOVA procedure in the SSPSX statistical package with option 3 (main effects only). *SPSSX Users' Guide* (Chicago, 1983), pp. 439–50. The analysis was replicated using the procedure GLM with statements MEANS and LSMEANS, in the SAS statistical package, and similar results were obtained. *SAS Users' Guide: Statistics* (Cary, NC, 1982), pp. 139–204.

Table 6. *Independent net effects of six factors on the accuracy of subsidy assessments*[1]

Factor	No. of cases (1)	Percent of probate valuation (2)	Deviation from mean (29.7 %) (3)	Beta (4)
Complexity of Wealth[2]				0.03
0–4	204	28.9	−0.8	
5–14	177	29.8	0.1	
15–	199	29.0	0.7	
Interval (subsidy–probate)				0.05
0–2 months	108	27.7	−2.0	
3–5 months	259	29.6	−0.13	
6–8 months	157	28.0	1.7	
9–11 months	56	29.0	−0.7	
Region				0.13*
Yorks/Lancs	20	33.3	3.6	
Salop/Staffs	56	23.6	−6.1	
Derbs/Notts	35	22.8	−6.9	
Lincs	184	30.1	0.4	
Leics etc.[3]	39	31.0	1.3	
Warw/Worcs	114	29.4	0.3	
Berks/Bucks/Wilts	53	32.1	2.4	
Hants	79	32.4	2.7	
Exemption limit				0.18
£1–2	179	25.1	−4.6	
£3	108	28.0	−1.7	
£5	155	30.1	0.4	
£10	138	36.5	6.8	
Period				0.24**
1524–42	20	48.7	19.0	
1543–45	177	33.1	3.4	
1546–47	130	32.2	2.5	
1549–57	121	27.6	−2.1	
1559–68	40	21.2	−8.5	
1571–72	92	22.1	−7.6	
Net Wealth				0.66**
£0–9	83	59.0	29.3	
£10–9	99	39.4	9.7	
£20–9	76	35.4	5.7	
£30–59	122	23.7	−6.0	
£60–99	138	16.2	−13.5	
£100–	62	9.9	−19.8	
Multiple R^2	0.48			

1 Adjusted for the effects of other factors.
2 Percentage of wealth in probate valuation exempt from assessment to the subsidy.
3 Includes Rutland (1), Cambs (2), Suffolk (2), Essex (1).
 * statistically significant at the 5 per cent level.
** statistically significant at the 1 per cent level.
Sources: see tables 2 and 3.

effects of any interconnections between them which otherwise would improperly distort the results.[77]

Each has been divided into a number of categories, for example, 'Region' comprises eight groups of counties, and six time periods are distinguished. The table shows for each category of each factor the number of cases (column 1), the percentage of the probate valuation which the subsidy assessments in that category on average attained (column 2), and the amount by which the figure for that category deviated above, or below, the overall mean figure of 29.7 per cent (column 3). If the accuracy of the subsidy assessment were strongly associated with a particular factor, we should find marked and systematic differences in the deviations for each category within the factor. For example, a decline in the accuracy of the assessments over time would appear in the table as a regular progression from large positive deviations above the average in the early periods to large negative deviations in the later period. Small or disorderly differences between the deviations for each category indicate that the factor is not systematically related to the variation in the accuracy of the subsidy assessments. The coherence of the relationship is measured formally by calculating the statistical significance of the effect of each factor, and the results are indicated by means of asterisks attached to the figures in the final column of the table, labelled 'beta'. Factors without asterisks are unlikely to be systematically related to variations in the accuracy of the subsidy assessments. The beta figures themselves are summary measures of the relative importance of each factor in accounting for the variation in the accuracy of the subsidy assessments.[78] The factors have been listed in the table in ascending order of importance and it is immediately

[77] This can only be achieved if each of the factors has the same proportional effect across the full range of values of the other factors. Where this is not so, as, for example, would be the case if the effect of region were not constant over time, the factors are said to 'interact' to produce a 'crossed effect' over and above the simple combination of their independent effects. If this occurs, it is impossible to estimate the independent effect of each factor net of the effects of the others. Tests were made for interactions between the factors using the more efficient GLM procedure in SAS (see previous note). No statistically significant crossed effects were found.

[78] More formally, beta is a standardised regression co-efficient in the sense used in multiple regression. It should be noted that the unequal numbers of cases in the different categories in the table means that the squares of the betas do not measure directly the proportion of the variance accounted for by each factor, and so do not sum to the R^2 figure given at the foot of the table. However the beta figures do properly represent the *proportional* differences in the degree to which the various factors account for the variance in the data.

apparent from their very low beta values that the first two factors, namely the complexity of wealth being valued and the interval between the two valuation dates, had no systematic influence on the accuracy of the assessments. While each of the remaining four factors included in the analysis appears to have been associated in a consistent manner with variations in the accuracy of the subsidy assessments, in the case of the next two factors listed in the table there is some doubt about the strength of the association.

Both the latter factors, the geographical region where the assessment was made and the level of the exemption limit in force, have respectable beta scores (0.13 and 0.18, respectively), and the figures in column 3 of the table show a coherent pattern of systematic deviations from the average for the accuracy of assessment associated with the various categories of each factor. It would seem that subsidy assessments were made a little more realistically than average in the north and in a central southern region, and somewhat less realistically than average in a belt of north midland counties running from Shropshire to Nottinghamshire. And it would also appear from the systematic progression in the deviations from average for the various levels of the minimum exemption limit that the accuracy of the assessments was indeed consistently reduced by any increase in the number of taxpayers to be assessed.[79] However, despite appearances, the exemption limit factor failed to attain statistical significance, indicating that overall its effect was weak when measured against all other sources of variation in the accuracy of the individual assessments.[80] Moreover, although the regional factor was statistically significant, the differences were small, and the interpretation of the largest of the differences, the apparent under assessment of the north midland counties, is perhaps less straightforward than might appear at first sight. Since all but three of the cases in that region came from the diocese of Lichfield, it is possible that it was not in fact the case that the subsidies were less adequately assessed there, but rather that probate valuations attained a more realistic level in that diocese.[81]

Each of the remaining two factors in the table, the wealth of the taxpayer and the period in which the assessment was made, was unambiguously associated with the accuracy of the subsidy assessments. Both factors achieved relatively high beta scores (0.66 and 0.24, respectively), and both attained high levels of statistical significance. The figures in column 2 of the table show that the accuracy of the assessments declined systematically over time from 48.7

---

[79] For the scale by which the numbers of assessments changed as a result of variations in the exemption limit, see note 25 above.

[80] If cases with missing subsidy assessments are included, with valuations arbitrarily set at 10s below the exemption limit (see note 72 above), not surprisingly the exemption limit emerges as the factor with the highest beta value, and is statistically significant at the 1 per cent level.

[81] Interpretation is further complicated by the fact that if cases with missing subsidy assessments are included, the deviations of Salop/Staffs and Derbs/Notts are reduced to 2.72 and 3.34, respectively.

per cent of the probate valuations in the period 1524–42 to 21.2 per cent in the first thirteen years of Elizabeth's reign.[82] The figures in column 3 of the table bring out the point that the assessments made in Henry VIII's reign were more accurate than the average for the whole period studied, while those made later were less accurate. In particular the assessments made before 1543 appear to have been considerably more accurate than was the case later, though it should be borne in mind that this result is based on only 20 cases. Thus, once the confounding effects of changes in other factors over time have been removed, it becomes apparent that the accuracy of the subsidy assessments of moveable goods experienced a similar decline between the reigns of Henry VIII and Elizabeth as was found in the case of assessments of annual incomes.

However, by far the most striking result to emerge from the analysis was the discovery that the factor with the strongest effect on the accuracy of the subsidy assessments was the wealth of the taxpayer. Indeed the beta scores in table 6 suggest that it accounted for almost three times more variation in the accuracy of the assessments, than could be attributed to time period, the next strongest factor. The figures for the deviations for each wealth category in column 3 of the table show a clear and substantial downward progression, with the poorest being assessed at a much higher than average percentage of their probate valuations, and the richest at a much lower than average percentage. Again, adding the deviations for each category to the overall mean, as in column 2 of the table, we find that once the effects of all other factors are held constant, those whose probated wealth was less than £10 were assessed in the subsidy at 59 per cent of their probate valuation, while those whose probated wealth was above £100 were assessed at only 10 per cent of their probate valuation. The allegations of Queen Elizabeth and her privy council that richer taxpayers were being more favourably treated than the poor in the later sixteenth century are amply confirmed. Throughout the entire period studied, from 1524 to 1572, an economic bias prevailed: the richer the taxpayer, the less his true wealth was captured by the subsidy assessments.[83]

Altogether, the six factors included in the analysis accounted for only about a half (48 per cent) of the variation in the accuracy of the assessments amongst the 580 cases studied.[84] While we might be able to improve on this figure if we could identify and measure other relevant factors, a certain proportion of the

---

[82] If cases with missing subsidy assessments are included, the figure for the 1543–5 period rises to a level much closer to that achieved in the earlier part of Henry VIII's reign. The accuracy of the assessments in the immediate post-Henrician period is also reduced. The deviations for the six periods become 20.1, 15.3, 2.1, −8.6, −5.0, −3.3. The beta figure, indicating the relative importance of time period, is substantially higher at 0.42.

[83] The strength of the relationship is further attested by the fact that it is present to the same degree in the data even before the effects of other factors are taken into account; and it is unchanged when cases with missing subsidy assessments are included in the analysis.

[84] Table 6: multiple $R^2 = 0.484$.

variation in the historical record will always resist our attempts to comprehend it. Each subsidy assessment and probate valuation will have been subject to the vagaries of chance, error and the accidents of personality. And further error will have been introduced in the course of this study, for example through the misidentification of individuals in the two sets of sources.

The results reported above are also limited by systematic errors and biases lurking in the sources. As has already been emphasised, neither the feodaries' surveys nor the probate inventories can be assumed to have provided true valuations of the wealth of individuals, and so may give an over-generous impression of the extent to which the subsidy assessments captured taxpayers' wealth. Moreover, since the accuracy of the subsidy assessments has to be measured relative to valuations in other sources, in principle the differences in accuracy noted above may have been produced by systematic differences in the accuracy of the alternative valuations rather than in the efficacy of the subsidy assessments. It has already been noted that this may have been so in the case of the apparent underassessment of the north midlands, which may merely reflect the ability of the authorities in the diocese of Lichfield to secure more realistic probate valuations.

On the other hand, this is less likely to have been the case with the other factors. It is improbable that the accuracy of *probate* valuations varied systematically with the number of people being assessed for the subsidy. Nor is it likely that the goods of richer people, though more completely specified in the inventories, were so much more rigorously valued than those of poorer people as to produce the steep gradient by wealth in the apparent accuracy of the subsidy assessments. And it is improbable that the accuracy of the valuations in both the probate inventories and the feodaries' surveys actually increased over time, thereby generating a spurious apparent decline in the accuracy of the subsidy assessments.

In a comparative study of historical sources, as has been attempted here, there is plenty of room for error, and the results deserve to be regarded with a sceptical eye. Yet the main features of the story of the accuracy of the subsidy assessments which have emerged from this analysis, notably the decline over time and the favouring of the rich over the poor, are consistent with contemporary evidence. Above all, they confirm for the population at large the conclusion that Helen Miller reached in the case of the peerage, namely that the enforcement of the assessment clauses in the subsidy acts was a very different matter under Henry VIII from the farce to which it had degenerated by the second half of Elizabeth's reign.

In principle, the directly assessed subsidy should have given the Tudors a means of raising taxes which kept pace with the rapid inflation that afflicted the sixteenth century. In practice, standards of assessment deteriorated and the yields of the taxes declined, so much so that by the end of Elizabeth's reign parliament was driven to granting 'double subsidies'. There seems no doubt that responsibility for the long drawn-out erosion of the subsidy in the later sixteenth century rests squarely on the commissioners, who supervised the assessments. Their failure to implement the subsidy acts is a mark of their unwillingness to put public obligation before private profit, whether in the narrow sense of their economic interests, or in the wider sense of the local political capital they could make from favourable assessments.

With the subsidies, as with many other matters, the crown was dependent on the leading social classes to implement national legislation; but in this case there was an additional dimension to the problem. The dismal fact is that the very privy councillors who were making patriotic speeches in parliament and writing to the commissioners requiring them in the name of the queen to improve the accuracy of the assessments, took care that they themselves were assessed at sums which bore increasingly little relation to their true wealth. For example, Winchester, as lord treasurer the senior financial official of the realm, persistently reduced his assessment despite his evident affluence, and his successor, Burghley, continued to quote the figure at which he was assessed before he was ennobled.[85] It was not a problem of the centre being unable to command the shires; despite the rhetoric, in the matter of fraudulent self-interest the centre was leading the way.

That a combination of personal self-interest and the exigencies of patronage politics conspired to undermine the directly assessed subsidy as a viable form of taxation under the later Tudors should, perhaps, not surprise us. After all, not only had direct assessment been tried in the past and abandoned as unworkable, but it was to be abandoned once more in the mid-seventeenth century and not be revived again until the end of the eighteenth century. What is remarkable about the Tudor period is not the collapse of direct assessment in the later sixteenth century, but the ability of the crown in the earlier decades of the century to secure the co-operation of the leading social classes in obtaining valuations of incomes and wealth which were much more realistic than could normally be achieved.

If the history of taxation in the later sixteenth century illustrates some of the limits of the Tudor state, its history in the reign of Henry VIII shows how political those limits were. In practice the crown could exercise no control over the subsidy commissioners, who were presiding over a system of taxation which was wide open to manipulation. Moreover, in the 1540s, along with others of their class, the commissioners were continually being asked to contribute by way of loans and non-parliamentary levies. Yet such was the political cohesion between the leading social classes and the crown that the former displayed an unparalleled willingness to operate a system of taxation, which, for its sophistication and attention to the principles of distributive justice, was several centuries ahead of its time. But it was a short-lived partnership: by the reign of Elizabeth relations between the crown and the political nation were no longer strong enough to hold the forces of individual and social advantage at bay.

[85] Miller, 'Subsidy assessment of the peerage', p. 22.

Bibliography of the writings of G. R. Elton, 1946–1986

Abbreviations

ARG	*Archiv für Reformationsgeschichte*
BIHR	*Bulletin of the Institute of Historical Research*
CHJ	*Cambridge Historical Journal*
EcHR	*Economic History Review*
EHR	*English Historical Review*
HJ	*Historical Journal*
JEH	*Journal of Ecclesiastical History*
P & P	*Past and Present*
TLS	*Times Literary Supplement*
TRHS	*Transactions of the Royal Historical Society*

BOOKS AND ARTICLES

1946

'The date of Caesar's Gallic proconsulate', *Journal of Roman Studies* 36, 18–42.

1949

'Two unpublished letters of Thomas Cromwell', *BIHR* 22, 35–7.
'The evolution of a Reformation statute', *EHR*, 64 174–97.

1950

'A note on the First Act of Annates', *BIHR* 23, 203–5.

1951

'Thomas Cromwell's decline and fall', *CHJ* 10, 150–85.
'The Commons' Supplication of 1532: parliamentary manoeuvres in the reign of Henry VIII', *EHR* 66, 507–34.

257

1952

'Parliamentary drafts 1529–40', *BIHR* 25, 117–32.
'The Sixteenth Century' in *Annual Bulletin of Historical Literature* (Historical Association).

1953

The Tudor Revolution in Government: Administrative Changes in the Reign of Henry VIII (Cambridge University Press).
'An early Tudor poor law', *EcHR* 2nd series, 6, 55–67.
'The Sixteenth Century' in *Annual Bulletin of Historical Literature* (Historical Association).

1954

'A further note on parliamentary drafts in the reign of Henry VIII', *BIHR* 27, 198–200.
'Informing for profit: a sidelight on Tudor methods of law-enforcement', *CHJ* 11, 149–67.
'King or minister? The man behind the Henrician Reformation', *History* 39, 216–32.
'The Sixteenth Century' in *Annual Bulletin of Historical Literature* (Historical Association).

1955

England Under the Tudors (London: Methuen).
'The Sixteenth Century' in *Annual Bulletin of Historical Literature* (Historical Association).

1956

'Thomas Cromwell', *History Today* (August).
'The quondam of Rievaulx', *JEH* 7, 45–60.
'Fifty years of Tudor history at London', *TLS* (6 Jan.).
'The political creed of Thomas Cromwell', *TRHS* 5th series, 6, 69–92.
'The Sixteenth Century' in *Annual Bulletin of Historical Literature* (Historical Association).

1958

(ed.) *The New Cambridge Modern History*, vol. II: *The Reformation* (Cambridge University Press).
Star Chamber Stories (London: Methuen).
'Henry VII: rapacity and remorse', *HJ* 1, 21–39.

1959

'The records of the conciliar courts in the 16th century', *The Amateur Historian* 4, 89–94.

1960

The Tudor Constitution: Documents and Commentary (Cambridge University Press).
'Henry VIII's Act of Proclamations', *EHR* 75, 208–22.

1961

'The Elizabethan Exchequer: war in the Receipt,' in *Elizabethan Government and Society*, ed. S. T. Bindoff, J. Hurstfield, C. H. Williams (London: Athlone Press), pp. 213–48.
'State planning in early Tudor England', *EcHR* 2nd series, 13, 433–9.
'Henry VII: a restatement', *HJ* 4, 1–29.
'Stuart Government', *P & P* 20, 76–82.

1962

The Reformation (BBC Publications).
Henry VIII: an Essay in Revision (Historical Association, Pamphlet G 51).

1963

Reformation Europe (London: Collins).
(ed.) *Ideas and Institutions in Western Civilization*, vol. III: *Renaissance and Reformation* (New York: Macmillan).
(ed. with G. Kitson Clark) *Guide to the Research Facilities in History in the Universities of Great Britain and Ireland* (Cambridge University Press).
'The teaching of history', *Cambridge Review* 84, 250.
'Anglo-French relations in 1522: a Scottish prisoner of war and his interrogation', *EHR* 78, 310–13.

1964

'The Tudor Revolution: a reply', *P & P* 29, 26–49.

1965

'Why the history of the early Tudor Council remains unwritten', *Annali della Fondazione Italiana per la Storia Amministrativa* 1, 268–96.
'A high road to civil war?' *From the Renaissance to the Counter-Reformation: Essays in Honor of Garrett Mattingley*, ed. C. H. Carter (New York: Random House), pp. 325–47.
'The problems and significance of administrative history in the Tudor period', *Journal of British Studies* 4 no. 2, 18–28.
Introduction to J. N. Figgis, *The Divine Right of Kings* (repr. Harper Torchbooks).
Introduction to A. F. Pollard, *Wolsey* (repr. Fontana Library).
'1555: a political retrospect', in *The Reformation Crisis*, ed. J. Hurstfield (London: Arnold).
'Government by edict?', *HJ* 8, 266–71.
'A revolution in Tudor history?' *P & P* 32, 103–9.

1966

Introduction to M. Creighton, *Queen Elizabeth* (repr. Crowell).

1967

The Practice of History (Sydney University Press).
'Thomas More and the opposition to Henry VIII', *Moreana* 15 & 16, 285–303.
(ed.) *Storia del Mondo Moderno*, vol. II.

1968

(ed.) *Ideas and Institutions in Western Civilization: Renaissance and Reformation*, 2nd edn. (New York: Macmillan).
The Future of the Past (Cambridge University Press).
'Thomas More and the opposition to Henry VIII', (repr. from Moreana 15 & 16), *BIHR* 41, 19–34.
'The law of treason in the early Reformation', *HJ* 11, 211–36.
'Reform by statute: Thomas Starkey's *Dialogue* and Thomas Cromwell's policy', *Proceedings of the British Academy*, 54, 165–88.
Review article on G. E. Aylmer, *The Struggle for the Constitution*, *Annali della Fondazione Italiana per la Storia Amministrativa* 2, 759–65.
'Interdisciplinary courses', *Cambridge Review* (26 Jan.).
'Graduate studies in the humanities', *Cambridge Review* (18 Oct.).

1969

The Sources of History: England 1200–1640 (London: Sources of History Ltd.).
'*The Body of the Whole Realm*': *Parliament and Representation in Medieval and Tudor England* (Charlottesville: University Press of Virginia).
'Literaturbericht über die englische Geschichte der Neuzeit', *Historische Zeitschrift*, Sonderheft 3.
'The King of Hearts', *HJ* 12, 158–63.
'The Good Duke', *HJ* 12, 702–6.
'A reply [to a review of *The Practice of History*]', *Journal of Historical Studies*, Winter 1968–9, 49–59.
'Second thoughts on history in the Universities', *History* 54, 60–7.
'Personal view', *The Listener* (27 Mar.).

1970

Political History: Principles and Practice (New York: Basic Books).
Modern Historians on British History 1485–1945: a Critical Bibliography (London: Methuen).
'Reformation in Church and State 1485–1603', *Encyclopaedia Americana* ('England').
'What sort of history should we teach?' *New Movements in the Study and Teaching of History*, ed. M. Ballard (London: Temple Smith), pp. 221–30.

1971

Europa im Zeitalter der Reformation, 2 vols. (Siebenstern).
'Government and society in Renaissance and Reformation Europe', in N. F. Cantor, ed., *Perspectives on the European Past: Conversations with Historians* (New York: Macmillan), pp. 228–51.
'Studying the history of parliament', *British Studies Monitor* 4, 3–12.
'Tudor historians', *The Listener* (30 Sept.).

1972

Policy and Police: the Enforcement of the Reformation in the Age of Thomas Cromwell (Cambridge University Press).
'Thomas More, councillor', *St Thomas More: Action and Contemplation*, ed. R. S. Sylvester (New Haven: Yale University Press), pp. 86–122.
'The rule of law in the sixteenth century', *Tudor Men and Institutions*, ed. A. J. Slavin (Baton Rouge: Louisiana State University Press), pp. 260–84.
'Reply [to J. H. Hexter]', *British Studies Monitor* 3, 16–22.

1973

Reform and Renewal: Thomas Cromwell and the Common Weal (Cambridge University Press).

1974

England under the Tudors, 2nd edn. (London: Methuen).
Studies in Tudor and Stuart Politics and Government, 2 vols. (Cambridge University Press).
La Europa de la Reforma (Siglo veintuino).
Political History: Japanese translation.
'Consultants' Report on Graduate Programs in History in the Province of Ontario.'
'Thomas Cranmer', 'Thomas Cromwell', 'Henry VIII' in *Encyclopaedia Britannica* (15th edn.).
'The early Journals of the House of Lords', *EHR* 89, 481–512.
'Tudor Politics: the points of contact. I. Parliament', *TRHS* 5th series, 24, 183–200.

1975

'Taxation for peace and war in early Tudor England', *War and Economic Development: Essays in Memory of David Joslin*, ed. J. M. Winter (Cambridge University Press), pp. 33–48.
'Thomas Cromwell and reform', *Annual Report of the Friends of Lambeth Library*.
'Tudor Politics: the points of contact. II The Council', *TRHS* 5th series, 25, 195–211.

1976

Ideas and Institutions in Western Civilisation, vol. III: *Renaissance and Reformation*, 3rd edn. (New York: Macmillan).

'Publishing history', *TLS* (25 June).
'Tudor Politics: the points of contact. III The Court', *TRHS* 5th series, 26, 211–28.
(ed.) *Annual Bibliography of British and Irish History: Publications for 1975* (Brighton: Harvester Press).

1977

Reform and Reformation: England 1509–1558 (London: Arnold).
'Introduction: crime and the historian', in J. S. Cockburn, ed., *Crime in England 1550–1800* (London: Methuen), pp. 1–14.
'Thomas Cromwell *redivivus*', *ARG* 68, 192–208.
'A new venture in history publishing', *British Book News* (December).
'Mid-Tudor finance', *HJ* 20, 737–40.
'The historian's social function', *TRHS* 5th series, 27, 197–211.
(ed.) *Annual Bibliography of British and Irish History: Publications for 1976* (Brighton: Harvester Press).

1978

'The sessional printing of statutes, 1484–1547', in *Wealth and Power in Tudor England: Essays Presented to S. T. Bindoff*, eds. E. W. Ives, R. J. Knecht and J. J. Scarisbrick (London: Athlone Press), pp. 68–86.
'England und die oberdeutsche Reformation,' *Zeitschrift für Kirchengeschichte*, 3–11.
(ed.) *Annual Bibliography of British and Irish History: Publications for 1977* (Brighton: Harvester Press).

1979

English Law in the Sixteenth Century: Reform in an Age of Change (London: Selden Society).
'Reform and the "Commonwealth-Men" of Edward VI's reign', in *The English Commonwealth 1547–1640: Essays in Politics and Society presented to Joel Hurstfield*, eds. P. Clark, A. G. R. Smith and N. Tyacke (Leicester University Press), pp. 23–38.
'The Rolls of Parliament 1449–1547', *HJ* 22, 1–29.
'Parliament in the sixteenth century: function and fortunes', *HJ* 22, 255–78.
'England and the continent in the sixteenth century', *Studies in Church History*, Subsidia 2, ed. D. Baker (Oxford: Blackwell), pp. 1–16.
'Catching up British history: 1 Tudors and early Stuarts', *TLS* (23 Nov.).
(ed.) *Annual Bibliography of British and Irish History: Publications for 1978* (Brighton: Harvester Press).

1980

'The real Thomas More?' in *Reformation Principle and Practice: Essays in Honour of A. G. Dickens*, ed. P. N. Brooks (London: Scolar Press), pp. 21–31.
'Politics and the Pilgrimage of Grace', in *After the Reformation: Essays in Honor of J. H. Hexter*, ed. B. Malament (Philadelphia: University of Pennsylvania Press), pp. 25–56.

'Enacting clauses and legislative initiative 1559–1581', *BIHR* 53, 183–91.
(ed.) *Annual Bibliography of British and Irish History: Publications for 1979* (Brighton: Harvester Press).

1981

'Cranmer, Thomas', *Theologische Realenzyklopädie*, vol. VIII.
'Arthur Hall, Lord Burghley and the antiquity of parliament', in *History and Imagination: Essays in Honour of H. R. Trevor-Roper*, eds. H. Lloyd-Jones, V. Pearl and B. Worden (London: Duckworth), pp. 83–103.
'Thomas More', in *Gestalten der Kirchengeschichte, Reformationszeit* I, ed. M. Greschat (Stuttgart: Kohlhammer), pp. 89–103.
(ed.) *Annual Bibliography of British and Irish History: publications for 1980* (Brighton: Harvester Press).

1982

The Tudor Constitution, 2nd edn. (Cambridge University Press).
Europa im Zeitalter der Reformation 1517–1559, 2nd edn. (Munich : C. H. Beck).
'Contentment and discontent on the eve of colonization', in *Early Maryland in a Wider World*, ed. D. A. Quinn (Detroit: Wayne State University Press), 105–18.
(ed.) *Annual Bibliography of British and Irish History: Publications for 1981* (Brighton: Harvester Press).
A Europa durante a Reforma 1517–1559 (Lisbon: Editorial Presença).
'Elisabeth I', *Theologische Realenzyklopädie*, vol. IX.

1983

Studies in Tudor and Stuart Politics, vol. III (Cambridge University Press).
England unter den Tudors (München: Callwey).
'Kann man sich auf Shakespeare verlassen? Das 15. Jahrhundert bei Shakespeare und in der Wirklichkeit', *Deutsche Shakespeare-Gesellschaft West: Jahrbuch 1983*, 27–39.
'The English parliament in the sixteenth century: estates and statutes', A. Cosgrove, J. I. McGuire, eds., *Parliament and Community*, Historical Studies 16 (Dublin: Appletree Press), pp. 69–95.
'Historians against History', *Cambridge Review* 104, 203–5.
With R. W. Fogel, *Which Way to the Past? Two Views of History* (New Haven and London: Yale University Press).
(ed.) *Annual Bibliography of British and Irish History: Publications for 1982* (Brighton: Harvester Press).

1984

The History of England (Cambridge University Press).
'Herbert Butterfield and the study of history', *HJ* 27, 729–43.
'Commemorating Luther', *JEH* 35, 614–19.
'Wales in parliament, 1542–1581', in *Welsh Society and Nationhood: Historical Essays presented to Glanmor Williams*, eds. R. R. Davies, R. A. Griffiths, I. G. Jones, K. O. Morgan (Cardiff: University of Wales Press), pp. 108–21.

'Lex terrae victrix: Der Rechtestreit in der englischen Frühreformation', *Zeitschrift der Savigny-Stiftung* 100, 217–36.
'Parliament', in C. A. Haigh, ed., *The Reign of Elizabeth I* (London: Macmillan), pp. 79–100.
'Persecution and toleration in the English Reformation', *Studies in Church History*, 21, ed. W. J. Sheils (Oxford: Blackwell), pp. 163–87.
'Auseinandersetzung und Zusammenarbeit zwischen Renaissance und Reformation in England', *Renaissance-Reformation: Gegensätze und Gemeinsamkeiten*, ed. A. Buck (Wolfenbüttler Abhandlungen 5: Weisbaden: Harrassowitz), pp. 217–25.
(ed.) *Annual Bibliography of British and Irish History: Publications for 1983* (Brighton: Harvester Press).

1985

F. W. Maitland (London: Weidenfeld).
'The State: government and politics under Elizabeth and James', in J. W. Andrews, ed., *William Shakespeare: his World, his Work, his Influence*, 3 vols. (New York: Scribner's), pp. 1–19.
'Once more, the History Faculty Building', *Cambridge Review* 106, 89–90.
(ed.) *Annual Bibliography of British and Irish History: Publications for 1984* (Brighton: Harvester Press).
'Political History', *History Today* (Jan.), 11–12.
'Europe and the Reformation,' in *History, Society and the Churches: Essays in Honour of Owen Chadwick*, eds. D. Beales and G. Best (Cambridge University Press), pp. 89–104.
'History according to St Joan', *The American Scholar* (autumn number).
'Luther and society', *Lutherjahrbuch* 52, 213–19.
'King Henry VII', *Transactions of the Hon. Society of Cymmrodorion*, 131–45.

1986

The Parliament of England 1559–1581 (Cambridge University Press).
'Revisionism Reassessed: The Tudor Revolution a Generation later', *Encounter* (July/ Aug.), 37–42.
'English national selfconsciousness and the parliament in the 16th century', in *Nationalismus in vorindustrieller Zeit*, ed. O. Dann (Munich: Oldenbourg), pp. 73–82.
'Piscatorial politics in the early parliament of Elizabeth I', in *Business Life and Public Policy: Essays in Honour of D. C. Coleman*, eds. N. McKendrick and R. B. Outhwaite (Cambridge University Press), pp. 1–20.
'Die europäische Reformation: mit oder ohne Luther?', in *Martin Luther: Probleme seiner Zeit*, eds. V. Press and D. Stievermann (Stuttgart: Klett-Cotta), pp. 43–57.
'Neale, Sir John Ernest', *Dictionary of National Biography 1971–80*, pp. 623–4.

Index